SCOTTISH COUNTRY DANCES

IN DIAGRAMS

First published 1955
Seventh Edition 1997
Large Print Edition 1998
Eighth Edition 2004

Pocket Edition ISBN 0 9519497 3 X

Large Print Edition ISBN 0 9519497 4 8

Copies of these books may be obtained from:-
Scottish Country Dances in Diagrams
C/o Sue Duckett
Corn Riggs
Hollands Lane
Kelsall
Tarporley
Cheshire
CW6 0QT
Please make cheques payable to
Scottish Country Dances in Diagrams

Preface

In 1967 the late Mr F.L. Pilling, who had produced in a duplicated format the first two editions of Scottish Country Dances in Diagrams, agreed that it should be taken over by our small committee. In subsequent editions of "The little green book" we have completely transformed the format. The coding system has been developed, the production changed to computer aided design, a large number of dances added and a separate large print edition produced. This eighth edition has an extra 78 dances compared with the seventh edition.

The membership of the committee has changed over the years, but our aims are unchanged - to produce for Scottish Country Dancers a book of dance diagrams, portrayed as simply as possible, to be used as an aide-mémoire. Anyone who wished to learn a dance should refer to the original printed instructions. The committee remains voluntary and unpaid; surplus funds are used for promoting Scottish country dancing by gifts to charities and projects.

The committee wishes to thank the many people who have assisted us by dancing new dances and verifying the coding. We acknowledge with gratitude the many suggestions made by dancers from many countries. We also wish to record the extensive work carried out by Sue Duckett in coding and producing the dance diagrams in the modern, adaptable and economical format. On with the dance!

Sue Duckett John Elsley Stephen O'Brien Trish Reid

Auld Lang Syne

Should auld acquaintance be forgot
And ncvcr brought to min'?
Should auld acquaintance be forgot,
And auld lang syne?

Chorus
For auld lang sync, my dcar,
For auld lang syne,
We'll tak a cup o' kindness yet,
For auld lang syne.

And there's a hand, my trusty fiere,
And gie's a hand o' thine:
And we'll tak a right guid-willie waught,
For auld lang syne.

ALTERNATIVE TITLE	TITLE IN 8th EDITION
Bonny Jocky	Kiss Me Quick, My Mither's Coming
Broun's Reel	Duke of Perth
Cameronian Rant	Greig's Pipes
Clever Lad	Reel of Glamis
Drops of Brandy	Strip the Willow
Duke is Welcome to Inverness	Lady MacIntosh's Rant
Flirt	C'est l'Amour
Graces	Three Bonnie Maidens
Inverness Country Dance	Speed the Plough
John Black's Daughter	Green Grow the Rashes
Just as I was in the Morning	Deuks Dang Ow'er My Daddy
Musselborough	Jenny Dang the Weaver
New Way of Gildon	General Stuart's Reel
Pease Strake	Duke of Perth
Reel Duine na Marachan	Menzies Rant
Tartan Plaidie	Highland Plaid
Uilliam Dona	Wicked Willy
Water Kelpie	Lady of the Lake
Waverley	Fergus McIver
Where Would Bonnie Annie Lie?	Red House

KEY TO THE SYMBOLS

○ Men	□ Women	↷1	Cast off one place
A	Allemande	↶1	Cast up one place
B	Balance in line	↓1	Lead (or dance) down one place
D	Pass back to back	↑1	Lead (or dance) up one place
DT	Double triangles	⑥	Six hands round and back
P	Poussette		Round to the left only
R	Repeat previous movement		Round to the right only
RA	Right hands across	)	Form arch
LA	Left hands across	→	Pass under arch
RL	Rights and lefts	○○	Reel of three
S	Set S↑ Set advancing	○○○	Reel of four
T	Turn	©©	Change reel of three. The dancers in tandem dance the normal track of the reel but at both outer points they each turn right about to change direction and leader
X	Cross over		
	Ladies' chain		
	Mens' chain		

Symbol	Meaning	Symbol	Meaning
┐	First corner position	┌	Second corner position
└	Partner's 1st corner position	┘	Partner's 2nd corner position
┌S┐	Set to corners	┌ST┐	Set and turn corners
└+┐	Turn corners, partner, corners, partner		
⇵	Retire and advance	↕	Advance ↑ and retire ↓
⇄	{ Lead down and back Dance down and back	HS	Highland Schottische Setting
※	Clap	PROM	Promenade
◇	Petronella movement for eight bars	CHAIN	Grand Chain
◇T	Petronella turn (2 bars)	HSP	Highland Schottische Poussette
◇D	Petronella in tandem (2 bars travelling)	□—○	Slip steps with both hands joined

Other formations are indicated by their usual names

Suffixes to Symbols

Suffix	Meaning	Suffix	Meaning
R	with Right hand	◉	Leading man's reel
L	with Left hand	↑	Advancing
B	with Both hands	↓	Retiring

Notes

Spaces between full vertical lines represent eight bars unless otherwise stated		Broken vertical line halves space into four bar sections	
	Movements bracketed are danced at the same time		Dance movement with hands joined
1 2 RL	Numbers above symbols indicate couples dancing	RL	Horizontal line halves a figure
2 3	Dancer follows route shown (full line for men broken line for women)		Dancers follow route shown (full line for men broken line for women)

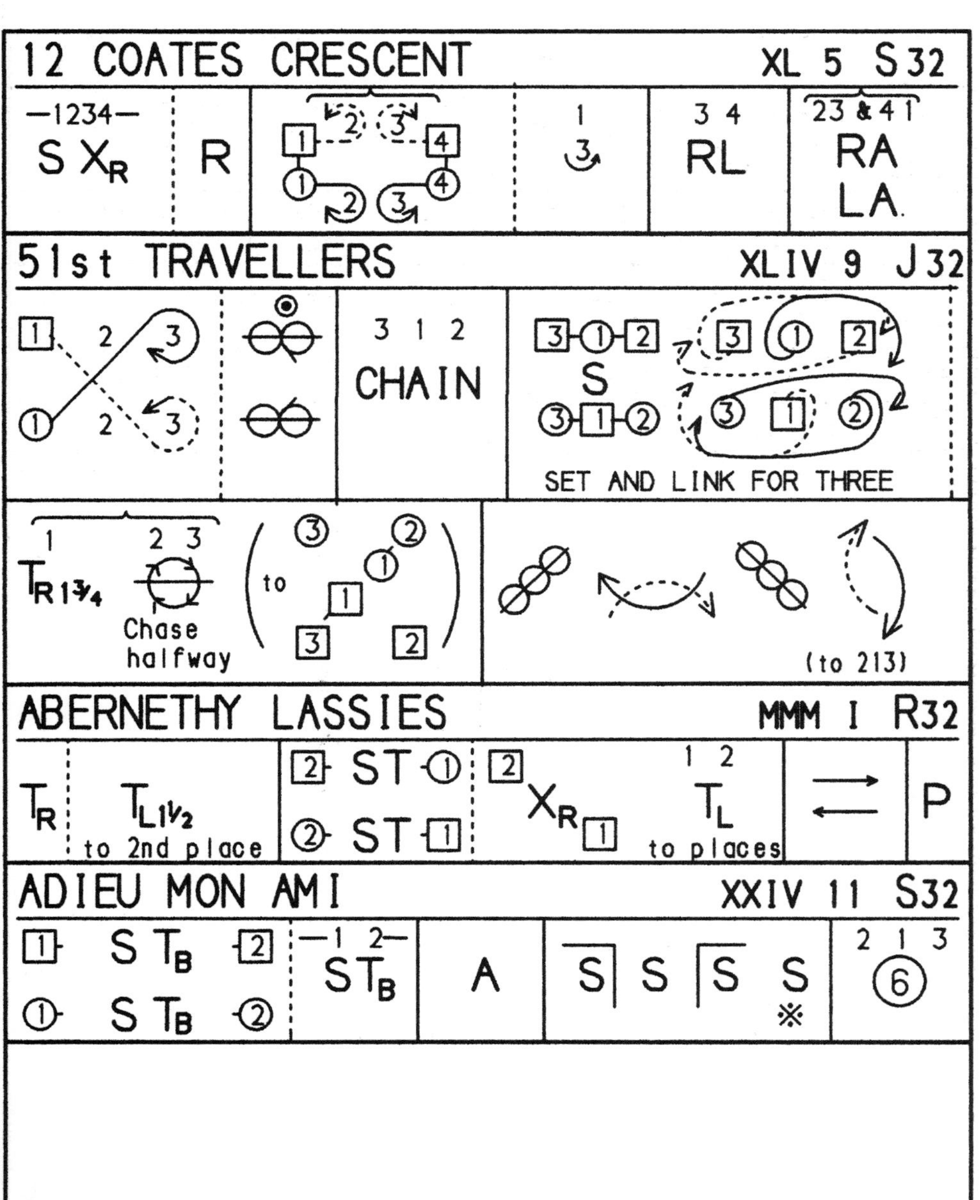
12 COATES CRESCENT
XL 5 S32
—1234—
S XR
R
1 3
RL
3 4
RA
LA
23 & 41
51st TRAVELLERS
XLIV 9 J32
3 1 2
CHAIN
S
SET AND LINK FOR THREE
1 2 3
TR 1¾
Chase halfway
to
(to 213)
ABERNETHY LASSIES
MMM I R32
TR
TL1½
to 2nd place
ST
XR
1 2
TL
to places
P
ADIEU MON AMI
XXIV 11 S32
S TB
—1 2—
STB
A
S S S S
2 1 3

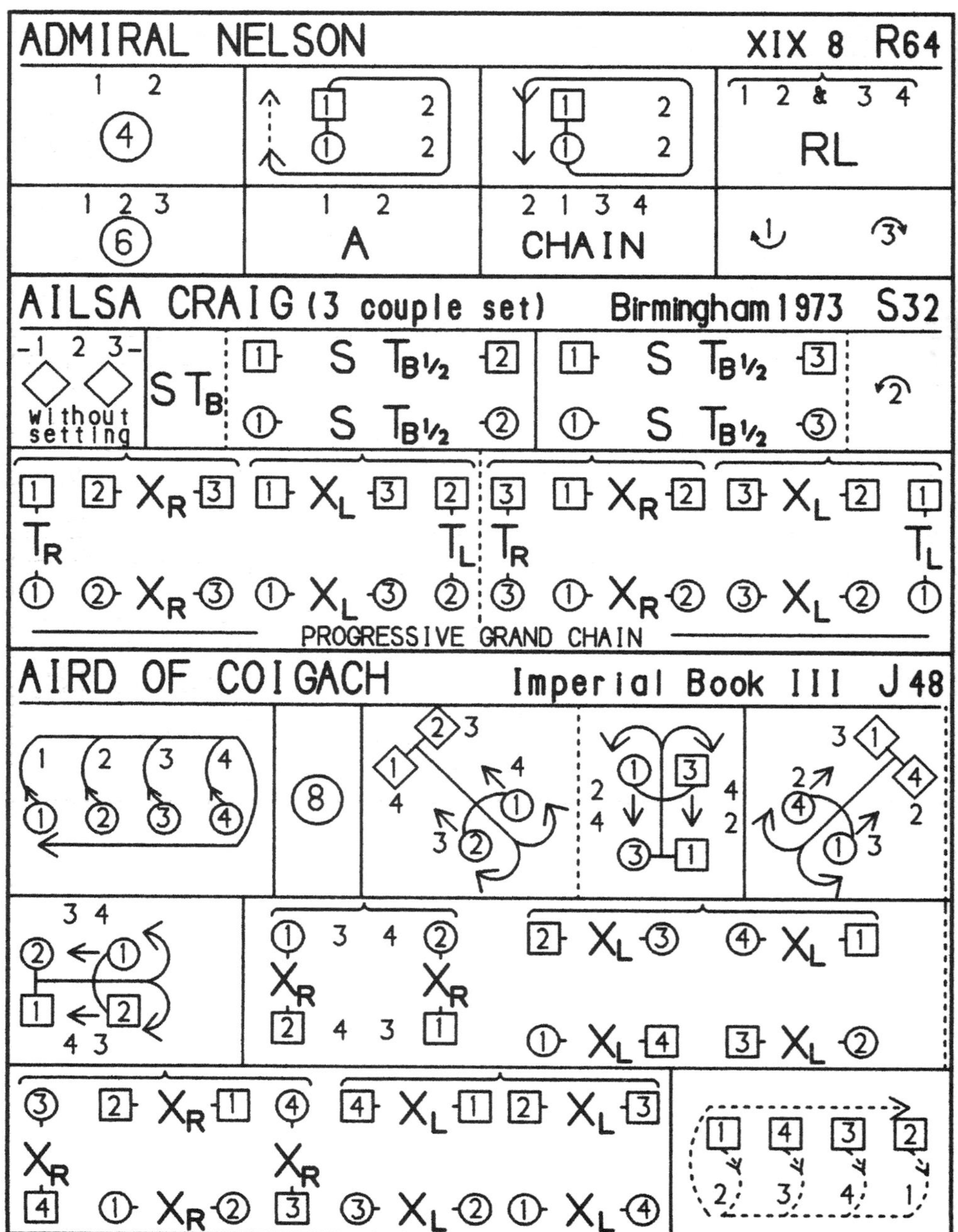

ADMIRAL NELSON
XIX 8 R64
RL
CHAIN
AILSA CRAIG (3 couple set)
Birmingham 1973 S32
without setting
PROGRESSIVE GRAND CHAIN
AIRD OF COIGACH
Imperial Book III J48

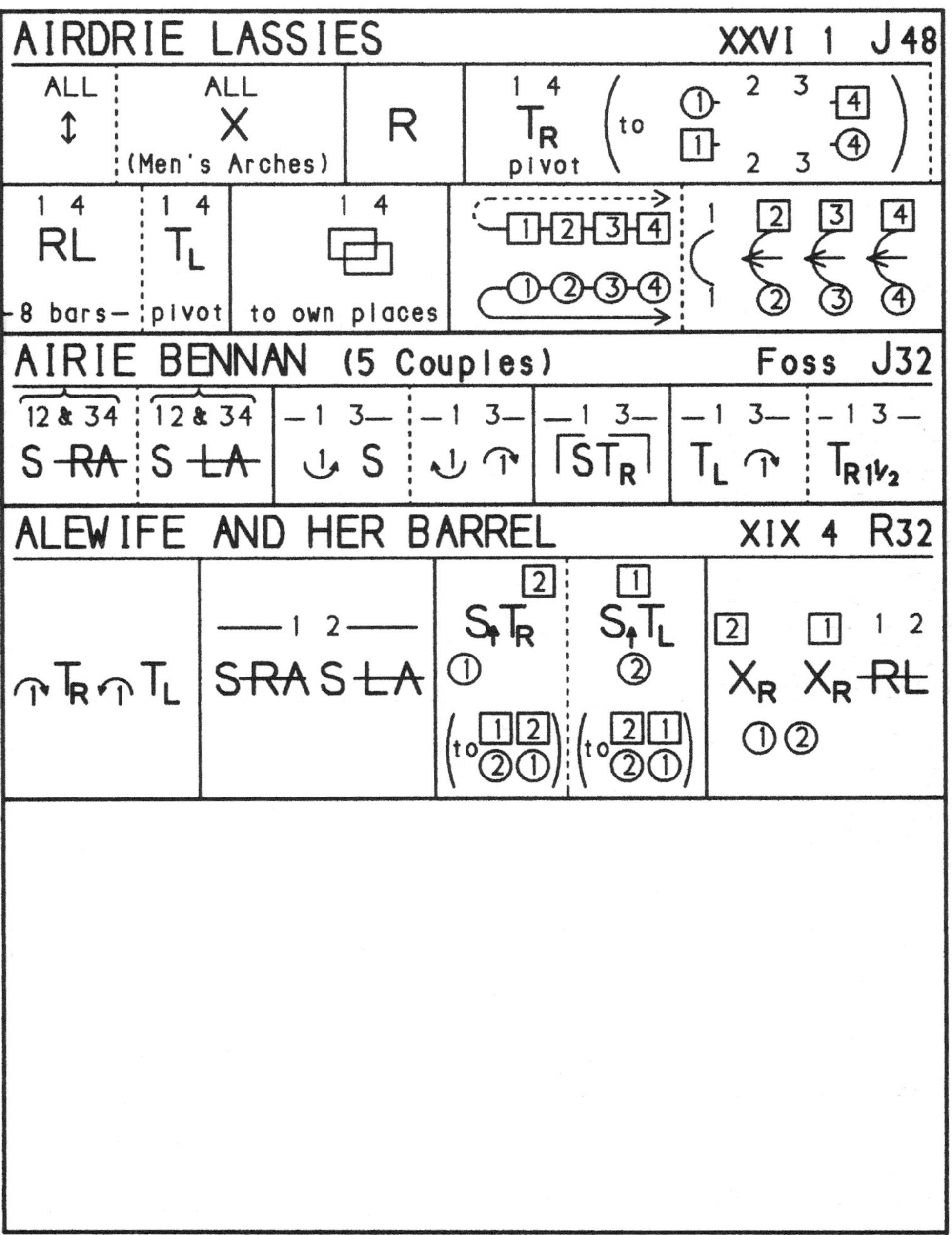

AIRDRIE LASSIES
XXVI 1 J48
ALL
ALL
X
(Men's Arches)
R
1 4
pivot
to
2 3
2 3
1 4
RL
-8 bars-
1 4
pivot
1 4
to own places
1
1
AIRIE BENNAN (5 Couples)
Foss J32
12 & 34
12 & 34
S
S
—1 3—
—1 3—
—1 3—
—1 3—
—1 3—
ALEWIFE AND HER BARREL
XIX 4 R32
1 2
to
to
1 2

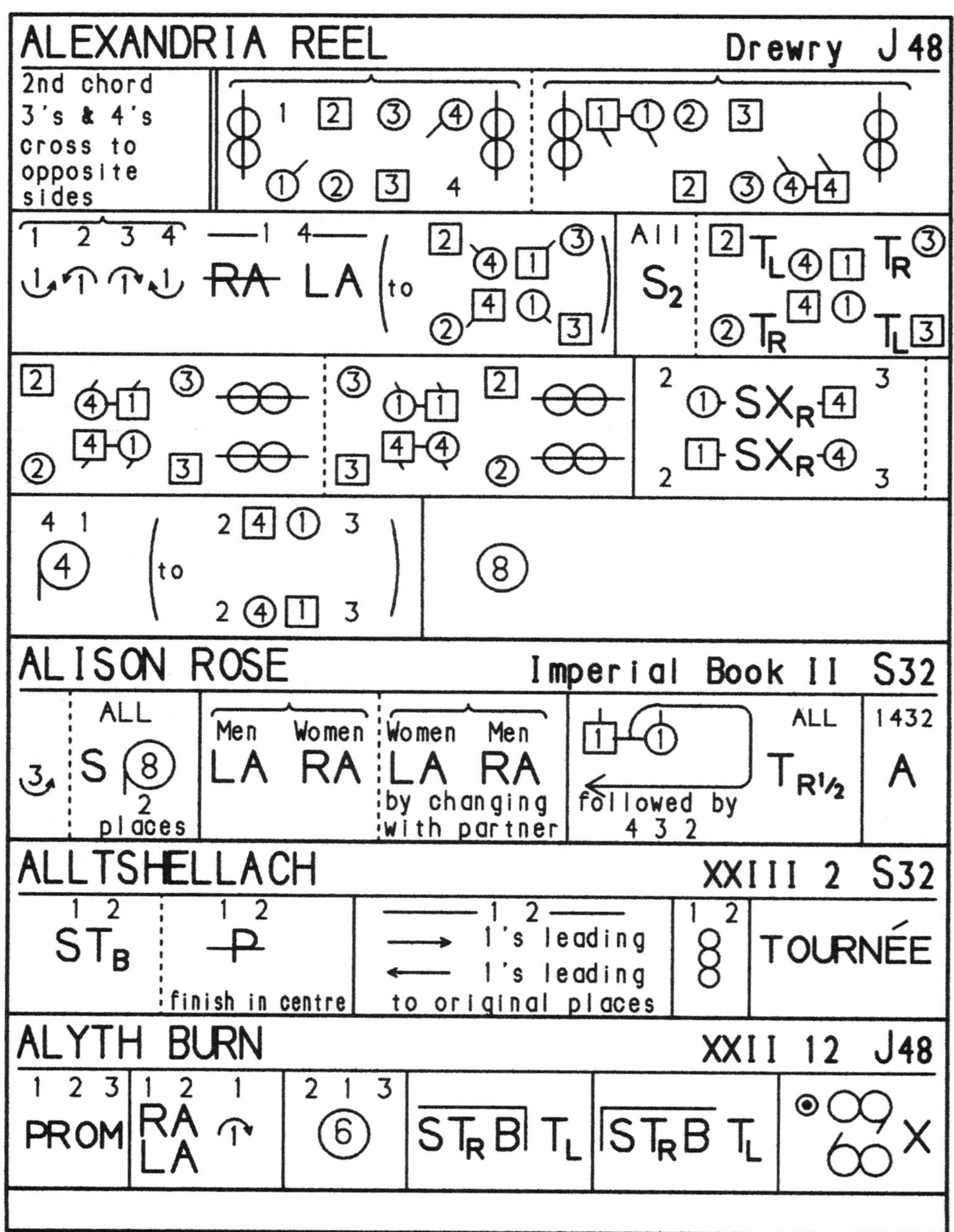
ALEXANDRIA REEL
Drewry J48
2nd chord
3's & 4's
cross to
opposite
sides
RA LA
to
All
S2
SXR
to
ALISON ROSE
Imperial Book II S32
ALL
S
2
places
Men Women
LA RA
Women Men
LA RA
by changing
with partner
followed by
4 3 2
ALL
1432
A
ALLTSHELLACH
XXIII 2 S32
STB
P
finish in centre
1's leading
1's leading
to original places
TOURNÉE
ALYTH BURN
XXII 12 J48
PROM
RA
LA
STRB TL
STRB TL
X

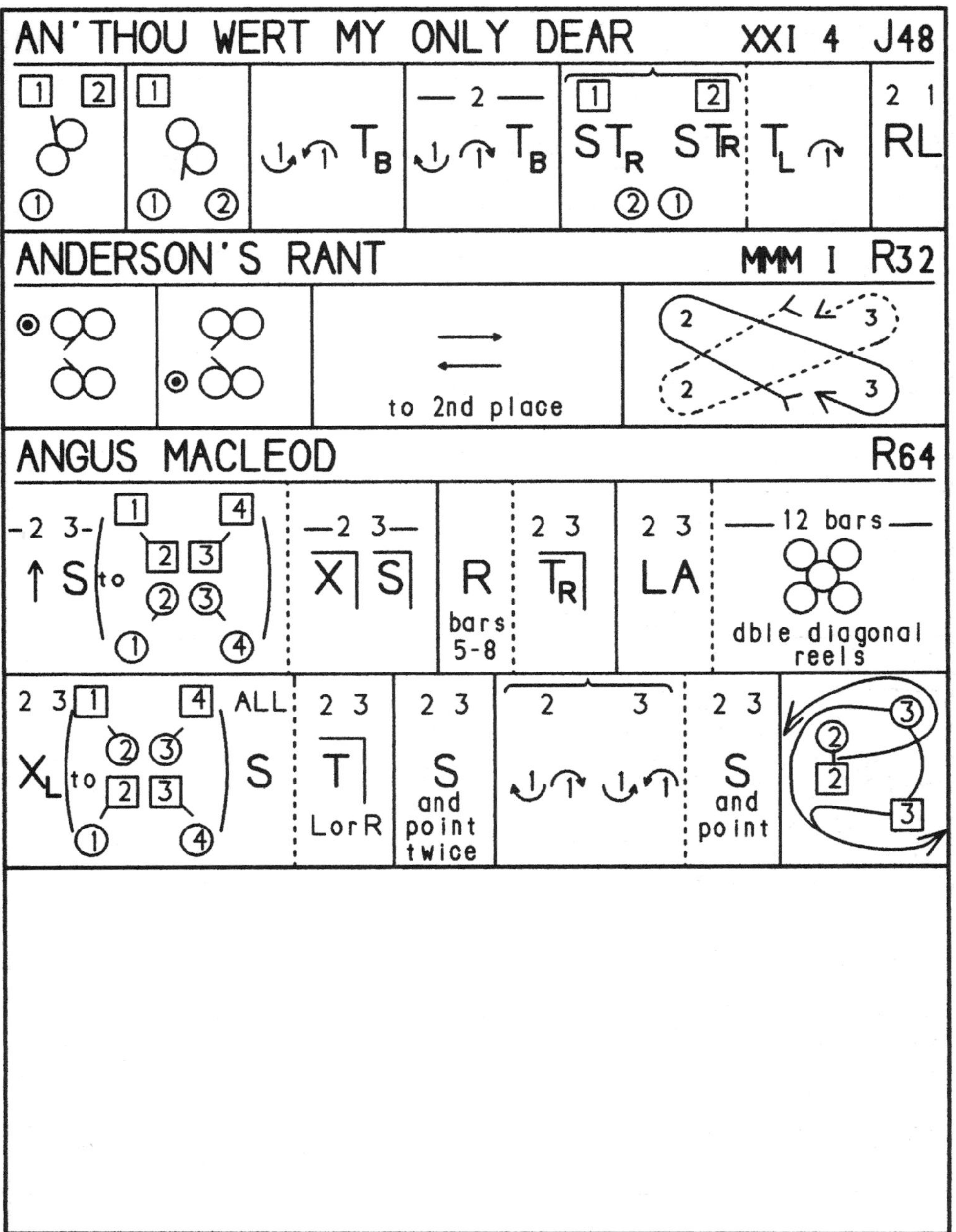
AN'THOU WERT MY ONLY DEAR
XXI 4 J48
ANDERSON'S RANT
MMM I R32
to 2nd place
ANGUS MACLEOD
R64
bars 5-8
12 bars
dble diagonal reels
ALL
LorR
and point twice
and point

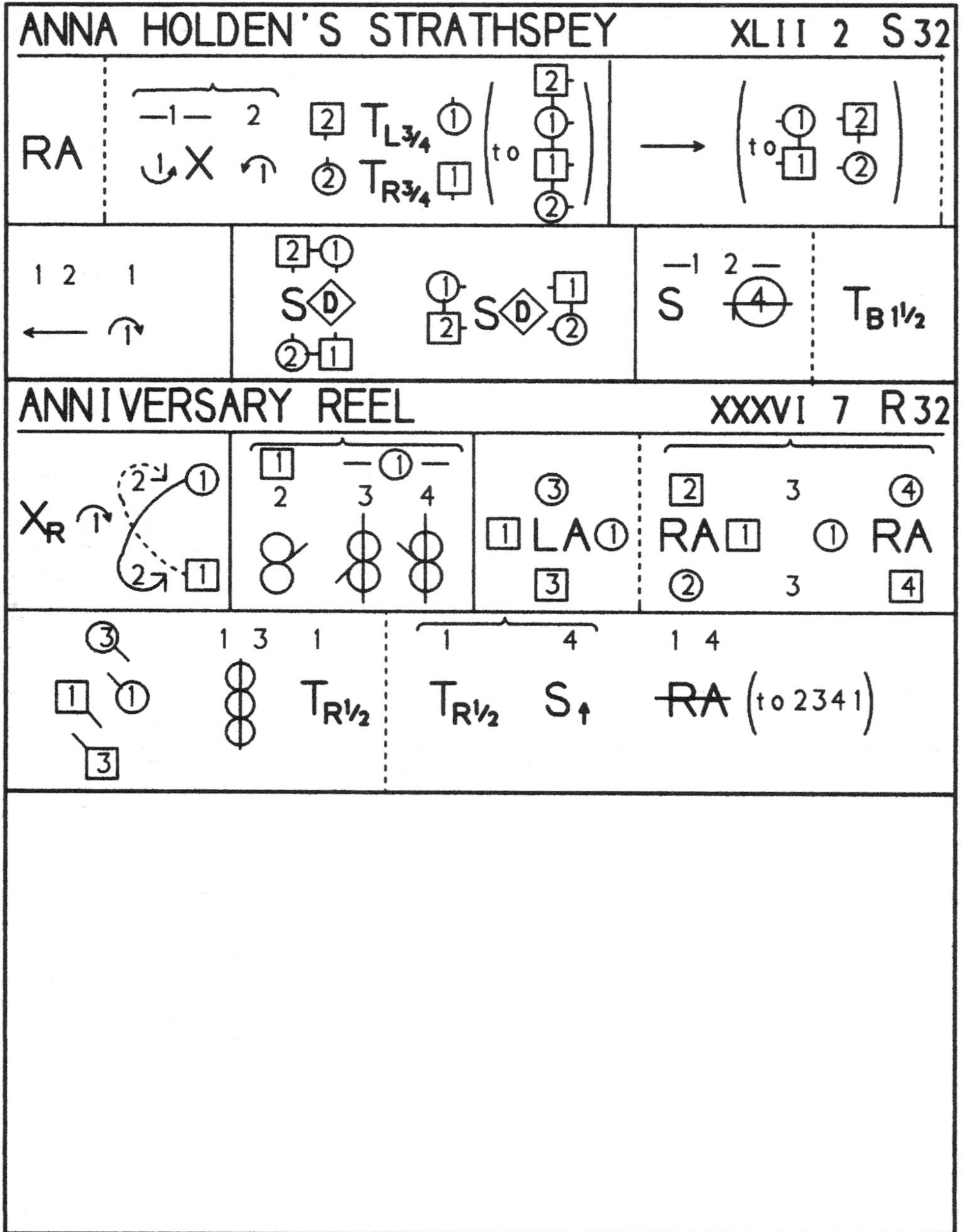
ANNA HOLDEN'S STRATHSPEY
XLII 2 S32
ANNIVERSARY REEL
XXXVI 7 R32

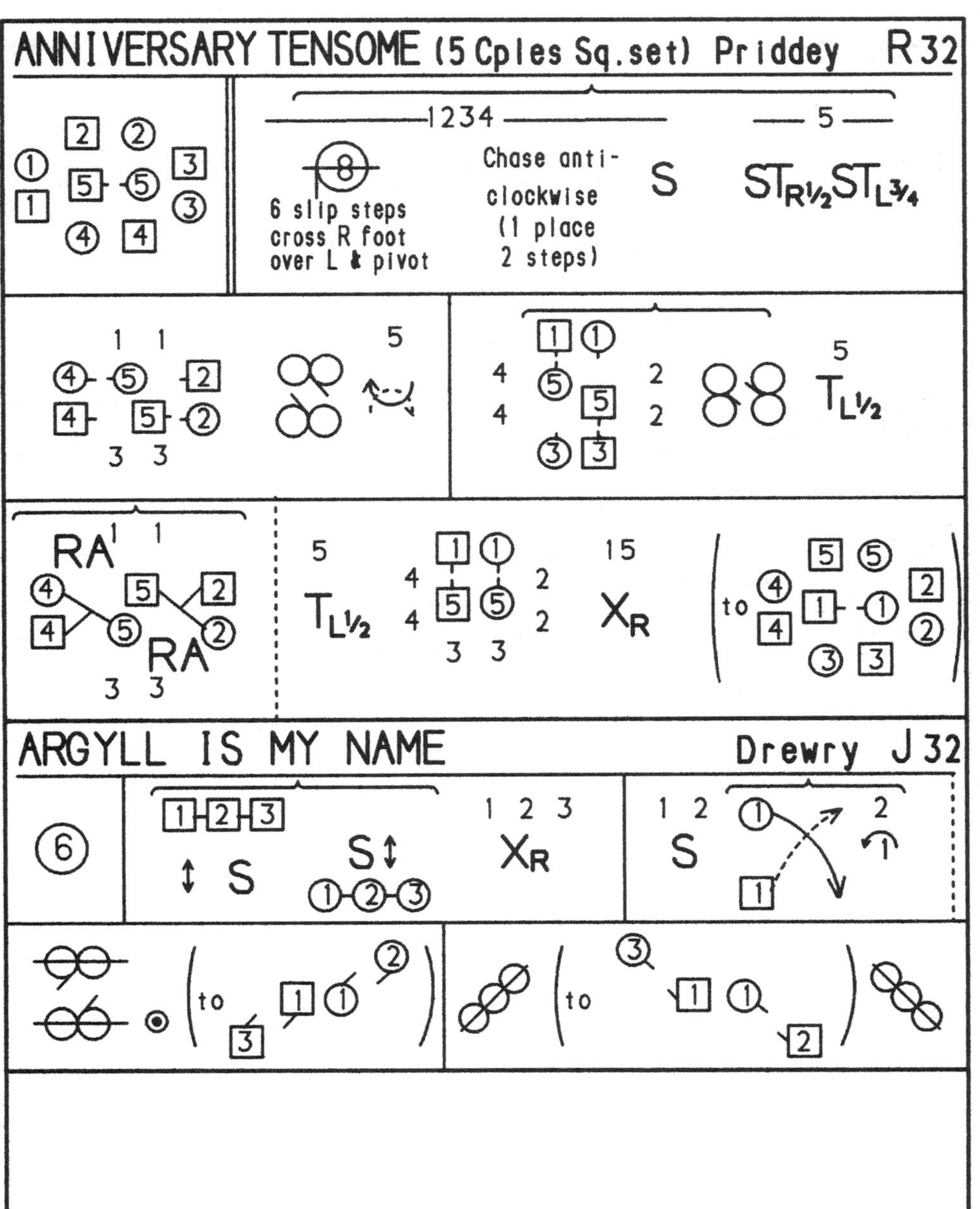
ANNIVERSARY TENSOME (5 Cples Sq.set) Priddey R32
1234
5
6 slip steps cross R foot over L & pivot
Chase anti-clockwise (1 place 2 steps)
S
ST R½ ST L¾
T L½
RA
RA
T L½
X R
to
ARGYLL IS MY NAME Drewry J32
6
S
S
X R
S
to
to

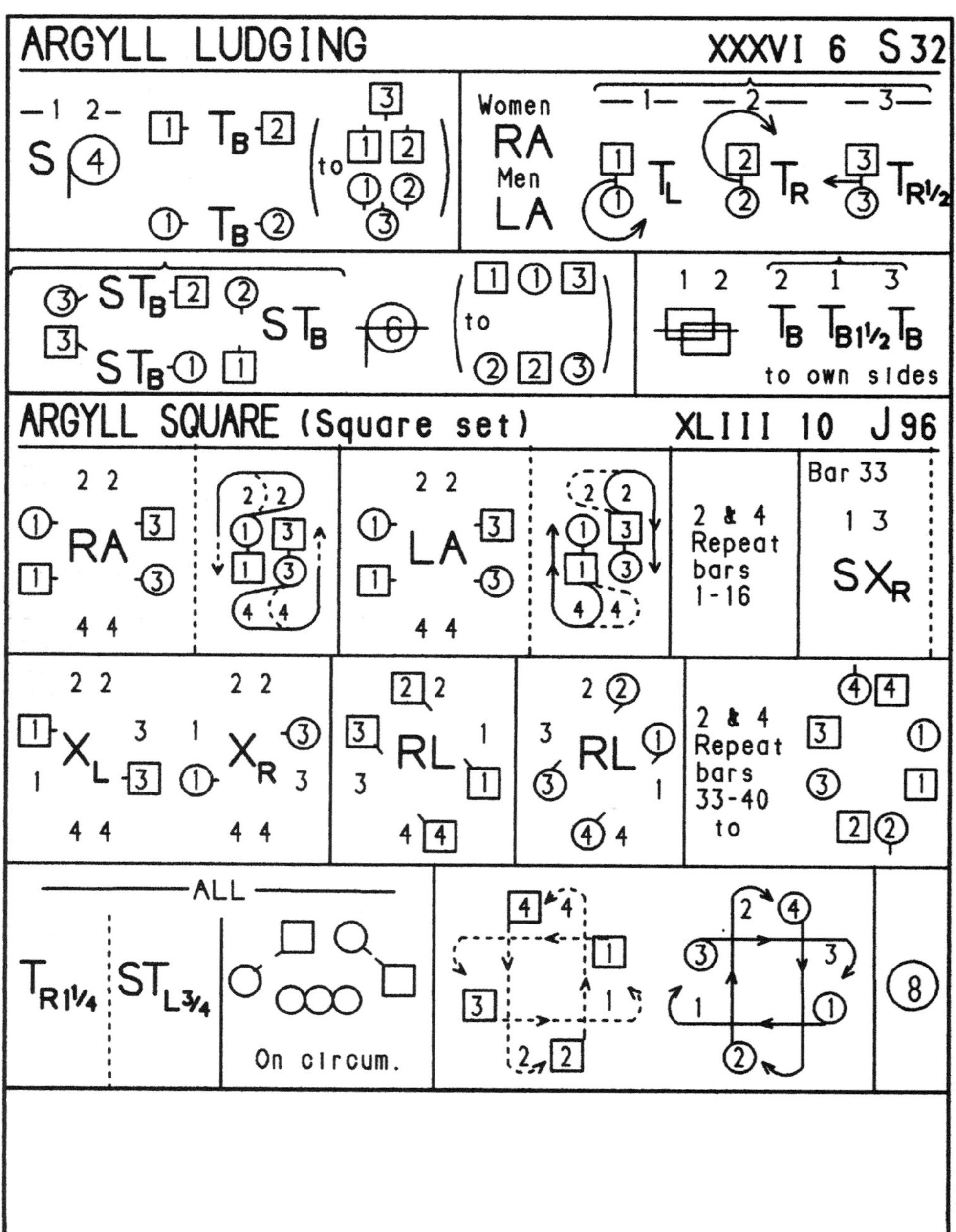
ARGYLL LUDGING
XXXVI 6 S32
—1 2—
S 4
TB
to
Women
RA
Men
LA
—1— —2— —3—
TL TR TR1½
STB
STB
STB
6
to
1 2
2 1 3
TB TB1½ TB
to own sides
ARGYLL SQUARE (Square set)
XLIII 10 J96
2 2
RA
4 4
2 2
LA
4 4
2 & 4
Repeat
bars
1-16
Bar 33
1 3
SXR
2 2
XL
3 1
XR
1 3
4 4
RL
RL
2 & 4
Repeat
bars
33-40
to
ALL
TR1¼
STL¾
On circum.
8

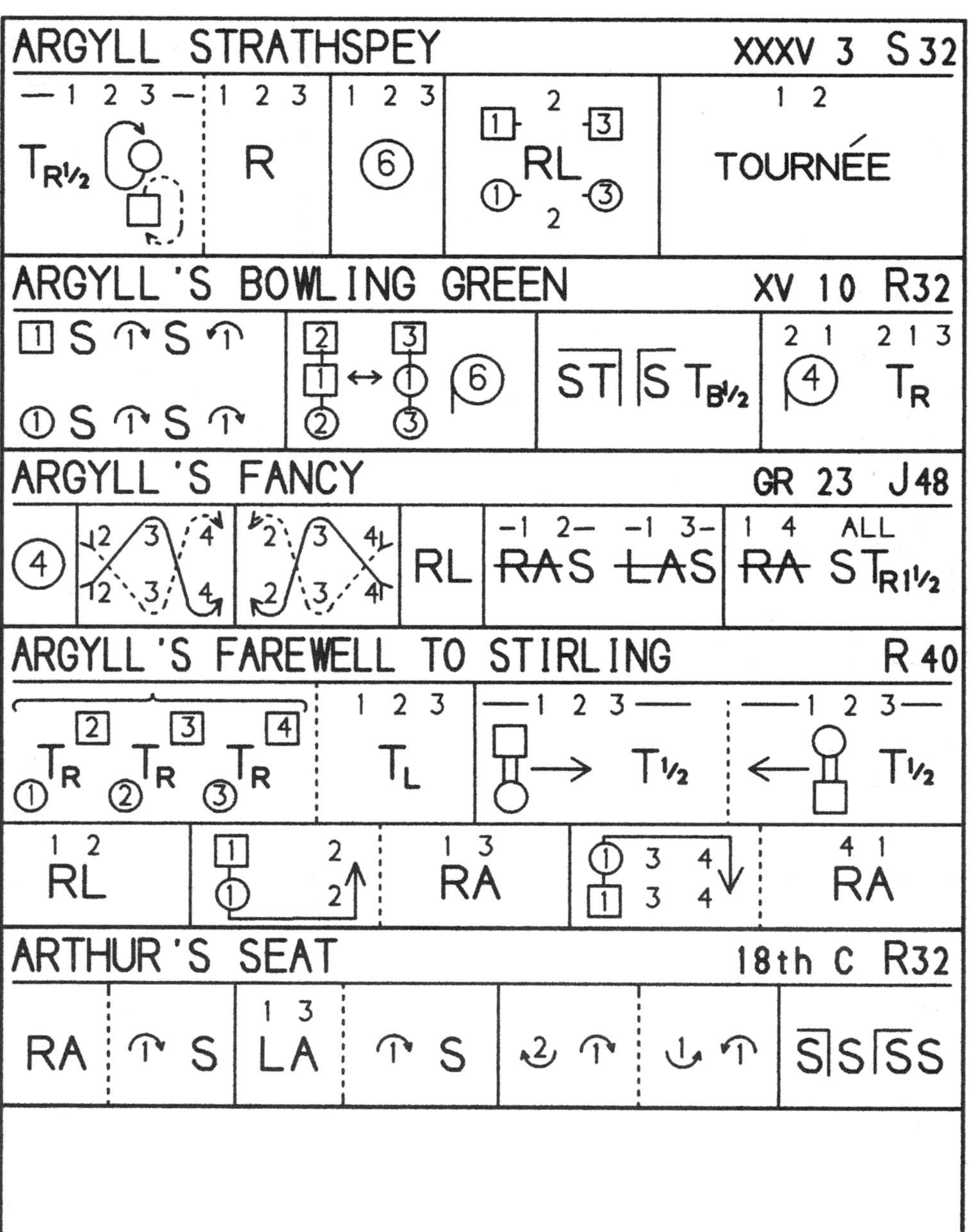
ARGYLL STRATHSPEY
XXXV 3 S32
TOURNÉE
ARGYLL'S BOWLING GREEN
XV 10 R32
ARGYLL'S FANCY
GR 23 J48
RL
RAS LAS
RA ALL
ARGYLL'S FAREWELL TO STIRLING
R 40
RL
RA
RA
ARTHUR'S SEAT
18th C R32
RA
LA

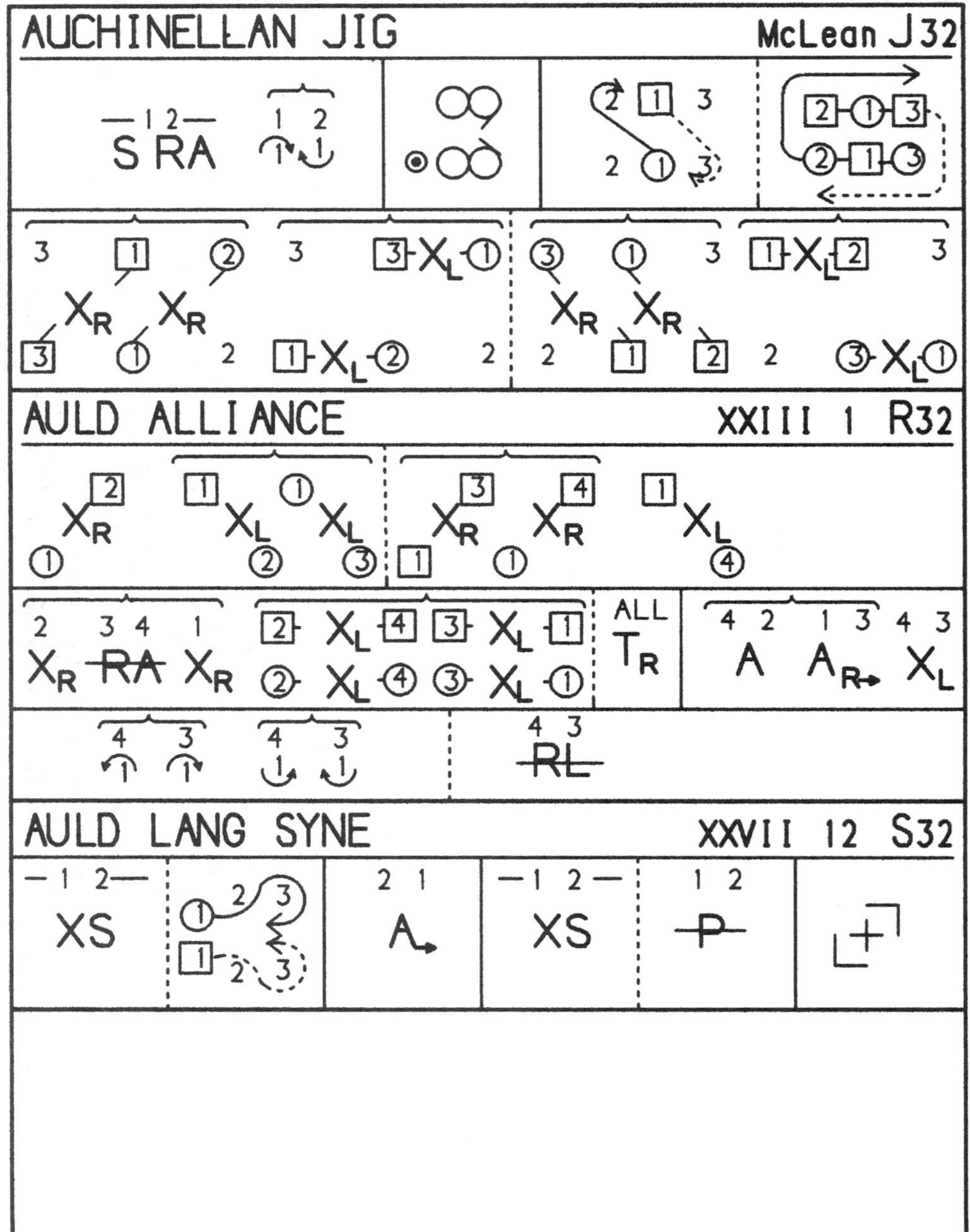
AUCHINELLAN JIG
McLean J32
AULD ALLIANCE
XXIII 1 R32
AULD LANG SYNE
XXVII 12 S32

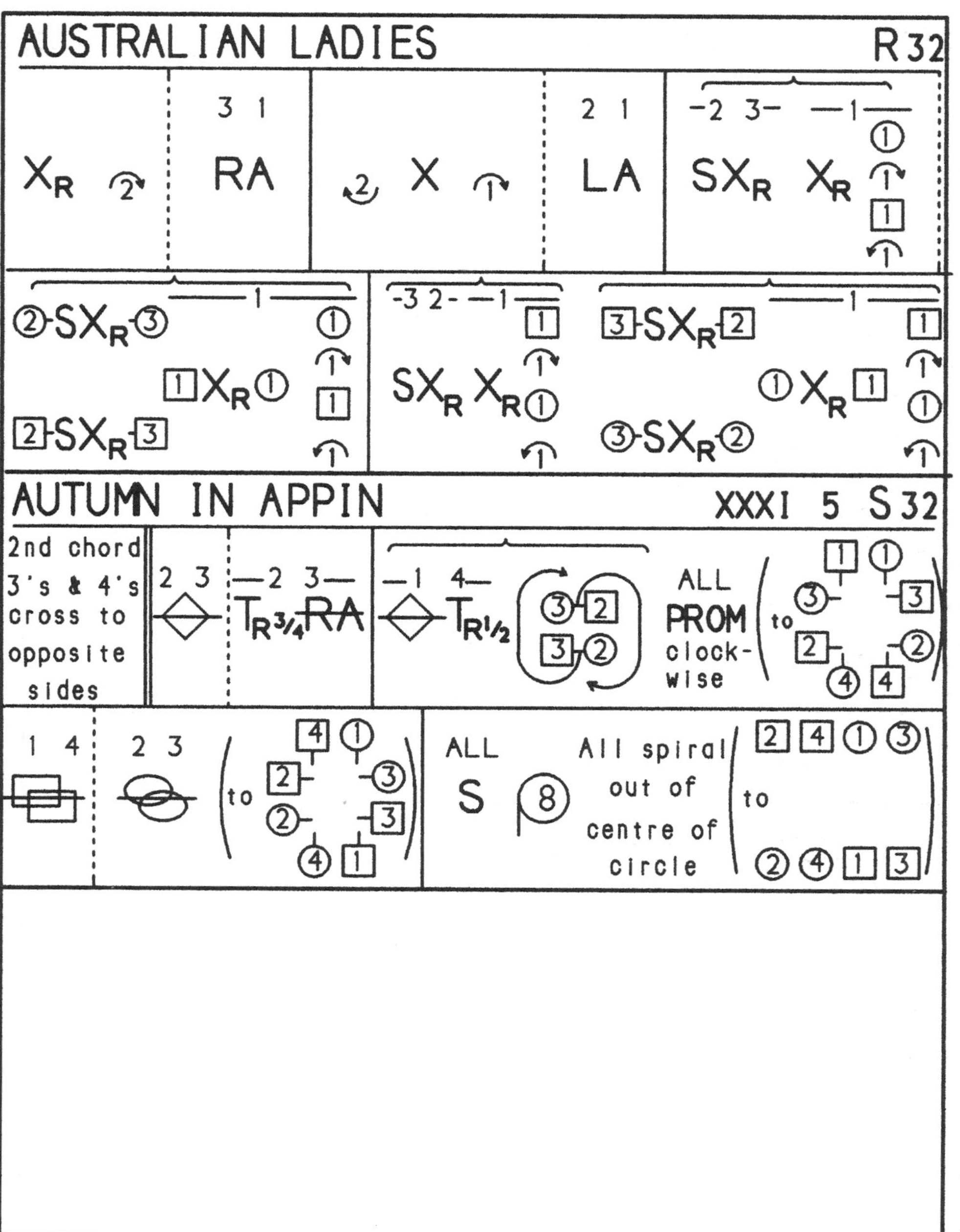

AUSTRALIAN LADIES
R32
3 1
RA
2 1
LA
-2 3-
SX
-3 2-
AUTUMN IN APPIN
XXXI 5 S32
2nd chord 3's & 4's cross to opposite sides
2 3
—2 3—
—1 4—
ALL
PROM
clock-wise
to
1 4
2 3
ALL
S
All spiral out of centre of circle

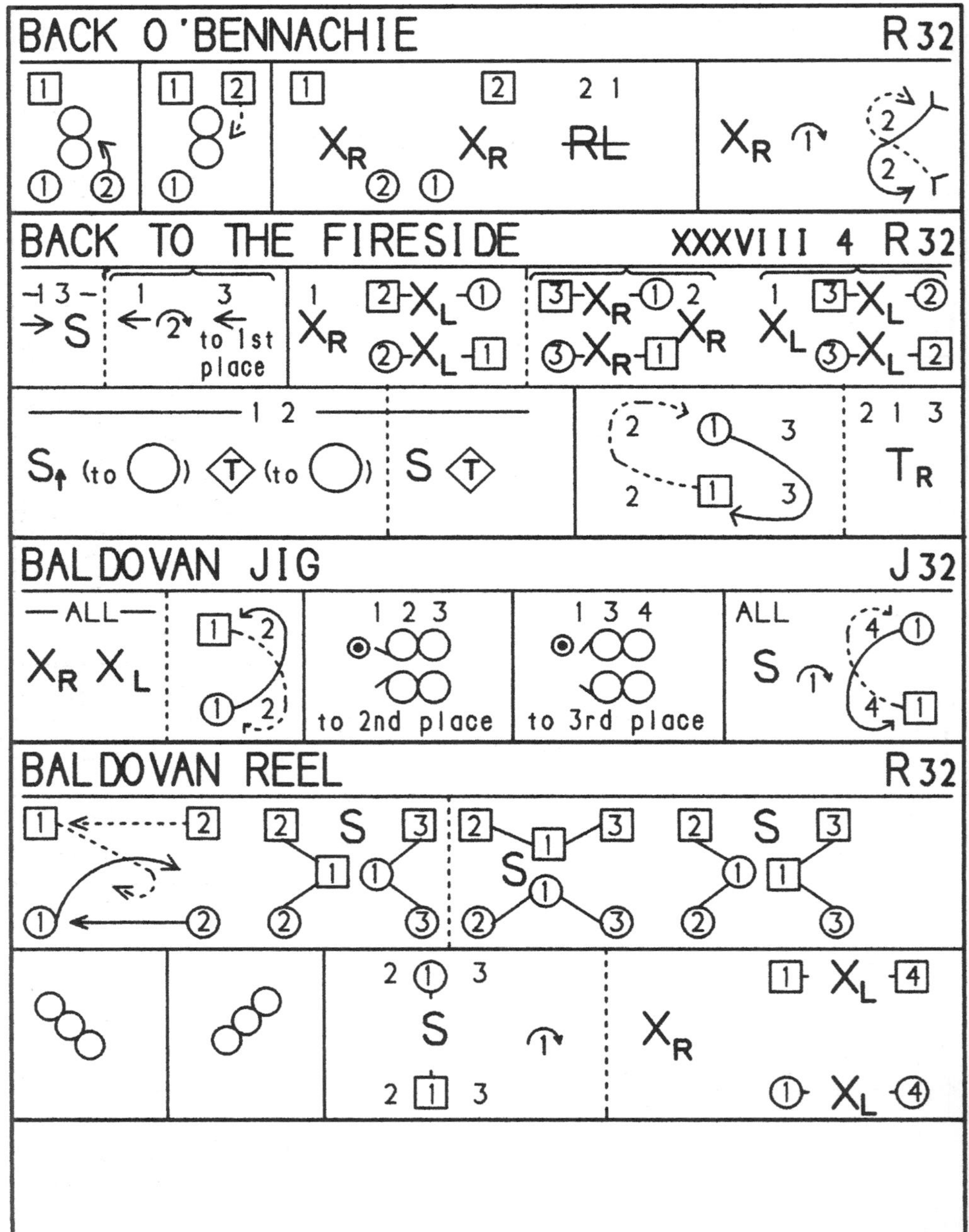
BACK O'BENNACHIE
R32
BACK TO THE FIRESIDE
XXXVIII 4
R32
to 1st place
BALDOVAN JIG
J32
ALL
to 2nd place
to 3rd place
ALL
BALDOVAN REEL
R32

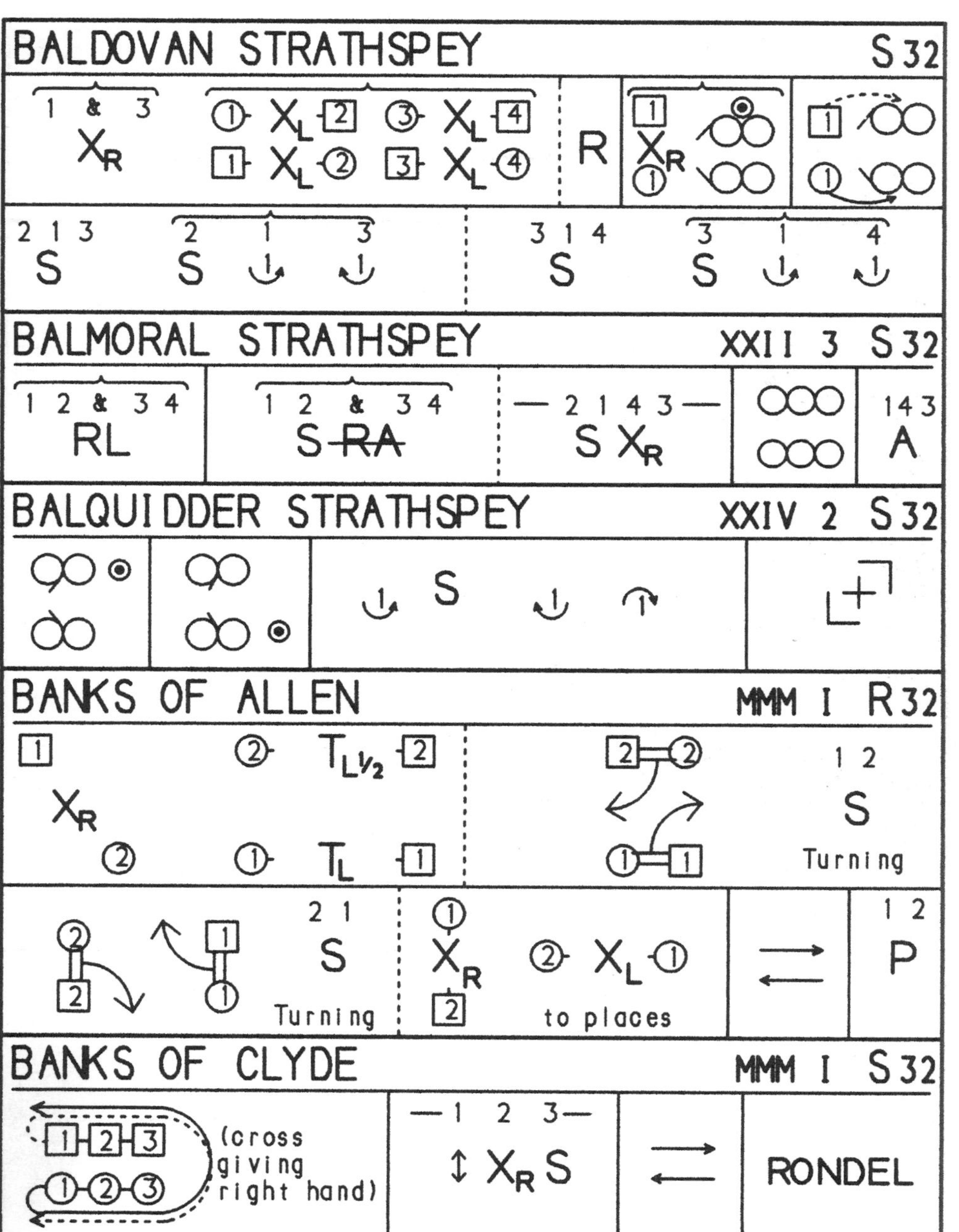
BALDOVAN STRATHSPEY
S 32
1 & 3
R
2 1 3
S
3 1 4
BALMORAL STRATHSPEY
XXII 3 S 32
1 2 & 3 4
RL
S RA
— 2 1 4 3 —
143
A
BALQUIDDER STRATHSPEY
XXIV 2 S 32
BANKS OF ALLEN
MMM I R 32
1 2
S
Turning
2 1
S
Turning
to places
1 2
P
BANKS OF CLYDE
MMM I S 32
(cross giving right hand)
— 1 2 3 —
RONDEL

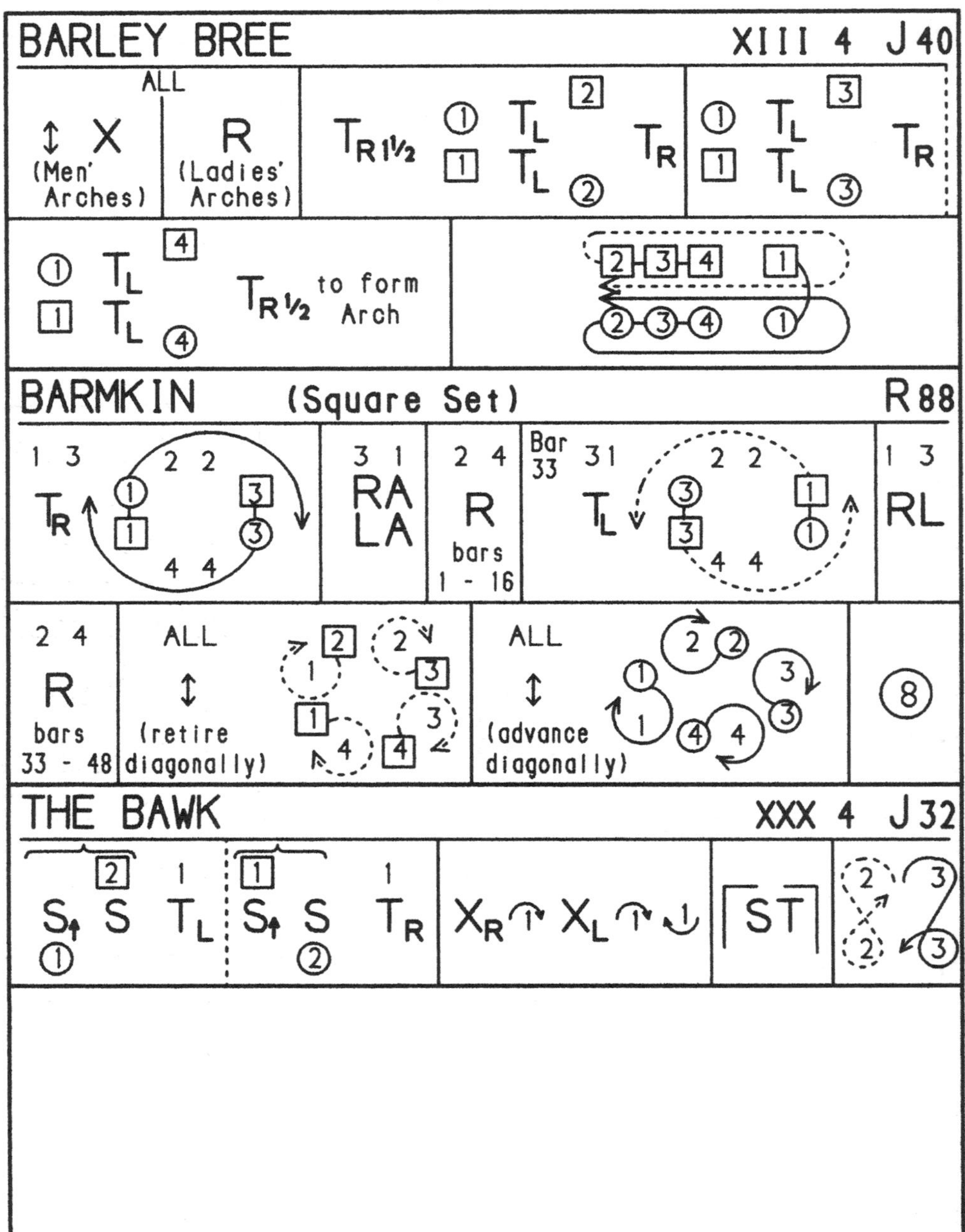
BARLEY BREE
XIII 4 J40
ALL
X
(Men' Arches)
R
(Ladies' Arches)
TR 1½
TL
TR
to form Arch
BARMKIN (Square Set)
R88
1 3
2 2
4 4
TR
3 1
RA
LA
2 4
R
bars 1 - 16
Bar 33
31
TL
1 3
RL
R
bars 33 - 48
ALL
(retire diagonally)
ALL
(advance diagonally)
8
THE BAWK
XXX 4 J32
S S TL
S S TR
XR XL
ST

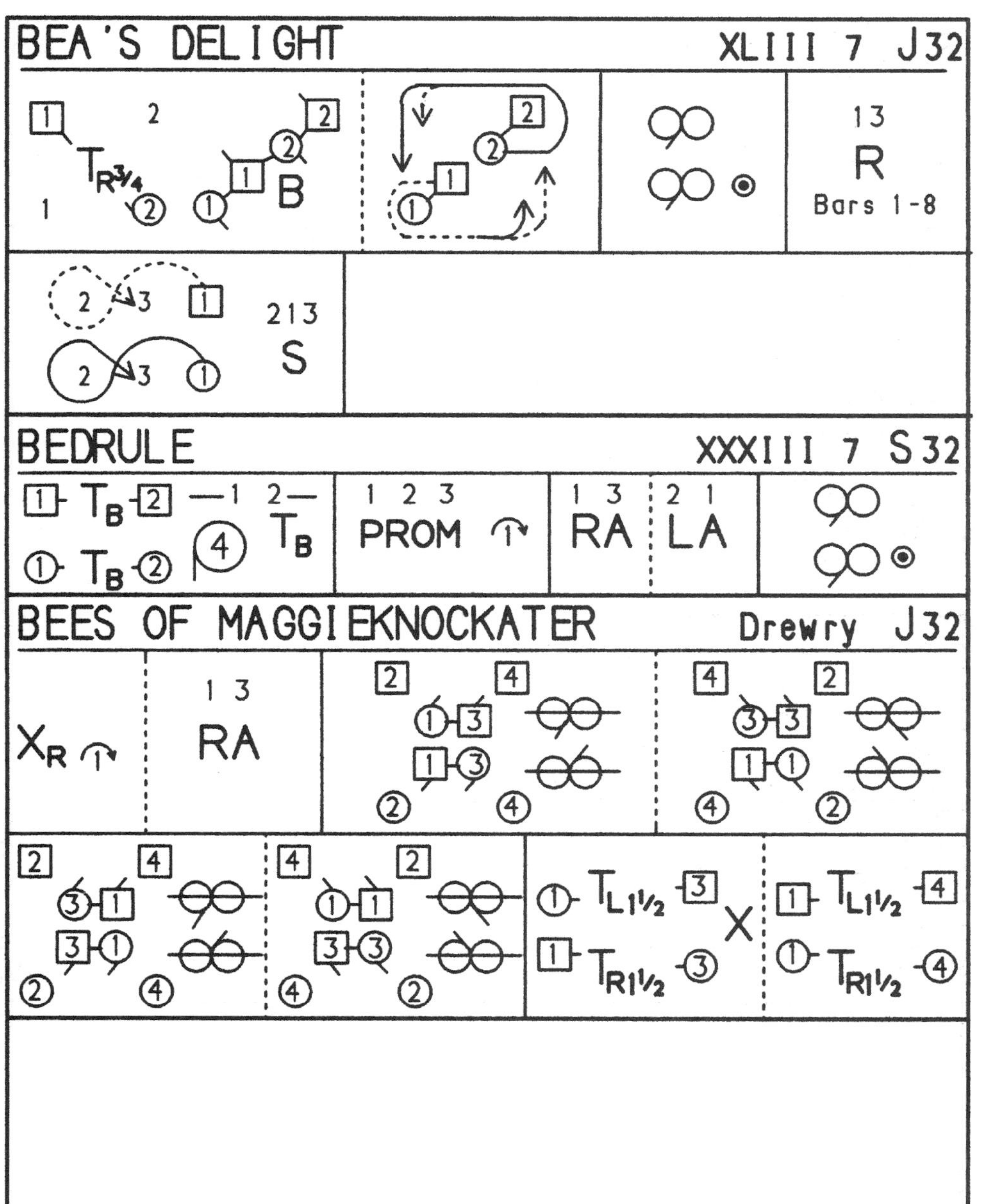
BEA'S DELIGHT
XLIII 7 J32
1
2
TR3/4
2
1
2
1
2
B
2
2
1
1
13
R
Bars 1-8
2
3
1
213
S
2
3
1
BEDRULE
XXXIII 7 S32
1
TB
2
—1 2—
1
TB
2
4
TB
1 2 3
PROM
1
1 3
RA
2 1
LA
BEES OF MAGGIEKNOCKATER
Drewry J32
XR
1
1 3
RA
2
4
1
3
1
3
2
4
4
2
3
3
1
1
4
2
2
4
3
1
3
1
2
4
4
2
1
1
3
3
4
2
1
TL1½
3
1
TR1½
3
X
1
TL1½
4
1
TR1½
4

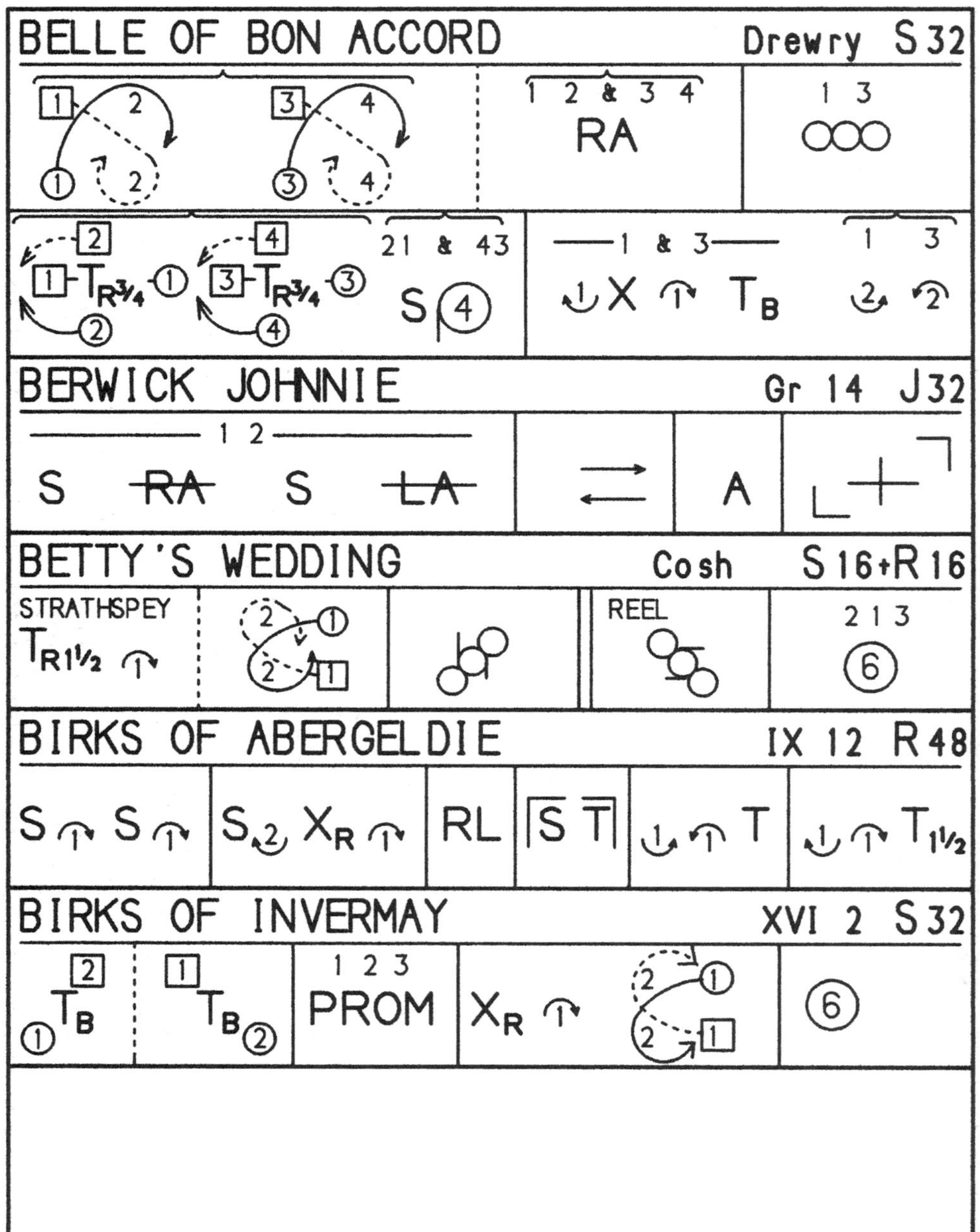
BELLE OF BON ACCORD
Drewry S32
1 2 & 3 4
RA
1 3
21 & 43
S 4
1 & 3
X
T_B
BERWICK JOHNNIE
Gr 14 J32
1 2
S RA S LA
A
BETTY'S WEDDING
Cosh S16+R16
STRATHSPEY
$T_{R1\frac{1}{2}}$
REEL
2 1 3
6
BIRKS OF ABERGELDIE
IX 12 R48
S S
S_2 X_R
RL
S T
T
$T_{1\frac{1}{2}}$
BIRKS OF INVERMAY
XVI 2 S32
T_B
T_B
1 2 3
PROM
X_R
6

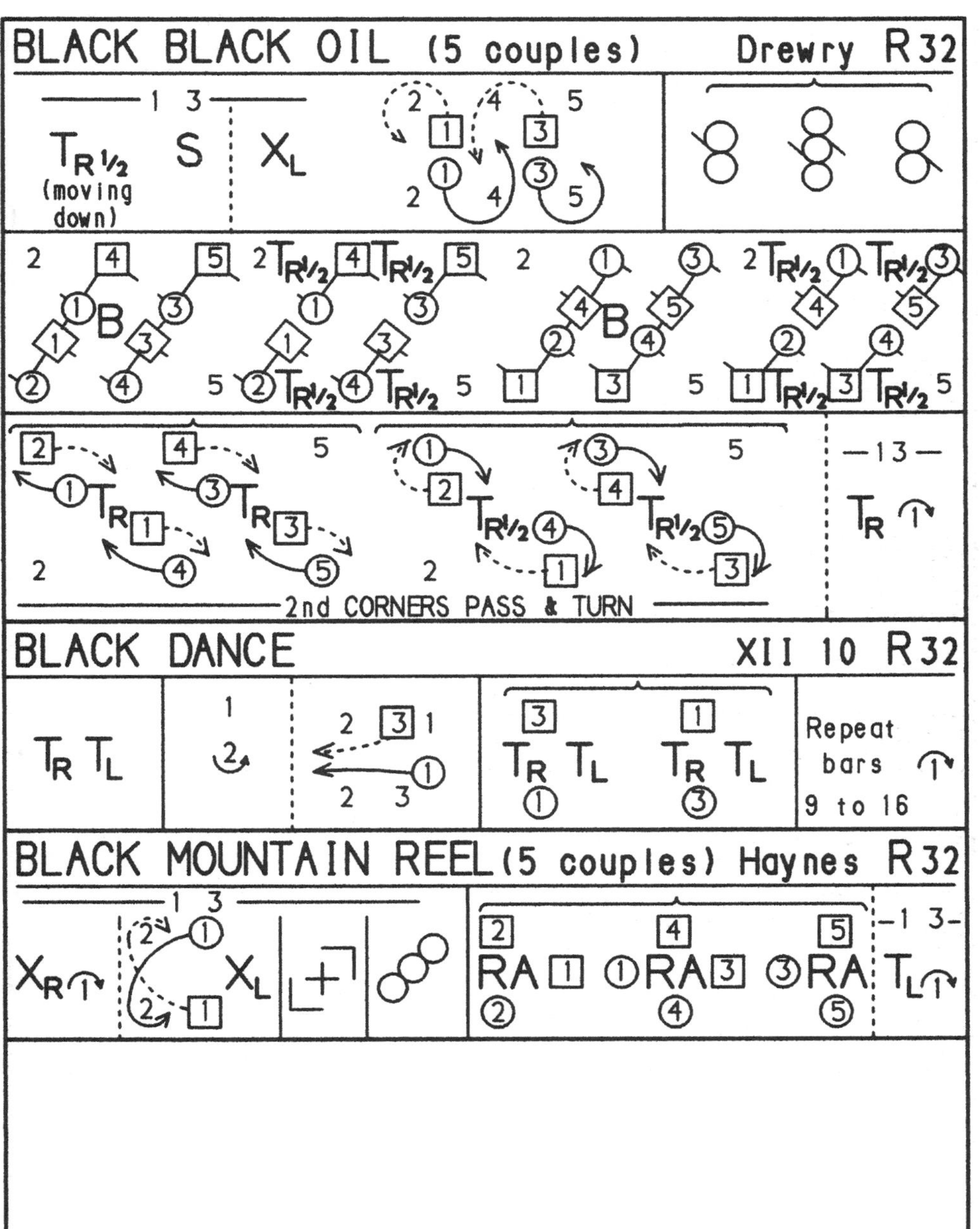
BLACK BLACK OIL (5 couples) Drewry R32
(moving down)
2nd CORNERS PASS & TURN
BLACK DANCE XII 10 R32
Repeat bars 9 to 16
BLACK MOUNTAIN REEL (5 couples) Haynes R32

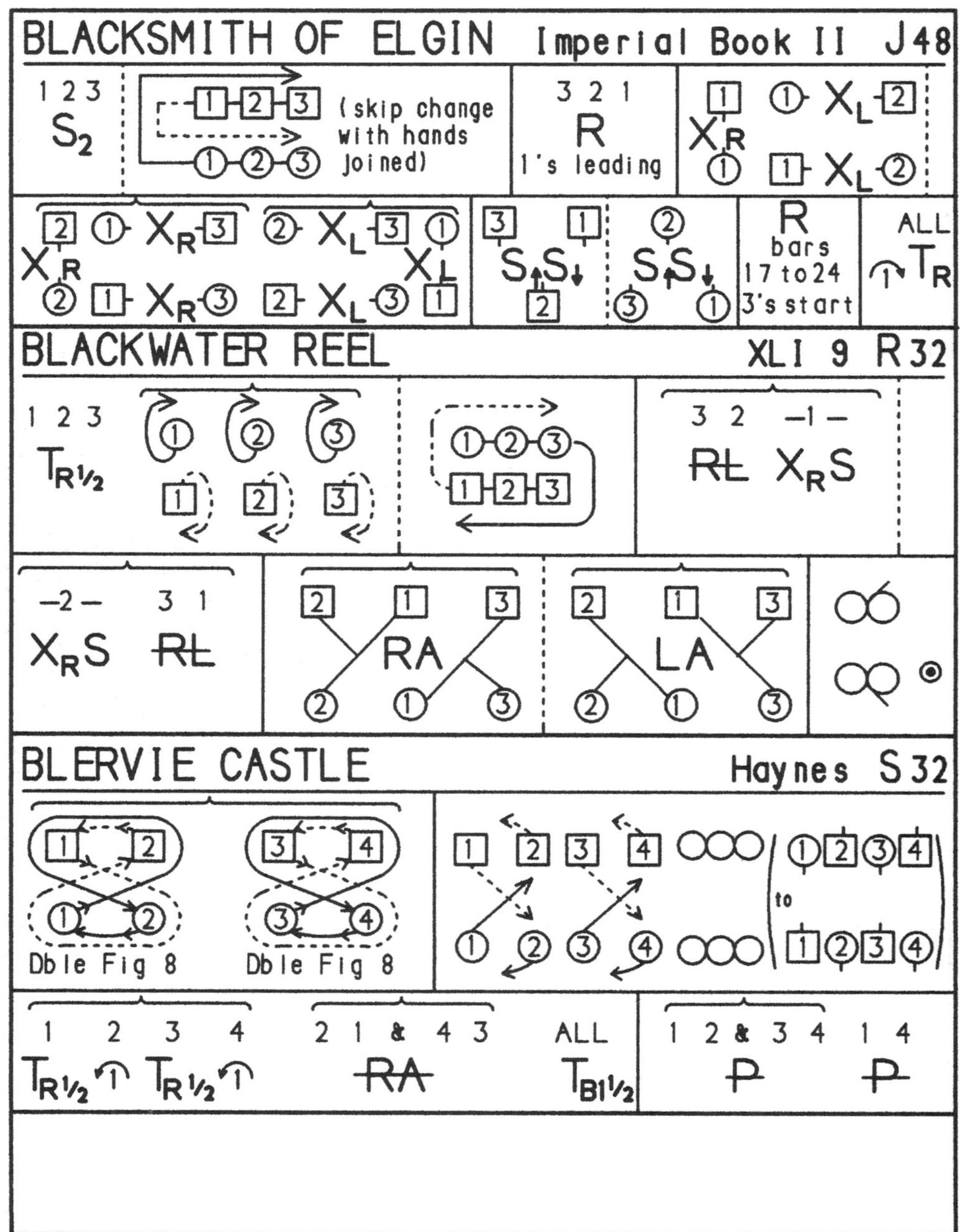
BLACKSMITH OF ELGIN
Imperial Book II
J48
1 2 3
S2
(skip change with hands joined)
3 2 1
R
1's leading
XR
XL
XR
XR
XL
XL
S S
S S
R
bars 17 to 24
3's start
ALL
TR
BLACKWATER REEL
XLI 9
R32
1 2 3
TR½
3 2 —1—
RL XRS
—2— 3 1
XRS RL
RA
LA
BLERVIE CASTLE
Haynes
S32
Dble Fig 8
Dble Fig 8
to
1 2 3 4
TR½ TR½
2 1 & 4 3
RA
ALL
TB1½
1 2 & 3 4
1 4
P
P

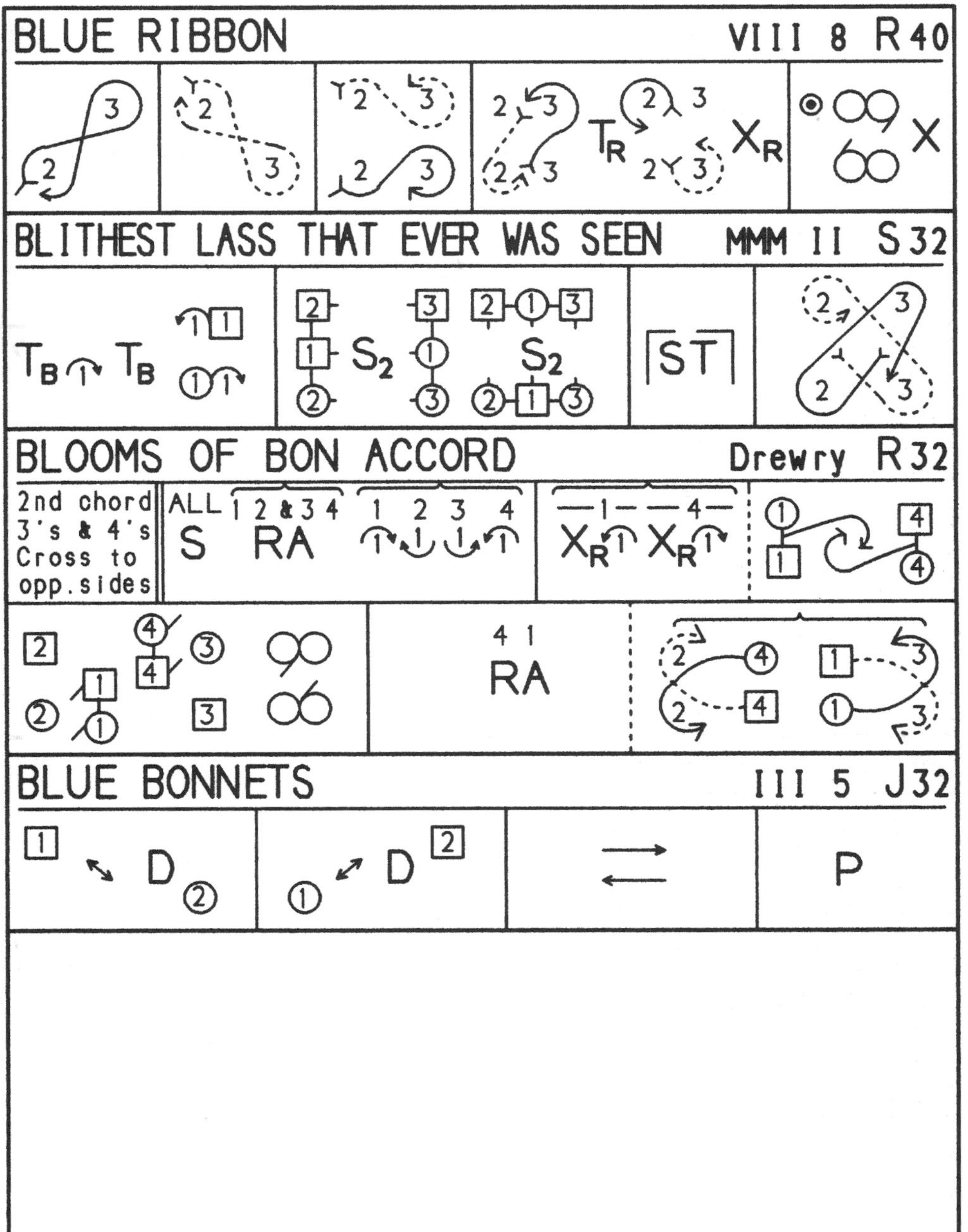
BLUE RIBBON
VIII 8 R40
BLITHEST LASS THAT EVER WAS SEEN
MMM II S32
BLOOMS OF BON ACCORD
Drewry R32
2nd chord
3's & 4's
Cross to
opp.sides
ALL
S
1 2 & 3 4
RA
4 1
RA
BLUE BONNETS
III 5 J32

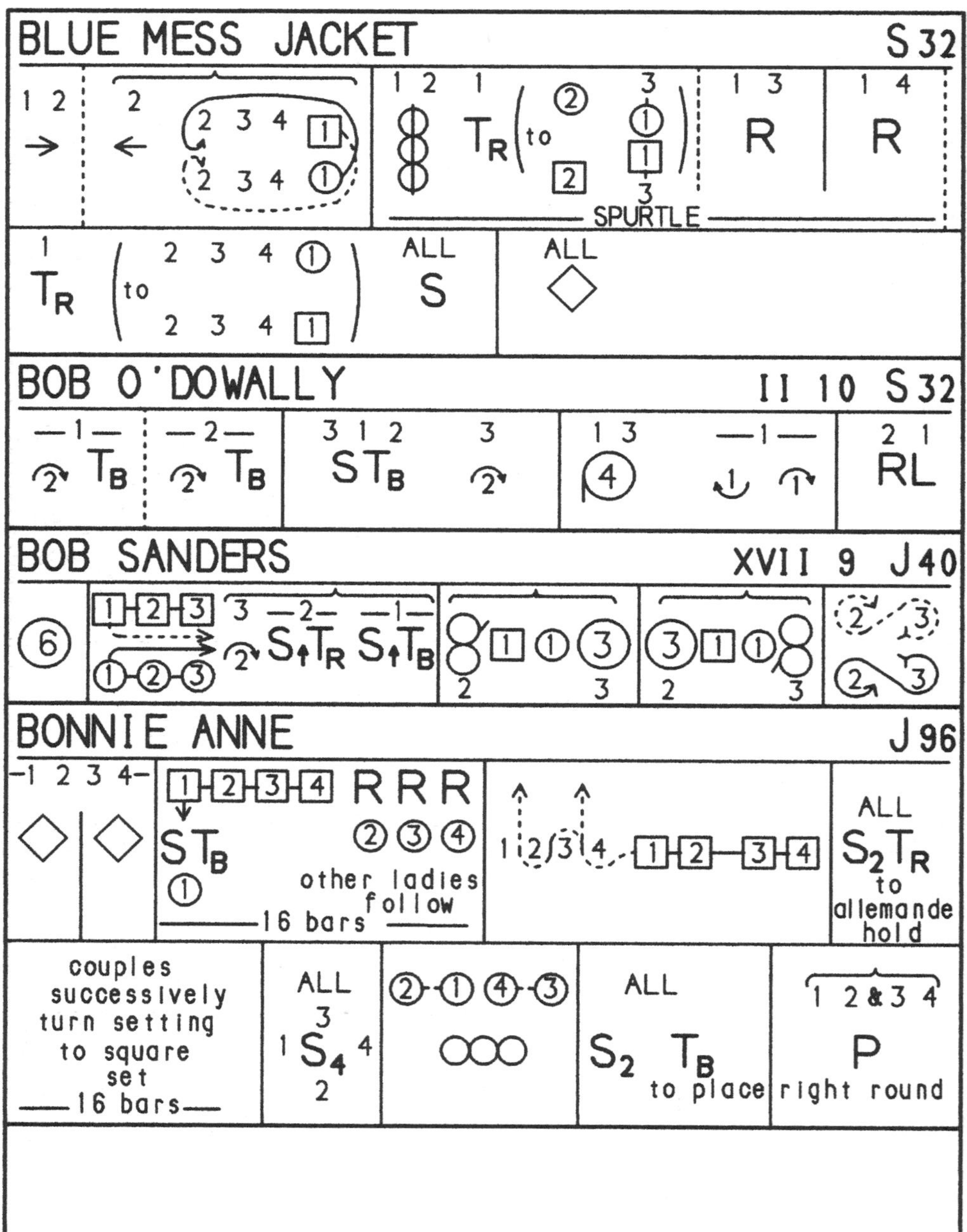
BLUE MESS JACKET
S 32
SPURTLE
ALL
S
BOB O'DOWALLY
II 10 S 32
RL
BOB SANDERS
XVII 9 J 40
BONNIE ANNE
J 96
R R R
other ladies follow
16 bars
ALL
to allemande hold
couples successively turn setting to square set
16 bars
ALL
to place
P
right round

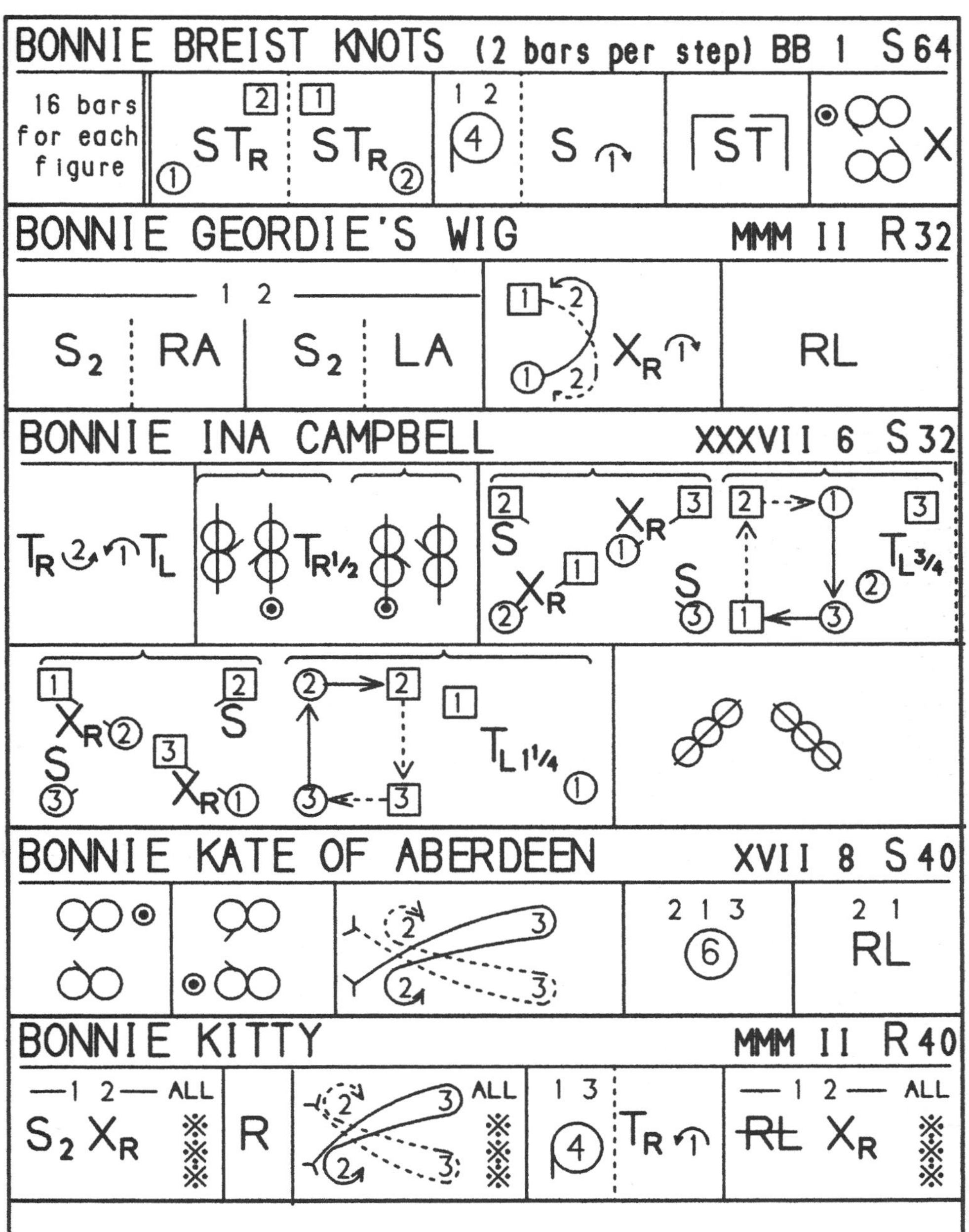
BONNIE BREIST KNOTS (2 bars per step) BB 1 S 64
16 bars for each figure
STR STR
1 2
4
S
ST
X
BONNIE GEORDIE'S WIG MMM II R 32
1 2
S2 RA S2 LA
XR
RL
BONNIE INA CAMPBELL XXXVII 6 S 32
TR TL
TR1/2
S XR XR S
TL3/4
XR S S XR
TL 1 1/4
BONNIE KATE OF ABERDEEN XVII 8 S 40
2 1 3
6
2 1
RL
BONNIE KITTY MMM II R 40
1 2 ALL
S2 XR
R
ALL
1 3
4
TR
1 2 ALL
RL XR

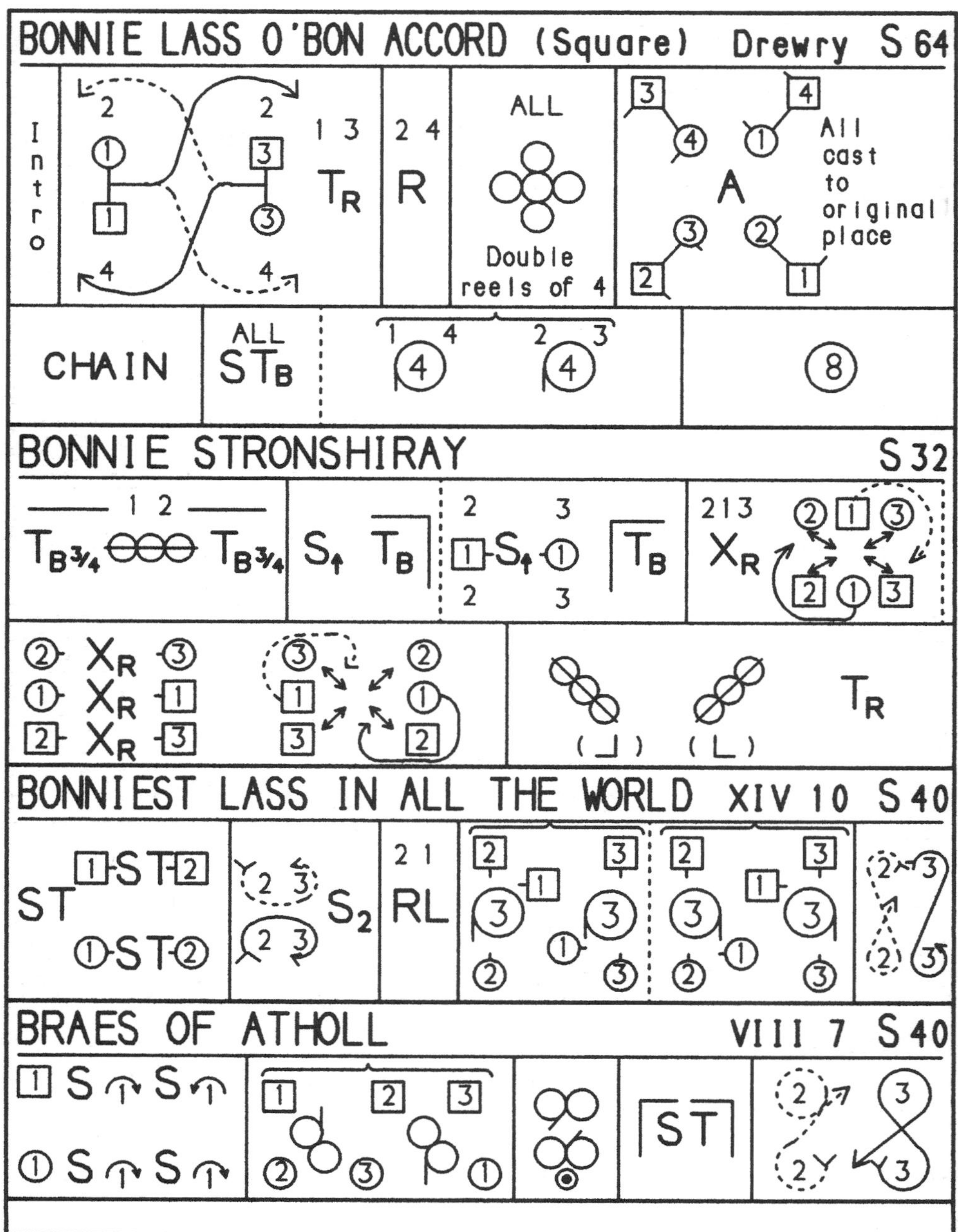
BONNIE LASS O'BON ACCORD (Square) Drewry S 64
Intro
1 3
T_R
2 4
R
ALL
Double reels of 4
A
All cast to original place
CHAIN
ALL
ST_B
8
BONNIE STRONSHIRAY S 32
1 2
$T_{B3/4}$
$T_{B3/4}$
T_B
X_R
X_R
T_R
BONNIEST LASS IN ALL THE WORLD XIV 10 S 40
ST
RL
S_2
BRAES OF ATHOLL VIII 7 S 40
ST

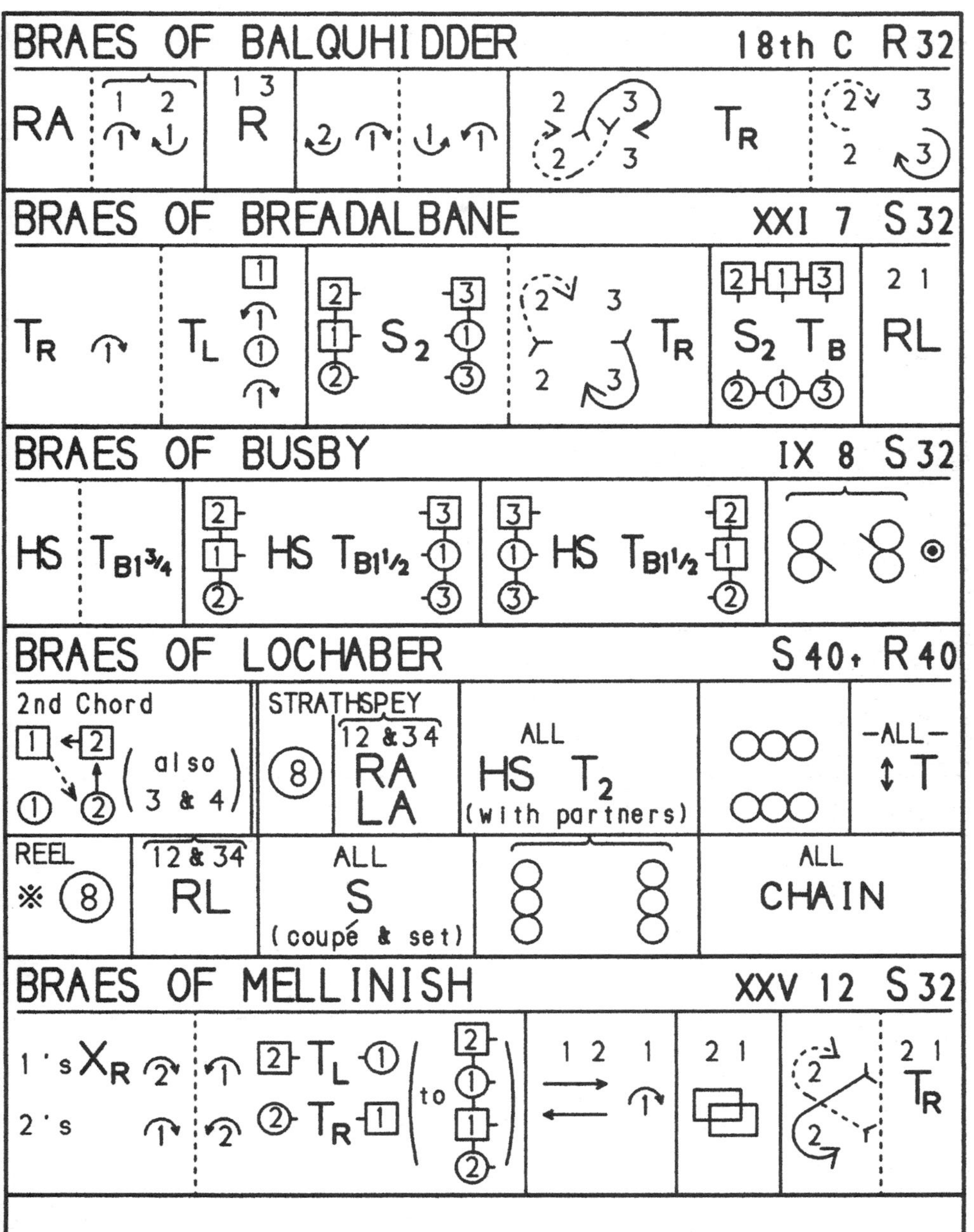
BRAES OF BALQUHIDDER
18th C R32
RA
R
TR
BRAES OF BREADALBANE
XXI 7 S32
TR
TL
S2
TR
S2 TB
RL
BRAES OF BUSBY
IX 8 S32
HS
TB1¾
HS TB1½
HS TB1½
BRAES OF LOCHABER
S40+ R40
2nd Chord
also
3 & 4
STRATHSPEY
12 & 34
RA
LA
ALL
HS T2
(with partners)
—ALL—
T
REEL
※
12 & 34
RL
ALL
S
(coupé & set)
ALL
CHAIN
BRAES OF MELLINISH
XXV 12 S32
1's XR
2's
TL
TR
to
TR

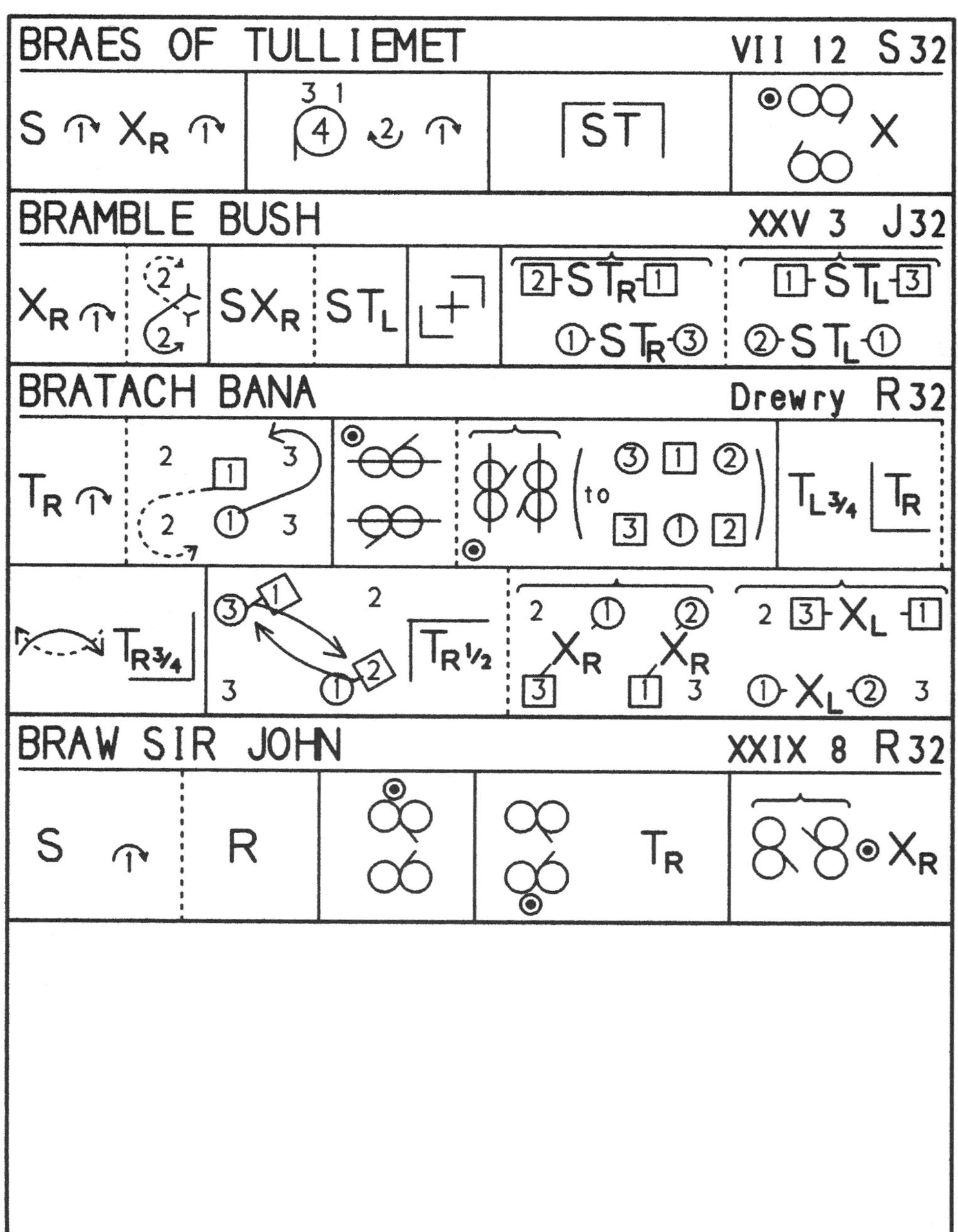
BRAES OF TULLIEMET
VII 12 S32
BRAMBLE BUSH
XXV 3 J32
BRATACH BANA
Drewry R32
BRAW SIR JOHN
XXIX 8 R32

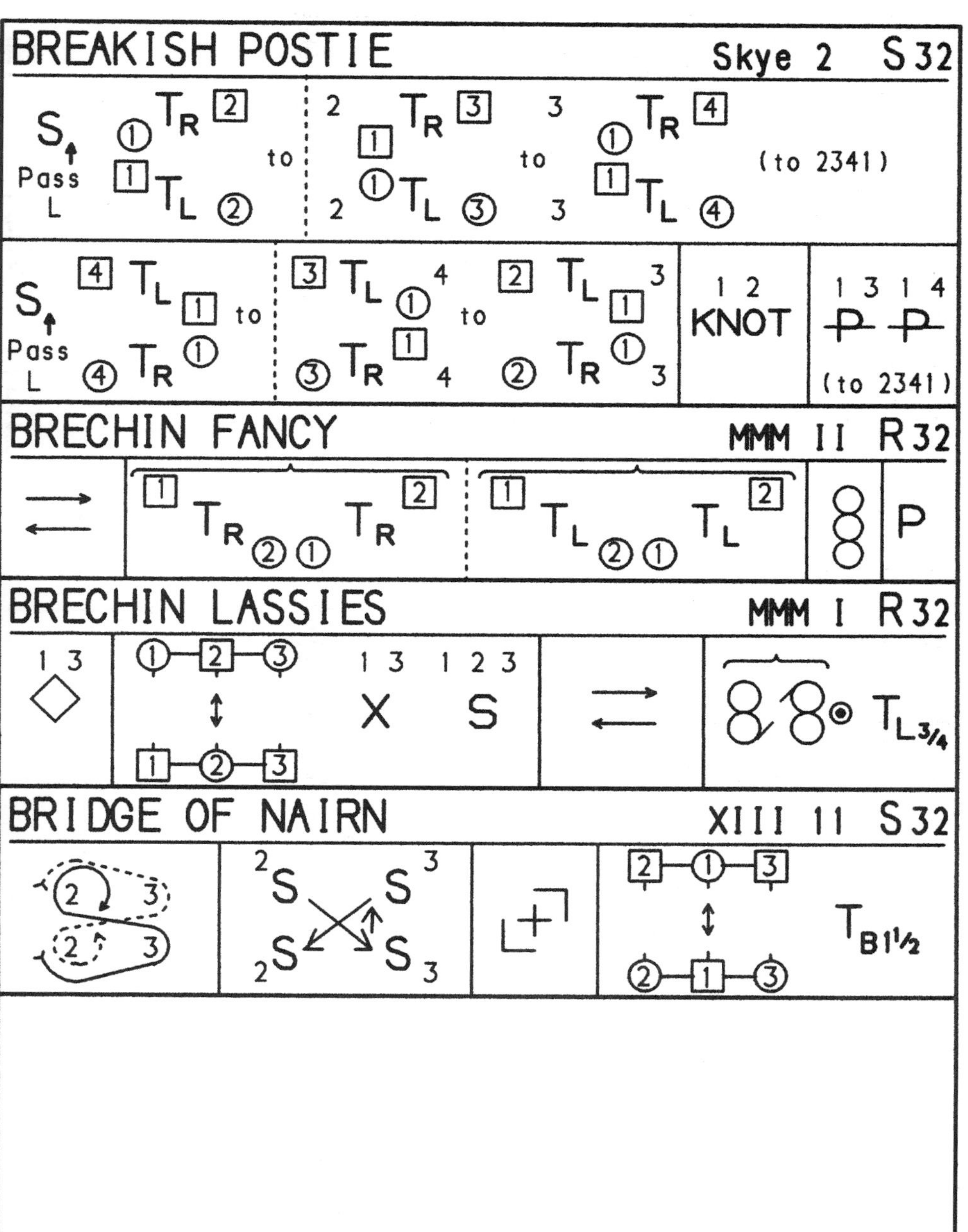
BREAKISH POSTIE
Skye 2 S32
Pass L
to
(to 2341)
KNOT
(to 2341)
BRECHIN FANCY
MMM II R32
BRECHIN LASSIES
MMM I R32
BRIDGE OF NAIRN
XIII 11 S32

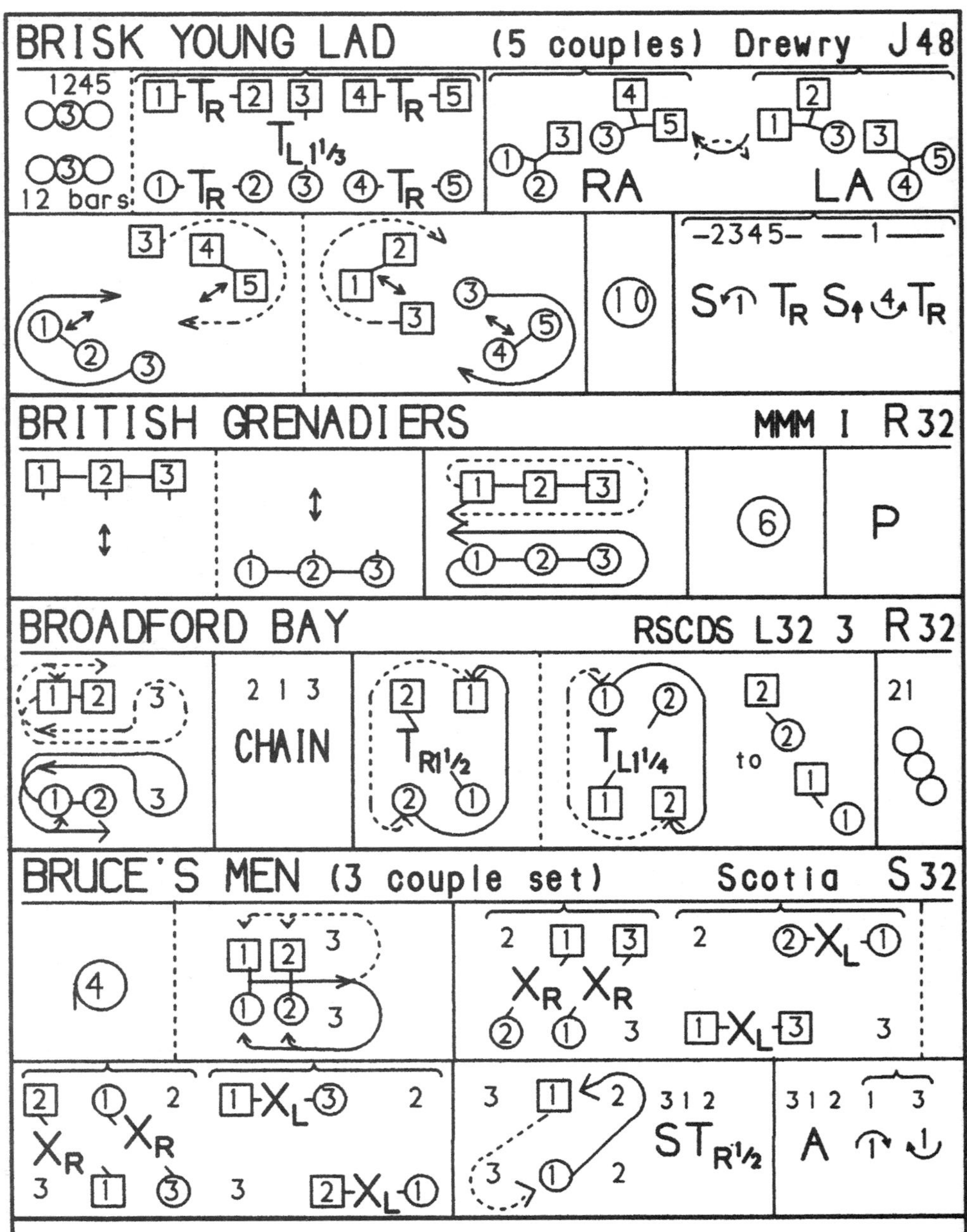
BRISK YOUNG LAD (5 couples) Drewry J48
1245
12 bars
TR
TL1⅓
RA
LA
-2345- —1—
S TR S 4 TR
10
BRITISH GRENADIERS MMM I R32
6
P
BROADFORD BAY RSCDS L32 3 R32
2 1 3
CHAIN
TR1½
TL1¼
to
21
BRUCE'S MEN (3 couple set) Scotia S32
4
XR XR
XL
XL
312
STR1½
312
A

BUCHAN EIGHTSOME (Square set) XXI 8 R400

(A) (8)	~~CHAIN~~	RA women inside	~~CHAIN~~ (to original places	LA men inside
(B) (7) [1] inside	[1] ST R ST L (3)	[1] [1] ST L ST R (4) (2)	with (1) & (3)	with (4) & (2)

Repeat (B) with [2] inside, then [3] [4] (1) (2) (3) (4)
Then repeat (A)

BURNIEBOOZLE R32

S (1) $T_{L1½}$	T_R	[2] S [3] [2] S (1) (1) [1] [3] (2) (2) S (3) [1] S (3) — DANCE TO EACH CORNER & SET —
Continue for another 8 bars	1 $T_{R1¼}$	(3) (2) ~~RL~~ [3] [2]

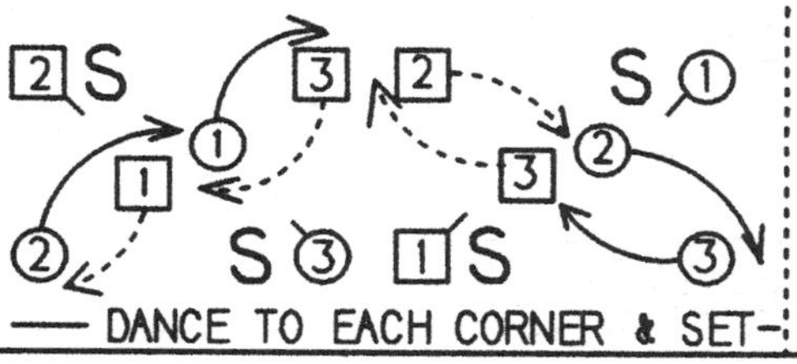

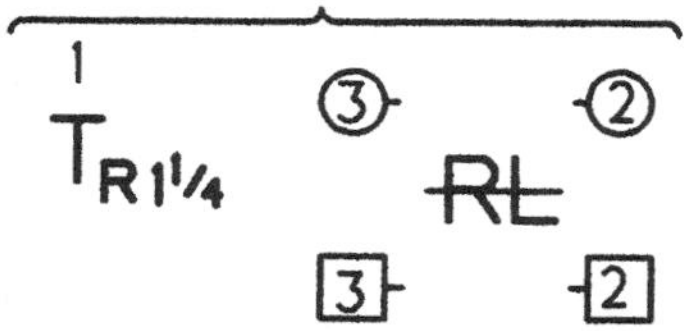

BURNS' HORNPIPE XXVII 4 H32

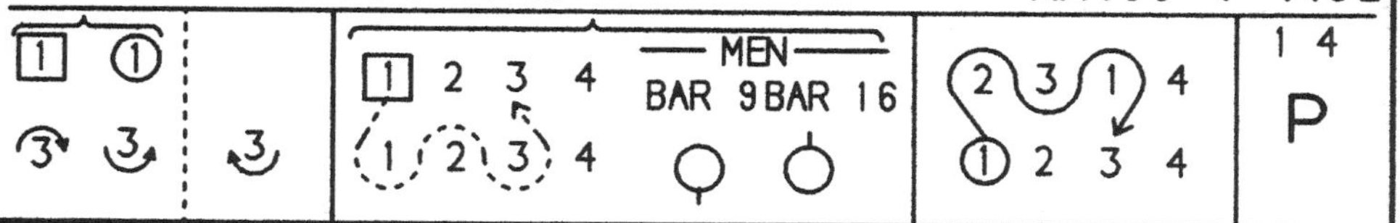

[1] (1) 3 3	3	[1] 2 3 4 1 2 3 4 — MEN — BAR 9 BAR 16	2 3 1 4 (1) 2 3 4	1 4 P

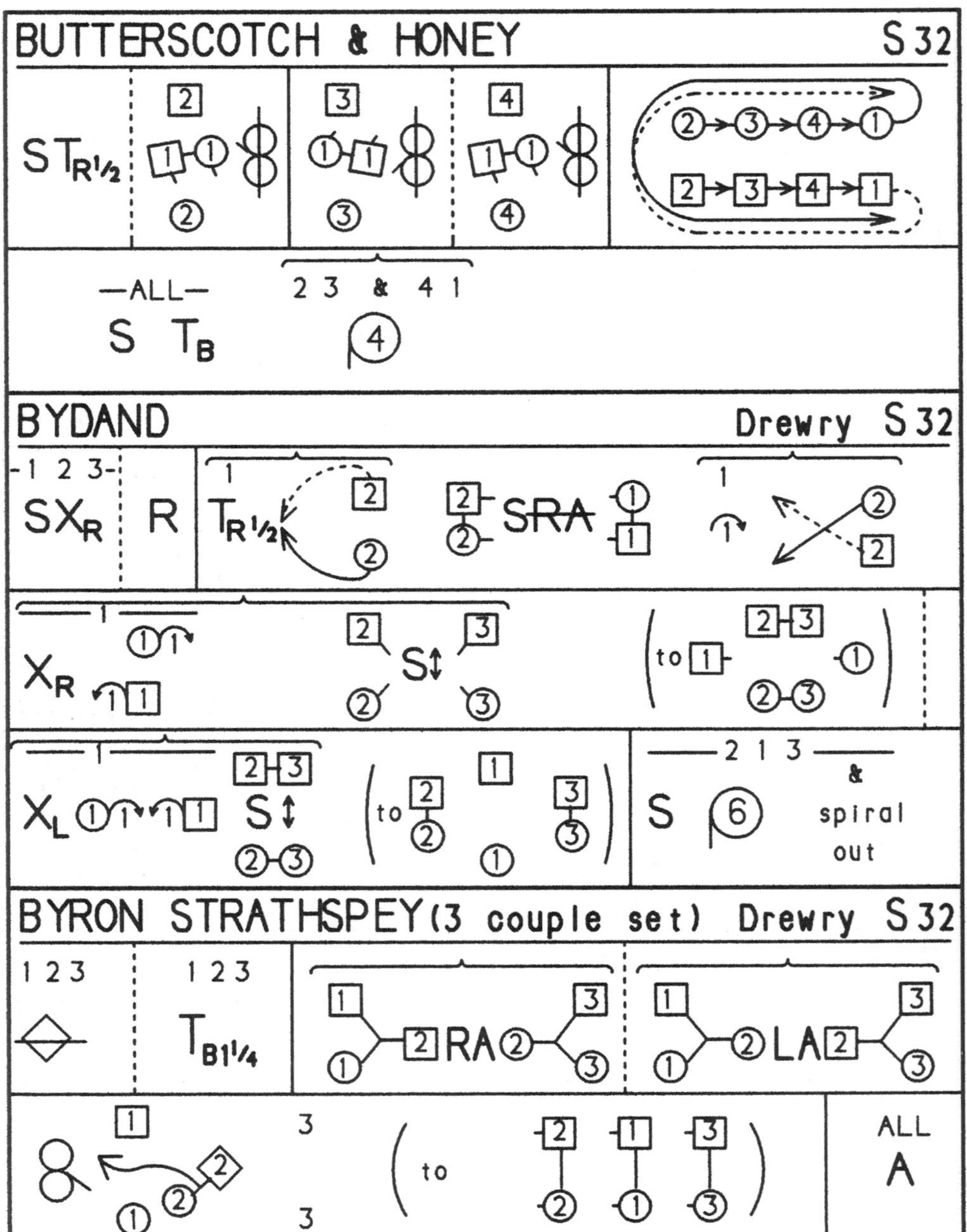

BUTTERSCOTCH & HONEY
S 32
ST R 1/2
2
3
4
1
ALL
S T B
2 3 & 4 1
4
BYDAND
Drewry S 32
1 2 3
SX R
R
T R 1/2
SRA
X R
S
to
X L
S
2 1 3
S
6
& spiral out
BYRON STRATHSPEY (3 couple set) Drewry S 32
1 2 3
1 2 3
T B1 1/4
RA
LA
3
to
3
ALL
A

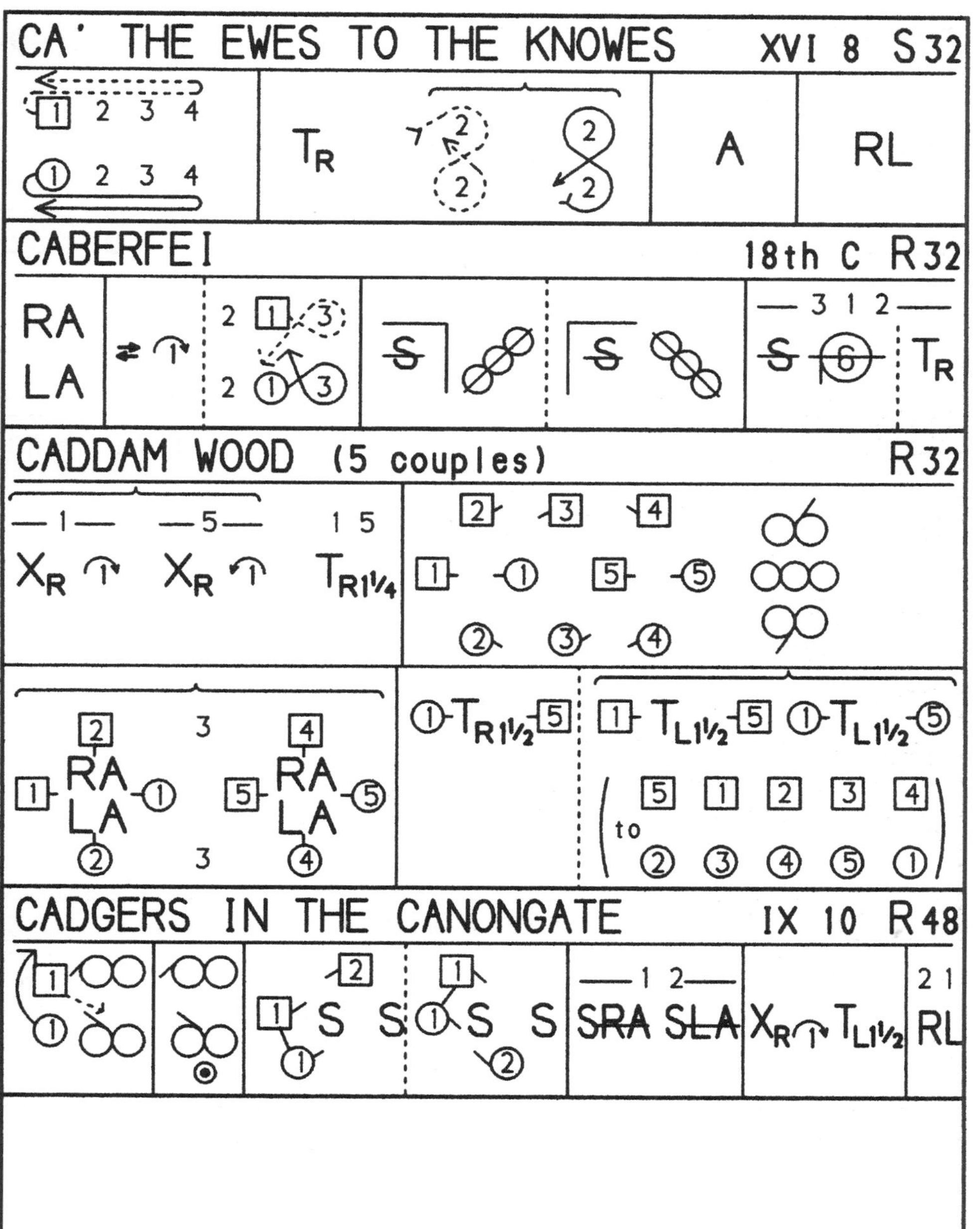
CA' THE EWES TO THE KNOWES
XVI 8 S32
1 2 3 4
1 2 3 4
TR
2
2
2
2
A
RL
CABERFEI
18th C R32
RA
LA
2 1 3
2 1 3
S
S
3 1 2
S 6
TR
CADDAM WOOD (5 couples)
R32
1
5
1 5
XR
XR
TR1¼
2 3 4
1 1 5 5
2 3 4
2 3 4
1 RA LA 1
5 RA LA 5
2 3 4 3
1 TR1½ 5
1 TL1½ 5 1 TL1½ 5
5 1 2 3 4
to
2 3 4 5 1
CADGERS IN THE CANONGATE
IX 10 R48
1
1
2
1 S S
1 S S
1
2
1 2
SRA SLA
XR TL1½
2 1
RL

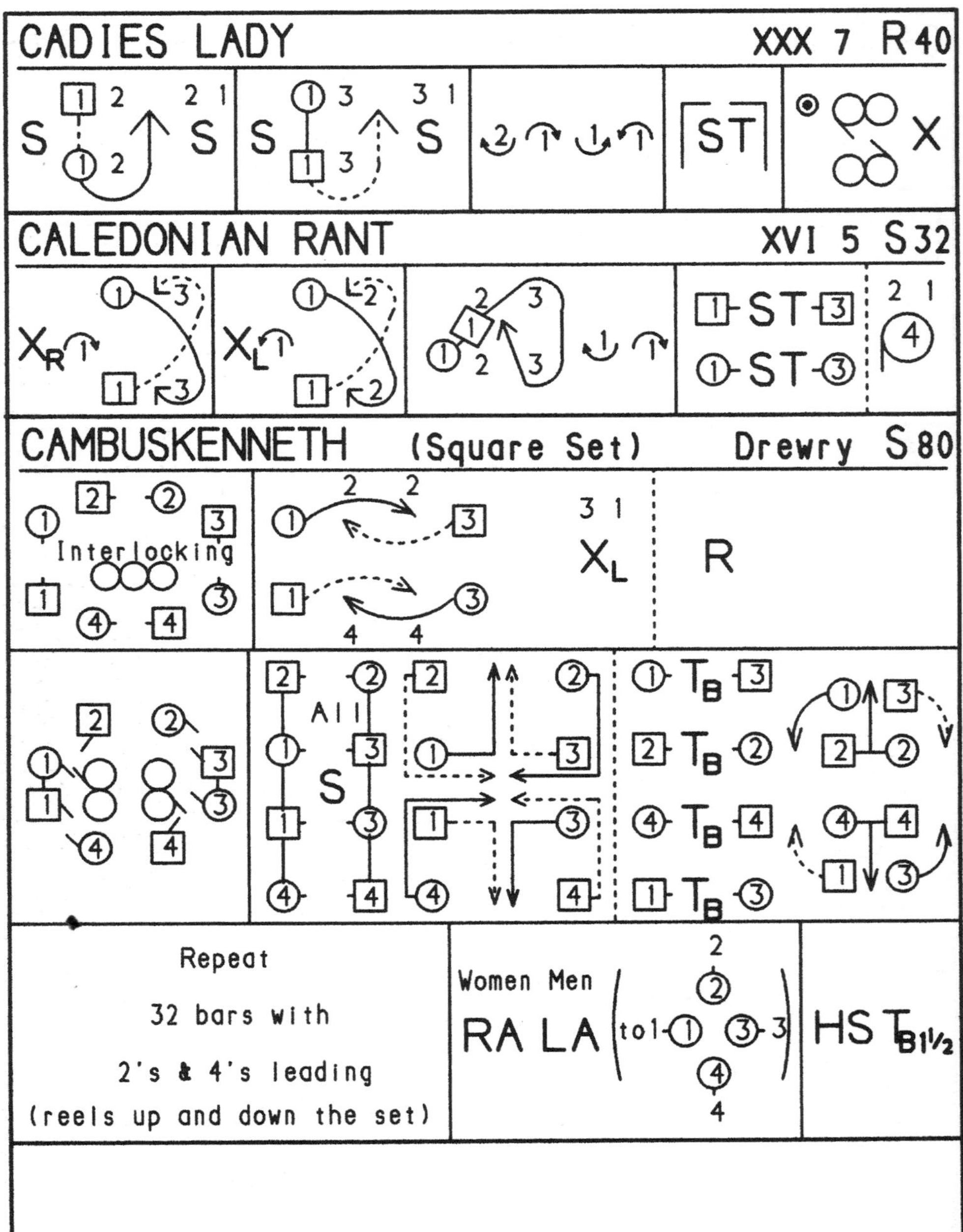
CADIES LADY
XXX 7 R40
CALEDONIAN RANT
XVI 5 S32
CAMBUSKENNETH (Square Set)
Drewry S80
Interlocking
All
Repeat
32 bars with
2's & 4's leading
(reels up and down the set)
Women Men
RA LA
to 1
HS

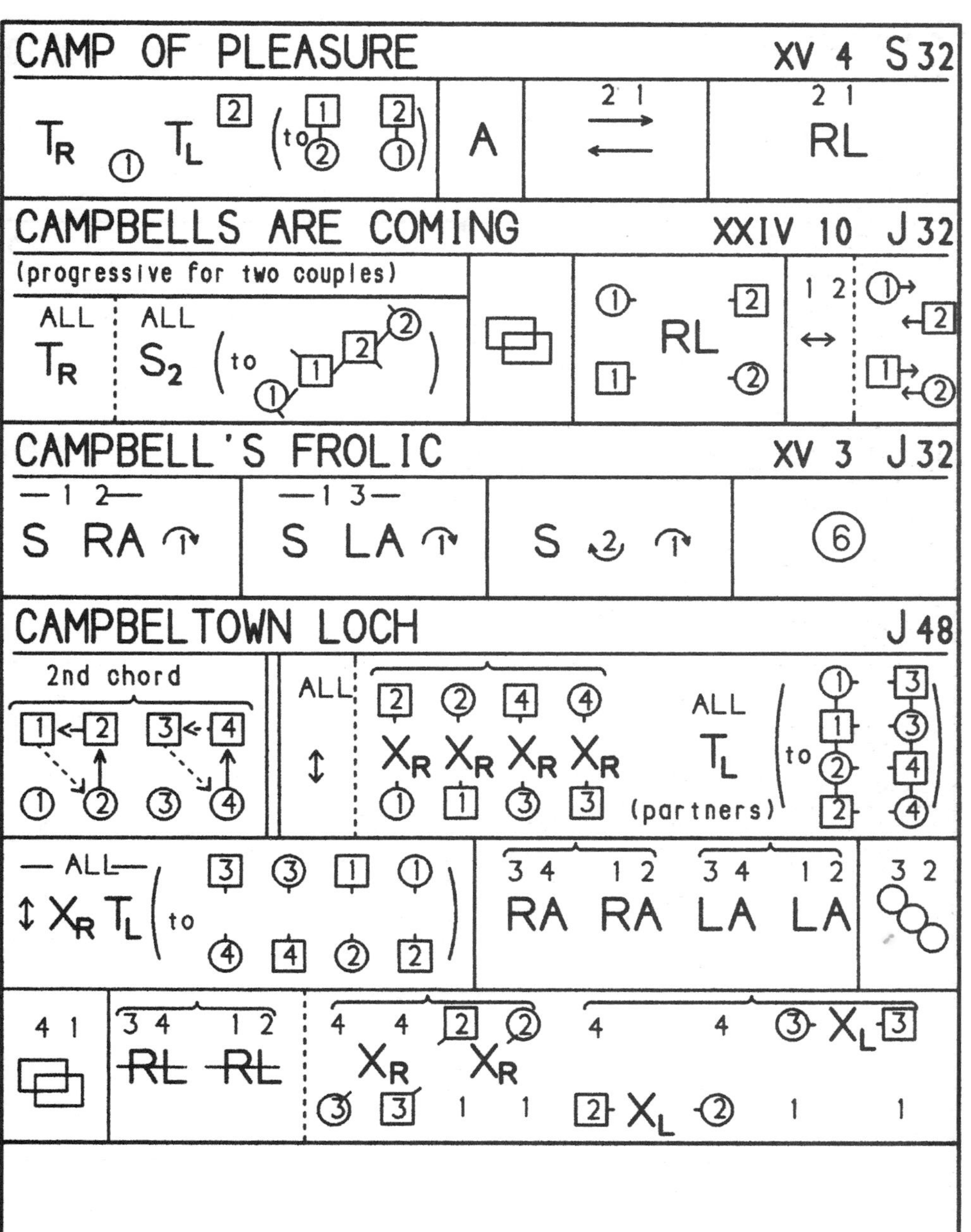
CAMP OF PLEASURE
XV 4 S32
A
RL
CAMPBELLS ARE COMING
XXIV 10 J32
(progressive for two couples)
ALL
ALL
to
RL
CAMPBELL'S FROLIC
XV 3 J32
S RA
S LA
S
CAMPBELTOWN LOCH
J48
2nd chord
ALL
ALL
to
(partners)
ALL
to
RA RA LA LA
RL RL

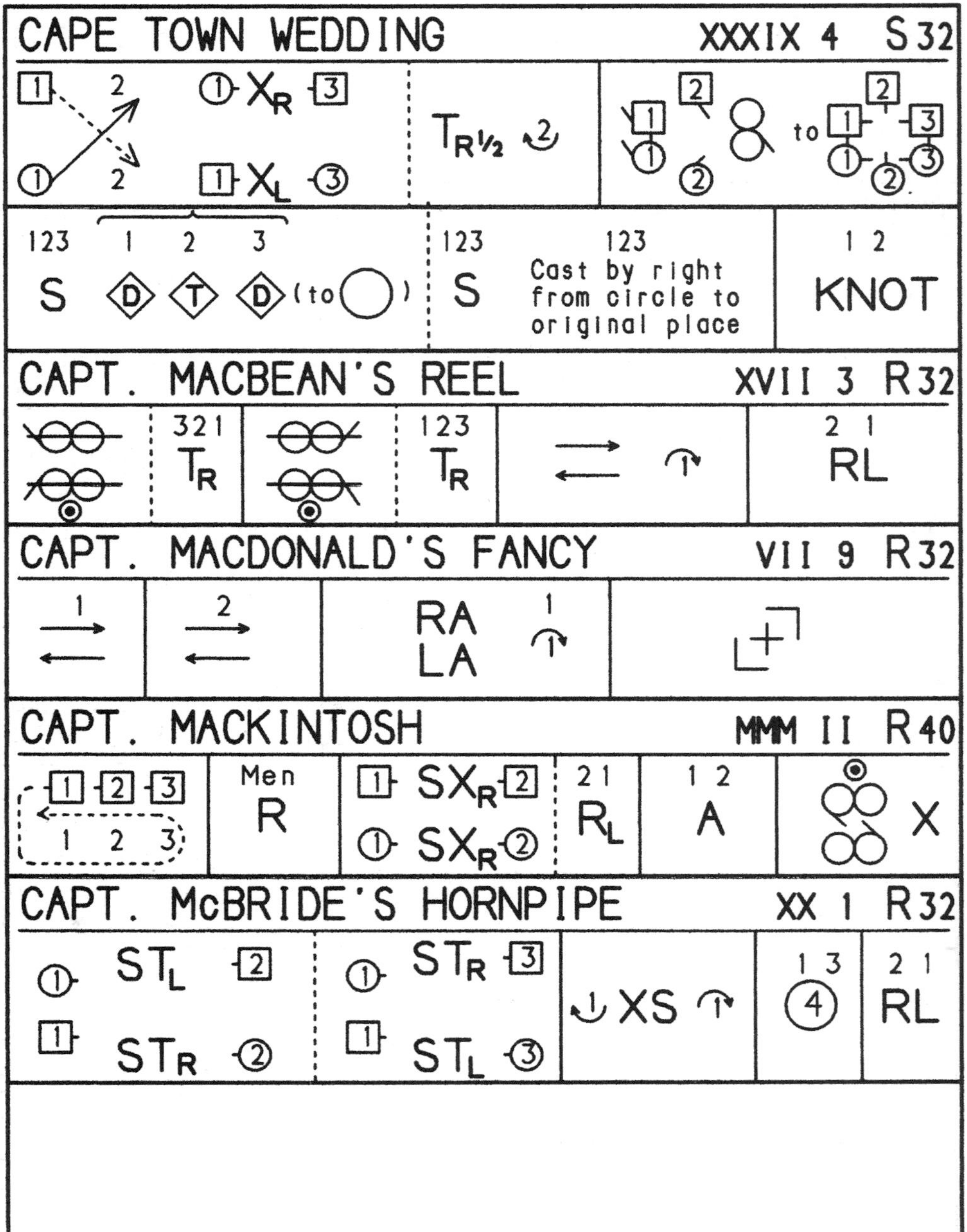
CAPE TOWN WEDDING
XXXIX 4 S32
Cast by right from circle to original place
KNOT
CAPT. MACBEAN'S REEL
XVII 3 R32
RL
CAPT. MACDONALD'S FANCY
VII 9 R32
RA
LA
CAPT. MACKINTOSH
MMM II R40
Men
R
A
CAPT. McBRIDE'S HORNPIPE
XX 1 R32
XS
RL

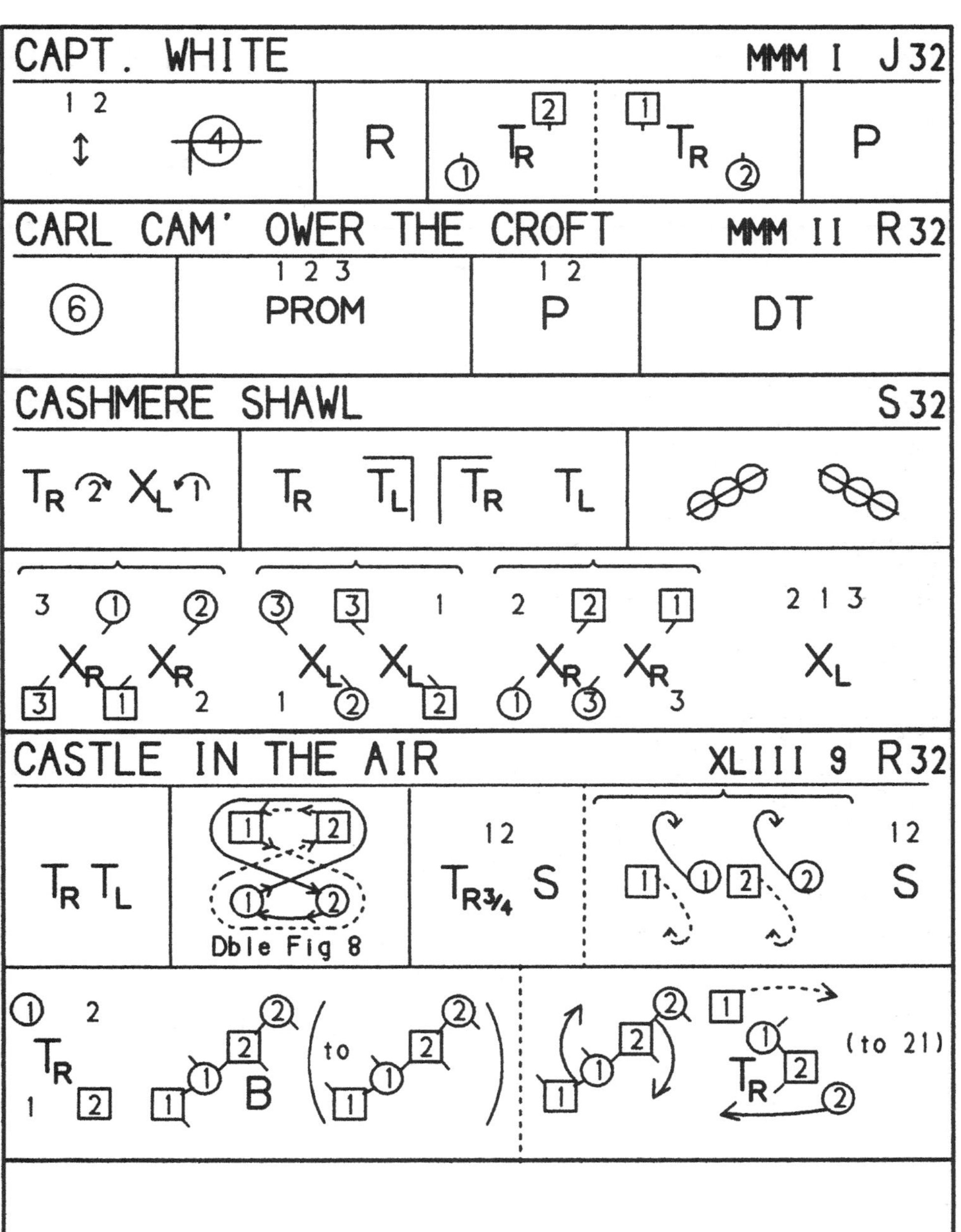
CAPT. WHITE
MMM I J32
1 2
R
P
CARL CAM' OWER THE CROFT
MMM II R32
6
1 2 3
PROM
1 2
P
DT
CASHMERE SHAWL
S32
CASTLE IN THE AIR
XLIII 9 R32
Dble Fig 8
12
S
B
to
(to 21)

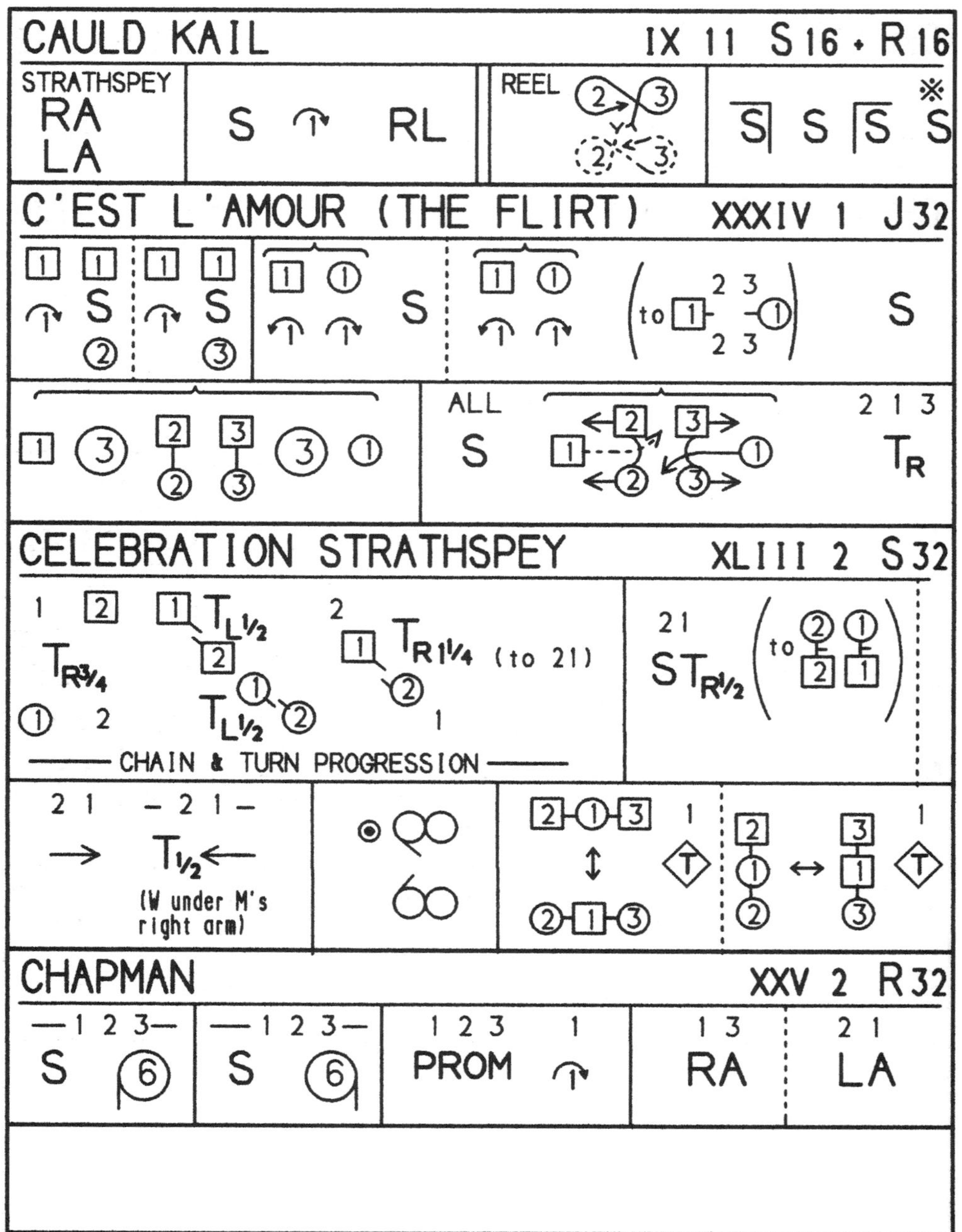
CAULD KAIL
IX 11 S16 + R16
STRATHSPEY
RA
LA
S
RL
REEL
S S S S
C'EST L'AMOUR (THE FLIRT)
XXXIV 1 J32
S S S
to
S
ALL
S
2 1 3
CELEBRATION STRATHSPEY
XLIII 2 S32
(to 21)
21
to
CHAIN & TURN PROGRESSION
2 1
– 2 1 –
(W under M's right arm)
CHAPMAN
XXV 2 R32
—1 2 3—
S
—1 2 3—
S
1 2 3
PROM
1
1 3
RA
2 1
LA

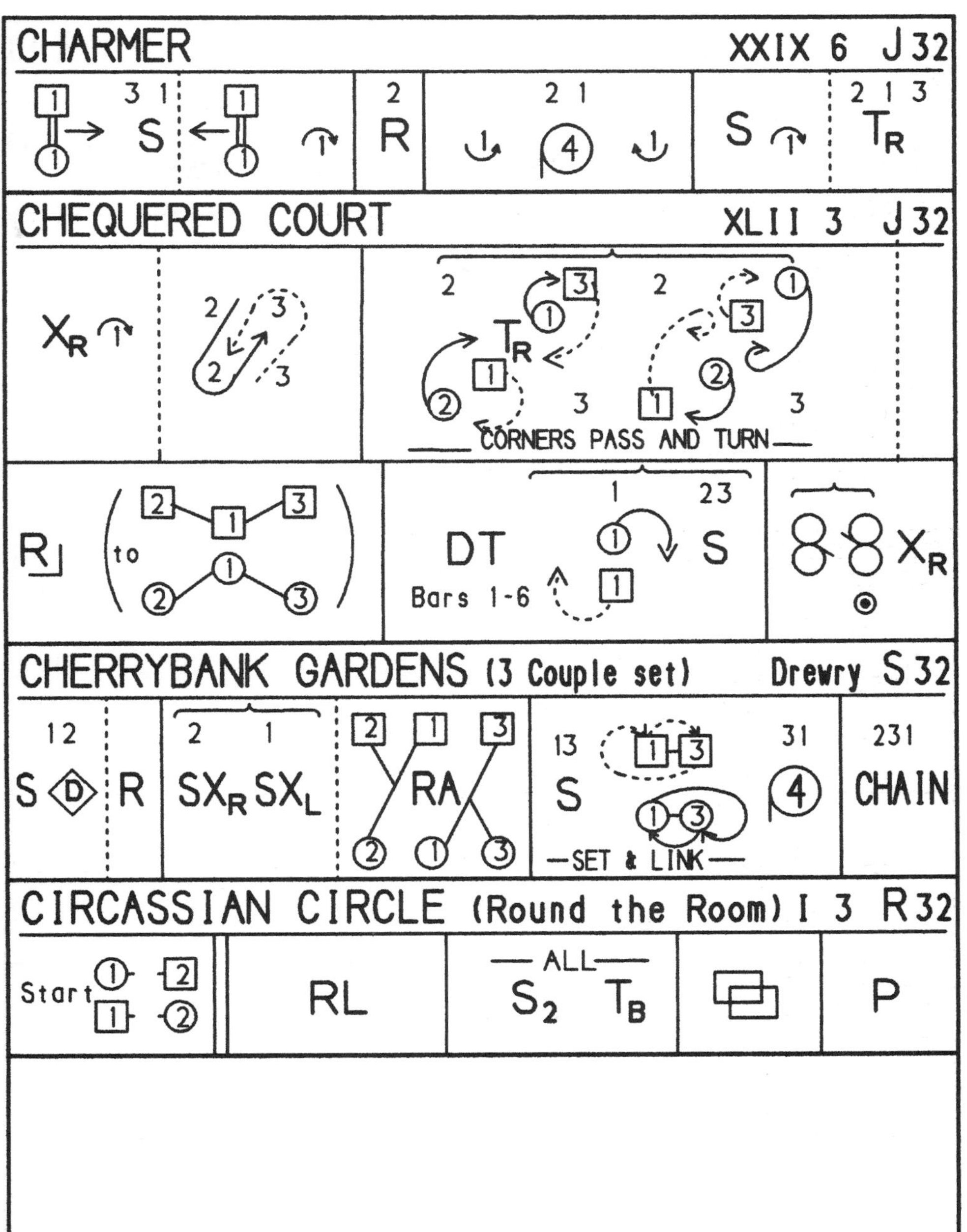
CHARMER
XXIX 6 J32
3 1
S
2
R
2 1
4
S
2 1 3
T R
CHEQUERED COURT
XLII 3 J32
X R
CORNERS PASS AND TURN
R
to
DT
Bars 1-6
1
23
S
X R
CHERRYBANK GARDENS (3 Couple set)
Drewry S32
12
S
D
R
2 1
SX R SX L
RA
13
S
31
4
231
CHAIN
—SET & LINK—
CIRCASSIAN CIRCLE (Round the Room) I 3 R32
Start
RL
—ALL—
S 2 T B
P

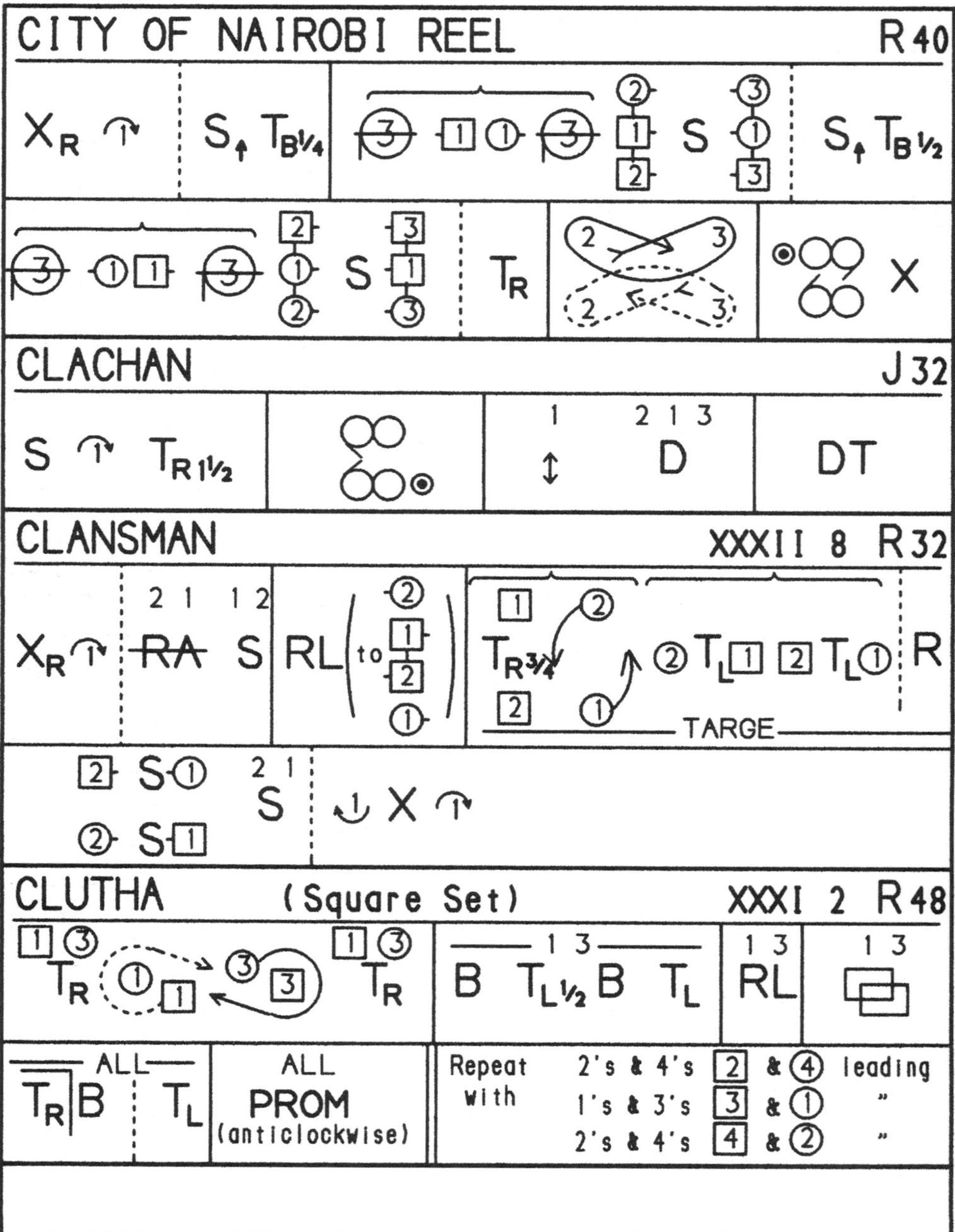
CITY OF NAIROBI REEL
R 40
CLACHAN
J 32
CLANSMAN
XXXII 8
R 32
TARGE
CLUTHA
(Square Set)
XXXI 2
R 48
ALL
ALL
PROM
(anticlockwise)
Repeat with
2's & 4's
leading
1's & 3's
"
2's & 4's
"

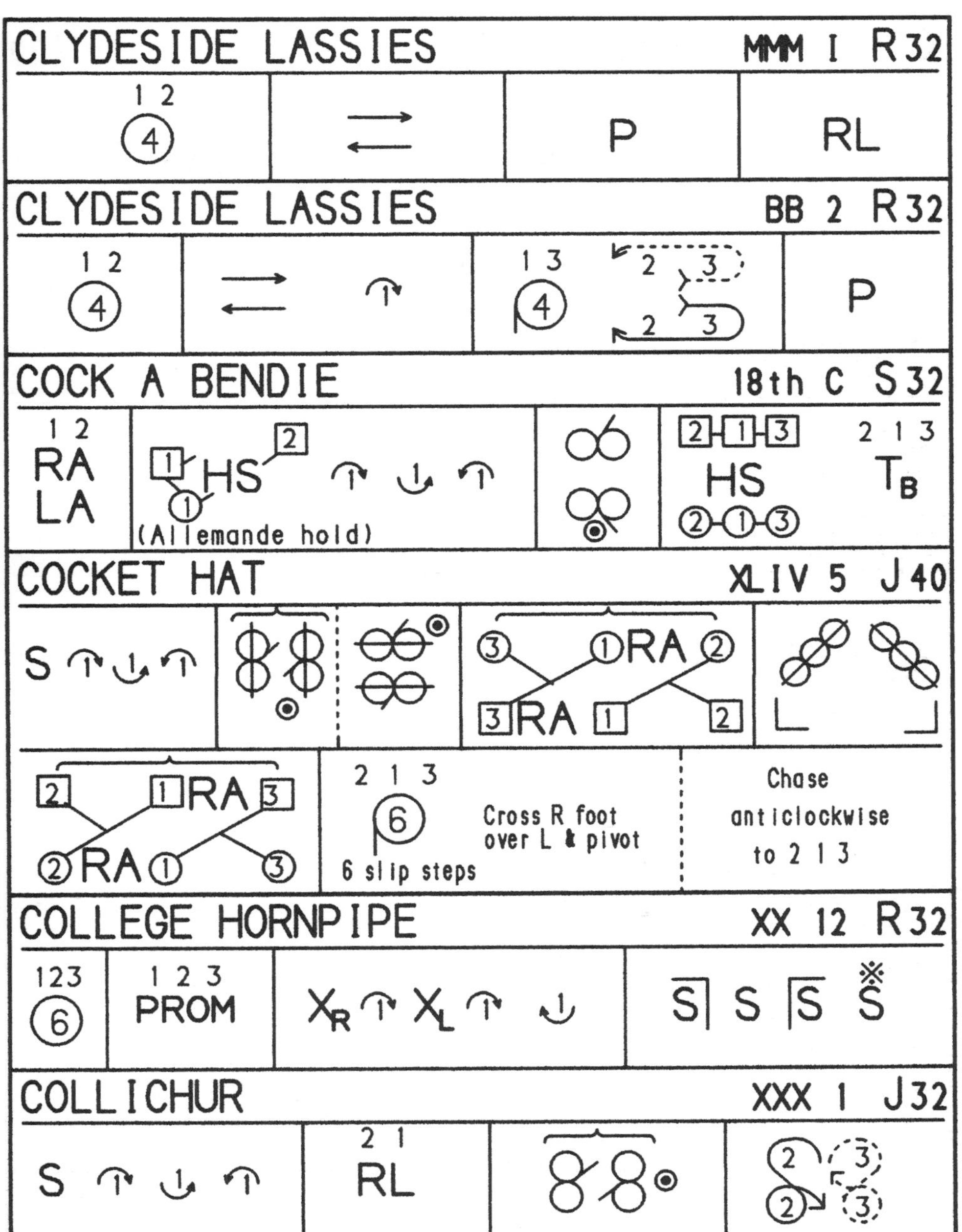

CLYDESIDE LASSIES
MMM I R32
1 2
4
P
RL
CLYDESIDE LASSIES
BB 2 R32
1 2
4
1 3
4
2 3
2 3
P
COCK A BENDIE
18th C S32
1 2
RA
LA
1
HS
2
1
(Allemande hold)
2-1-3
HS
2-1-3
2 1 3
T_B
COCKET HAT
XLIV 5 J40
S
3
1 RA 2
3 RA 1
2
2
1 RA 3
2 RA 1
3
2 1 3
6
6 slip steps
Cross R foot
over L & pivot
Chase
anticlockwise
to 2 1 3
COLLEGE HORNPIPE
XX 12 R32
123
6
1 2 3
PROM
X_R
X_L
S S S S
COLLICHUR
XXX 1 J32
S
2 1
RL
2 3
2 3

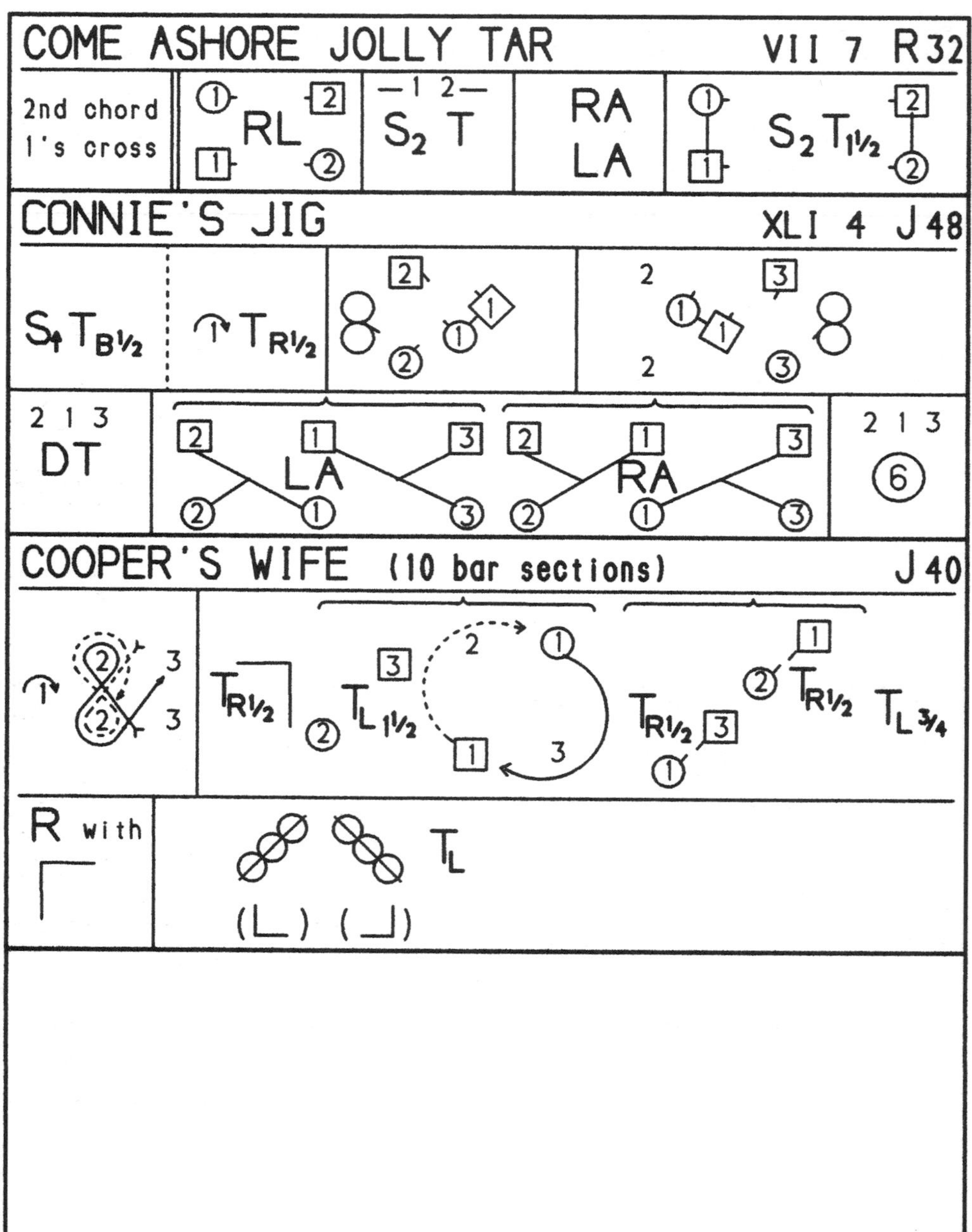
COME ASHORE JOLLY TAR
VII 7 R32
2nd chord
1's cross
RL
1 2
S2 T
RA
LA
S2 T1½
CONNIE'S JIG
XLI 4 J48
S4 TB½
TR½
2 1 3
DT
LA
RA
2 1 3
6
COOPER'S WIFE (10 bar sections)
J40
TR½
TL 1½
TR½
TR½
TL ¾
R with
TL

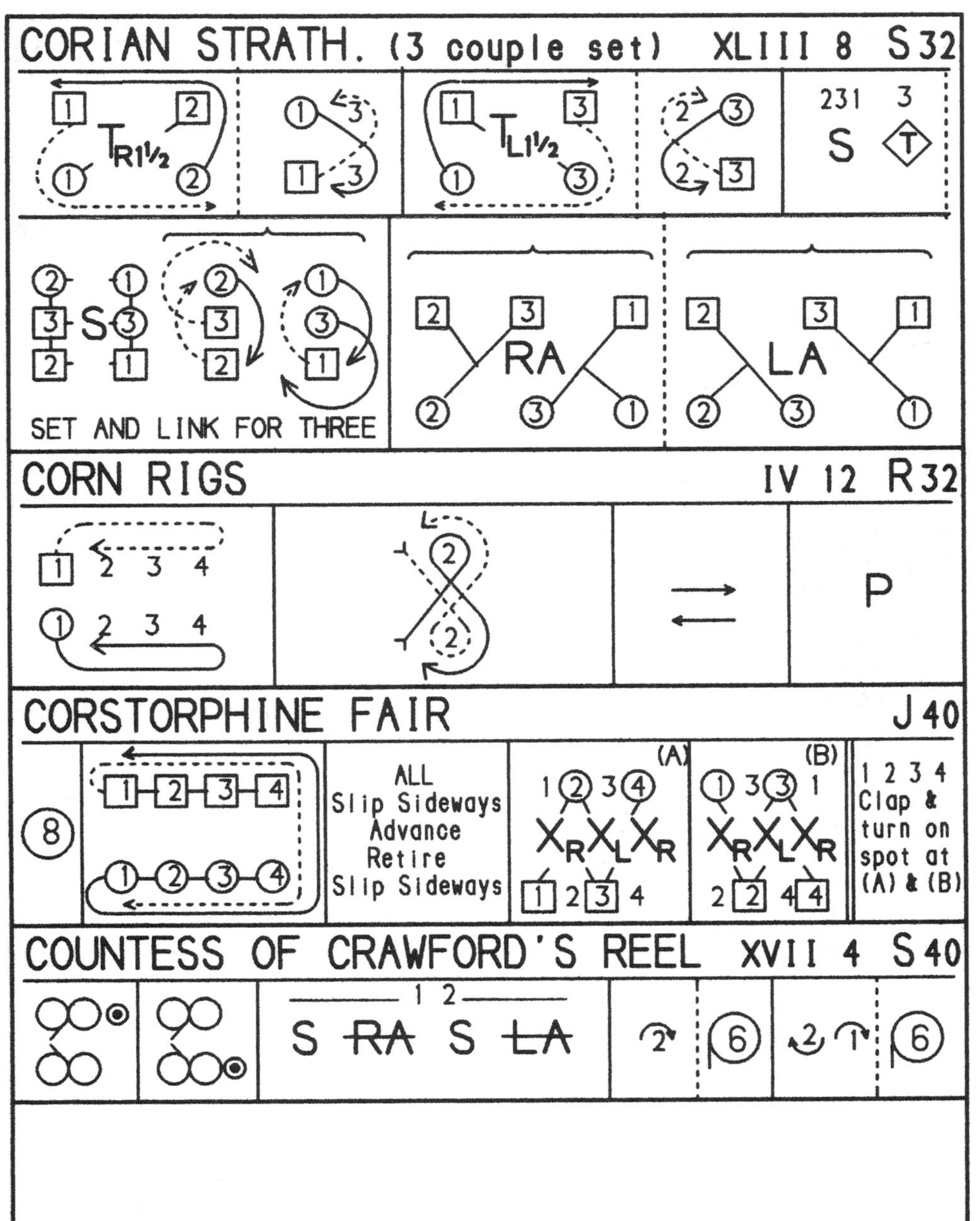

CORIAN STRATH. (3 couple set) XLIII 8 S32
T R1½
T L1½
231 3
S T
SET AND LINK FOR THREE
RA
LA
CORN RIGS IV 12 R32
P
CORSTORPHINE FAIR J40
8
ALL
Slip Sideways
Advance
Retire
Slip Sideways
(A)
(B)
1 2 3 4
Clap &
turn on
spot at
(A) & (B)
COUNTESS OF CRAWFORD'S REEL XVII 4 S40
1 2
S RA S LA
6

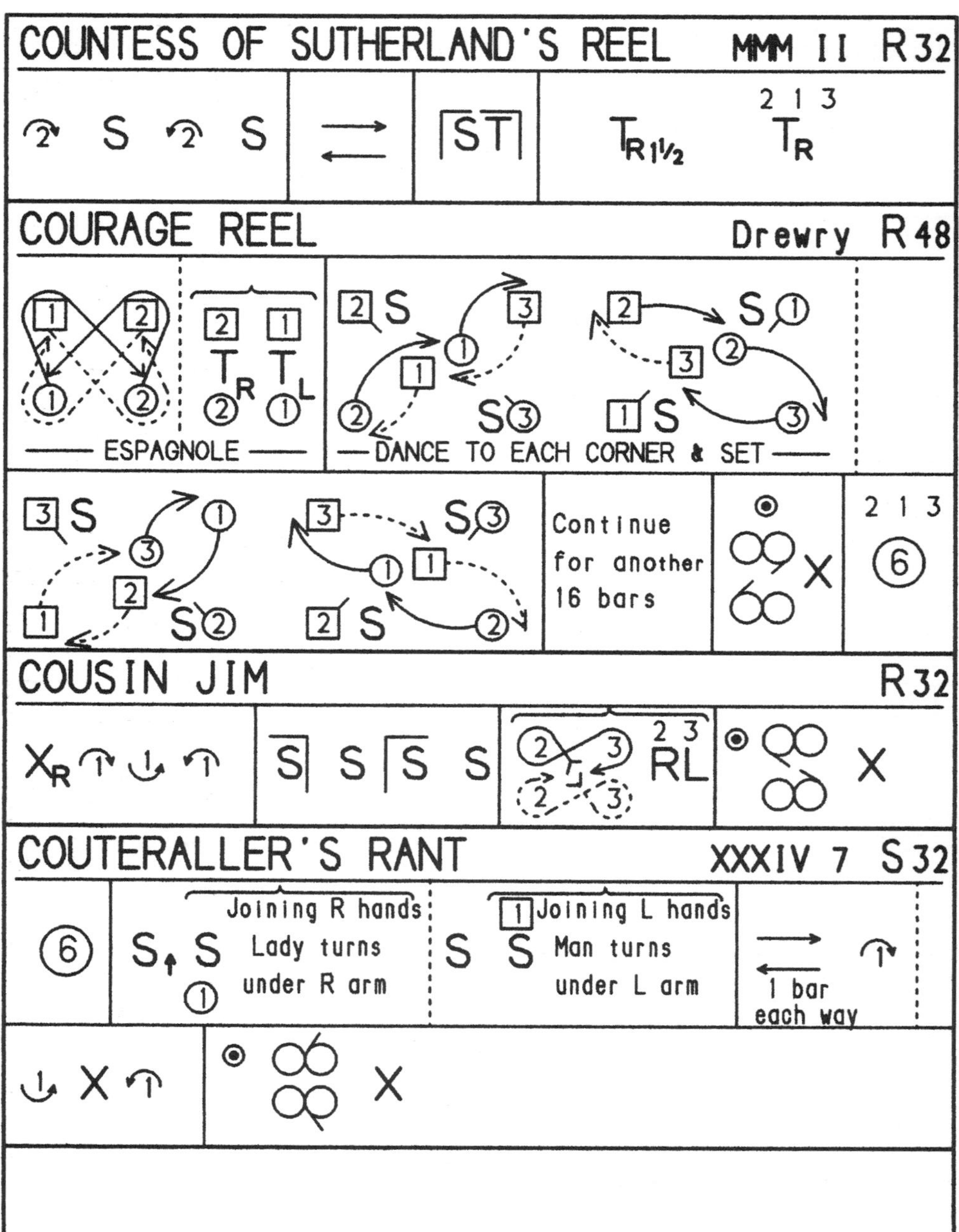
COUNTESS OF SUTHERLAND'S REEL
MMM II R32
S S
ST
T R 1½
2 1 3
T R
COURAGE REEL
Drewry R48
ESPAGNOLE
DANCE TO EACH CORNER & SET
Continue
for another
16 bars
2 1 3
6
COUSIN JIM
R32
X R
S S S S
2 3
RL
X
COUTERALLER'S RANT
XXXIV 7 S32
6
Joining R hands
Lady turns
under R arm
Joining L hands
Man turns
under L arm
1 bar
each way
X
X

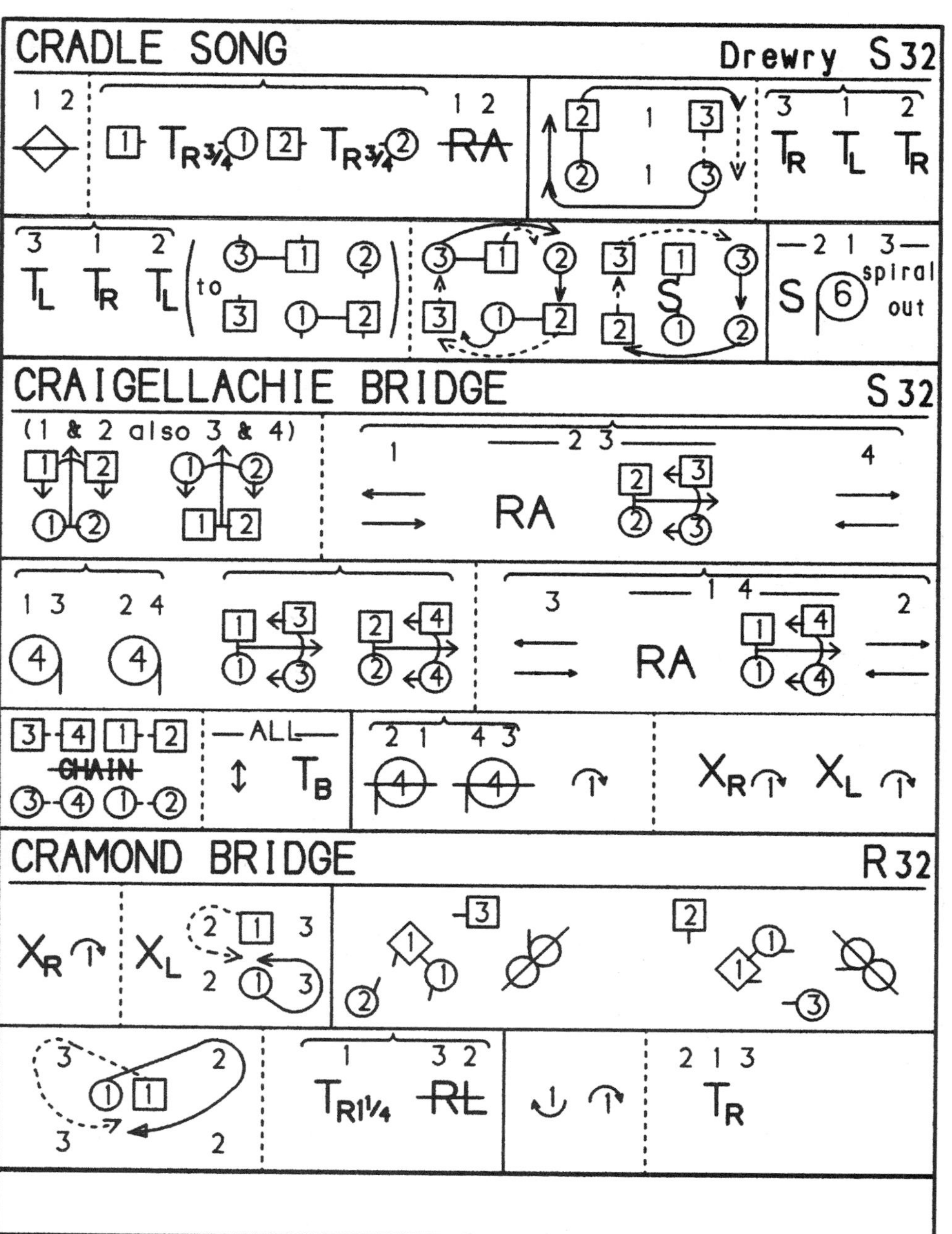
CRADLE SONG
Drewry S 32
CRAIGELLACHIE BRIDGE
S 32
(1 & 2 also 3 & 4)
CRAMOND BRIDGE
R 32

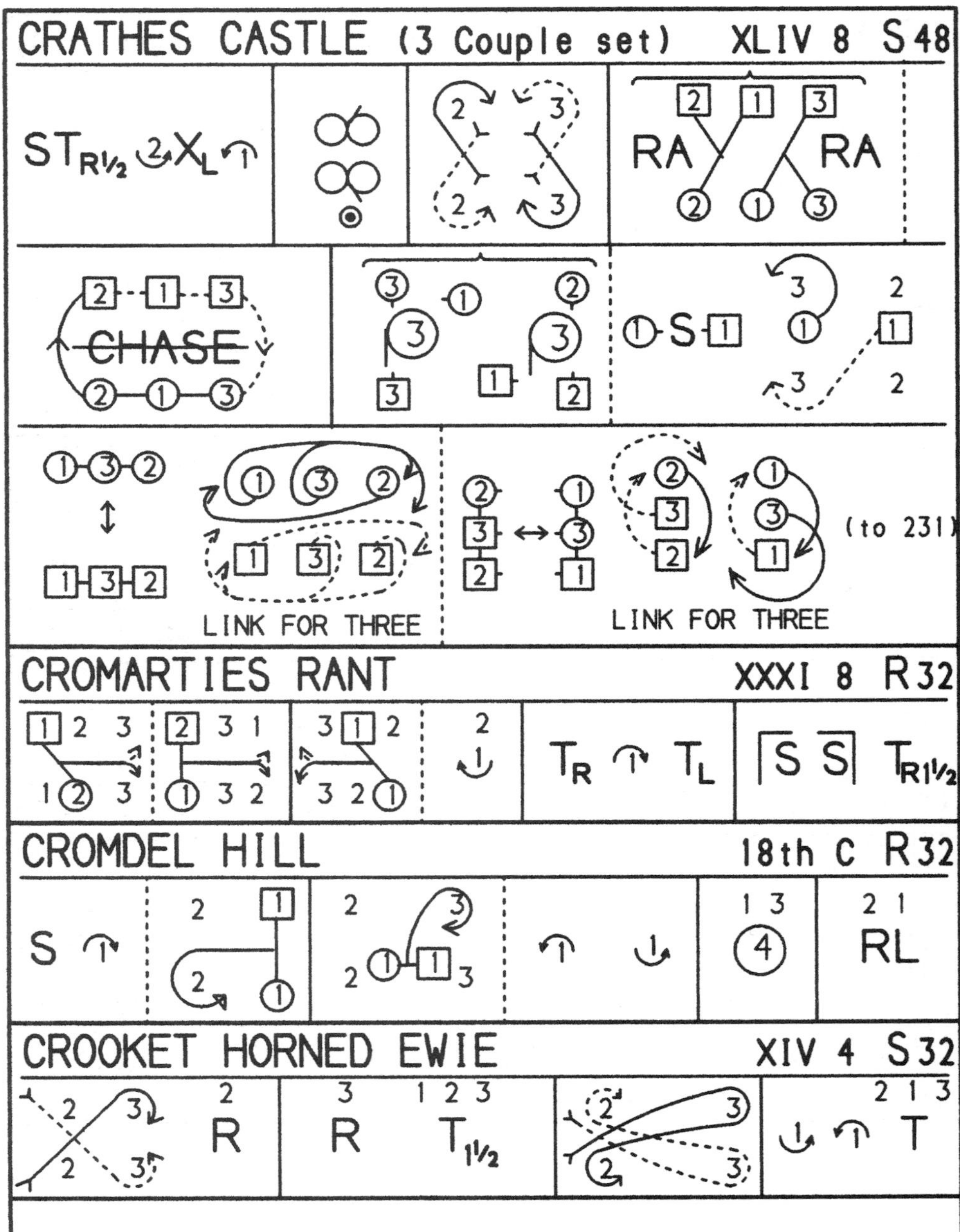
CRATHES CASTLE (3 Couple set) XLIV 8 S48
RA RA
CHASE
LINK FOR THREE
LINK FOR THREE
(to 231)
CROMARTIES RANT XXXI 8 R32
CROMDEL HILL 18th C R32
RL
CROOKET HORNED EWIE XIV 4 S32

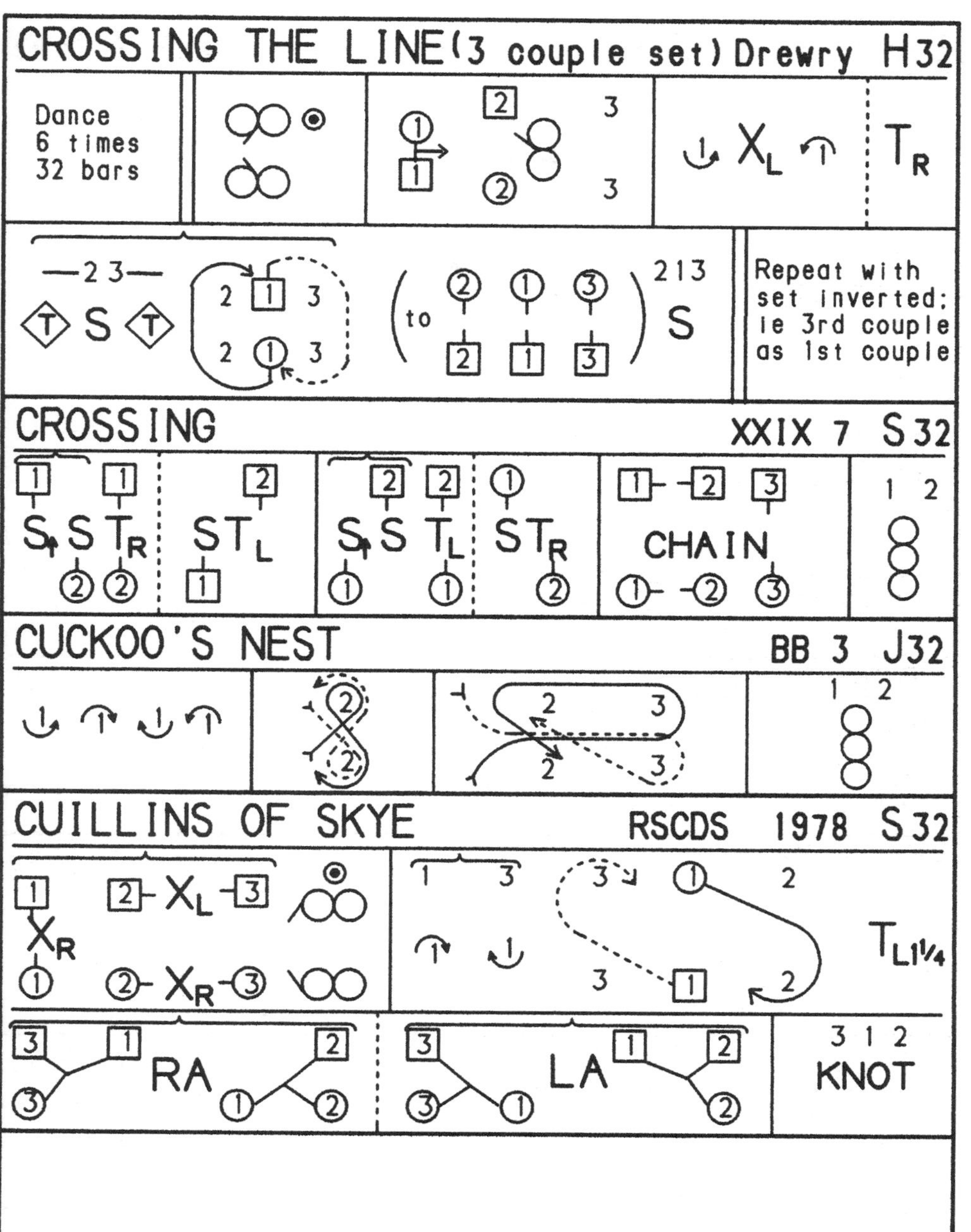
CROSSING THE LINE (3 couple set) Drewry H32
Dance
6 times
32 bars
Repeat with
set inverted:
ie 3rd couple
as 1st couple
CROSSING XXIX 7 S32
CHAIN
CUCKOO'S NEST BB 3 J32
CUILLINS OF SKYE RSCDS 1978 S32
RA
LA
KNOT

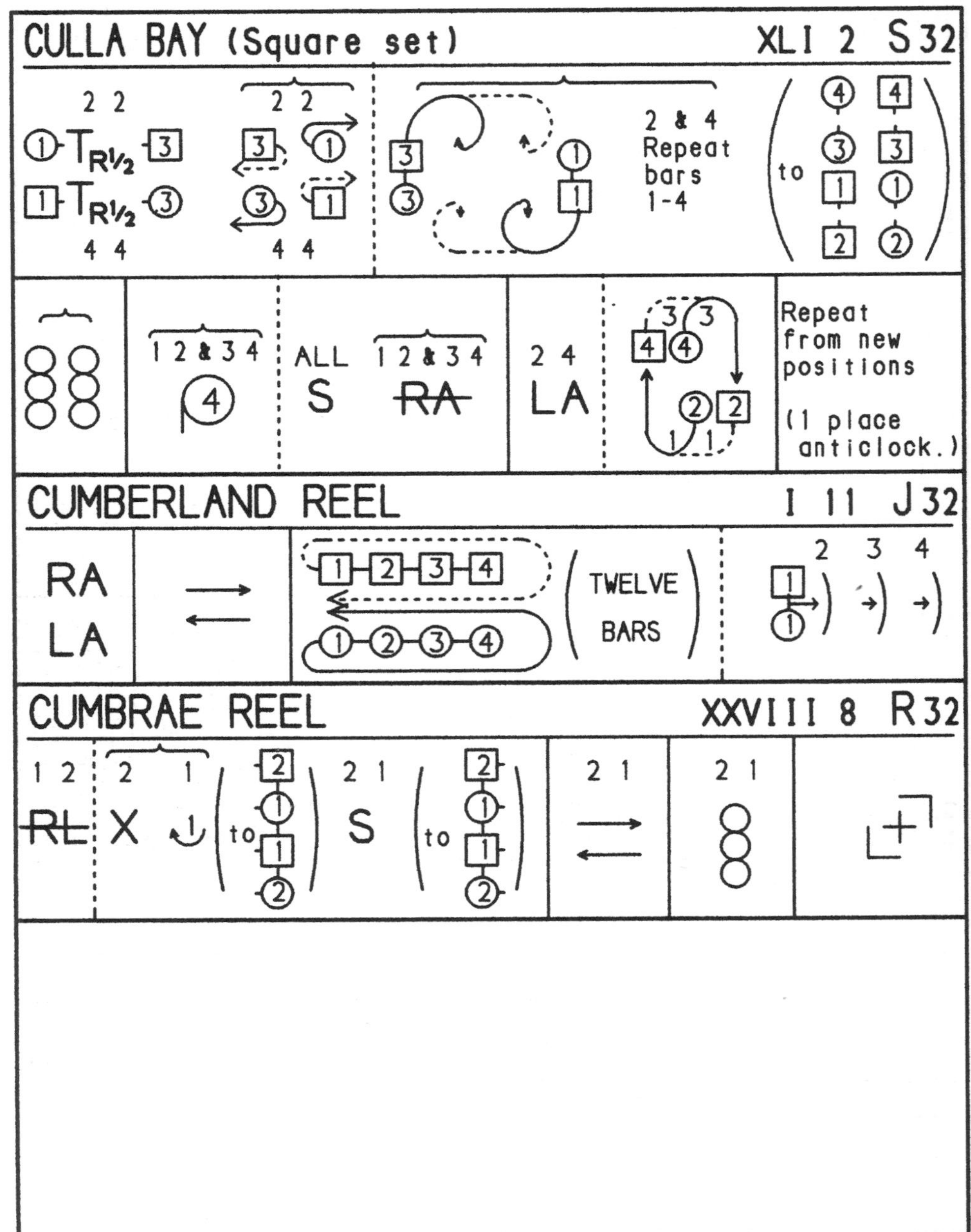

CULLA BAY (Square set)
XLI 2 S32
2 2
T R½
4 4
2 & 4
Repeat
bars
1-4
to
1 2 & 3 4
ALL
S
RA
2 4
LA
Repeat
from new
positions
(1 place
anticlock.)
CUMBERLAND REEL
I 11 J32
RA
LA
TWELVE
BARS
2 3 4
CUMBRAE REEL
XXVIII 8 R32
1 2
RL
2 1
X
to
2 1
S
to
2 1
2 1

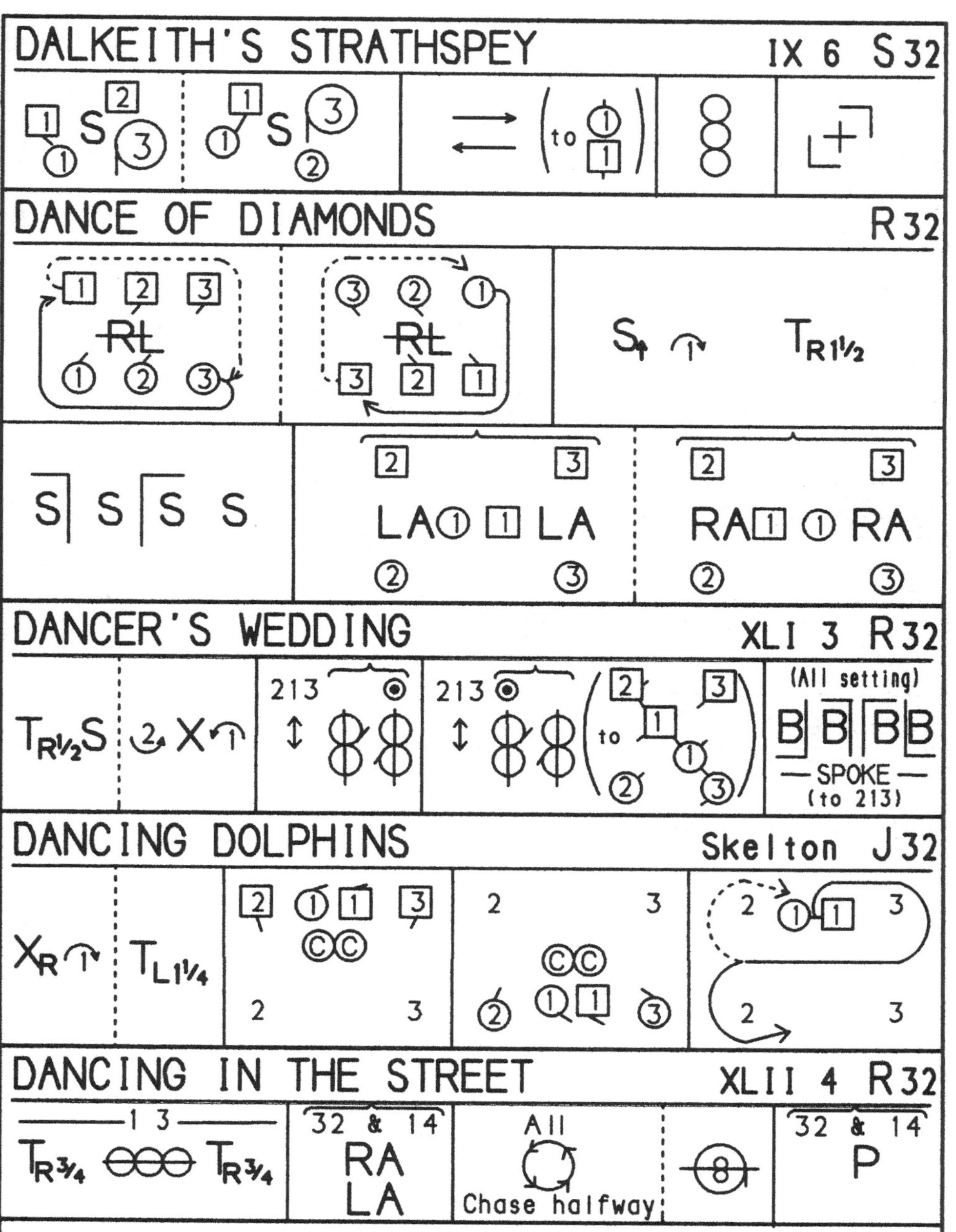
DALKEITH'S STRATHSPEY
IX 6 S32
S
S
to
DANCE OF DIAMONDS
R32
RL
RL
S
T R1½
S S S S
LA LA
RA RA
DANCER'S WEDDING
XLI 3 R32
T R½ S
X
213
213
to
(All setting)
B B B B
SPOKE
(to 213)
DANCING DOLPHINS
Skelton J32
X R
T L1¼
2 3
DANCING IN THE STREET
XLII 4 R32
1 3
T R¾ T R¾
32 & 14
RA
LA
All
Chase halfway
32 & 14
P

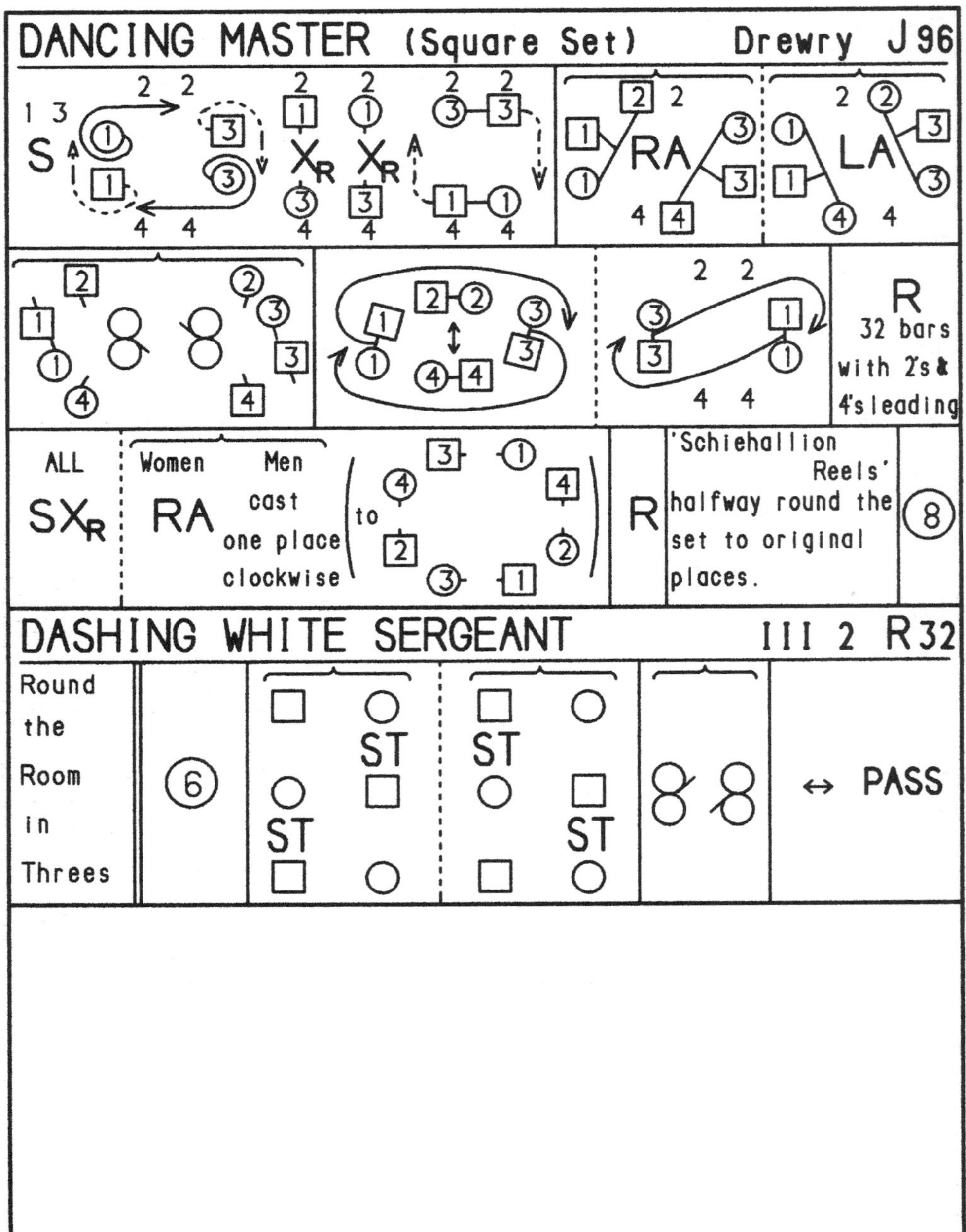
DANCING MASTER (Square Set)
Drewry J96
S
XR XR
RA
LA
R
32 bars
with 2's &
4's leading
ALL
SXR
Women
Men
RA
cast
one place
clockwise
to
R
'Schiehallion
Reels'
halfway round the
set to original
places.
8
DASHING WHITE SERGEANT
III 2 R32
Round
the
Room
in
Threes
6
ST
ST
ST
ST
↔ PASS

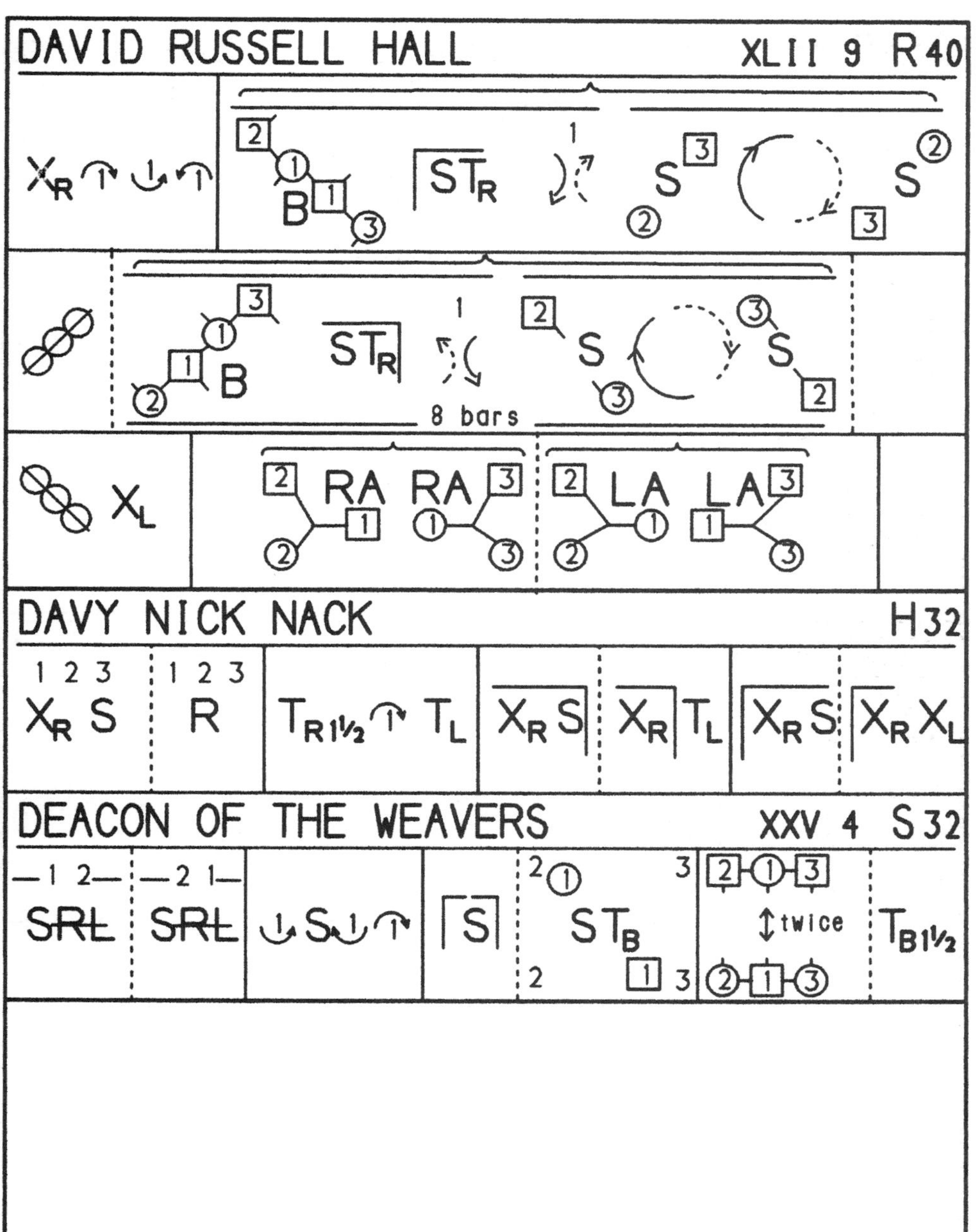

DAVID RUSSELL HALL
XLII 9 R40
B
ST R
S
S
8 bars
RA RA
LA LA
DAVY NICK NACK
H32
1 2 3
X R S
R
T R 1½
T L
DEACON OF THE WEAVERS
XXV 4 S32
SRL
S
ST B
twice
T B 1½

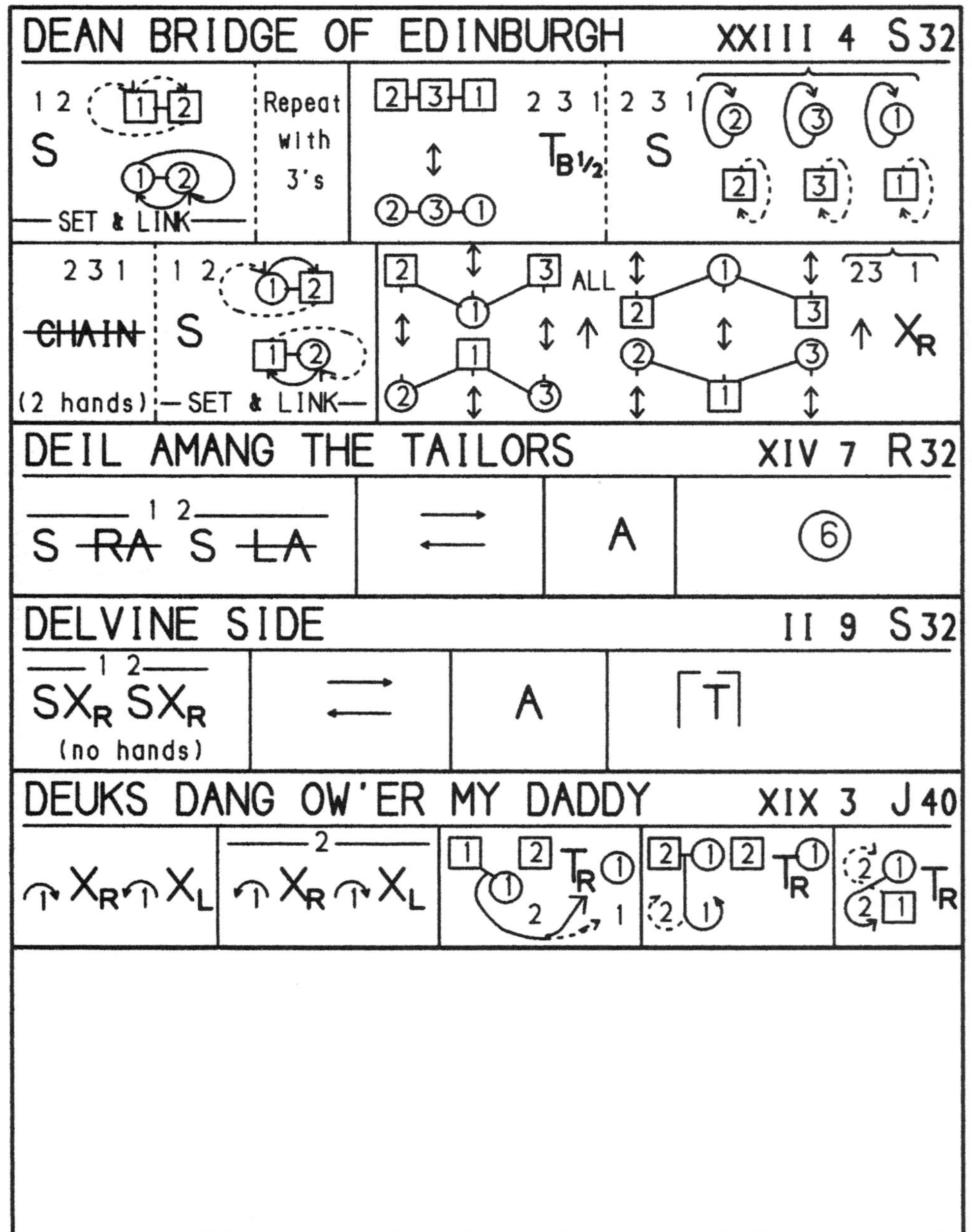

DEAN BRIDGE OF EDINBURGH
XXIII 4 S32
1 2
S
SET & LINK
Repeat with 3's
2 3 1
$T_{B 1/2}$
2 3 1
S
2 3 1
CHAIN
(2 hands)
1 2
S
SET & LINK
ALL
23 1
X_R
DEIL AMANG THE TAILORS
XIV 7 R32
1 2
S RA S LA
A
6
DELVINE SIDE
II 9 S32
1 2
SX_R SX_R
(no hands)
A
T
DEUKS DANG OW'ER MY DADDY
XIX 3 J40
X_R X_L
2
X_R X_L
T_R
T_R
T_R

DIAMOND JUBILEE — XXXI 1 J32

1 / 4		
$T_{R1½}$ ↷1 $T_{R1½}$ ↶1	① T_L ④ 1 T_L 4	○○○ ○○○ (to 2 4 1 3 / 2 4 1 3)

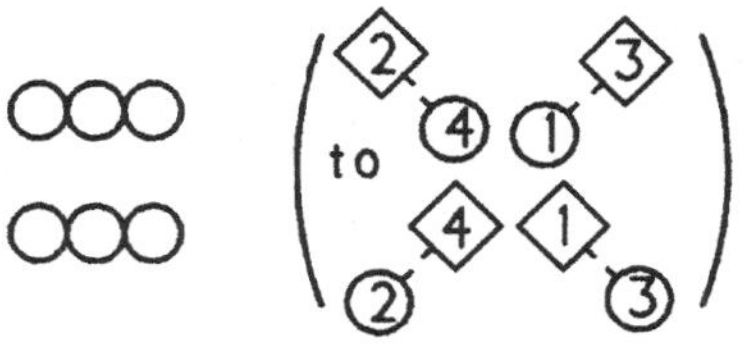

ALL	4 1 · 2 3	2 4 1 3
SX_R SX_L	RA SX_R	SX_R

DONALD BANE — XVII 12 S32

	1 2	1 3		
○○ ○○ ⊙	RA ↷1	LA	⑥	S S S S

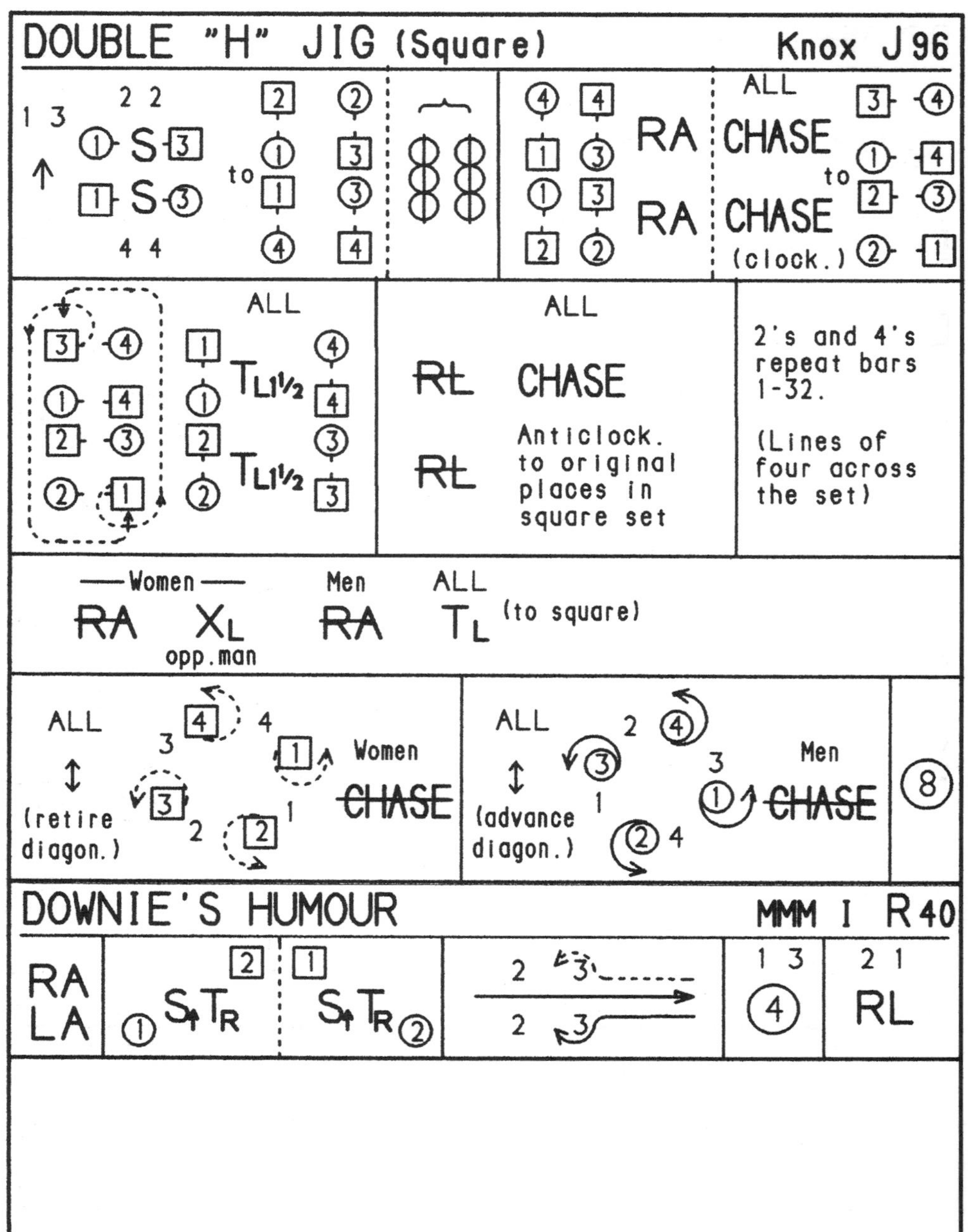
DOUBLE "H" JIG (Square)
Knox J96
1 3
2 2
S
S
4 4
to
RA
RA
ALL
CHASE
CHASE
(clock.)
to
ALL
$T_{L1½}$
$T_{L1½}$
ALL
RL
CHASE
RL
Anticlock. to original places in square set
2's and 4's repeat bars 1-32.
(Lines of four across the set)
Women
RA
X_L
opp.man
Men
RA
ALL
T_L
(to square)
ALL
(retire diagon.)
Women
CHASE
ALL
(advance diagon.)
Men
CHASE
8
DOWNIE'S HUMOUR
MMM I R40
RA
LA
$S T_R$
$S T_R$
1 3
4
2 1
RL

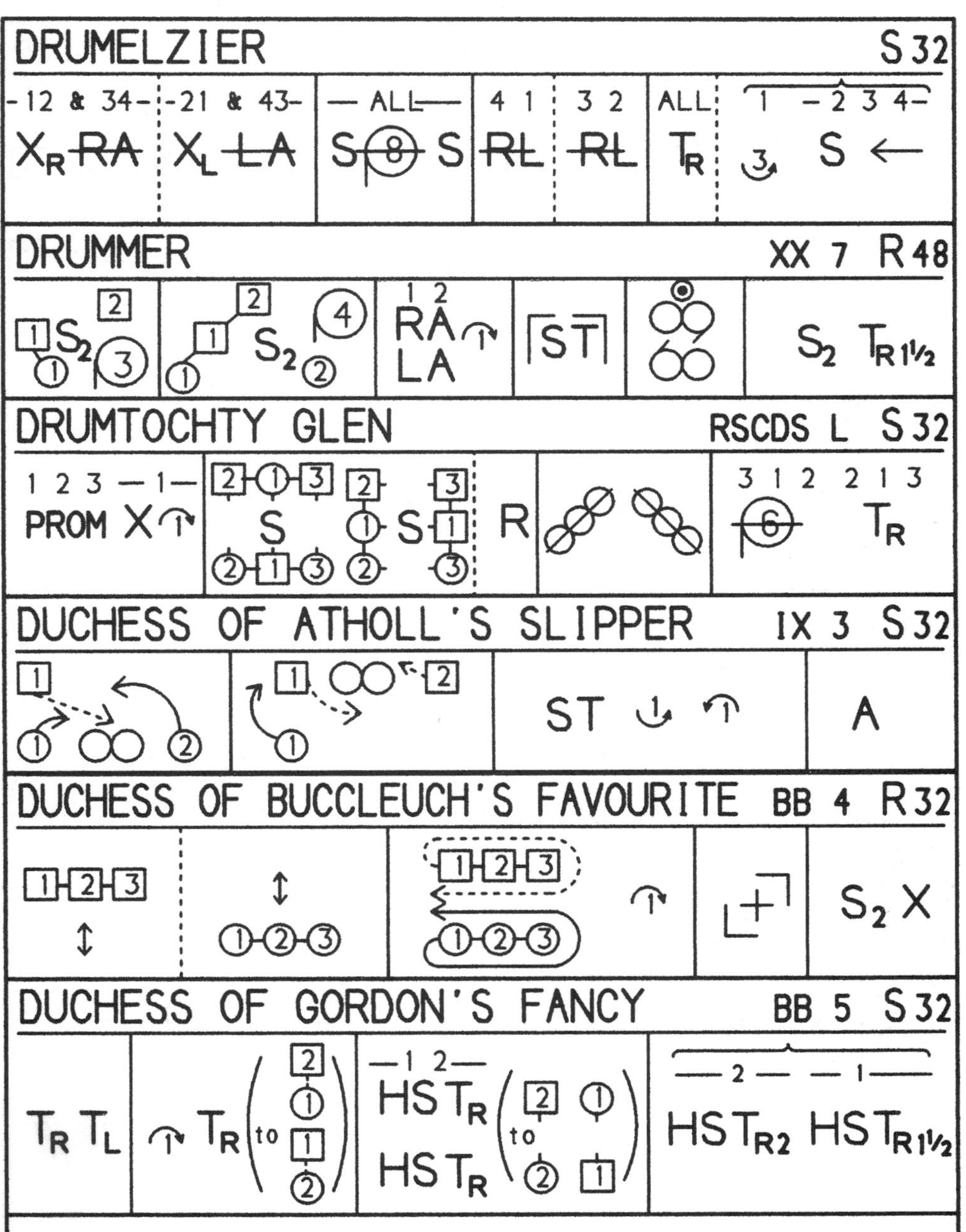
DRUMELZIER S 32
-12 & 34- -21 & 43- — ALL— 4 1 3 2 ALL 1 -2 3 4-
DRUMMER XX 7 R 48
DRUMTOCHTY GLEN RSCDS L S 32
1 2 3 —1— 3 1 2 2 1 3
PROM
DUCHESS OF ATHOLL'S SLIPPER IX 3 S 32
DUCHESS OF BUCCLEUCH'S FAVOURITE BB 4 R 32
DUCHESS OF GORDON'S FANCY BB 5 S 32
—1 2— —2— —1—

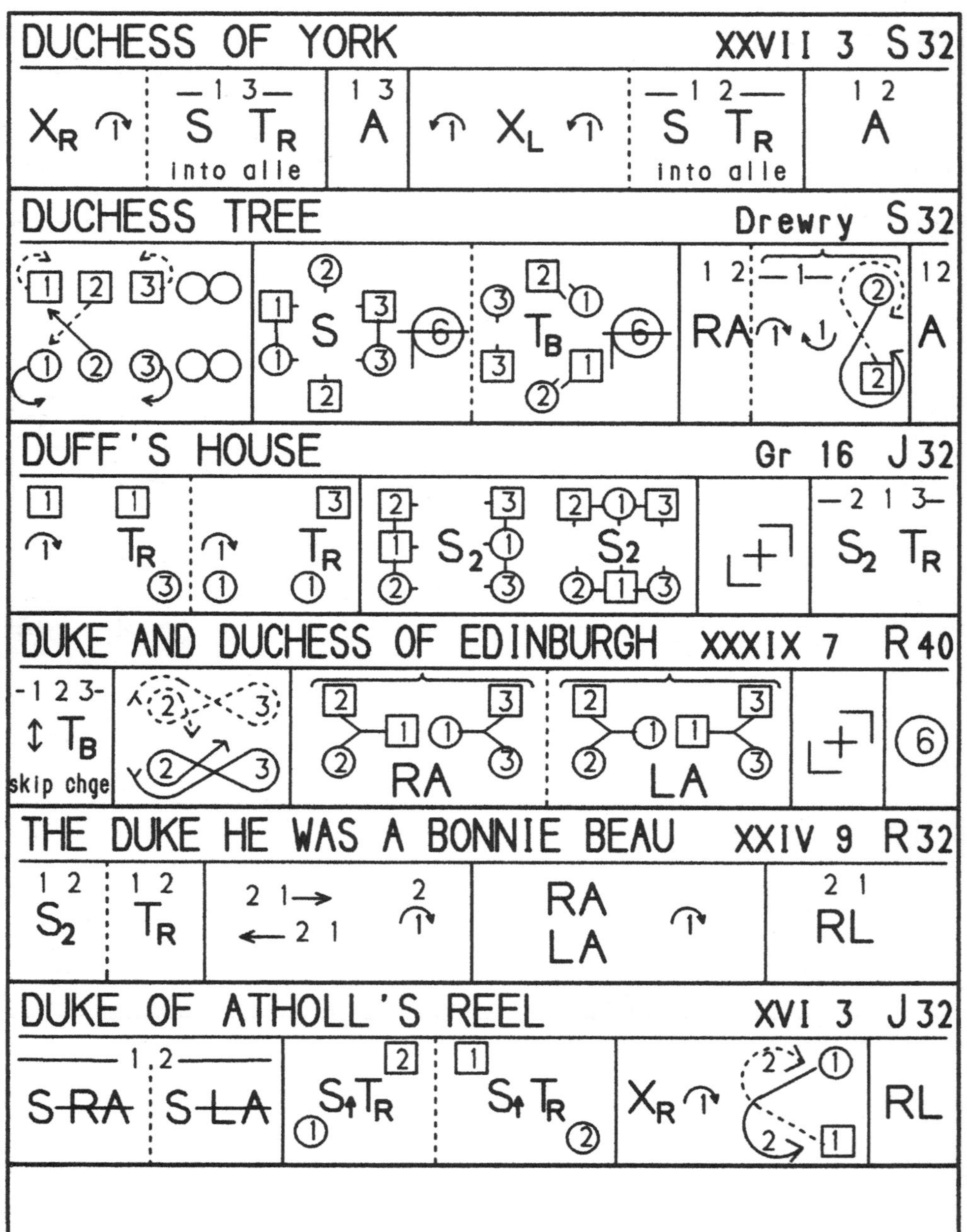
DUCHESS OF YORK
XXVII 3 S32
X R
—1 3—
S T R
into alle
1 3
A
X L
—1 2—
S T R
into alle
1 2
A
DUCHESS TREE
Drewry S32
S
T B
1 2
RA
—1—
12
A
DUFF'S HOUSE
Gr 16 J32
T R
T R
S 2
S 2
—2 1 3—
S 2 T R
DUKE AND DUCHESS OF EDINBURGH
XXXIX 7 R40
-1 2 3-
T B
skip chge
RA
LA
THE DUKE HE WAS A BONNIE BEAU
XXIV 9 R32
1 2
S 2
1 2
T R
2 1→
←2 1
RA
LA
2 1
RL
DUKE OF ATHOLL'S REEL
XVI 3 J32
1,2
S RA
S LA
S T R
S T R
X R
RL

DUKE OF HAMILTON'S REEL V 8 S32

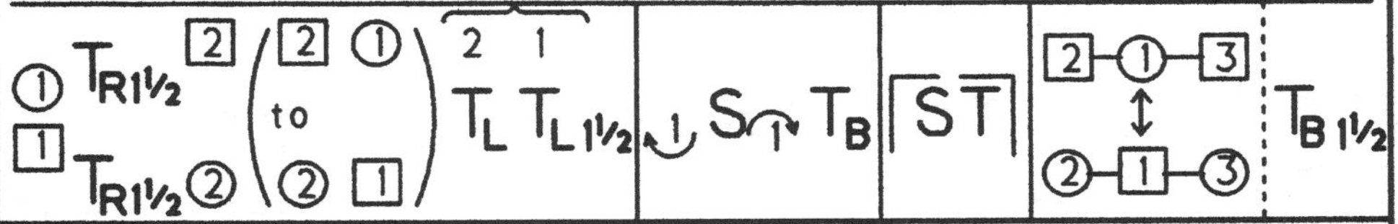

① $T_{R1½}$ [2] ([2] ① to ② [1]) 2 1 T_L $T_{L1½}$ | S | T_B | ST | [2]-①-[3] ↕ ②-[1]-③ | $T_{B1½}$

[1] $T_{R1½}$ ②

DUKE OF PERTH I 8 R32

T_R | T_L | ST | X

DUMBARTON DRUMS V 2 R32

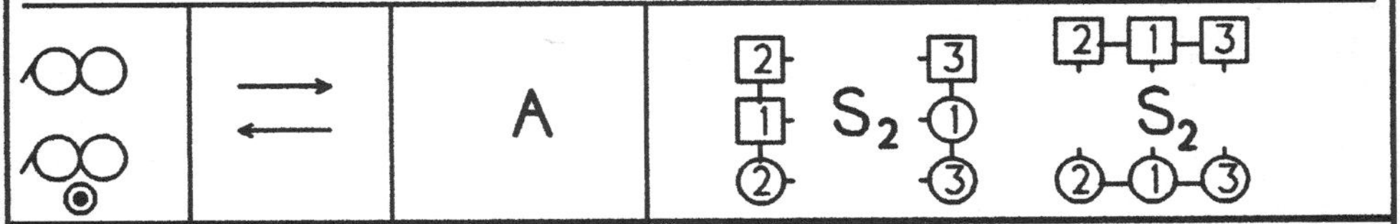

A | [2] [1] ② S_2 [3] ① ③ | [2]-[1]-[3] S_2 ②-①-③

DUNDEE REEL BB 6 J40

1 2 3 RA LA | ST | [2]-①-[3] ↕ ②-[1]-③ $T_{1½}$

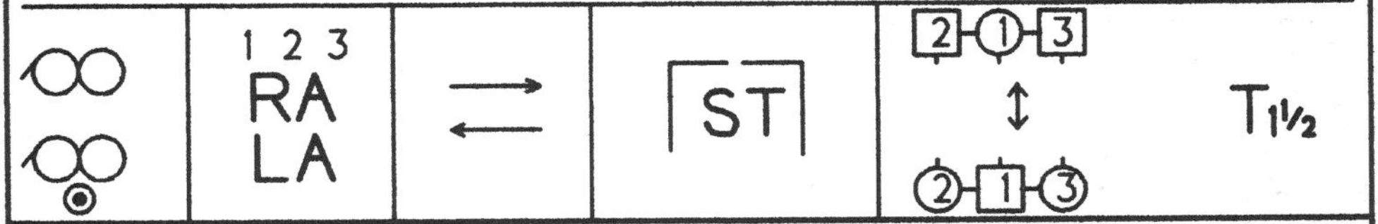

DUNDEE WHALER S32

2 4 | 12 & 34 | 1 3 | ② X_L [1] | ① X_R [2] [1] X_R [3] | ③ X_L ① ④ X_L [1] ① X_R [4]

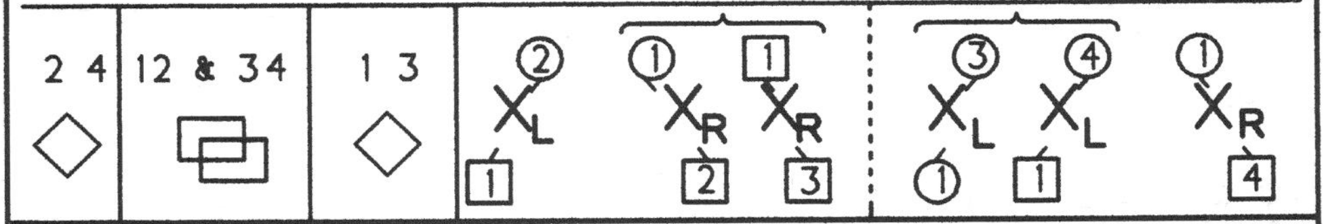

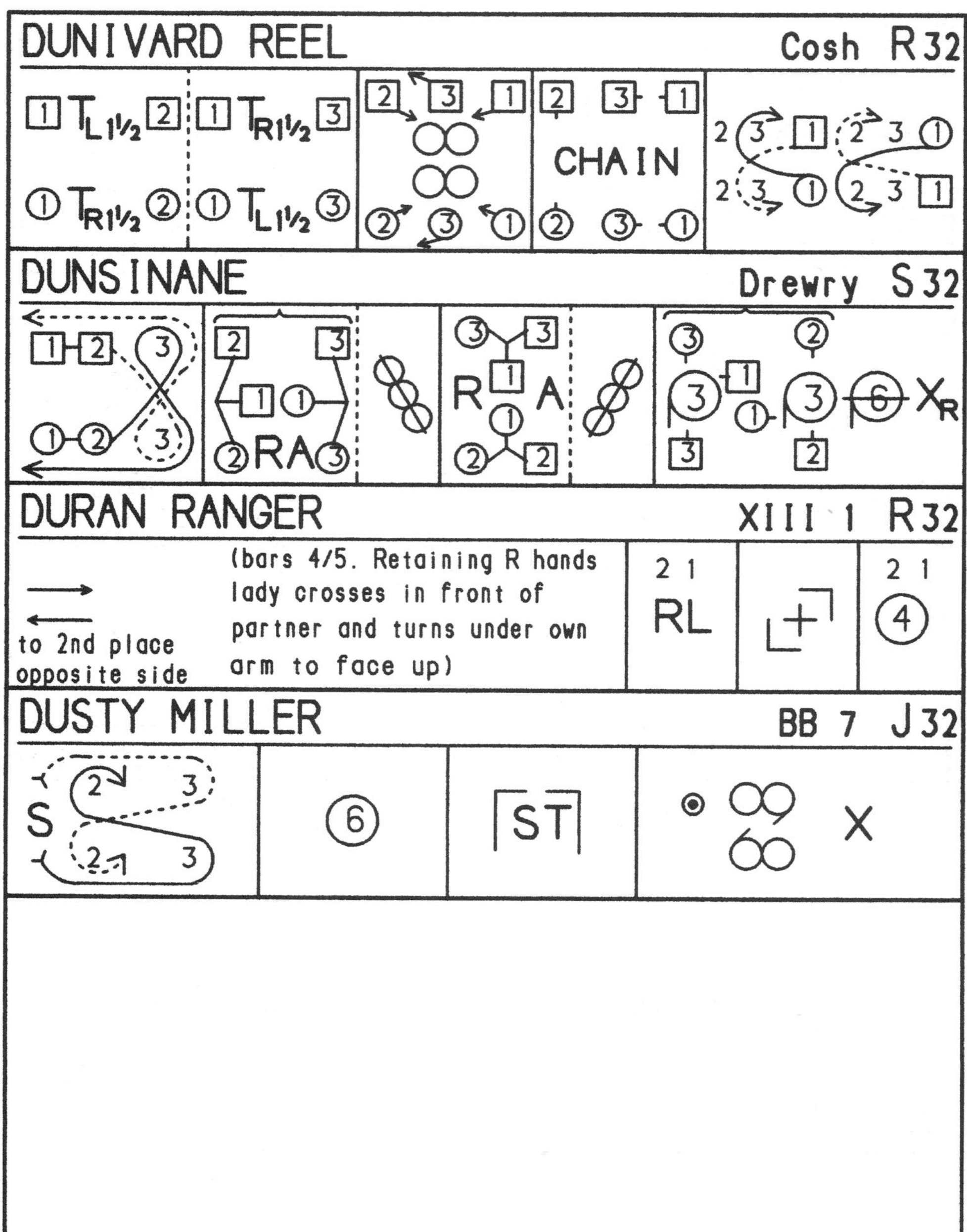
DUNIVARD REEL
Cosh R32
CHAIN
DUNSINANE
Drewry S32
RA
R A
DURAN RANGER
XIII 1 R32
to 2nd place opposite side
(bars 4/5. Retaining R hands lady crosses in front of partner and turns under own arm to face up)
2 1
RL
DUSTY MILLER
BB 7 J32
S
ST
X

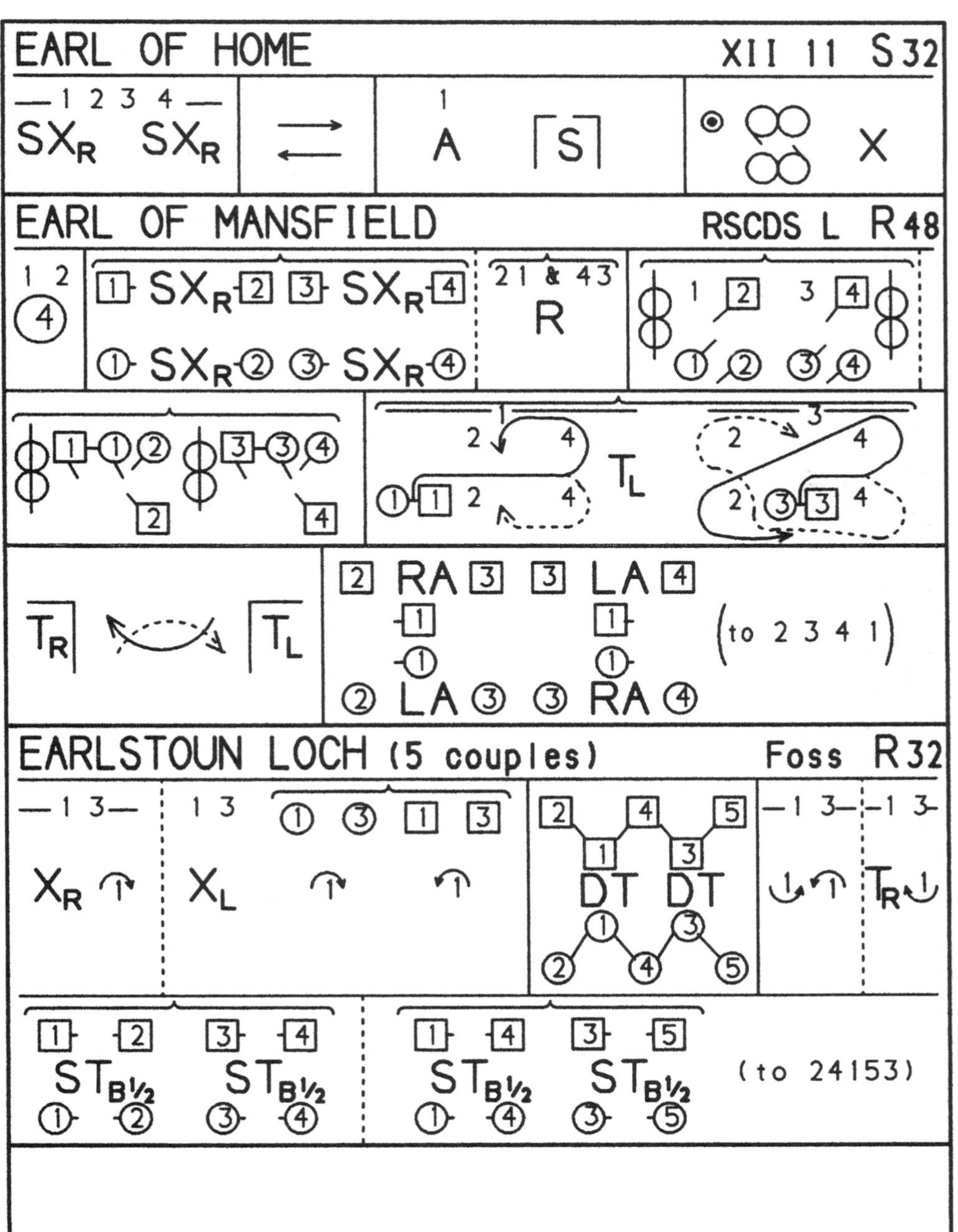

EARL OF HOME
XII 11 S32
1 2 3 4
SXR SXR
1
A
S
X
EARL OF MANSFIELD
RSCDS L R48
1 2
4
1 SXR 2 3 SXR 4
1 SXR 2 3 SXR 4
21 & 43
R
1 2 3 4
1 2 3 4
1 1 2 3 3 4
2 4
TL
TR
TL
2 RA 3 3 LA 4
1 1
1 1
2 LA 3 3 RA 4
(to 2 3 4 1)
EARLSTOUN LOCH (5 couples)
Foss R32
1 3
XR
1 3
XL
1 3 1 3
2 4 5
1 3
DT DT
1 3
2 4 5
1 3
1 3
TR
1 2 3 4
STB½ STB½
1 2 3 4
1 4 3 5
STB½ STB½
1 4 3 5
(to 24153)

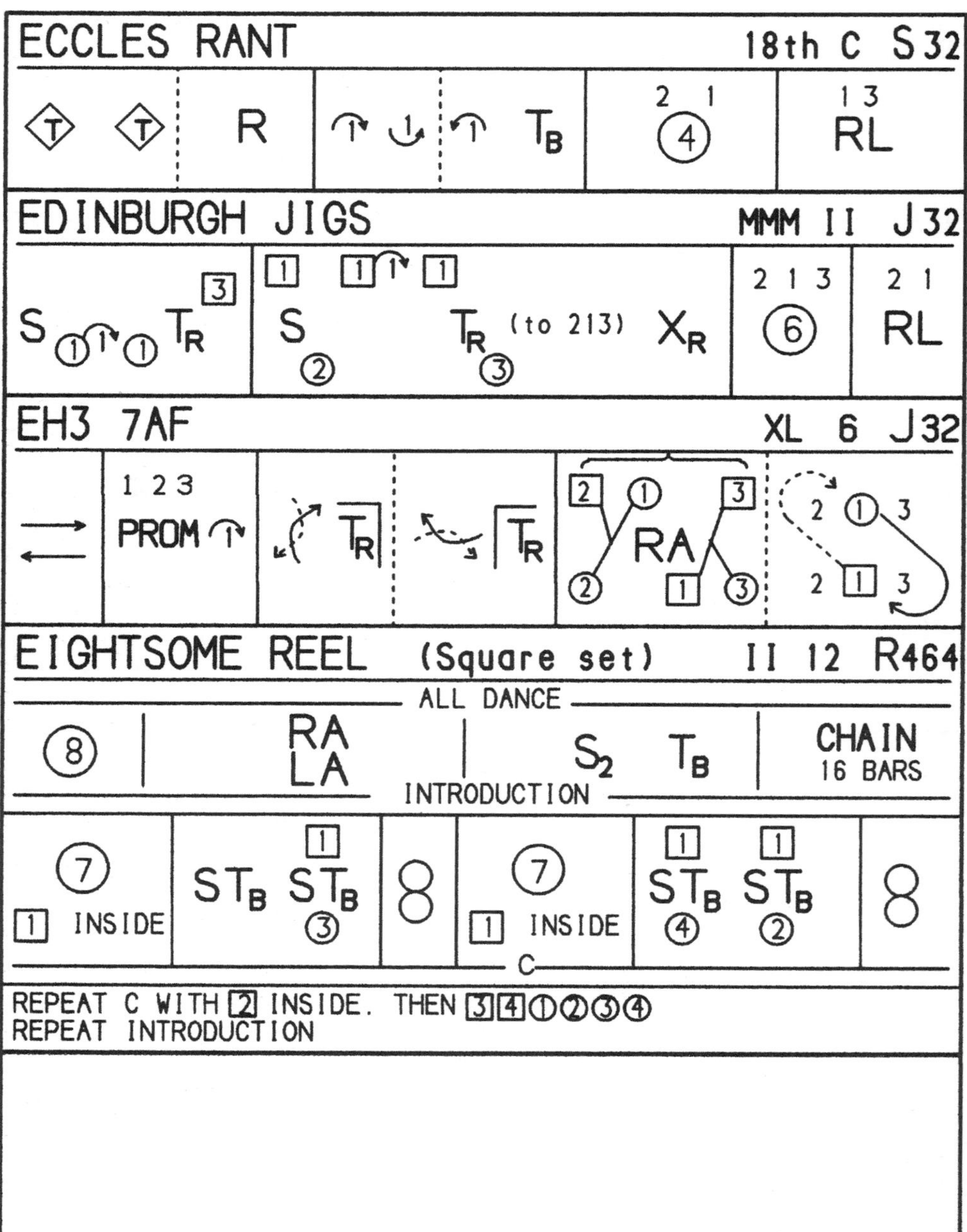
ECCLES RANT
18th C S32
T T R TB
2 1
4
1 3
RL
EDINBURGH JIGS
MMM II J32
S 1 1 1 TR 3
1 1 1 1
S 2
TR 3 (to 213) XR
2 1 3
6
2 1
RL
EH3 7AF
XL 6 J32
1 2 3
PROM
TR
TR
2 1 3
RA
2 1 3
2 1 3
2 1 3
EIGHTSOME REEL (Square set)
II 12 R464
ALL DANCE
8
RA
LA
S2 TB
CHAIN
16 BARS
INTRODUCTION
7
1 INSIDE
ST B ST B
1
3
8
7
1 INSIDE
1 1
ST B ST B
4 2
8
C
REPEAT C WITH 2 INSIDE. THEN 3 4 1 2 3 4
REPEAT INTRODUCTION

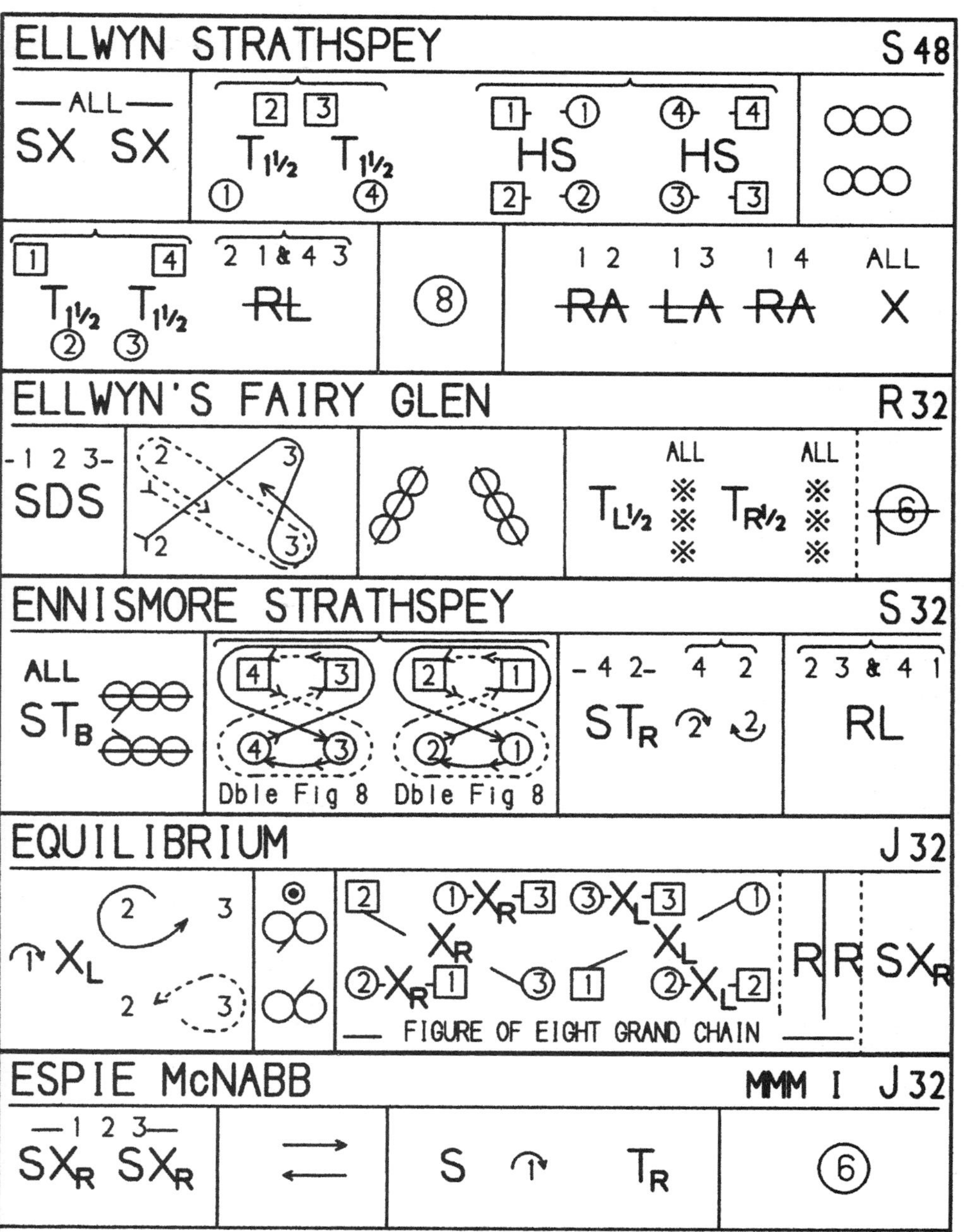
ELLWYN STRATHSPEY
S 48
ALL
SX SX
2 3
T 1½ T 1½
1 4
1 1 4 4
HS HS
2 2 3 3
1 4
T 1½ T 1½
2 3
2 1 & 4 3
RL
8
1 2 1 3 1 4 ALL
RA LA RA X
ELLWYN'S FAIRY GLEN
R 32
-1 2 3-
SDS
2 3
2 3
ALL ALL
T L½ T R½
6
ENNISMORE STRATHSPEY
S 32
ALL
ST B
4 3 2 1
4 3 2 1
Dble Fig 8 Dble Fig 8
-4 2- 4 2
ST R 2 2
2 3 & 4 1
RL
EQUILIBRIUM
J 32
X L
2 3
2 3
2 1 X R 3 3 X L 3 1
X R X L
2 X R 1 3 1 2 X L 2
FIGURE OF EIGHT GRAND CHAIN
R R SX R
ESPIE McNABB
MMM I J 32
1 2 3
SX R SX R
S T R
6

EXPRESS				XX 11 J 40
⊙	⊙	⇄	A	DT

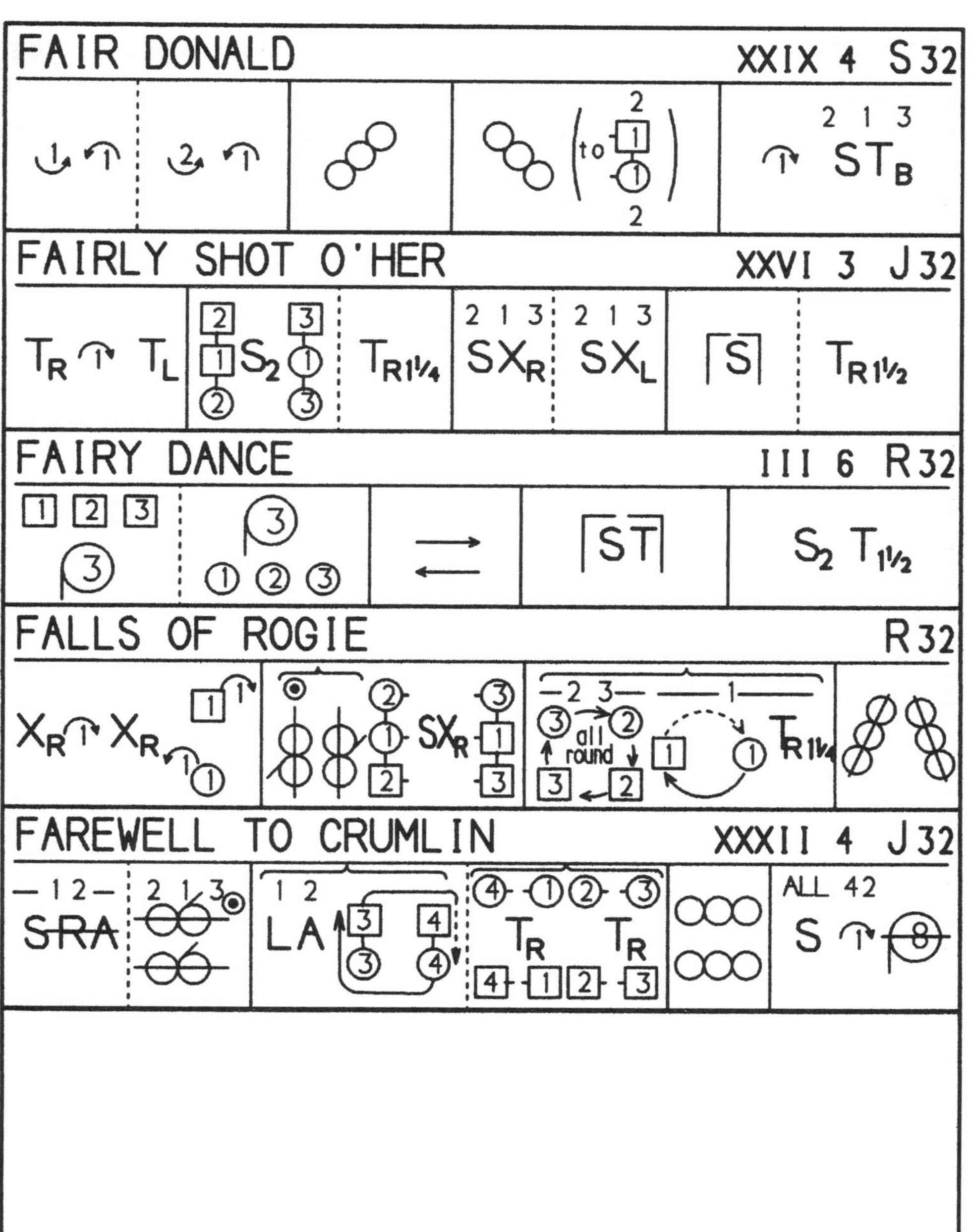
FAIR DONALD
XXIX 4 S32
FAIRLY SHOT O'HER
XXVI 3 J32
FAIRY DANCE
III 6 R32
FALLS OF ROGIE
R32
FAREWELL TO CRUMLIN
XXXII 4 J32

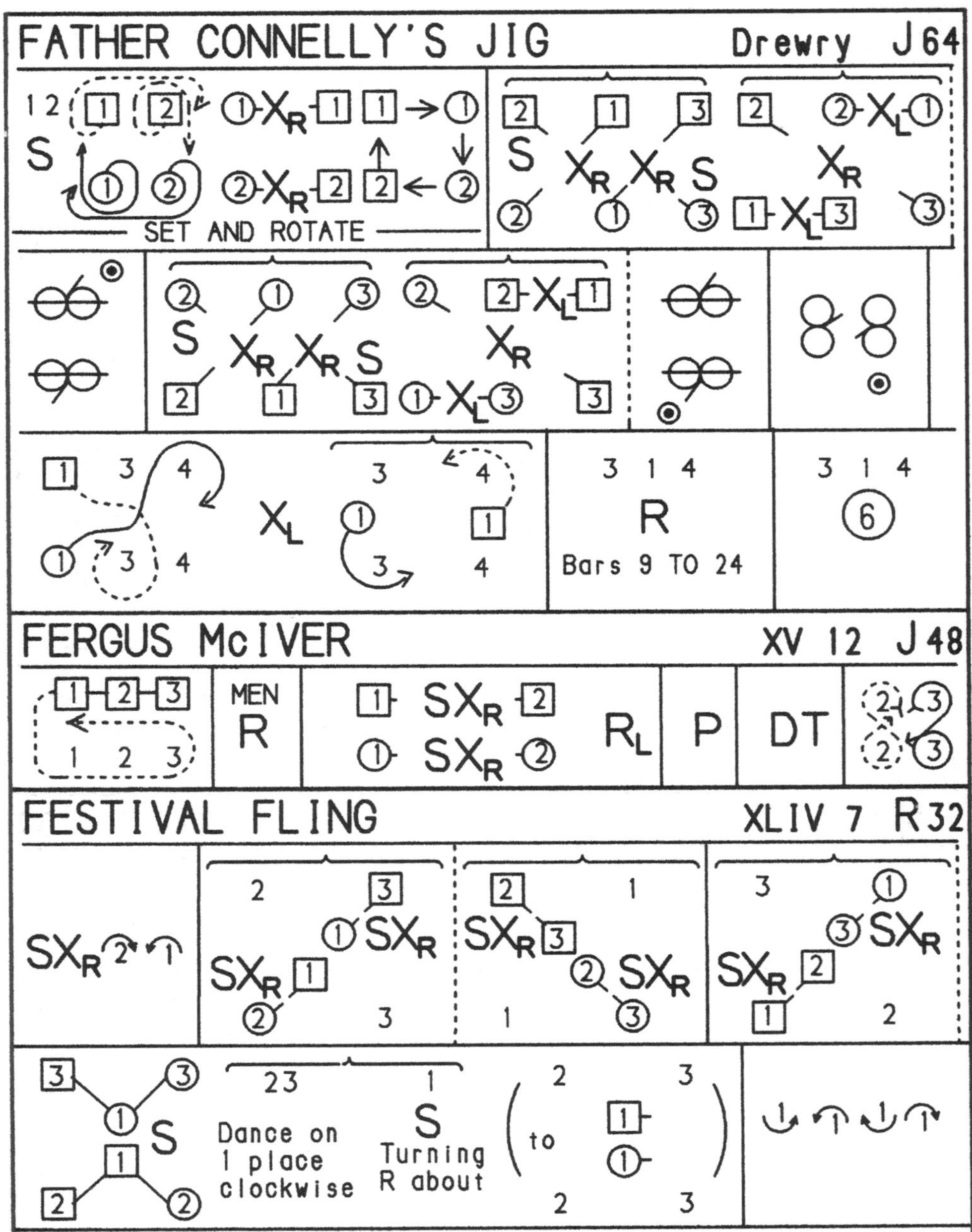
FATHER CONNELLY'S JIG
Drewry J64
SET AND ROTATE
Bars 9 TO 24
FERGUS McIVER
XV 12 J48
MEN
FESTIVAL FLING
XLIV 7 R32
Dance on
1 place
clockwise
Turning
R about
to

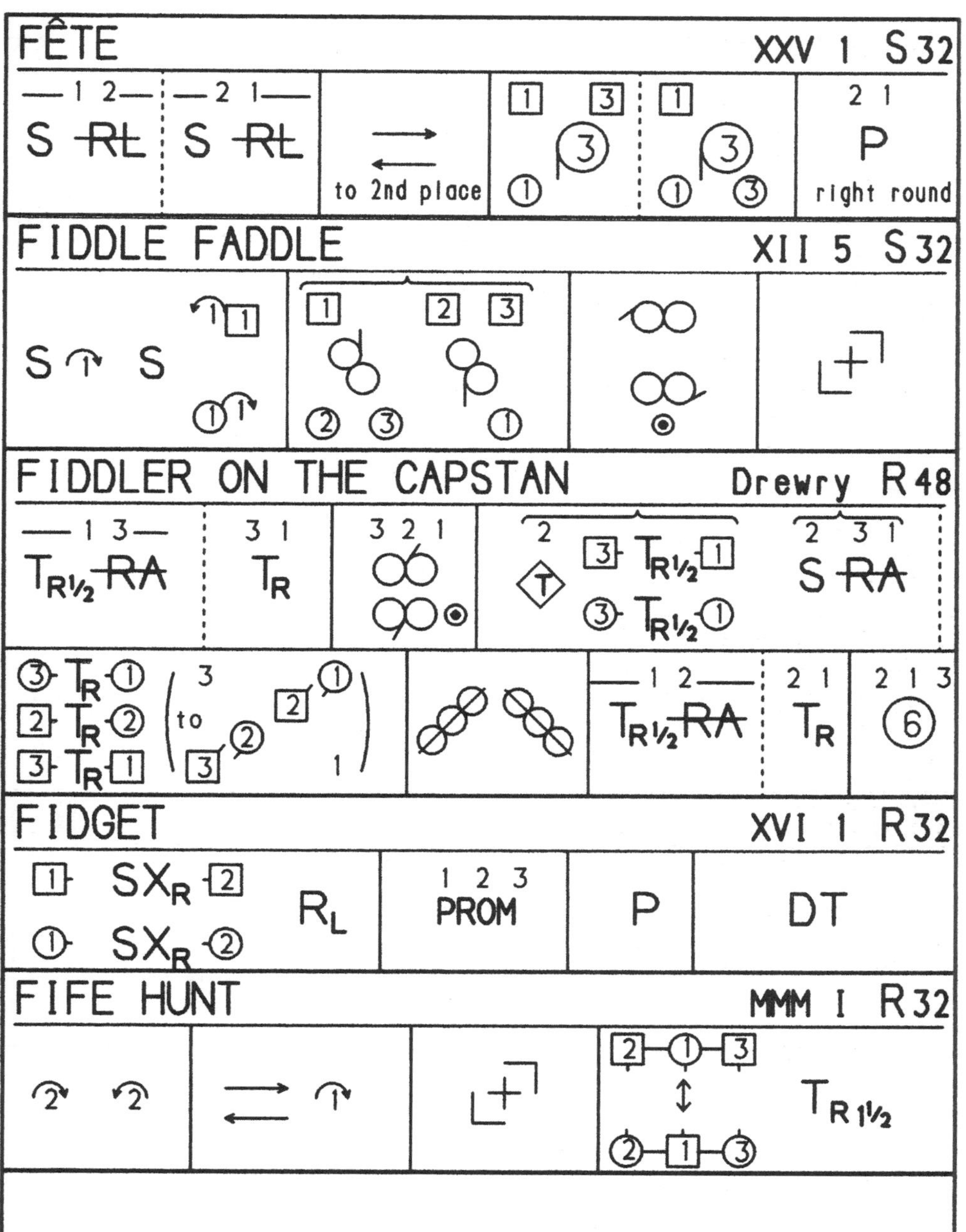
FÊTE
XXV 1 S32
to 2nd place
right round
FIDDLE FADDLE
XII 5 S32
FIDDLER ON THE CAPSTAN
Drewry R48
to
FIDGET
XVI 1 R32
PROM
DT
FIFE HUNT
MMM I R32

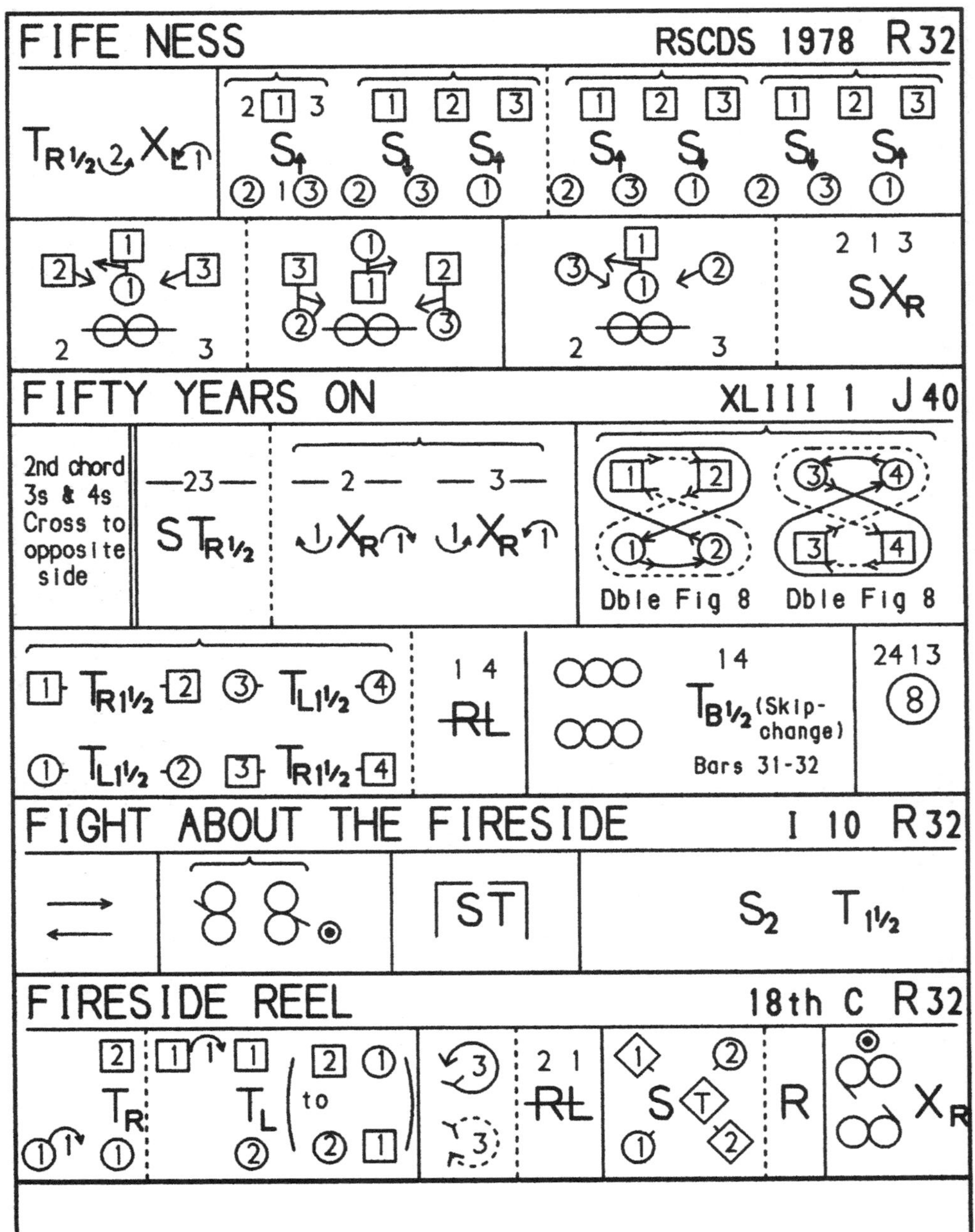
FIFE NESS
RSCDS 1978 R32
FIFTY YEARS ON
XLIII 1 J40
2nd chord 3s & 4s Cross to opposite side
Dble Fig 8
Dble Fig 8
(Skip-change)
Bars 31-32
FIGHT ABOUT THE FIRESIDE
I 10 R32
FIRESIDE REEL
18th C R32

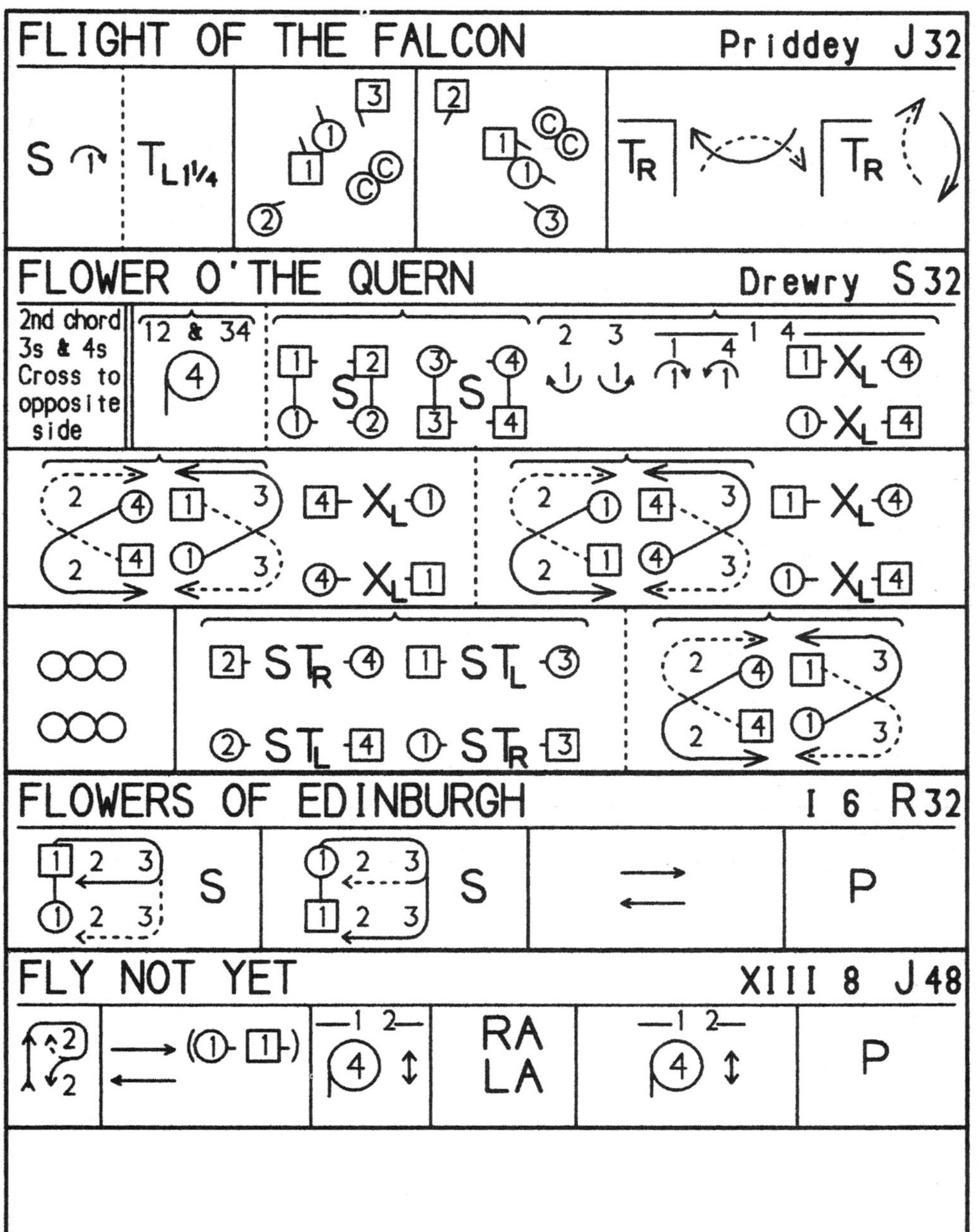
FLIGHT OF THE FALCON
Priddey J32
FLOWER O'THE QUERN
Drewry S32
2nd chord 3s & 4s Cross to opposite side
12 & 34
FLOWERS OF EDINBURGH
I 6 R32
FLY NOT YET
XIII 8 J48
RA
LA

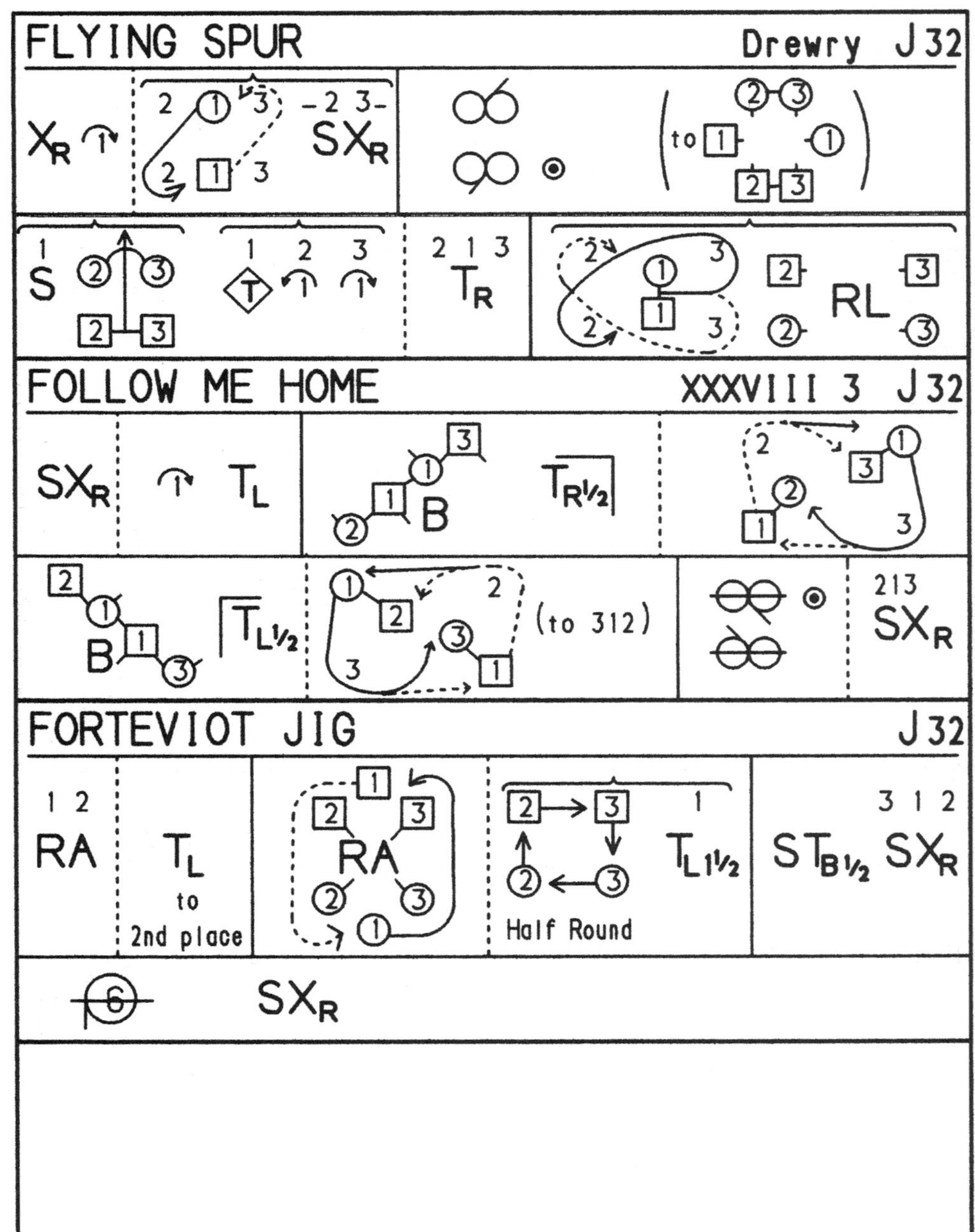
FLYING SPUR
Drewry J32
X_R
SX_R
to
RL
FOLLOW ME HOME
XXXVIII 3 J32
SX_R
T_L
B
$T_{R1/2}$
$T_{L1/2}$
(to 312)
213
SX_R
FORTEVIOT JIG
J32
RA
T_L
to
2nd place
RA
$T_{L1 1/2}$
Half Round
3 1 2
$ST_{B1/2}$ SX_R
SX_R

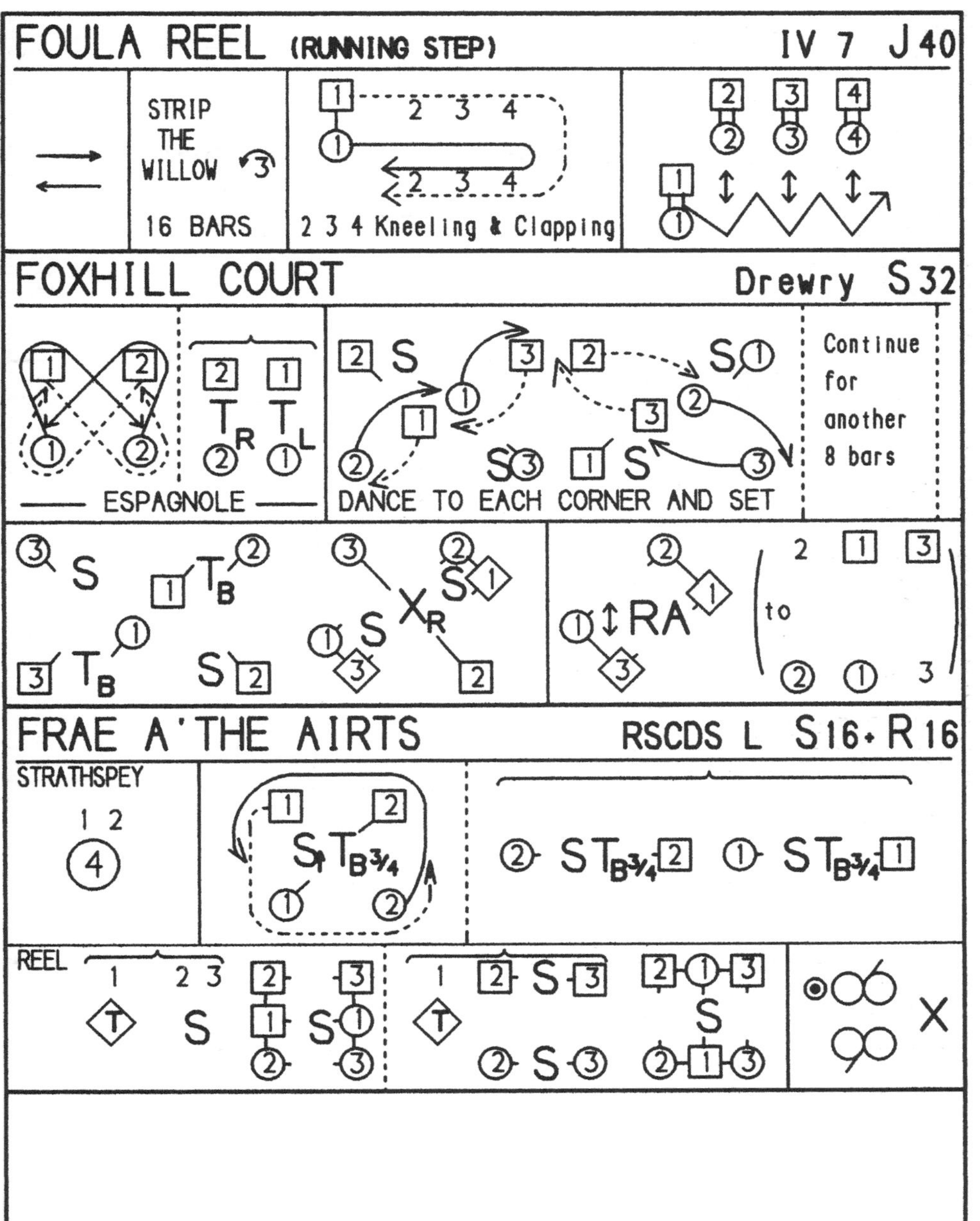
FOULA REEL (RUNNING STEP)
IV 7 J 40
STRIP THE WILLOW
16 BARS
2 3 4 Kneeling & Clapping
FOXHILL COURT
Drewry S 32
ESPAGNOLE
DANCE TO EACH CORNER AND SET
Continue for another 8 bars
FRAE A'THE AIRTS
RSCDS L S16+R16
STRATHSPEY
REEL

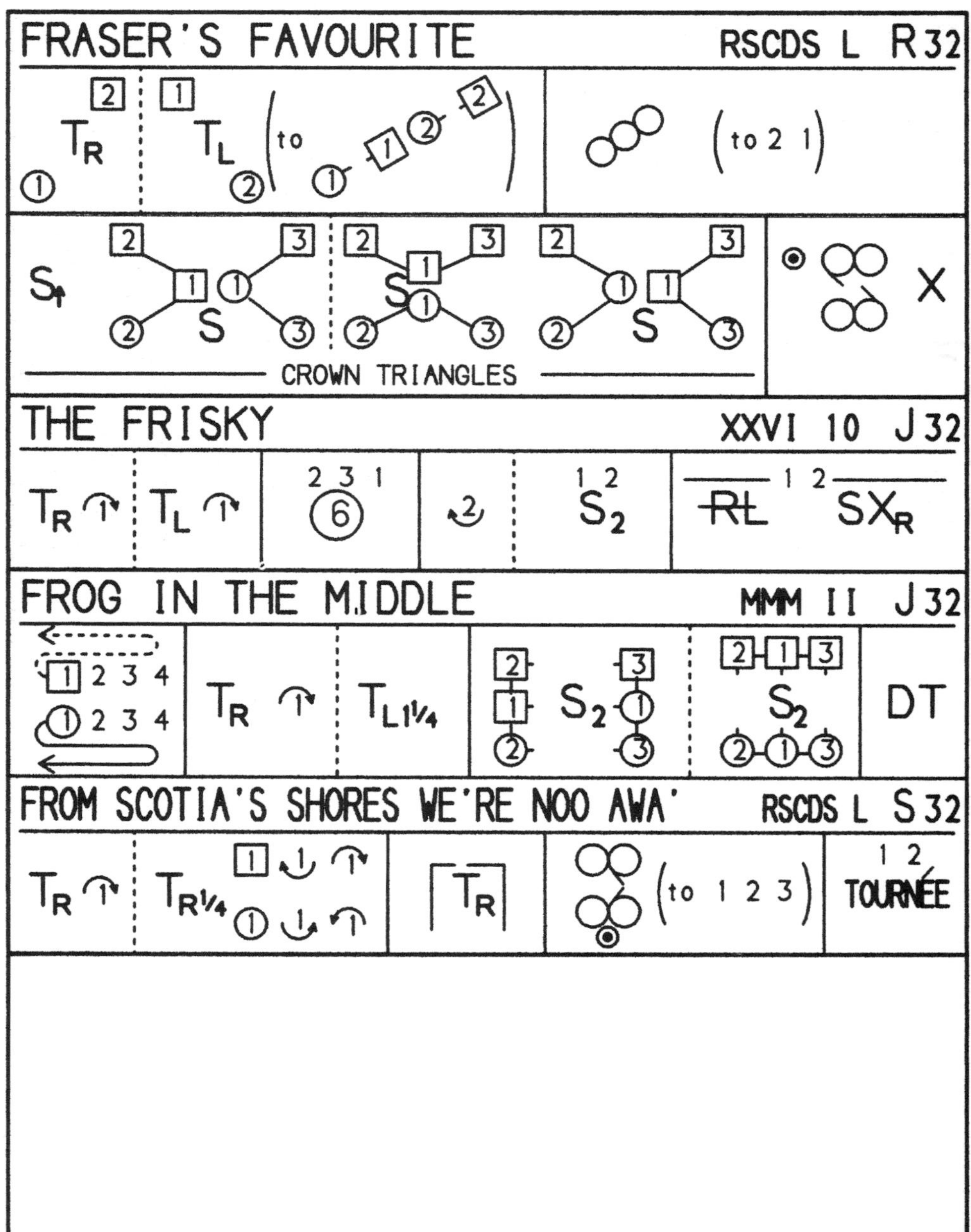
FRASER'S FAVOURITE
RSCDS L R32
to
to 2 1
CROWN TRIANGLES
THE FRISKY
XXVI 10 J32
2 3 1
6
1 2
FROG IN THE MIDDLE
MMM II J32
1 2 3 4
1 2 3 4
DT
FROM SCOTIA'S SHORES WE'RE NOO AWA'
RSCDS L S32
to 1 2 3
1 2
TOURNÉE

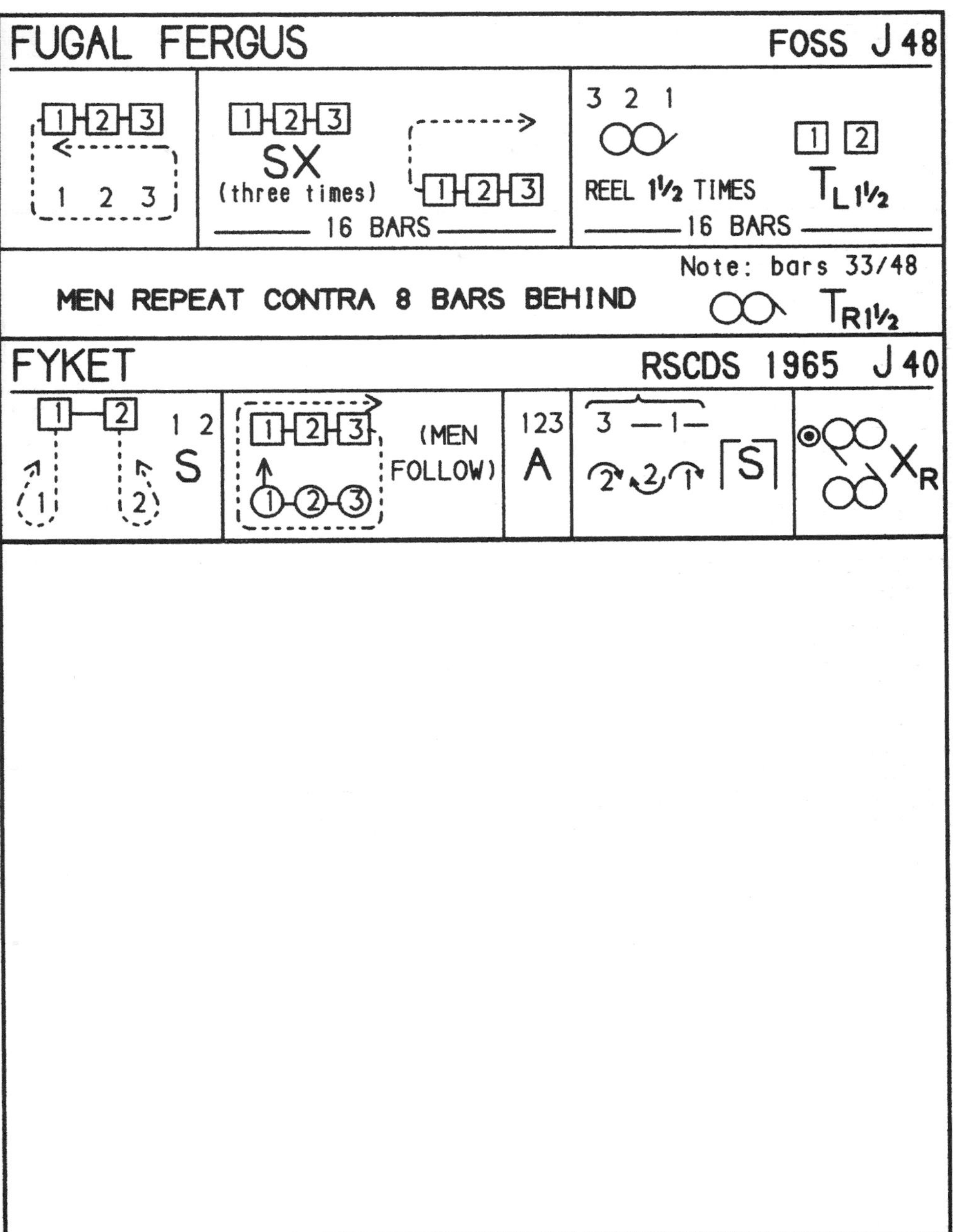
FUGAL FERGUS
FOSS J 48
1 2 3
1 2 3
SX
(three times)
1 2 3
1 2 3
16 BARS
3 2 1
1 2
REEL 1½ TIMES
TL 1½
16 BARS
Note: bars 33/48
MEN REPEAT CONTRA 8 BARS BEHIND
TR1½
FYKET
RSCDS 1965 J 40
1 2
1 2
S
1 2
1 2 3
(MEN FOLLOW)
1 2 3
123
A
3 —1—
2 2 1
S
XR

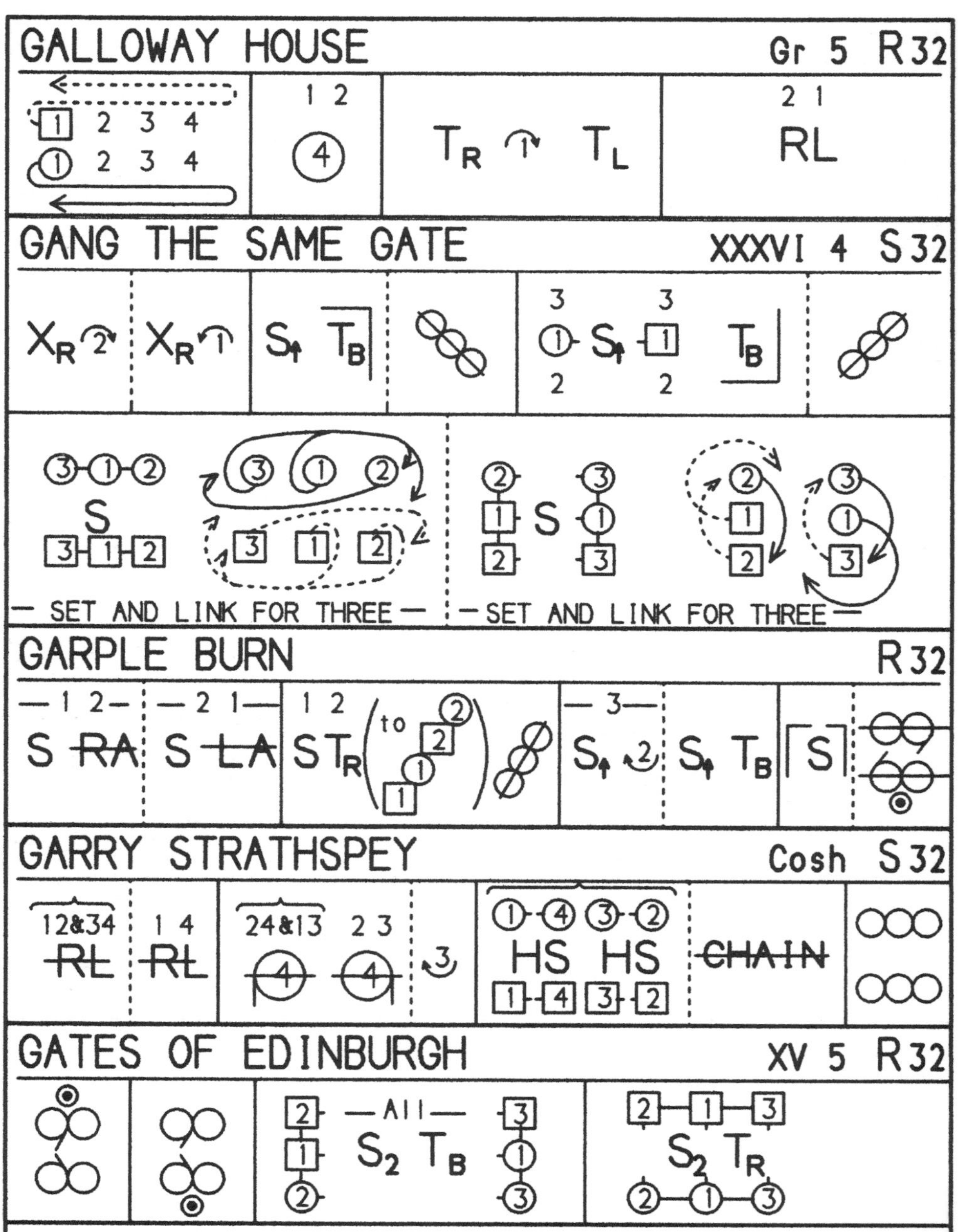
GALLOWAY HOUSE
Gr 5 R32
GANG THE SAME GATE
XXXVI 4 S32
SET AND LINK FOR THREE
SET AND LINK FOR THREE
GARPLE BURN
R32
GARRY STRATHSPEY
Cosh S32
CHAIN
GATES OF EDINBURGH
XV 5 R32
All

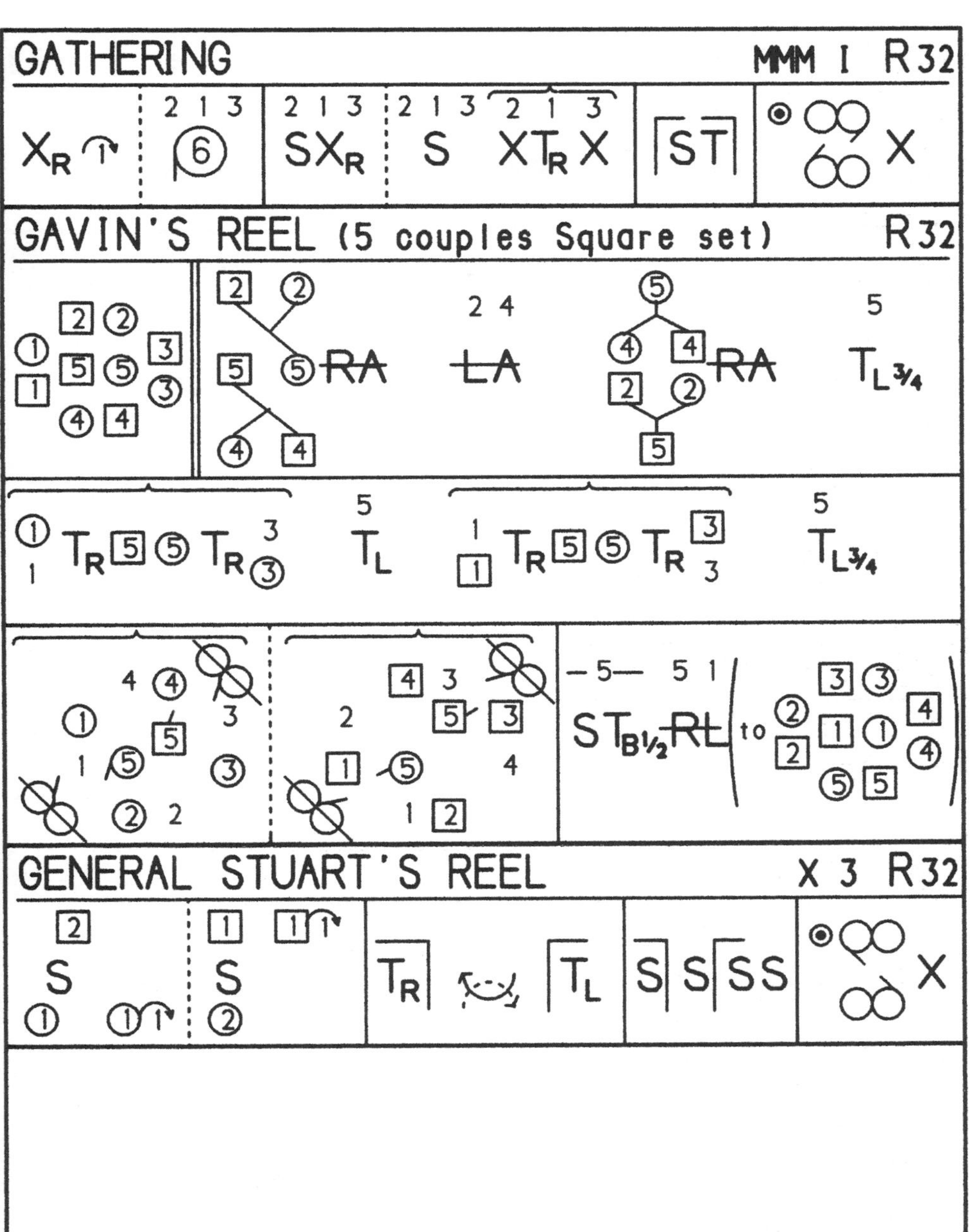
GATHERING
MMM I R32
GAVIN'S REEL (5 couples Square set)
R32
to
GENERAL STUART'S REEL
X 3 R32

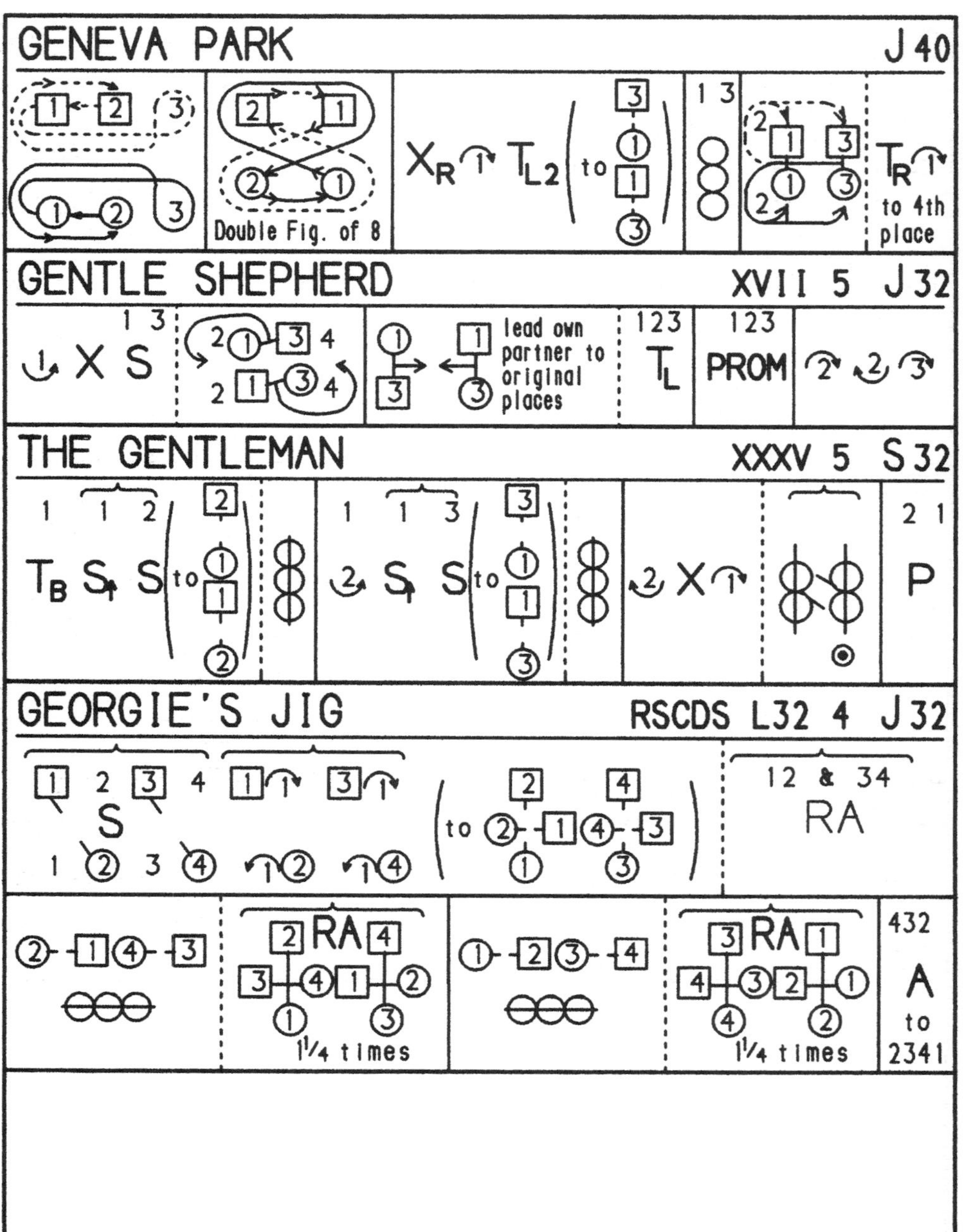
GENEVA PARK
J 40
Double Fig. of 8
to 4th place
GENTLE SHEPHERD
XVII 5 J32
lead own partner to original places
PROM
THE GENTLEMAN
XXXV 5 S32
GEORGIE'S JIG
RSCDS L32 4 J32
12 & 34
RA
1¼ times
1¼ times
432
A
to
2341

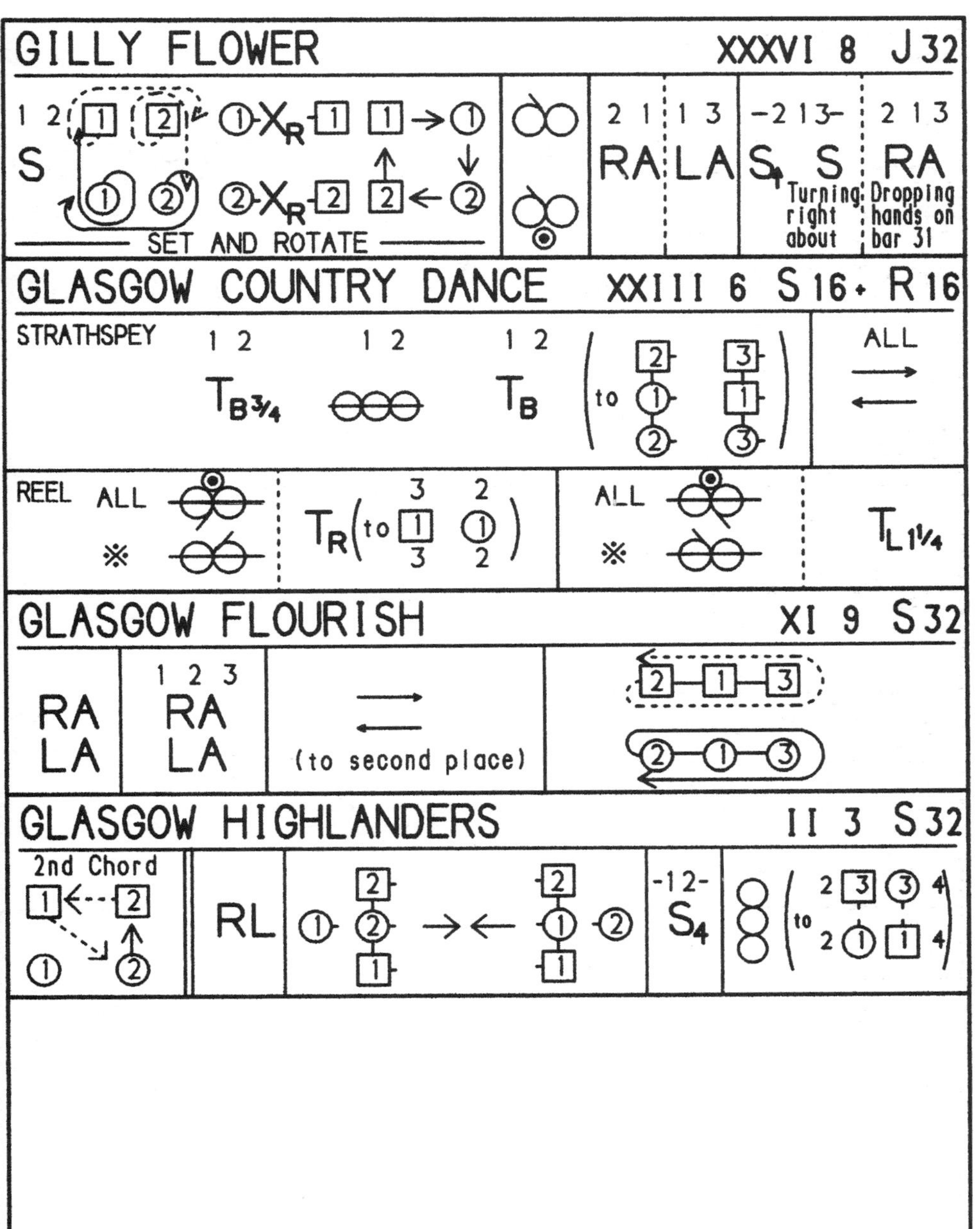
GILLY FLOWER
XXXVI 8 J32
1 2
S
SET AND ROTATE
2 1
RA
1 3
LA
-2 1 3-
S S
Turning right about
2 1 3
RA
Dropping hands on bar 31
GLASGOW COUNTRY DANCE
XXIII 6 S16 + R16
STRATHSPEY
1 2
1 2
1 2
to
ALL
REEL
ALL
※
to
ALL
※
GLASGOW FLOURISH
XI 9 S32
RA
LA
1 2 3
RA
LA
(to second place)
GLASGOW HIGHLANDERS
II 3 S32
2nd Chord
RL
-1 2-
to

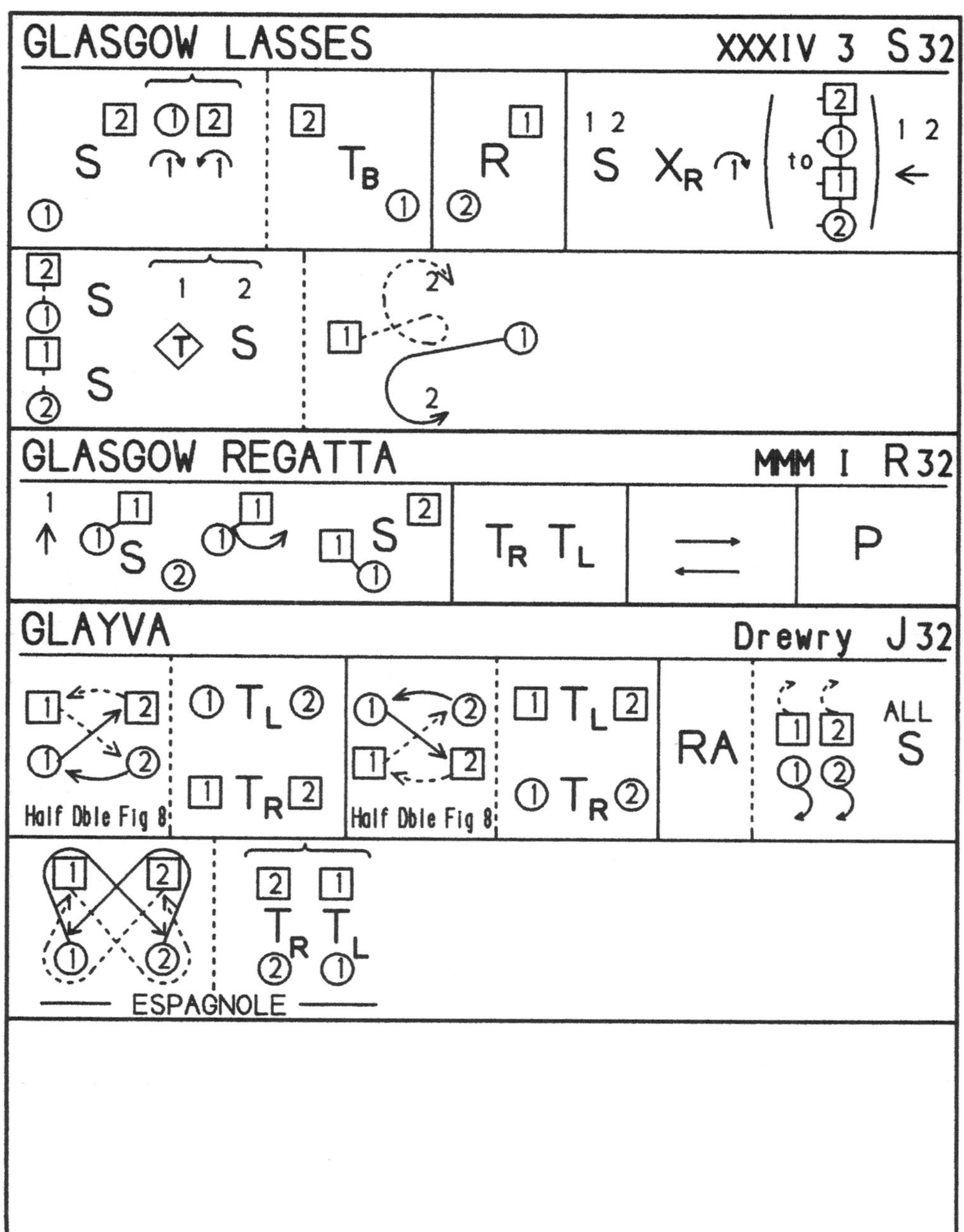
GLASGOW LASSES
XXXIV 3 S32
GLASGOW REGATTA
MMM I R32
GLAYVA
Drewry J32
Half Dble Fig 8
Half Dble Fig 8
RA
ALL S
ESPAGNOLE

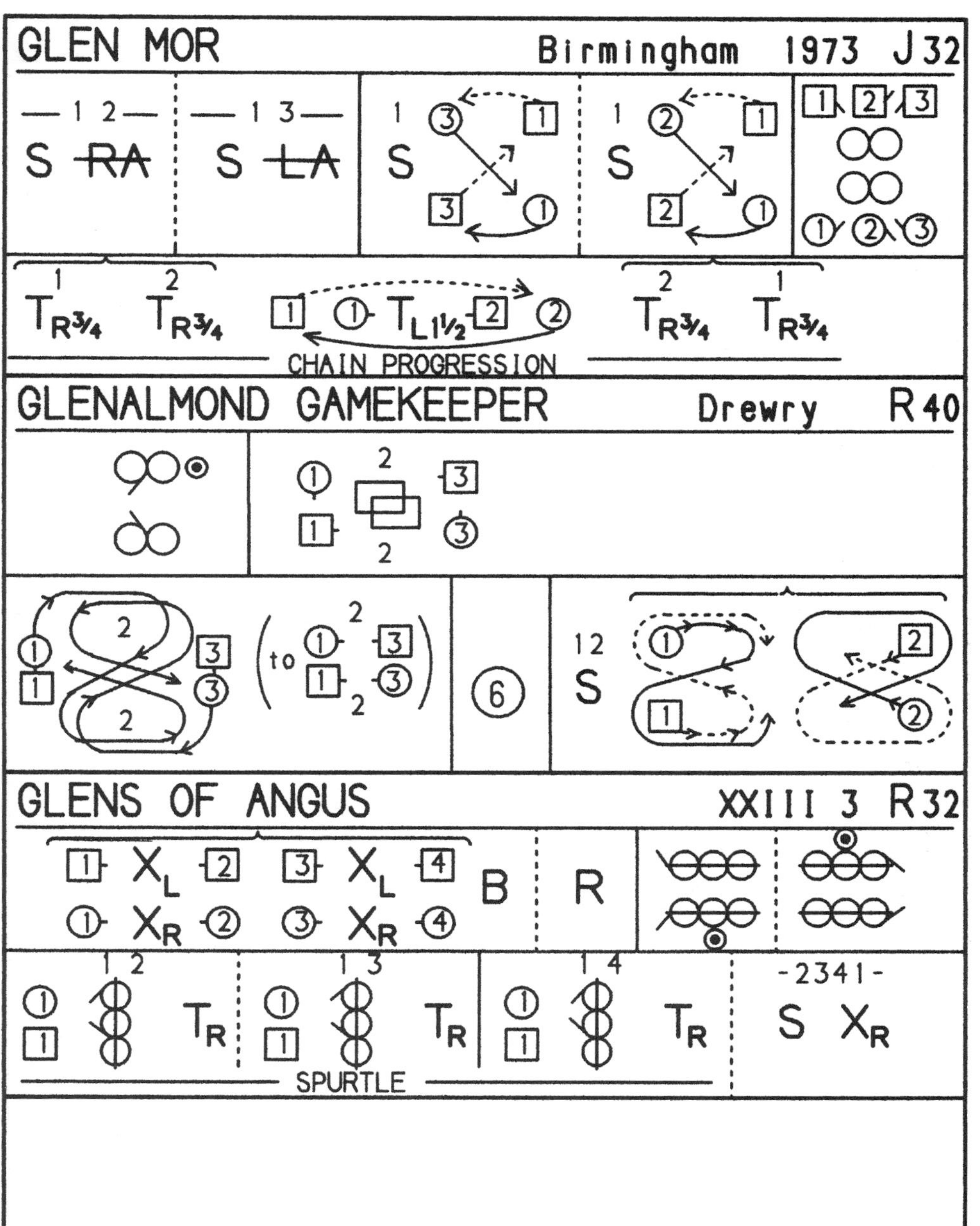
GLEN MOR
Birmingham 1973 J32
S RA
S LA
S
S
CHAIN PROGRESSION
GLENALMOND GAMEKEEPER
Drewry R40
to
S
GLENS OF ANGUS
XXIII 3 R32
B
R
SPURTLE
-2341-
S

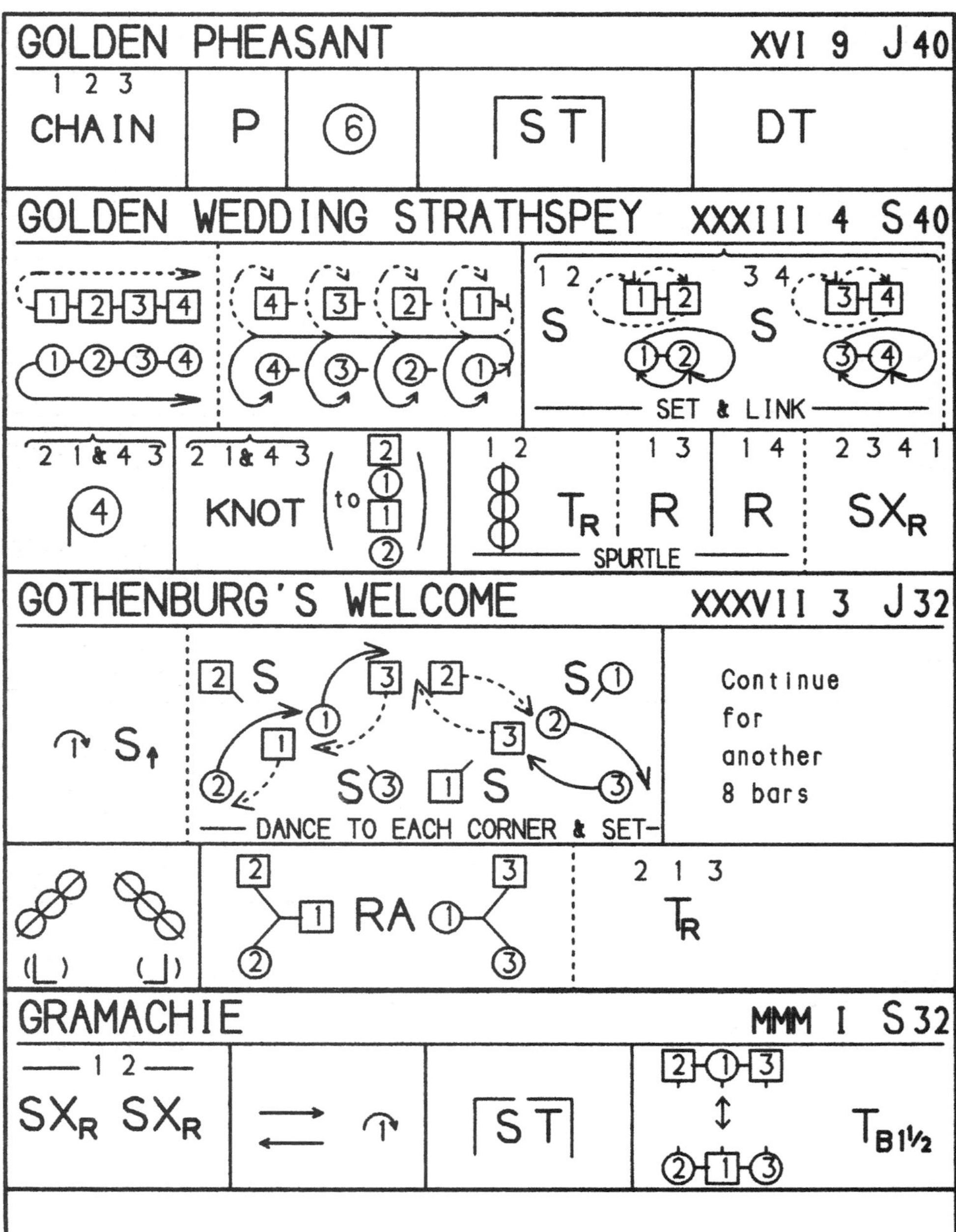

GOLDEN PHEASANT
XVI 9 J40
1 2 3
CHAIN
P
6
ST
DT
GOLDEN WEDDING STRATHSPEY
XXXIII 4 S40
1 2
S
3 4
S
SET & LINK
2 1 & 4 3
4
2 1 & 4 3
KNOT
to
1 2
T R
1 3
R
1 4
R
2 3 4 1
SX R
SPURTLE
GOTHENBURG'S WELCOME
XXXVII 3 J32
S
DANCE TO EACH CORNER & SET
Continue
for
another
8 bars
RA
2 1 3
T R
GRAMACHIE
MMM I S32
1 2
SX R SX R
ST
T B1½

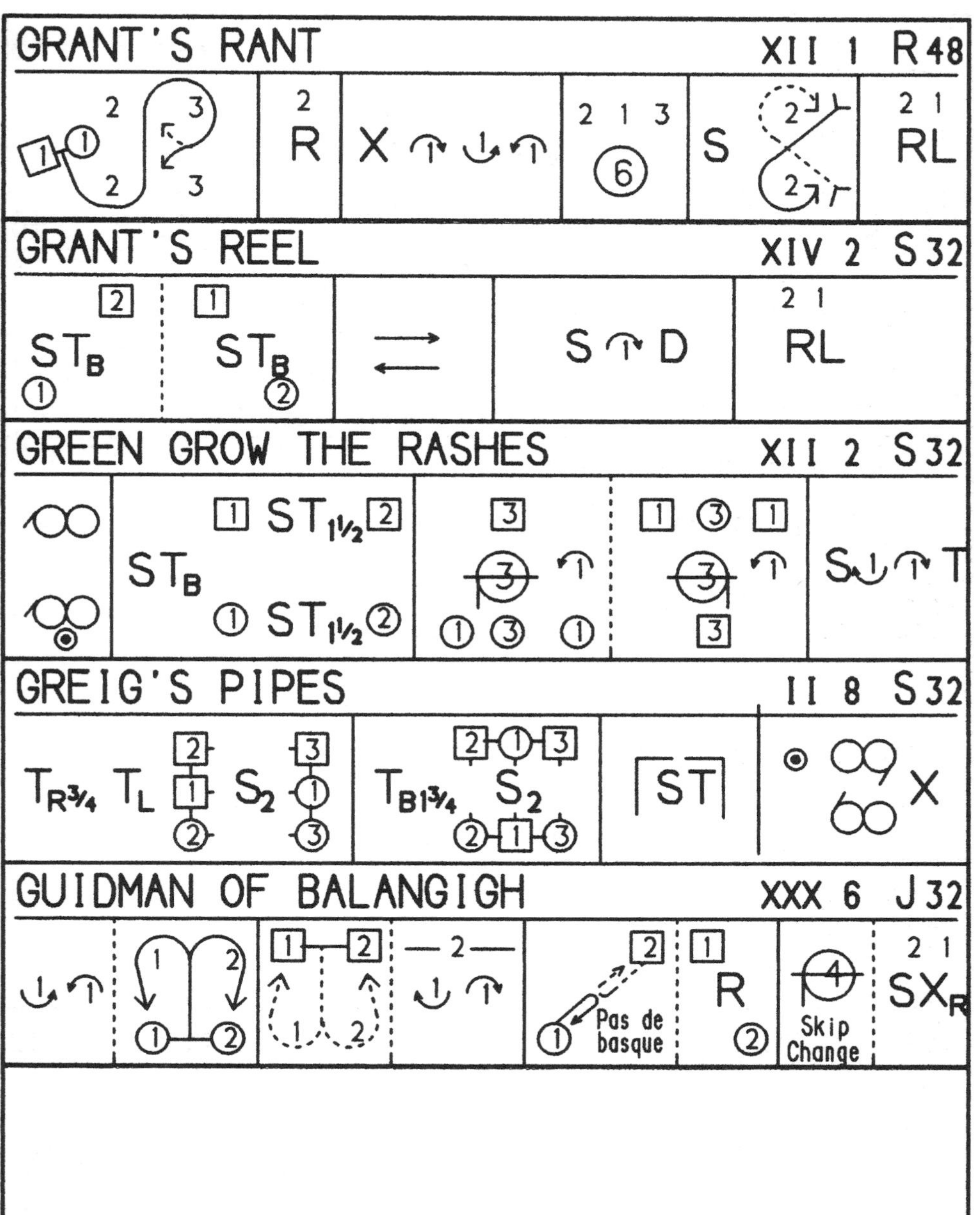
GRANT'S RANT
XII 1 R48
R
X
S
RL
GRANT'S REEL
XIV 2 S32
ST
S D
RL
GREEN GROW THE RASHES
XII 2 S32
ST
S T
GREIG'S PIPES
II 8 S32
T
S
ST
X
GUIDMAN OF BALANGIGH
XXX 6 J32
Pas de basque
R
Skip Change
SX

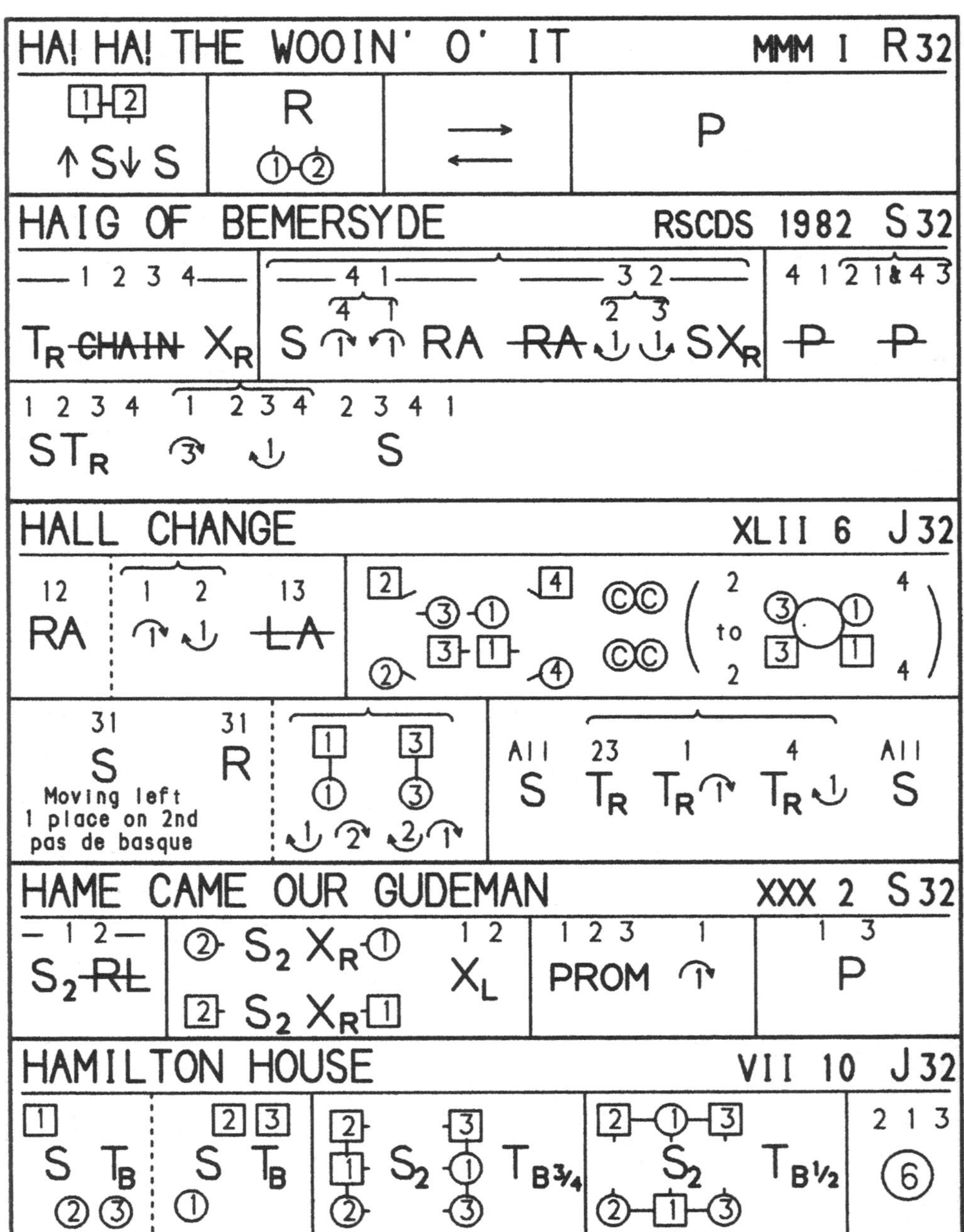
HA! HA! THE WOOIN' O' IT
MMM I R32
HAIG OF BEMERSYDE
RSCDS 1982 S32
CHAIN
HALL CHANGE
XLII 6 J32
to
Moving left
1 place on 2nd
pas de basque
All
HAME CAME OUR GUDEMAN
XXX 2 S32
PROM
HAMILTON HOUSE
VII 10 J32

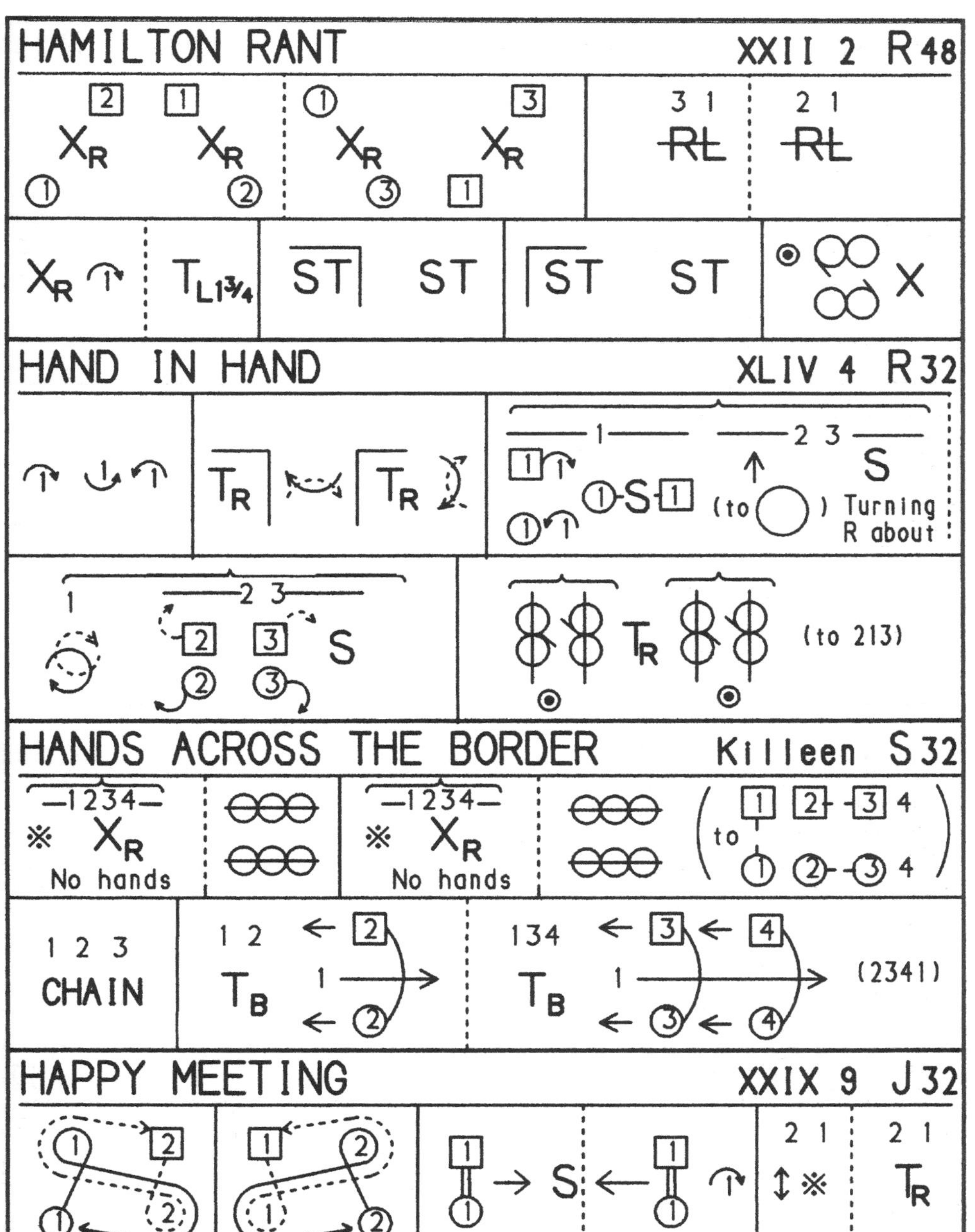
HAMILTON RANT
XXII 2 R48
HAND IN HAND
XLIV 4 R32
Turning R about
(to 213)
HANDS ACROSS THE BORDER
Killeen S32
No hands
No hands
CHAIN
(2341)
HAPPY MEETING
XXIX 9 J32

HAPPY RETURNS
MMM II R32

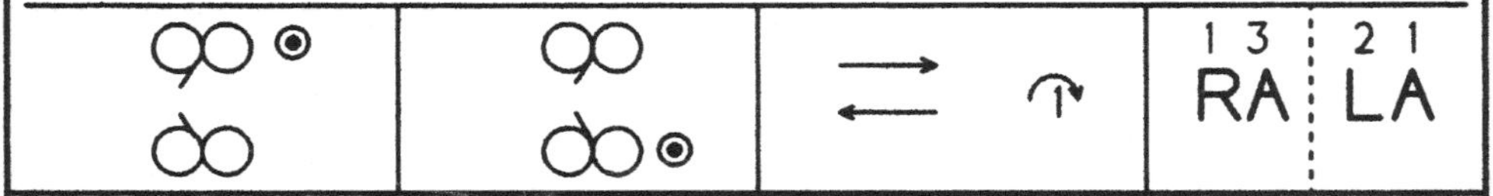

			1 3 RA ⋮ 2 1 LA

HASTE TO THE WEDDING
XXV 6 J32

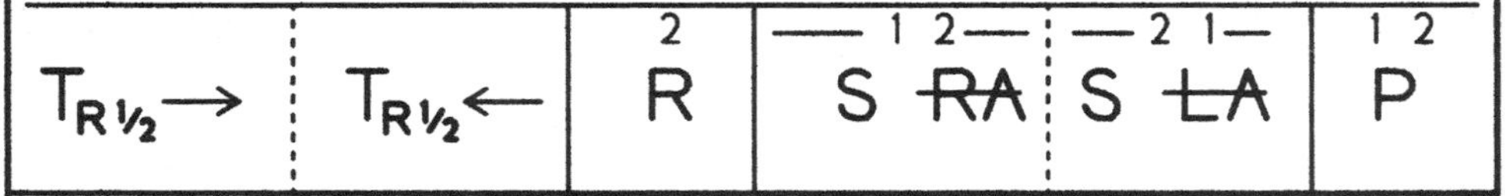

$T_{R\,1/2}$ → ⋮ $T_{R\,1/2}$ ←	2 R	1 2 S RA ⋮ 2 1 S LA	1 2 P

HAUNT OF THE GNOMES (Square Set) Drewry S64

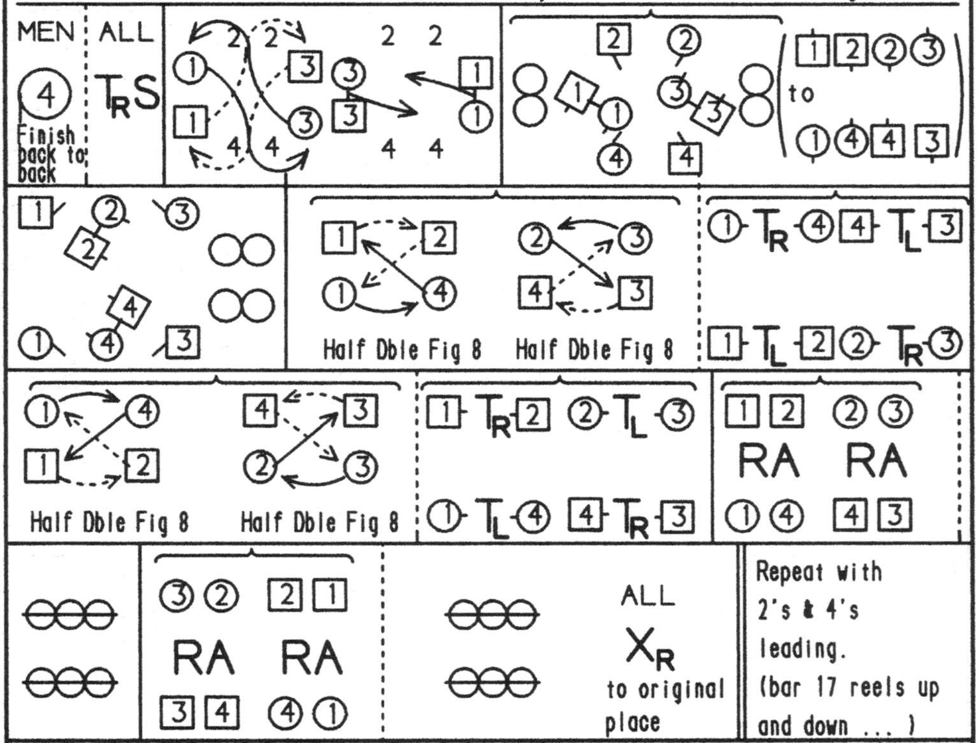

MEN ⋮ ALL
4 Finish back to back ⋮ T_RS

2 2 2 2 3 3 1 1 3 3 1 1 4 4 4 4

2 2 1 1 3 3 4 4 (1 2 2 3 to 1 4 4 3)

1 2 3 2 4 1 4 3

1 2 1 4 — Half Dble Fig 8; 2 3 4 3 — Half Dble Fig 8 ⋮ 1 T_R 4 4 T_L 3 / 1 T_L 2 2 T_R 3

1 4 1 2 — Half Dble Fig 8; 4 3 2 3 — Half Dble Fig 8 ⋮ 1 T_R 2 2 T_L 3 / 1 T_L 4 4 T_R 3 ⋮ 1 2 2 3 RA RA 1 4 4 3

3 2 2 1 RA RA 3 4 4 1 ⋮ ALL X_R to original place

Repeat with 2's & 4's leading. (bar 17 reels up and down ...)

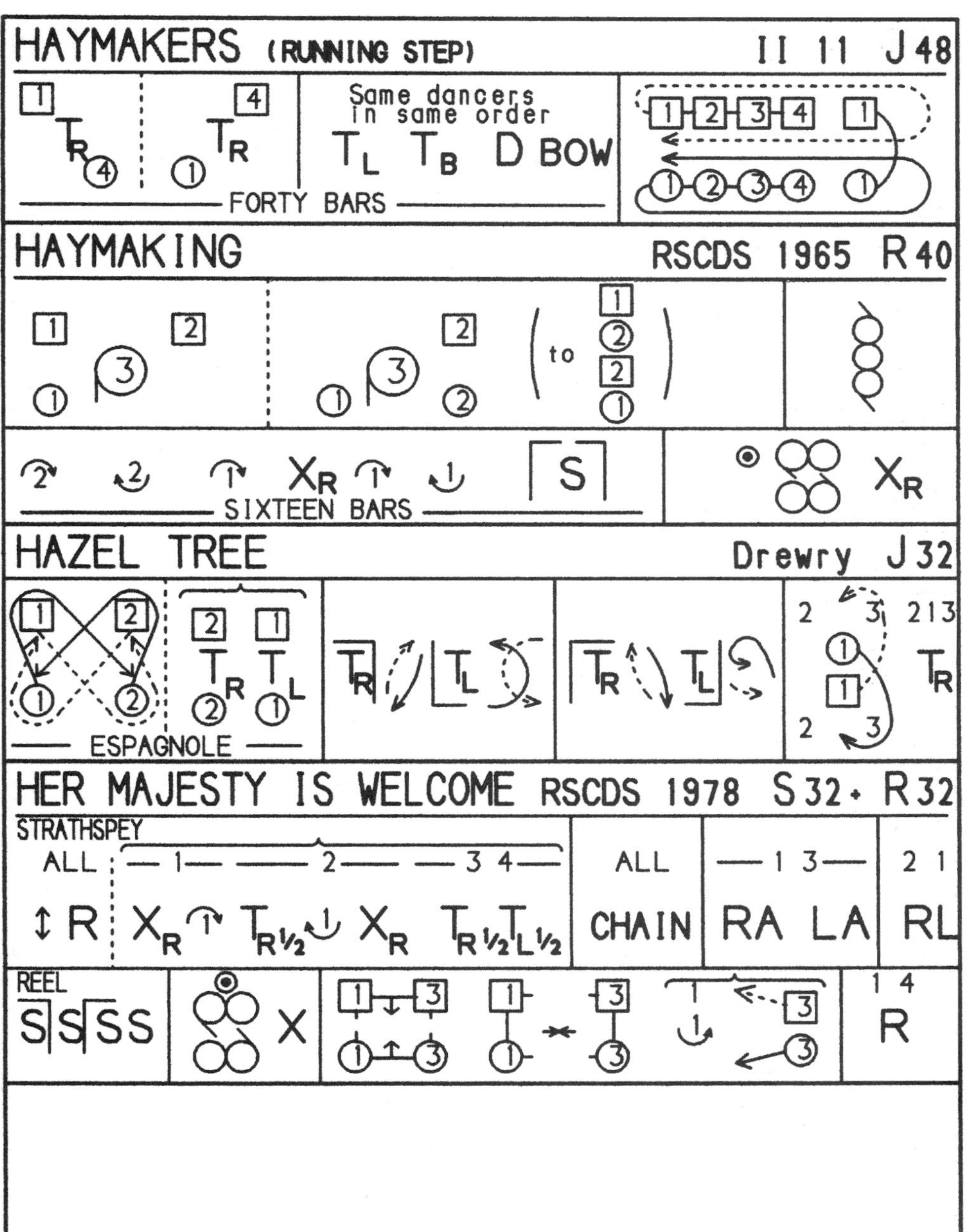

HAYMAKERS (RUNNING STEP) II 11 J48
1 TR 4
4 TR 1
Same dancers in same order
TL TB D BOW
FORTY BARS
1 2 3 4 1
1 2 3 4 1
HAYMAKING RSCDS 1965 R40
1 2 3 1
2 3 1 2
to 1 2 2 1
2 2 1 XR 1 S
SIXTEEN BARS
XR
HAZEL TREE Drewry J32
1 2 1 2
ESPAGNOLE
2 1 TR TL 2 1
TR TL
TR TL
2 3 213 1 1 2 3 TR
HER MAJESTY IS WELCOME RSCDS 1978 S32 + R32
STRATHSPEY
ALL — 1 — — 2 — — 3 4 —
↕ R XR 1 TR½ 1 XR TR½ TL½
ALL CHAIN
— 1 3 — RA LA
2 1 RL
REEL
S S S S S
X
1 3 1 3 1 3 1 3
1 3
1 4 R

HEREFORD SILVER JUBILEE H32

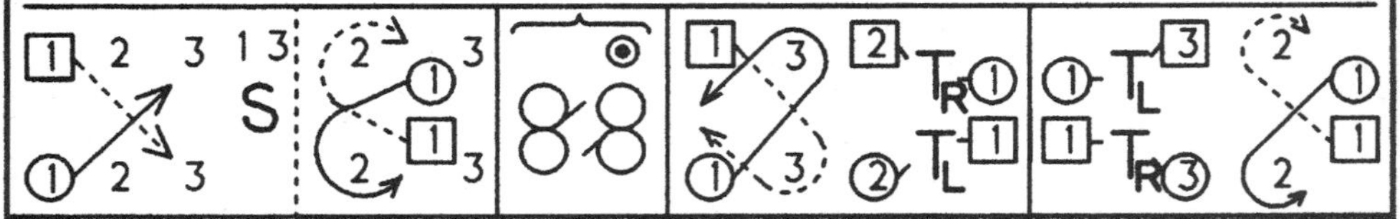

1 2 3 1 3 S 1 2 3	2 3 1 1 3 2	8 8	1 3 1 3	2 T_R 1 2 T_L 1	1 T_L 3 1 T_R 3	2 1 1 2

HIGH ROAD TO WIGTON MMM I R32

1 2 1 2 · 1 2 1 2	RA LA	→ ←	P

HIGHLAND FAIR Gr 6 J32

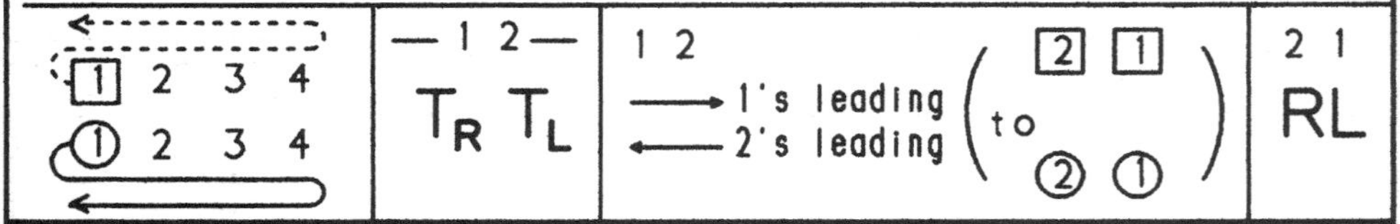

1 2 3 4 · 1 2 3 4	— 1 2 — T_R T_L	1 2 → 1's leading ← 2's leading to (2 1 · 2 1)	2 1 RL

HIGHLAND LADDIE IV 9 R32

S 2 · 2 3 X_R	2 S 1	ST ST	2 1 3 B_2 2 1 3 · 2 1 3 T_R

HIGHLAND LASS XXX 3 R32

1 · 8 8	1 1 · 8 8	2 1 RL	1 1 · 2 1 3 T_R

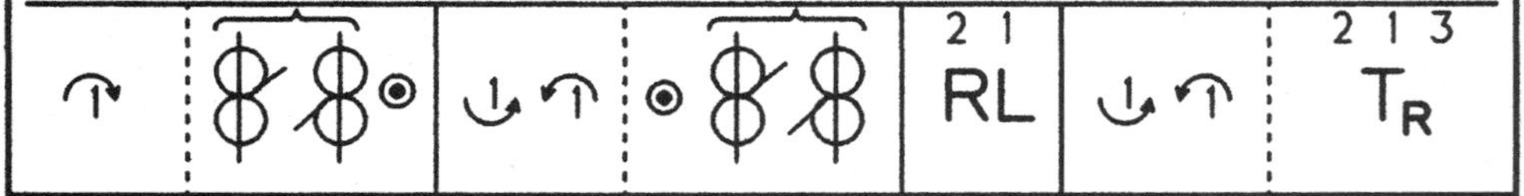

HIGHLAND PLAID VII 8 S32

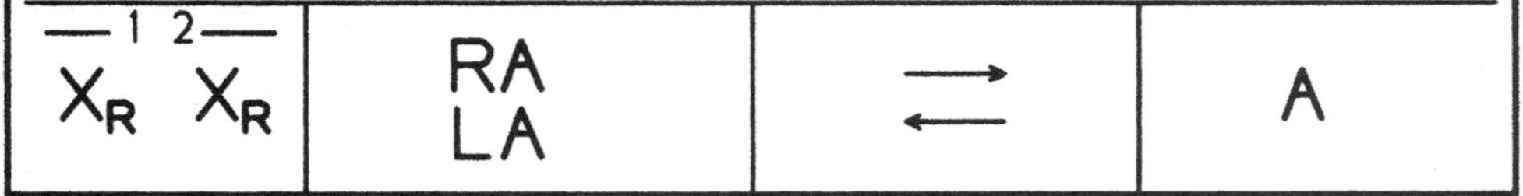

— 1 2 — X_R X_R	RA LA	→ ←	A

HIGHLAND RAMBLER R40

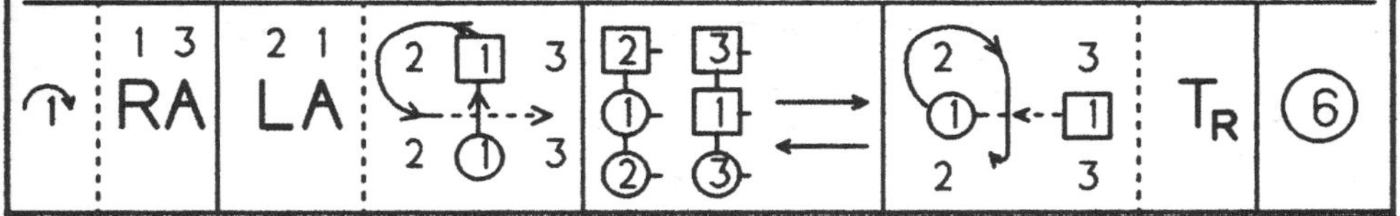

↷ ⋮ 1 3 RA	2 1 LA ⋮ 2 1 3 / 2 1 3	2 3 / 1 1 / 2 3 ⇄	2 3 / 1 1 / 2 3 ⋮	T_R	⑥

HIGHLAND REEL (Sixes round the room) XIII 5 R32

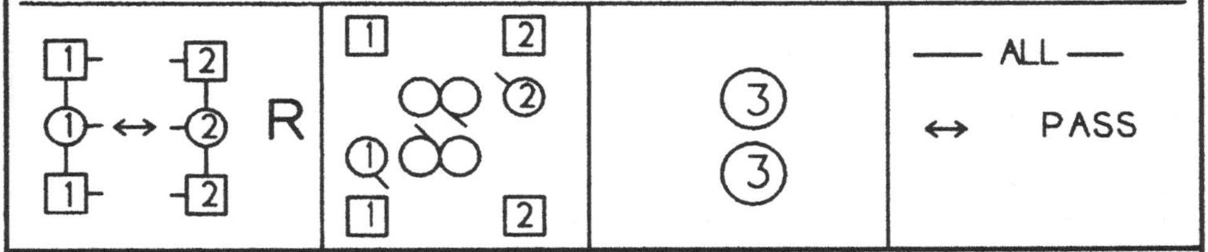

1 2 / 1 ↔ 2 / 1 2 R	1 2 / 2 / 1 / 1 2	③ ③	— ALL — ↔ PASS

HIGHLANDMAN KISSED HIS MOTHER MMM I R32

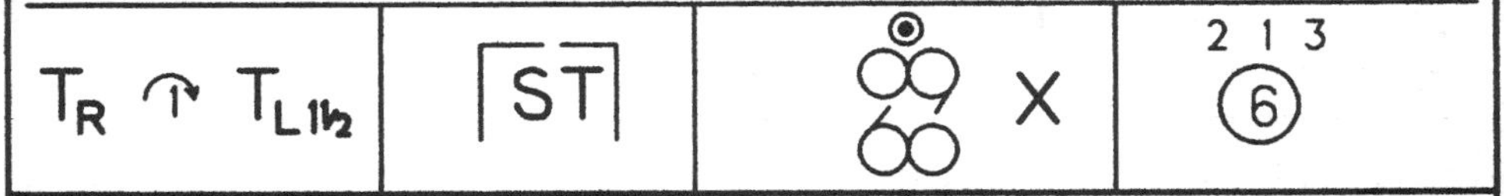

T_R ↷ $T_{L1½}$	ST	X	2 1 3 ⑥

HIGHLANDMAN KISSED HIS MOTHER BB 9 R32

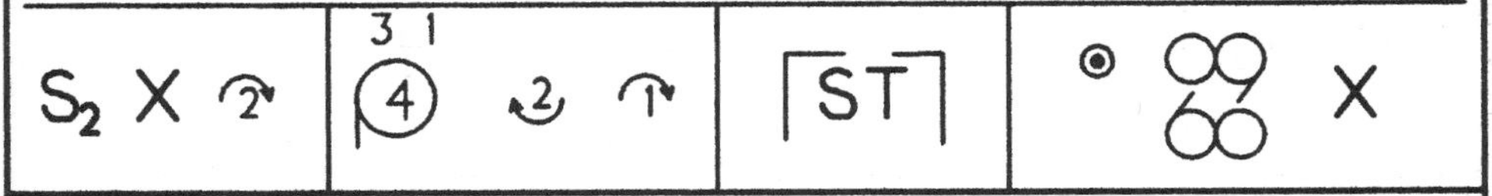

S_2 X ↷2	3 1 ④ ↶2 ↷	ST	X

HOGMANAY JIG J32

1 2 3 SX_R ①②③ / 1 2 3	3 2 1 SX_L ③②① / 3 2 1	3 1 2 321 X_R X_R X_R S ① ③ ②	1's X_L to begin snow-ball chain 1's T_R to 2nd

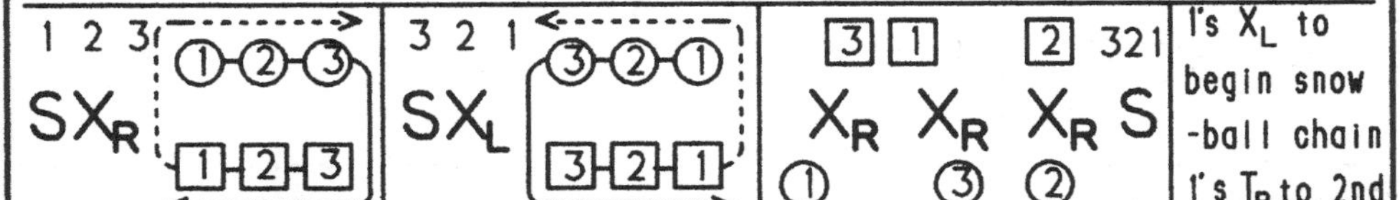

HOLLIN BUSS XXIV 8 J32

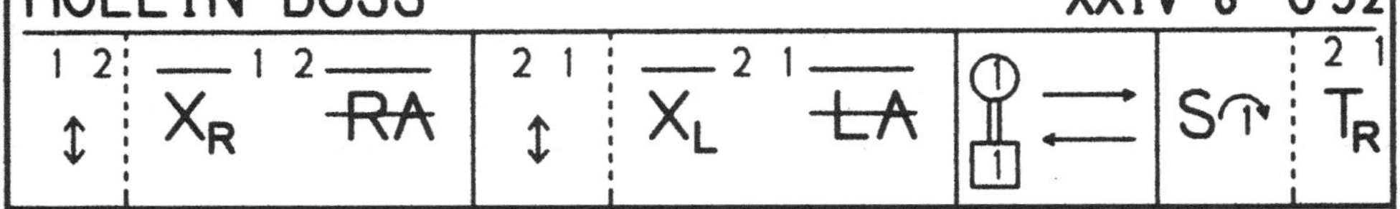

1 2 ⋮ ↕	1 2 X_R ~~RA~~	2 1 ⋮ ↕	2 1 X_L ~~LA~~	① / 1 ⇄	S↷ ⋮	2 1 T_R

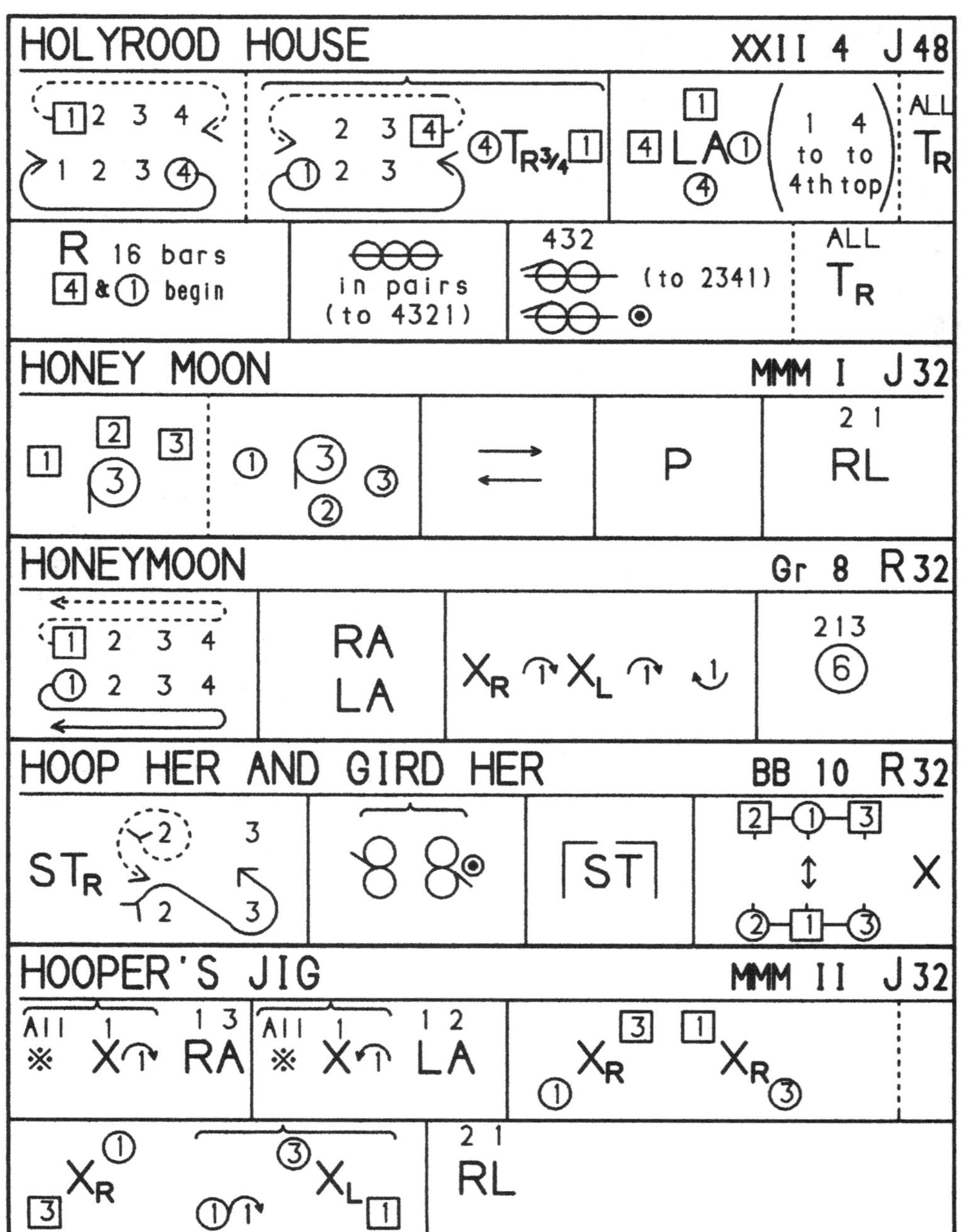
HOLYROOD HOUSE
XXII 4 J 48
ALL
16 bars
begin
in pairs
(to 4321)
432
(to 2341)
ALL
HONEY MOON
MMM I J 32
HONEYMOON
Gr 8 R 32
RA
LA
213
HOOP HER AND GIRD HER
BB 10 R 32
ST
HOOPER'S JIG
MMM II J 32
All
RA
All
LA
RL

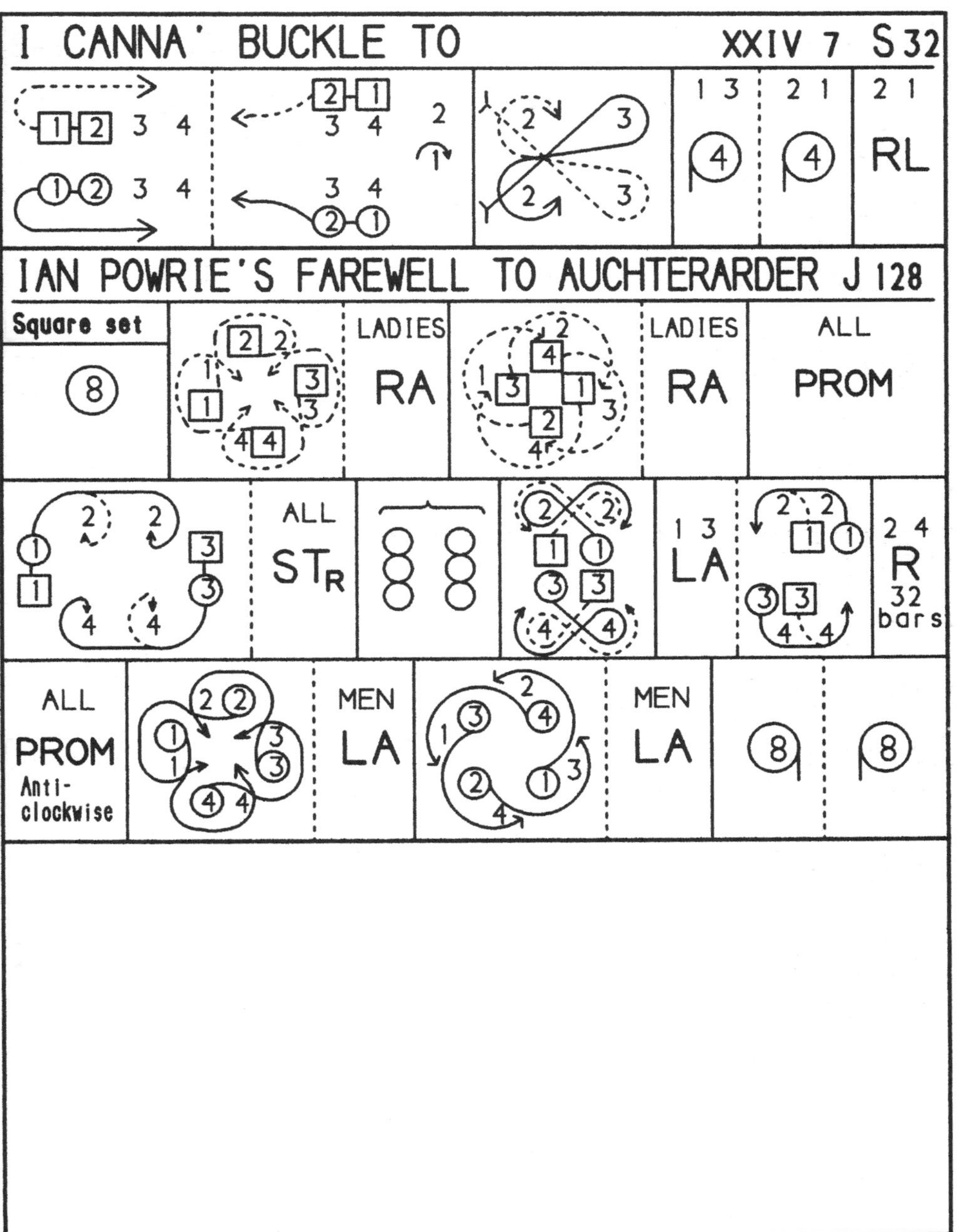
I CANNA' BUCKLE TO
XXIV 7 S 32
1 2 3 4
2 1
3 4
2
1
2 3
2 3
1 3
4
2 1
4
2 1
RL
IAN POWRIE'S FAREWELL TO AUCHTERARDER J 128
Square set
8
LADIES
RA
LADIES
RA
ALL
PROM
ALL
ST R
1 3
LA
2 4
R
32
bars
ALL
PROM
Anti-
clockwise
MEN
LA
MEN
LA
8
8

ICE CAP (Square Set) Scotia 3 S96

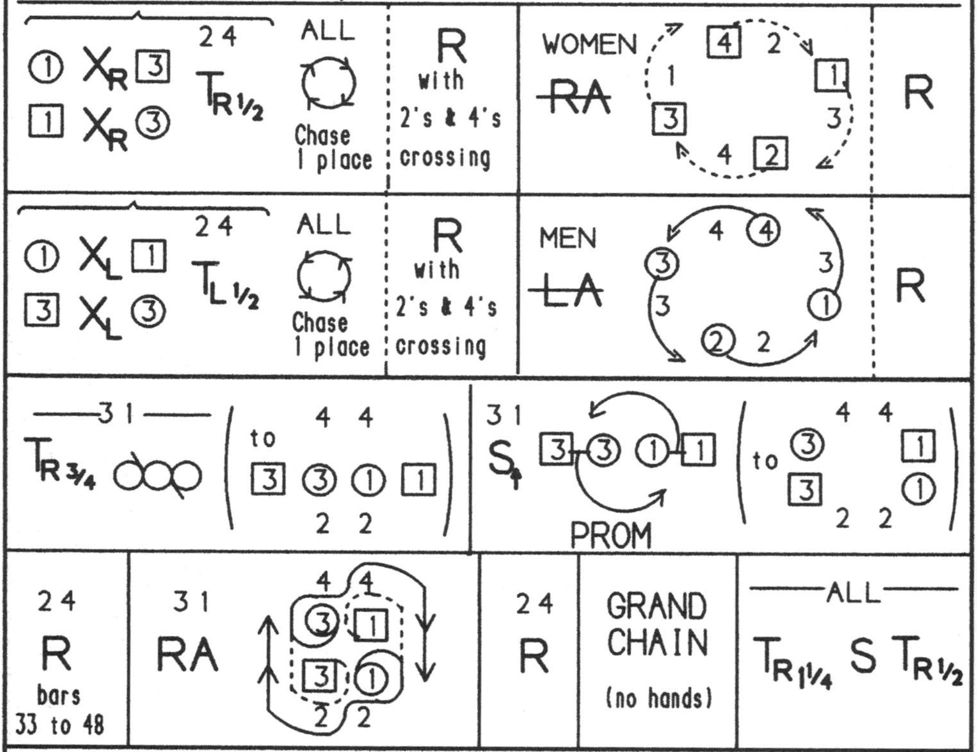

① X_R [3] / [1] X_R ③ — 2 4 $T_{R\,1/2}$	ALL — Chase 1 place	R with 2's & 4's crossing	WOMEN RA (struck) — 1, [4], 2, [1], 3, [2], 4, [3]	R
① X_L [1] / [3] X_L ③ — 2 4 $T_{L\,1/2}$	ALL — Chase 1 place	R with 2's & 4's crossing	MEN LA (struck) — ④ 4, 3, ①, ② 2, 3, ③	R

3 1 $T_{R\,3/4}$ (to 4 4 / [3] ③ ① [1] / 2 2)	3 1 S [3]③ ①[1] PROM (to 4 4 / ③ [1] / [3] ① / 2 2)

2 4 R bars 33 to 48	3 1 RA — 4 4 / ③ [1] / [3] ① / 2 2	2 4 R	GRAND CHAIN (no hands)	ALL $T_{R\,1\frac{1}{4}}$ S $T_{R\,1/2}$

I'LL GANG NAE MAIR TAE YON TOON XV 2 S40

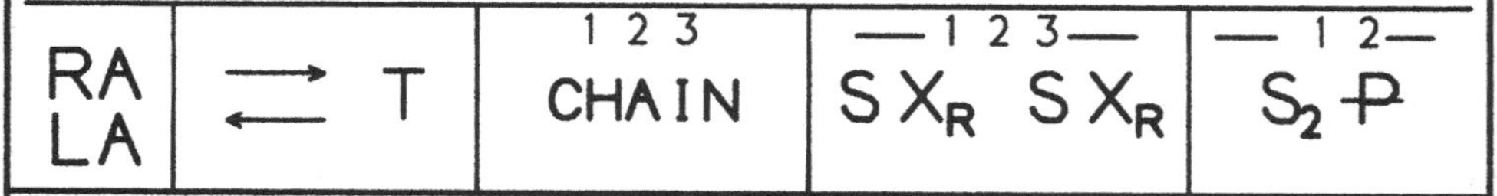

RA LA	⇄ T	1 2 3 CHAIN	1 2 3 S X_R S X_R	1 2 S_2 P

I'LL MAK' YE FAIN TO FOLLOW ME VI 10 J32

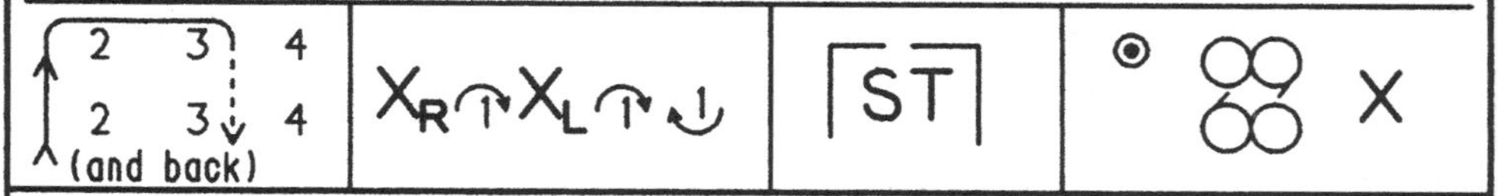

2 3 4 / 2 3 4 (and back)	X_R X_L	ST	X

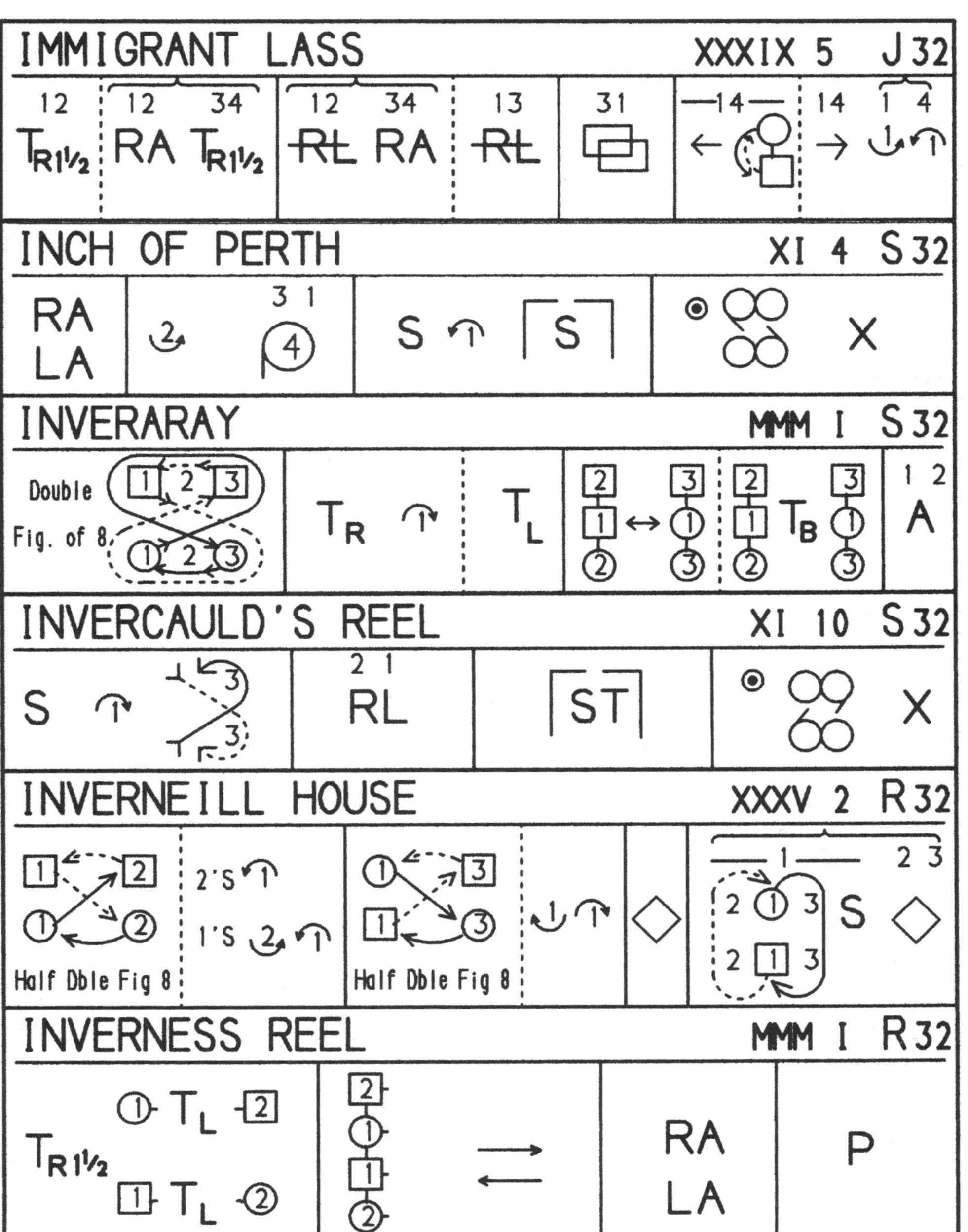

IMMIGRANT LASS
XXXIX 5 J32
INCH OF PERTH
XI 4 S32
INVERARAY
MMM I S32
Double Fig. of 8
INVERCAULD'S REEL
XI 10 S32
INVERNEILL HOUSE
XXXV 2 R32
Half Dble Fig 8
INVERNESS REEL
MMM I R32

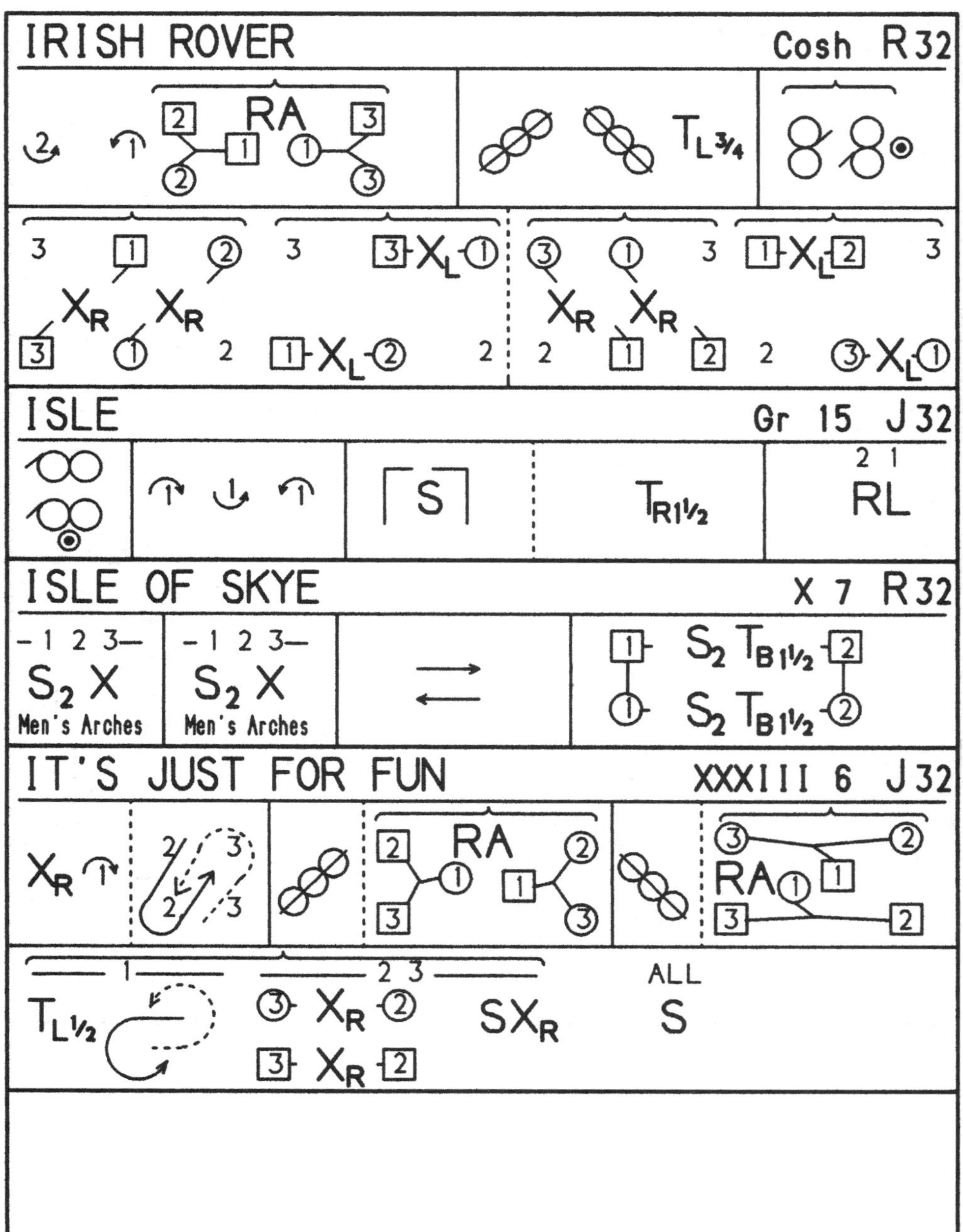
IRISH ROVER
Cosh R32
RA
T L 3/4
X R
X L
ISLE
Gr 15 J32
S
T R 1½
2 1
RL
ISLE OF SKYE
X 7 R32
-1 2 3-
S 2 X
Men's Arches
-1 2 3-
S 2 X
Men's Arches
S 2 T B 1½
S 2 T B 1½
IT'S JUST FOR FUN
XXXIII 6 J32
X R
RA
RA
1
T L ½
2 3
X R
X R
SX R
ALL
S

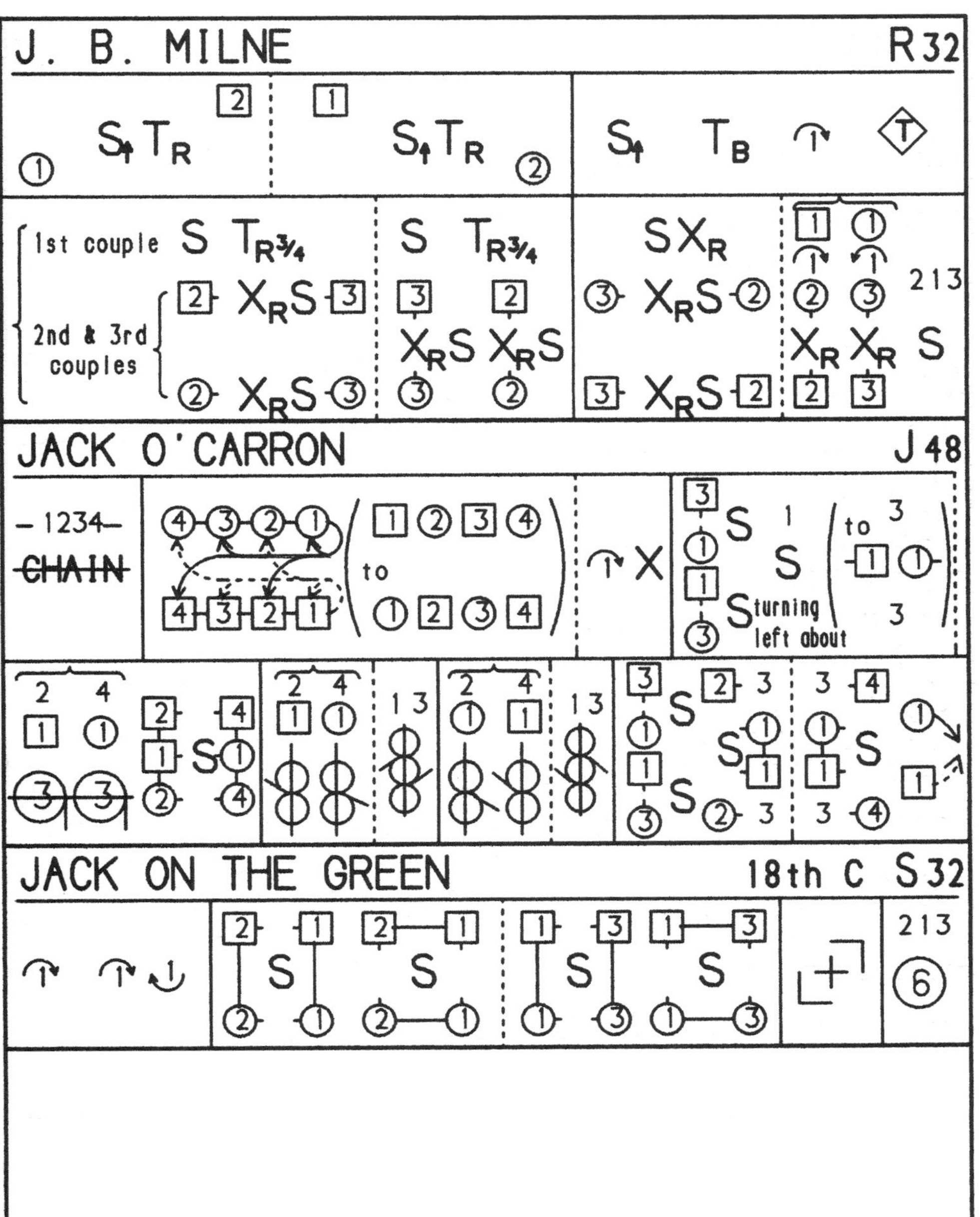
J. B. MILNE
R32
1st couple
2nd & 3rd couples
213
JACK O'CARRON
J48
1234
CHAIN
to
turning left about
JACK ON THE GREEN
18th C
S32
213

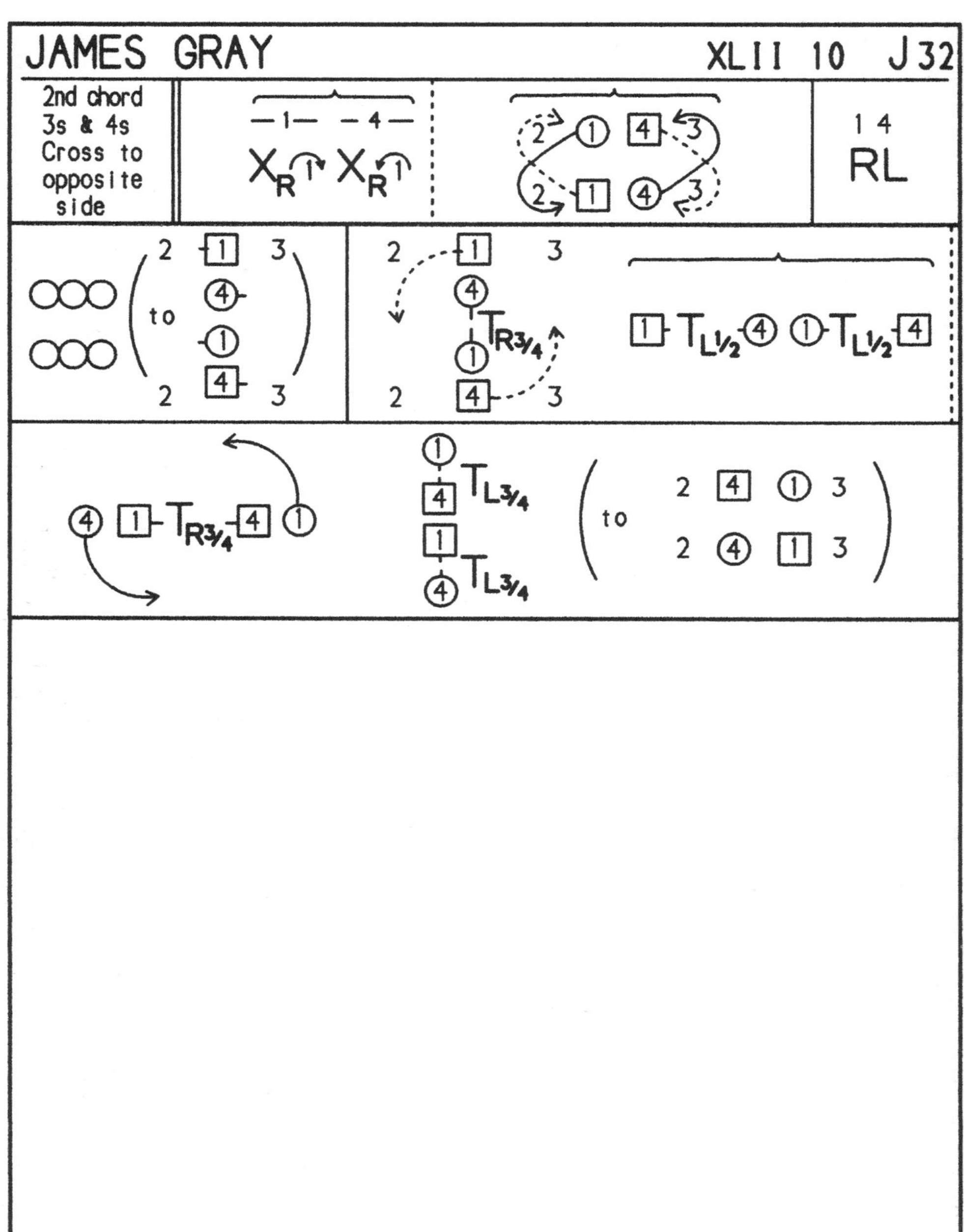
JAMES GRAY
XLII 10 J32
2nd chord
3s & 4s
Cross to
opposite
side
RL
to
to

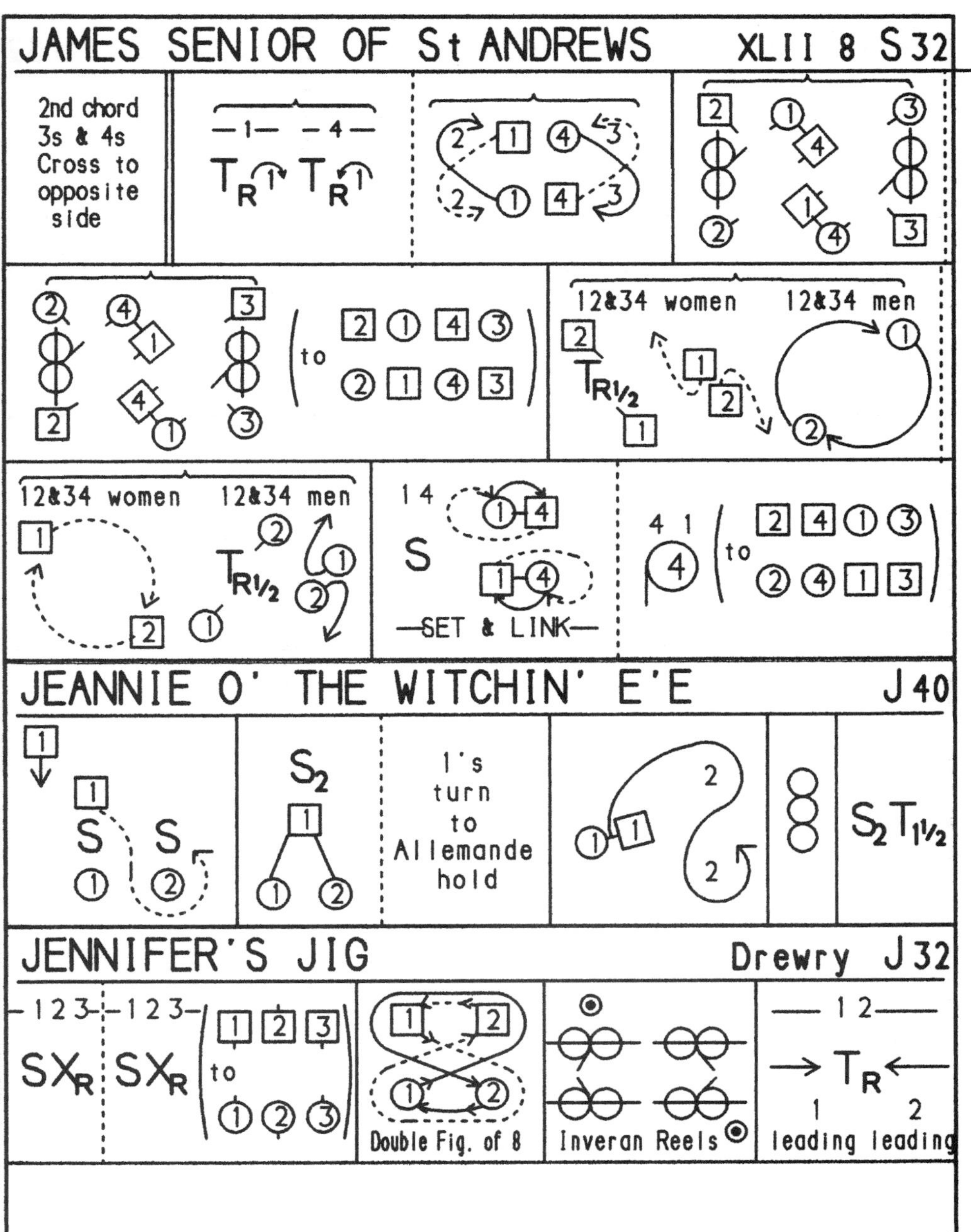

JAMES SENIOR OF St ANDREWS
XLII 8 S32
2nd chord
3s & 4s
Cross to
opposite
side
to
12&34 women
12&34 men
S
SET & LINK
JEANNIE O' THE WITCHIN' E'E
J40
1's
turn
to
Allemande
hold
JENNIFER'S JIG
Drewry J32
to
Double Fig. of 8
Inveran Reels
leading leading

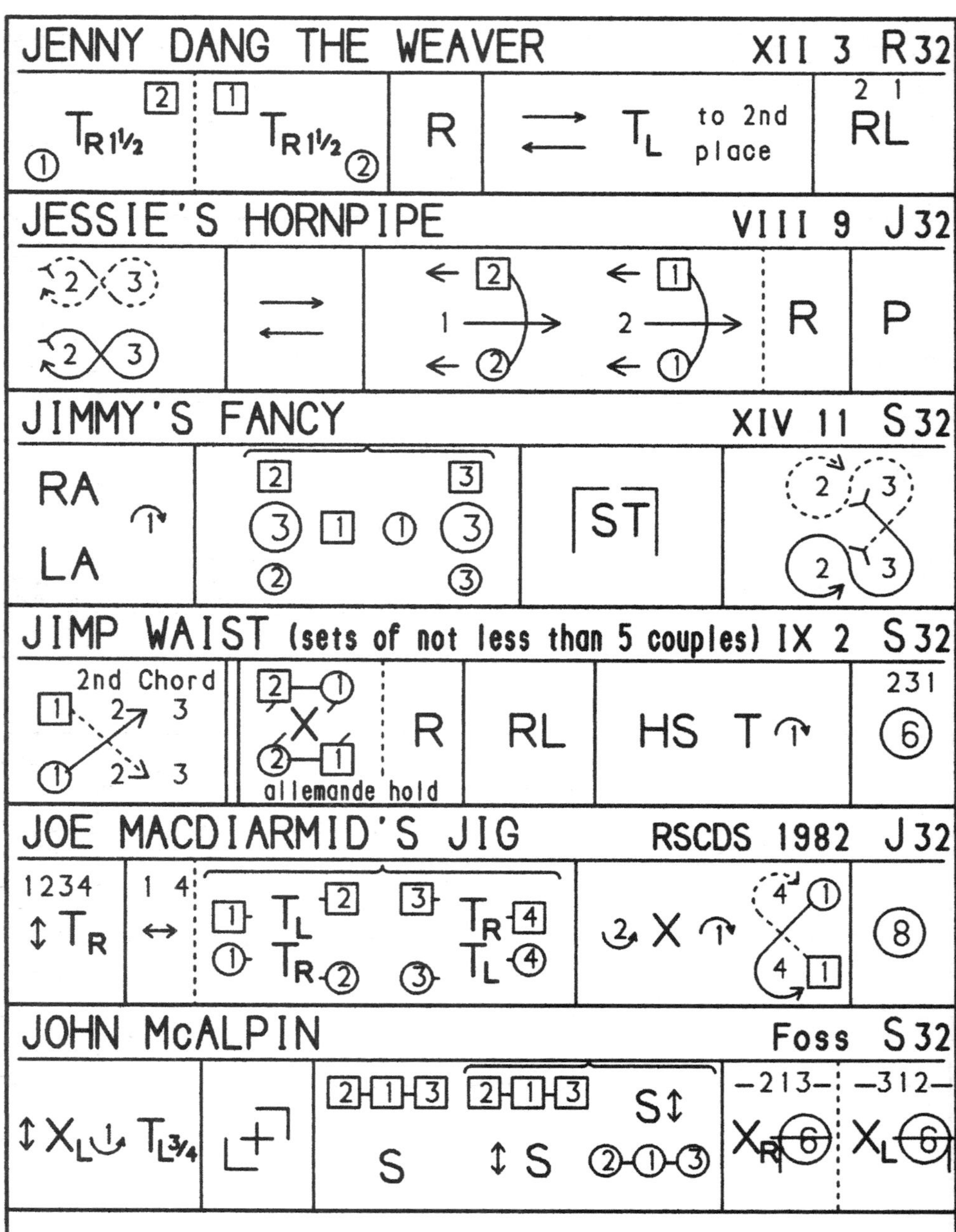
JENNY DANG THE WEAVER
XII 3 R32
2
1
TR1½
TR1½
1
2
R
TL
to 2nd place
2 1
RL
JESSIE'S HORNPIPE
VIII 9 J32
2 3
2 3
2
1
1
2
2
1
R
P
JIMMY'S FANCY
XIV 11 S32
RA
LA
2
3
3
1
1
3
2
3
ST
2 3
2 3
JIMP WAIST (sets of not less than 5 couples) IX 2 S32
2nd Chord
1
2 3
1
2 3
2
1
X
2
1
allemande hold
R
RL
HS T
231
6
JOE MACDIARMID'S JIG
RSCDS 1982 J32
1234
TR
1 4
1 TL 2
3 TR 4
1 TR 2
3 TL 4
2 X
4 1
4 1
8
JOHN McALPIN
Foss S32
XL TL¾
2 1 3
2 1 3
S
S
S
2 1 3
–213–
XR 6
–312–
XL 6

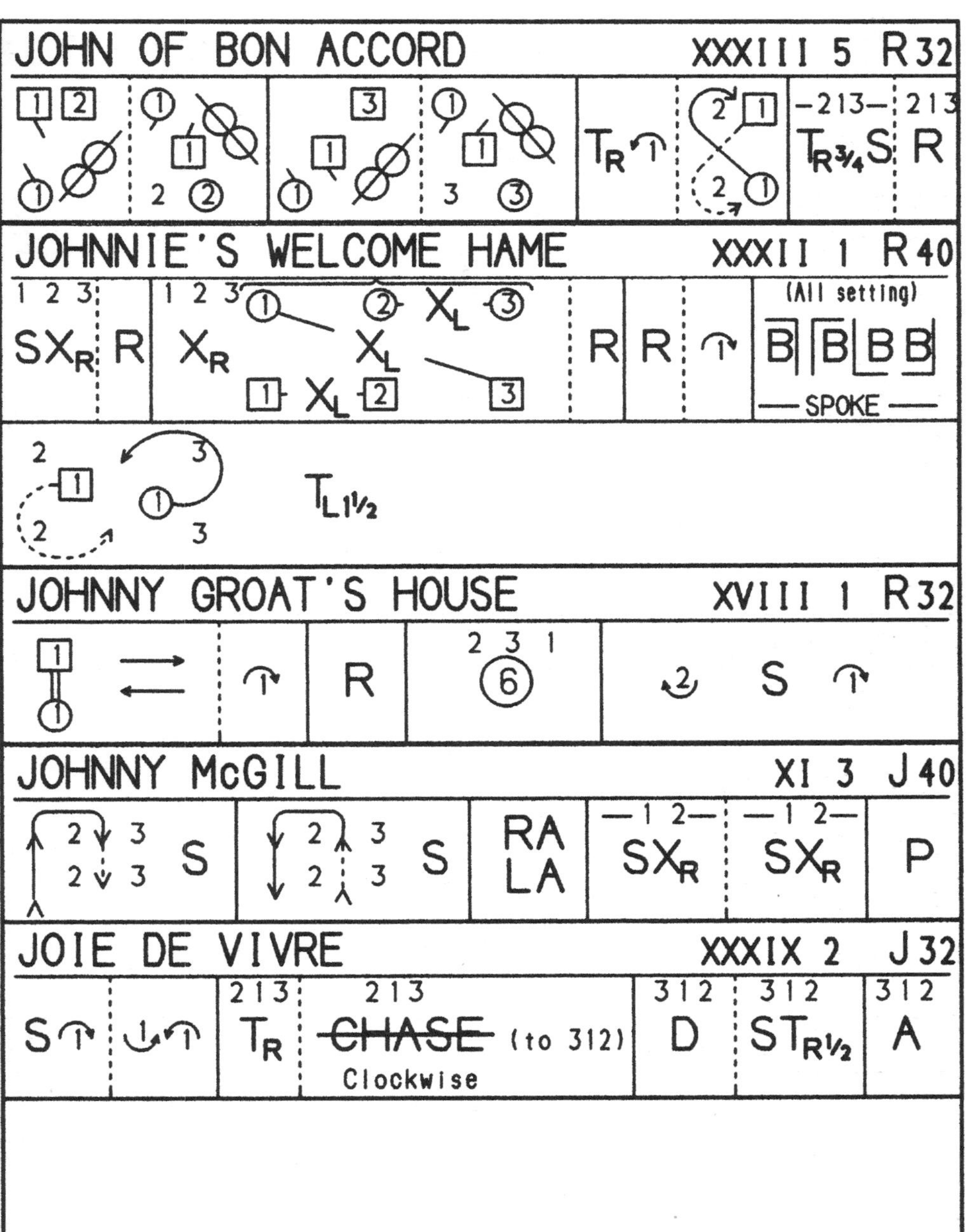
JOHN OF BON ACCORD XXXIII 5 R32
1 2 1 1 2 2 3 1 1 1 3 3
TR 1
2 1 2 1
—213— 213
TR¾ S R
JOHNNIE'S WELCOME HAME XXXII 1 R40
1 2 3
SXR R
1 2 3
1 2 XL 3
XR XL
1 XL 2 3
R R
(All setting)
B B B B
SPOKE
2 1 3 1 2 3
TL1½
JOHNNY GROAT'S HOUSE XVIII 1 R32
1 1
R
2 3 1
6
2 S
JOHNNY McGILL XI 3 J40
2 3 2 3 S
2 3 2 3 S
RA LA
—1 2— SXR
—1 2— SXR
P
JOIE DE VIVRE XXXIX 2 J32
S
213 TR
213 CHASE (to 312)
Clockwise
312 D
312 STR½
312 A

JUBILEE JIG

RSCDS L J32

[3] ↻ ST_R (1) (1)	[1] [1] ↻ ST_L (3)	[2] [1] [3] RA RA SX_L (2) (1) (3)	[2] (1) [3] RA RA SX_L (2) [1] (3)

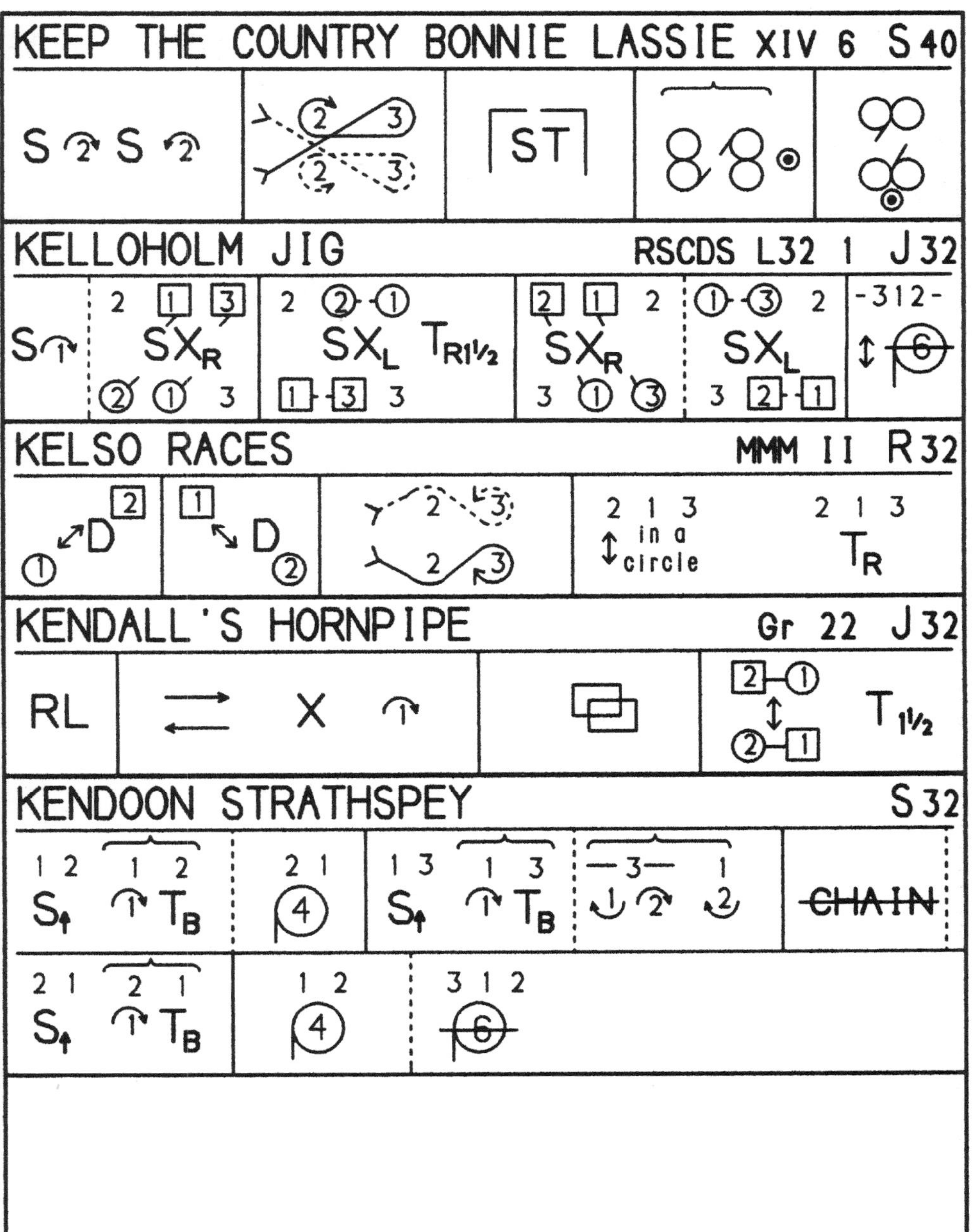
KEEP THE COUNTRY BONNIE LASSIE XIV 6 S 40
S 2 S 2
2 3
2 3
ST
KELLOHOLM JIG RSCDS L32 1 J 32
S 1
2 1 3
SX R
2 1 3
2 2 1
SX L T R1½
1 3 3
2 1 2
SX R
3 1 3
1 3 2
SX L
3 2 1
-312-
6
KELSO RACES MMM II R 32
2
1 D
1
D 2
2 3
2 3
2 1 3
in a circle
2 1 3
T R
KENDALL'S HORNPIPE Gr 22 J 32
RL
X 1
2 1
2 1
T 1½
KENDOON STRATHSPEY S 32
1 2 1 2
S 1 T B
2 1
4
1 3 1 3
S 1 T B
—3— 1
1 2 2
CHAIN
2 1 2 1
S 1 T B
1 2
4
3 1 2
6

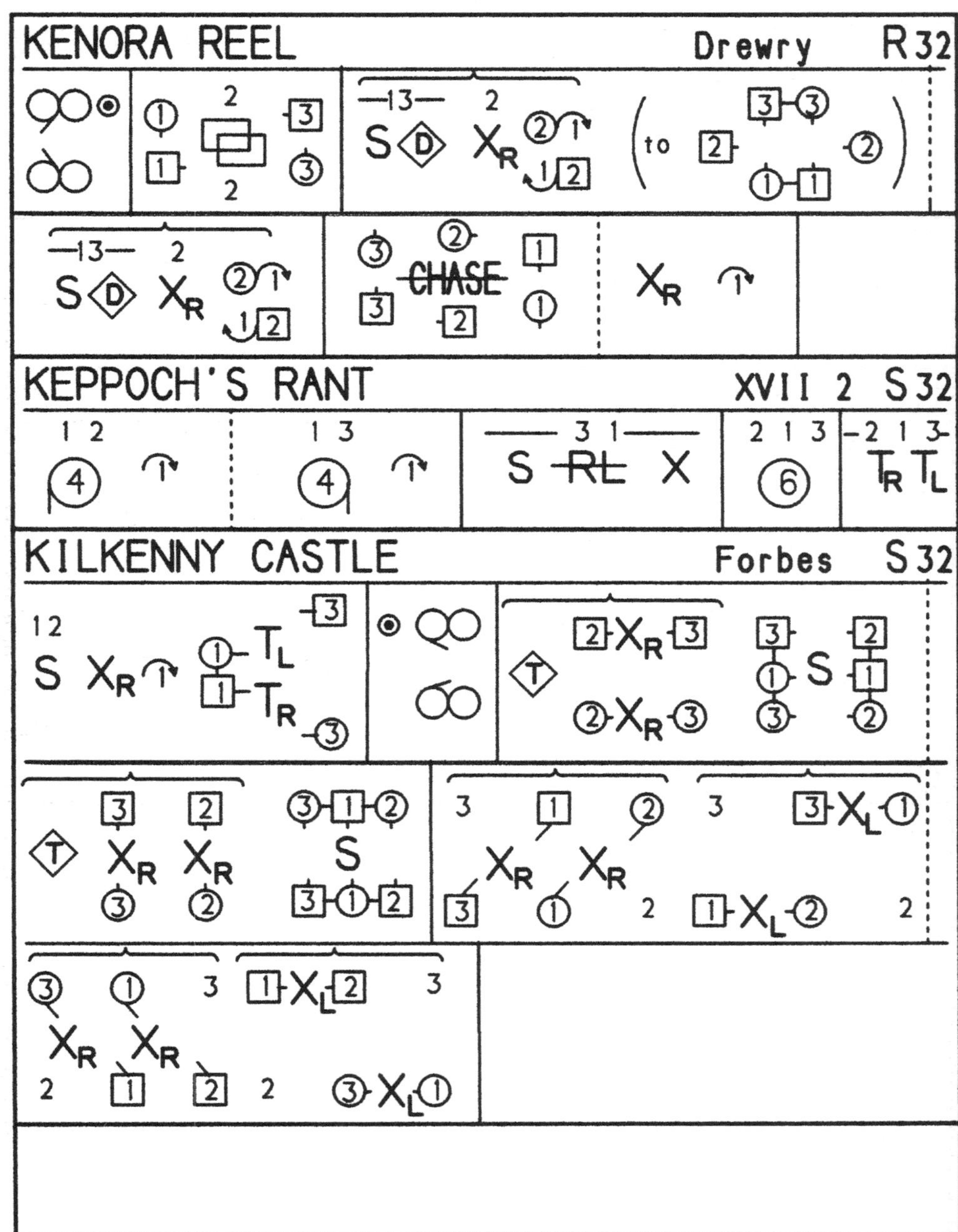
KENORA REEL
Drewry
R32
to
CHASE
KEPPOCH'S RANT
XVII 2
S32
KILKENNY CASTLE
Forbes
S32

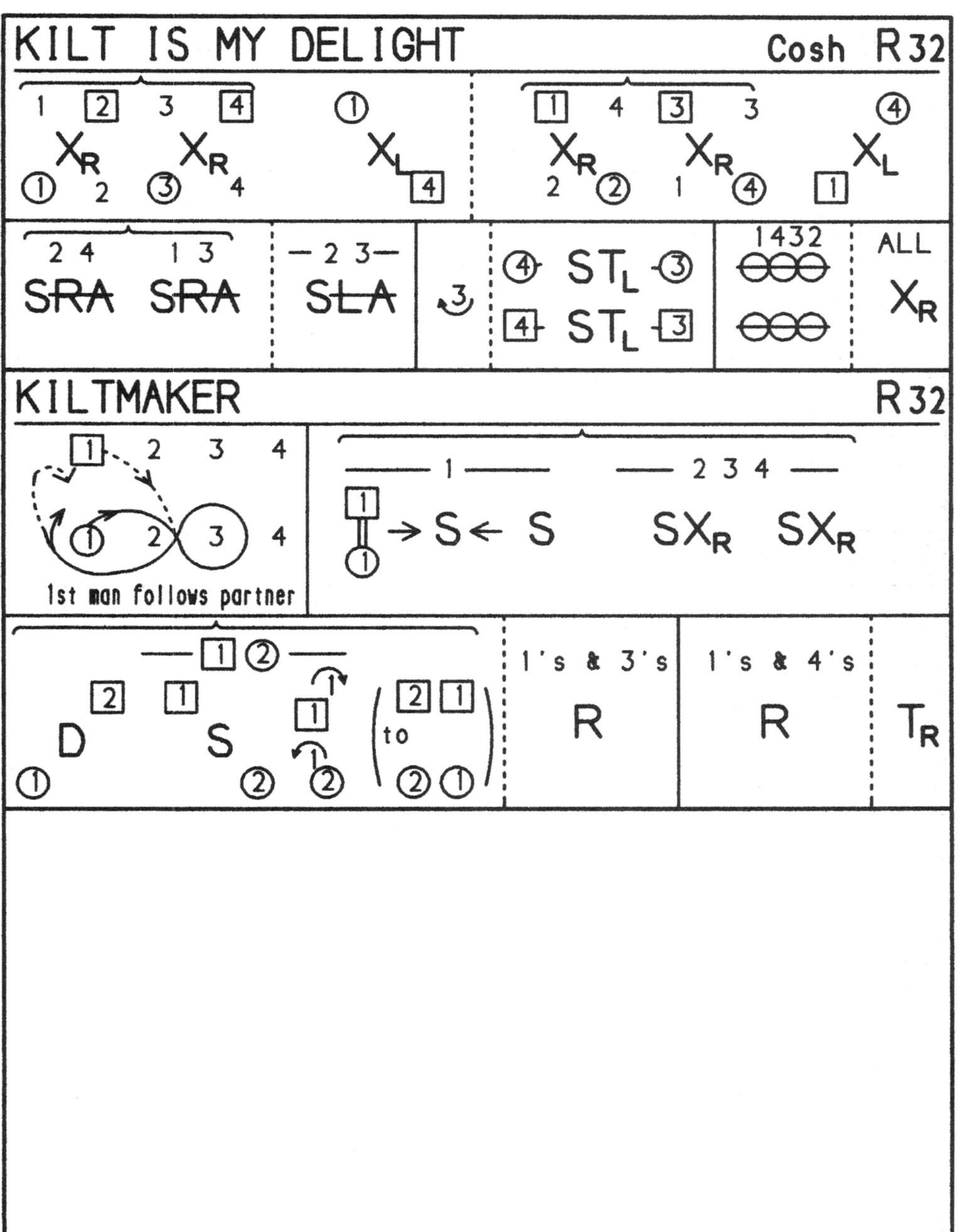
KILT IS MY DELIGHT
Cosh R32
1 2 3 4
1 2 3 4
XR XR XL
1 4 3 3 4
2 2 1 4 1
XR XR XL
2 4 1 3
SRA SRA
2 3
SLA
3
4 STL 3
4 STL 3
1432
ALL
XR
KILTMAKER
R32
1 2 3 4
1 2 3 4
1st man follows partner
1
2 3 4
1
→S← S
1
SXR SXR
1 2
2 1
D
1
S
2
1
1
2
2 1
to
2 1
1's & 3's
R
1's & 4's
R
TR

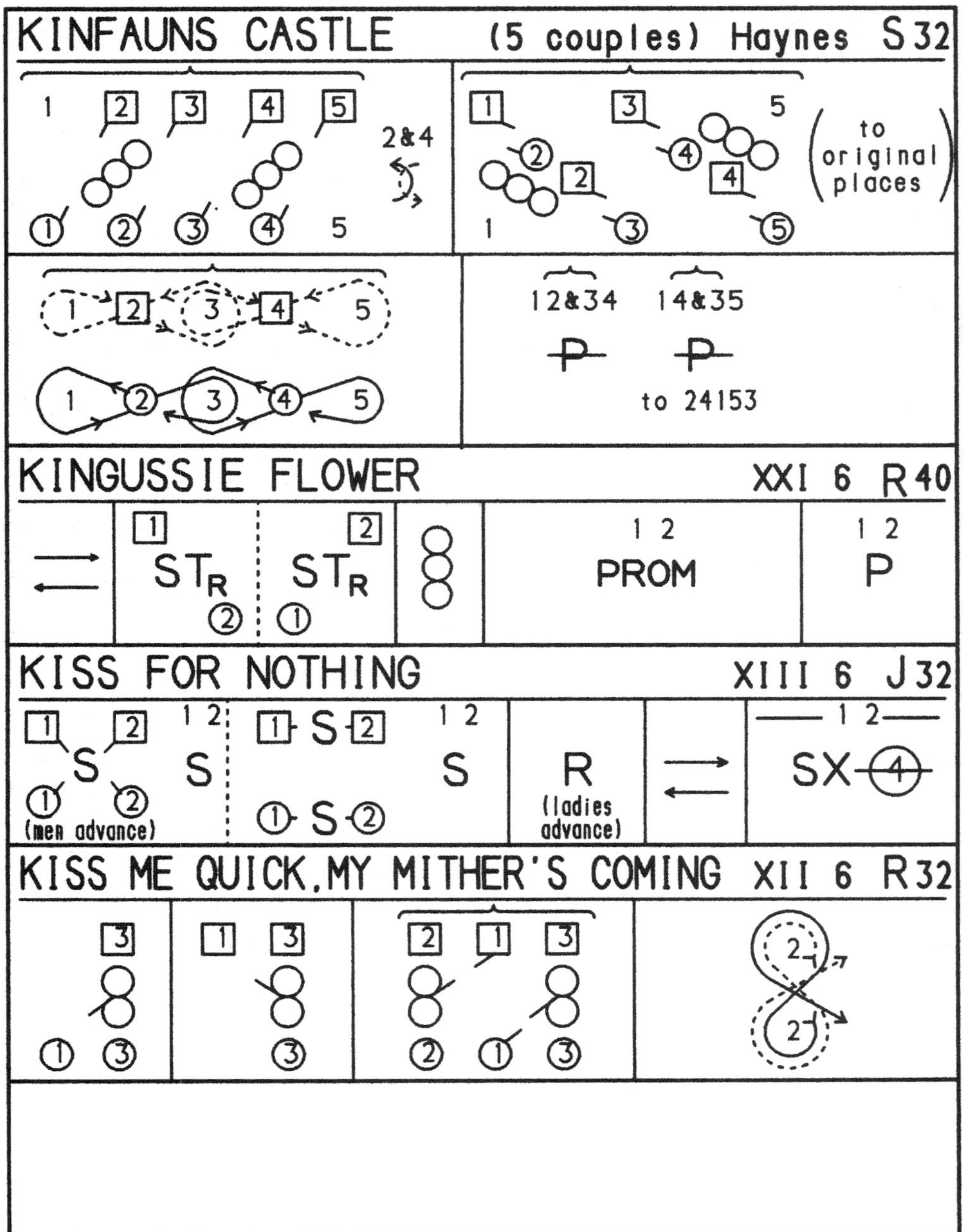
KINFAUNS CASTLE (5 couples) Haynes S32
2&4
to original places
12&34 14&35
P P
to 24153
KINGUSSIE FLOWER XXI 6 R40
ST R
ST R
1 2
PROM
1 2
P
KISS FOR NOTHING XIII 6 J32
S
(men advance)
1 2
S
S
1 2
S
S
R
(ladies advance)
1 2
SX
KISS ME QUICK, MY MITHER'S COMING XII 6 R32

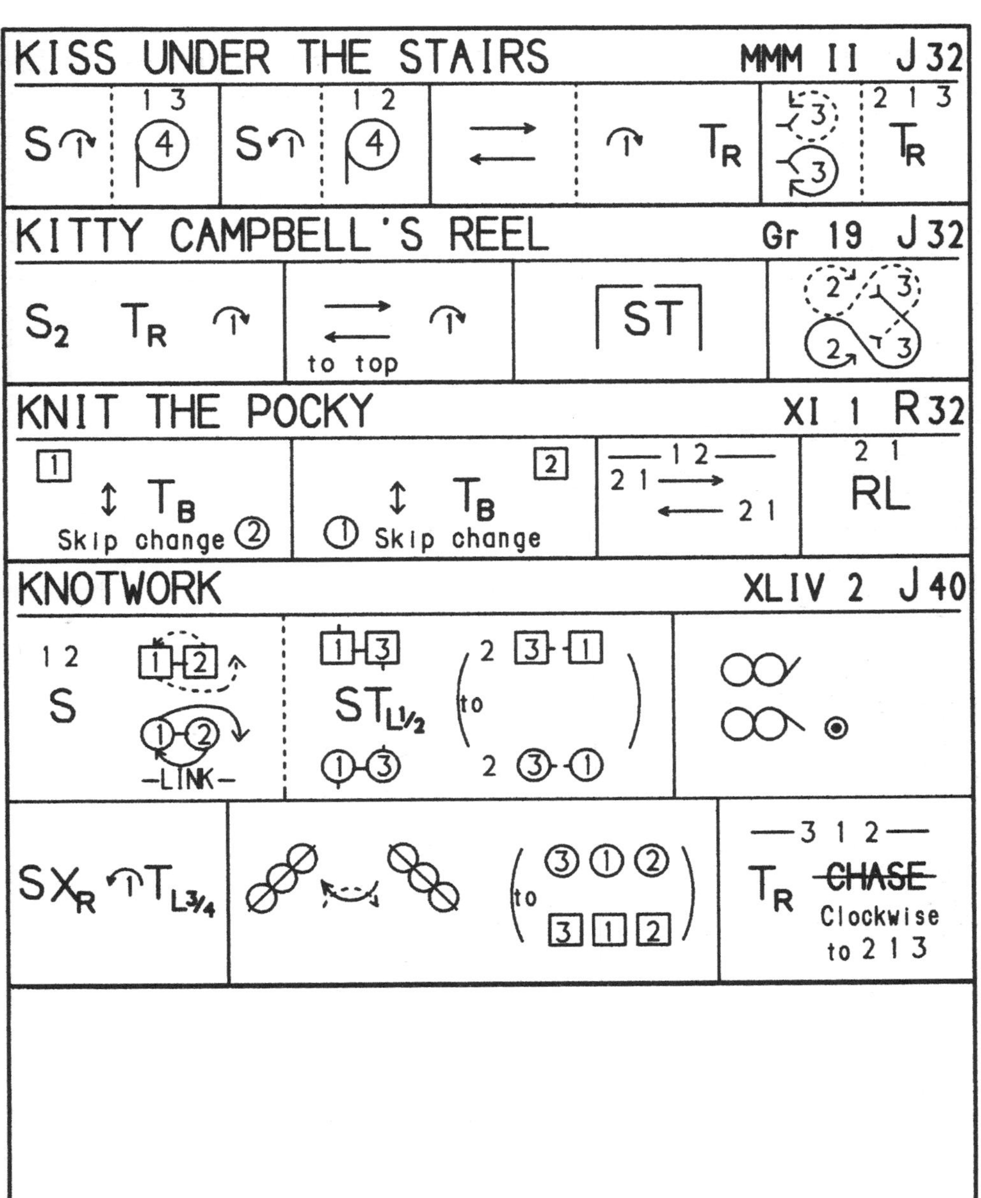
KISS UNDER THE STAIRS
MMM II J32
KITTY CAMPBELL'S REEL
Gr 19 J32
to top
ST
KNIT THE POCKY
XI 1 R32
Skip change
Skip change
RL
KNOTWORK
XLIV 2 J40
-LINK-
to
to
CHASE
Clockwise
to 2 1 3

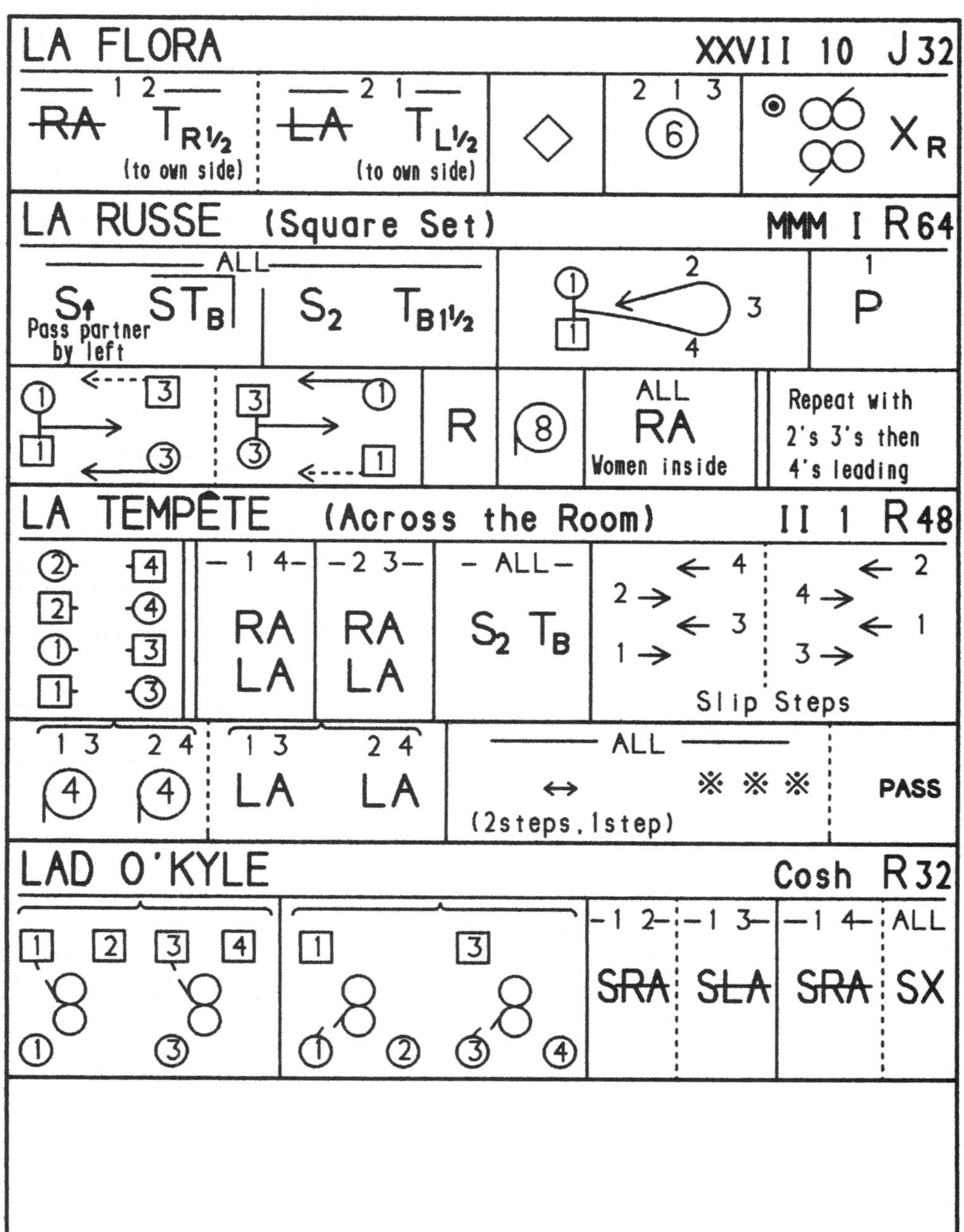
LA FLORA
XXVII 10 J32
1 2
RA
T R1½
(to own side)
2 1
LA
T L1½
(to own side)
2 1 3
6
X R
LA RUSSE (Square Set)
MMM I R64
ALL
S
ST B
Pass partner by left
S2
T B1½
1
2
3
4
1
P
3
1
3
3
1
R
8
ALL
RA
Women inside
Repeat with
2's 3's then
4's leading
LA TEMPÊTE (Across the Room)
II 1 R48
2
4
2
4
1
3
1
3
1 4
2 3
ALL
RA
LA
RA
LA
S2 T B
4
2
3
1
2
4
1
3
Slip Steps
1 3
2 4
4
4
1 3
2 4
LA
LA
ALL
(2steps, 1step)
PASS
LAD O'KYLE
Cosh R32
1
2
3
4
1
3
1
3
1
2
3
4
1 2
1 3
1 4
ALL
SRA
SLA
SRA
SX

LADDIES O'DUNSE — BB 11 J48

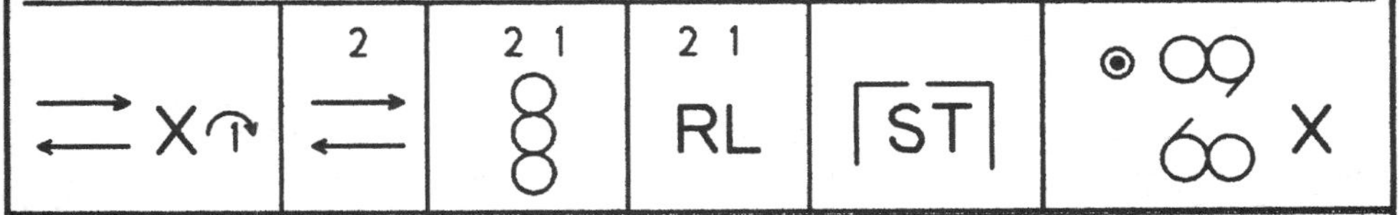

	2	2 1	2 1		
⇄ X ↻	⇄	8	RL	⌈ST⌉	⊙ X

LADIES' FANCY — XIII 12 J32

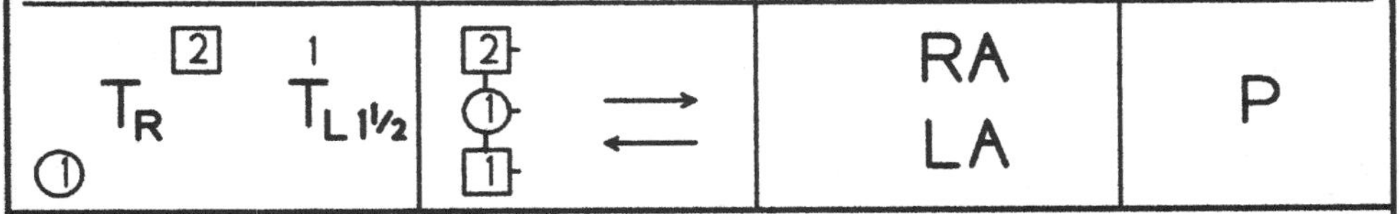

[2] 1 T_R $T_{L1½}$ (1)	[2] (1) [1] ⇄	RA LA	P

LADIES OF DINGWALL — MMM II R48

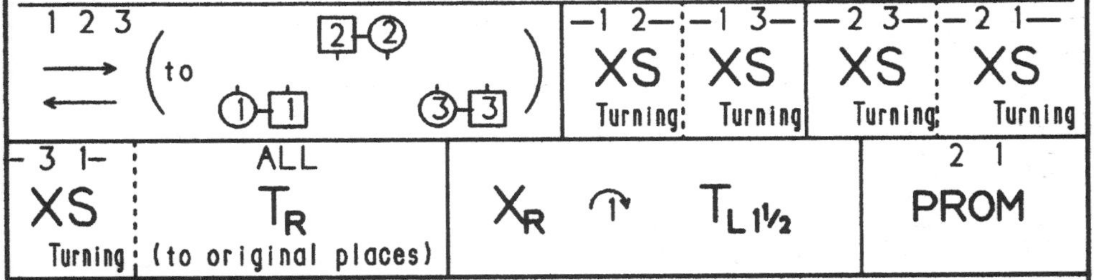

1 2 3 ⇄ (to [2]-(2) (1)-[1] (3)-[3])	–1 2– XS Turning	–1 3– XS Turning	–2 3– XS Turning	–2 1– XS Turning

– 3 1– XS Turning	ALL T_R (to original places)	X_R ↻ $T_{L1½}$	2 1 PROM

LADIES OF DUNSE — XXVI 11 R40

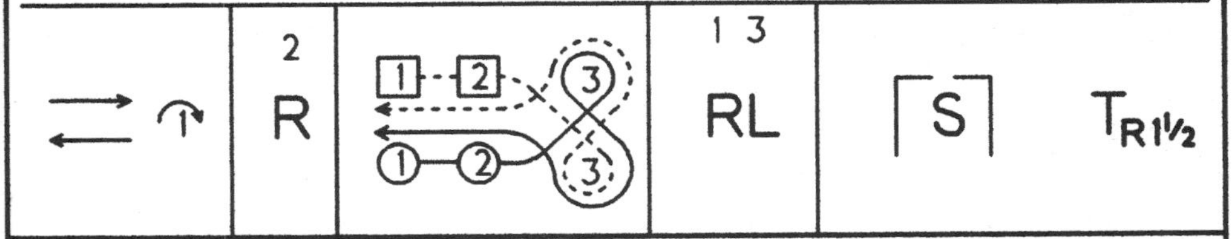

	2		1 3	
⇄ ↻	R	[1] [2] (1) (2) (3) (3)	RL	⌈S⌉ $T_{R1½}$

LADS OF SALTCOATS — MMM II R32

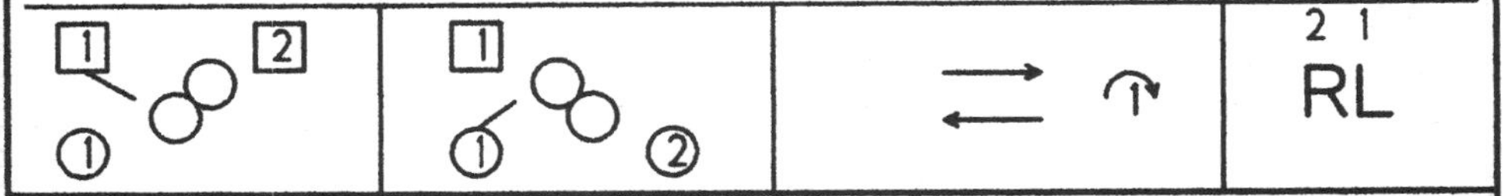

			2 1
[1] [2] (1)	[1] (1) (2)	⇄ ↻	RL

LADY AUCKLAND'S REEL — XVIII 2 S32

	1 T_B 2 · 1 2 T_B	MEN R	⇄	A

LADY BAIRD'S REEL — XVIII 3 R32

1 2 3 PROM	P	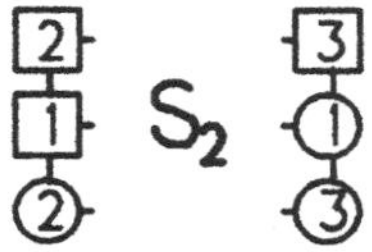	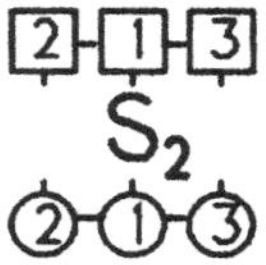	DT

LADY CATHERINE BRUCE'S REEL — Gr 7 J32

⇄	A		2 1 (4)

LADY CHARLOTTE BRUCE — MMM II S32

1 2 3 ↕ (twice)	1 2 3 ~~CHAIN~~	R	⇄ ↻	2 1 3 (6)

LADY DUMFRIES — MMM I R32

RL	1 2 → 1's leading ← 2's leading	2 1 3 SX_R	2 1 3 SX_R	DT

LADY GLASGOW — MMM I S32

1 2 3 SX_R $ST_{R\frac{1}{2}}$	1 2 3 PROM	S ↻ D	2 1 3 (6)

LADY HOME'S JIG — MMM I J32

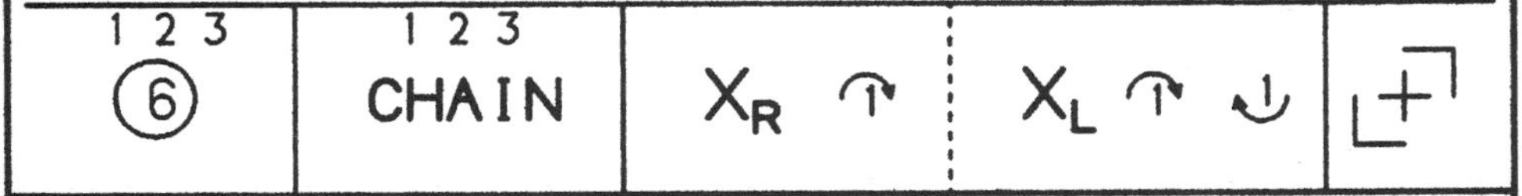

1 2 3 ⑥	1 2 3 CHAIN	X_R	X_L	

LADY JEAN MURRAY'S RANT — X 4 S32

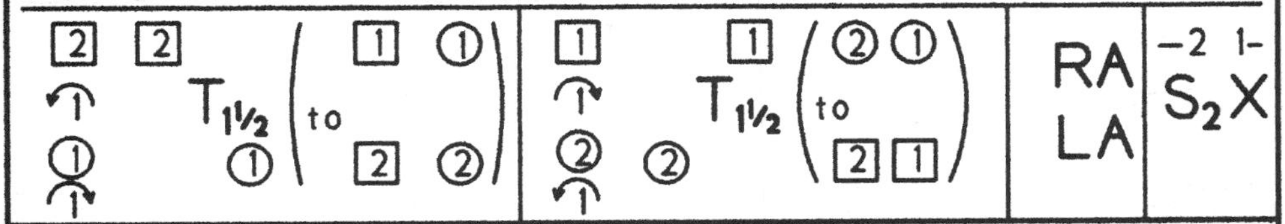

[2] [2] ① ① $T_{1½}$ ([1] ① to [2] ②)	[1] [1] ② ② $T_{1½}$ (② ① to [2] [1])	RA LA	−2 1− S_2X

LADY LOUISA MACDONALD'S STRATHSPEY — XVIII 4 S32

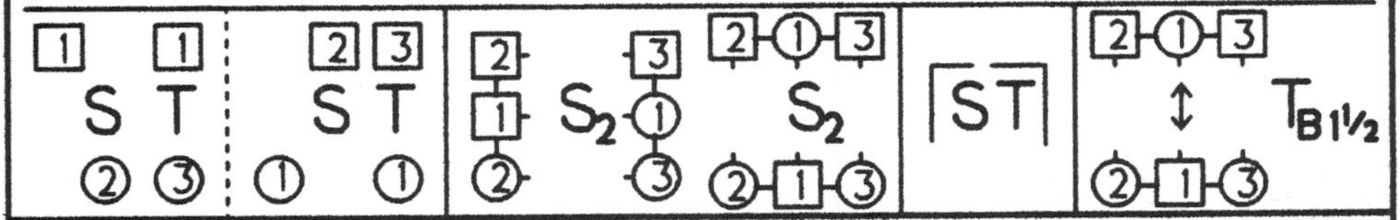

[1] [1] S T ② ③	[2] [3] S T ① ①	[2] [1] ② S_2 [3] ① ③ S_2 [2]①[3] ②[1]③	ST	[2]①[3] ↕ $T_{B1½}$ ②[1]③

LADY LUCY RAMSAY — MMM II S32

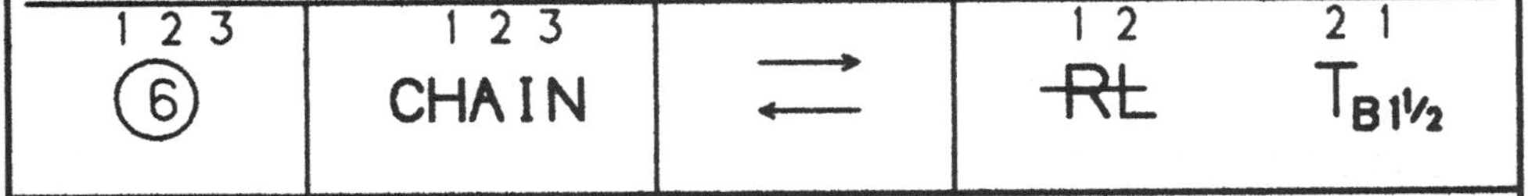

1 2 3 ⑥	1 2 3 CHAIN	⇄	1 2 RL 2 1 $T_{B1½}$

LADY MACINTOSH'S RANT — III 9 S32

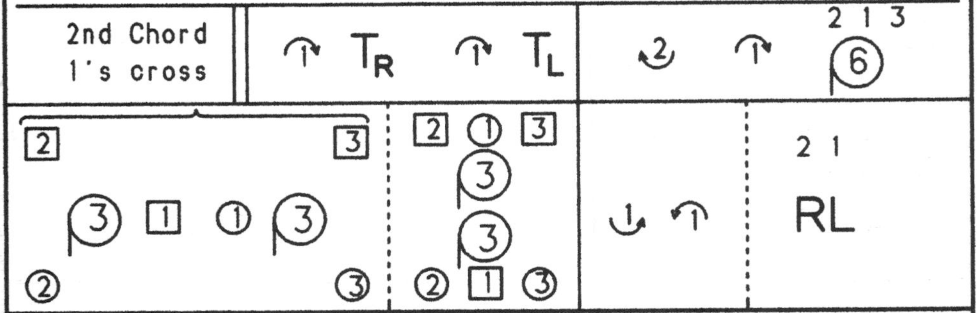

2nd Chord 1's cross	T_R T_L	2 1 3 ⑥
[2] [3] ③ [1] ① ③ ② ③	[2] ① [3] ③ ③ ② [1] ③	2 1 RL

LADY MARY COCHRANE'S REEL — XXVI 4 R32

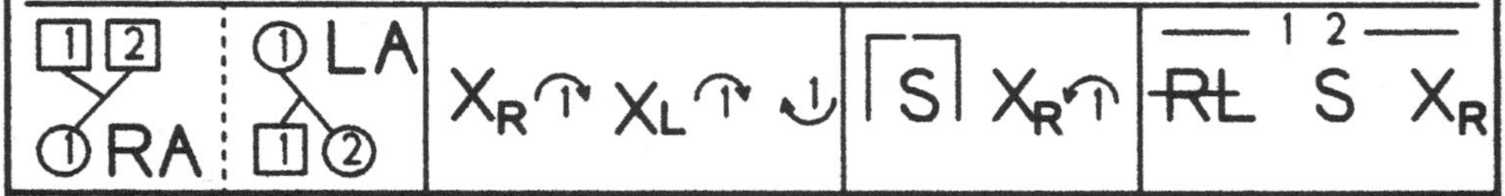

1 2 / 1 RA ⋮ 1 LA / 1 2	X_R 1 X_L 1 1	S X_R 1	1 2 RL S X_R

LADY MARY MENZIES' REEL — VII 5 R32

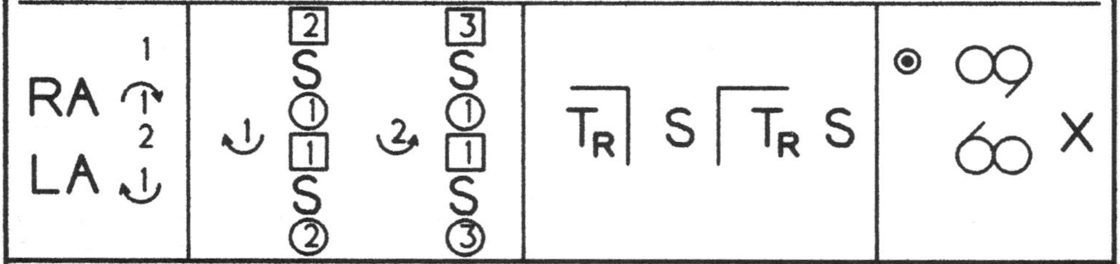

RA 1 2 LA 1	1 2 S 1 1 S 2 — 2 3 S 1 1 S 3	T_R S T_R S	X

LADY MAXWELL'S REEL — XXVI 8 S16 + R16

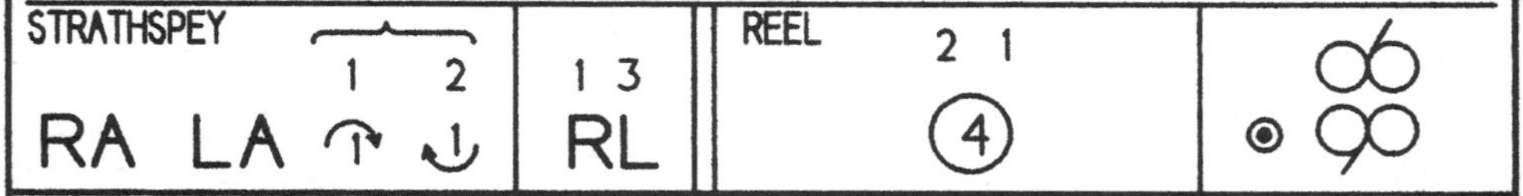

STRATHSPEY RA LA 1 2	1 3 RL	REEL 2 1 4	

LADY OF THE LAKE — XXV 8 H32

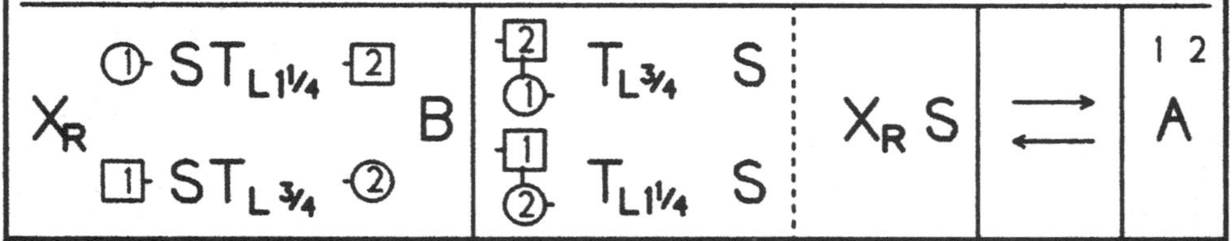

X_R 1 $ST_{L1\frac{1}{4}}$ 2 / 1 $ST_{L\frac{3}{4}}$ 2 B	2 1 $T_{L\frac{3}{4}}$ S / 1 2 $T_{L1\frac{1}{4}}$ S	X_R S	⇄	1 2 A

LADY SOPHIA ANNE OF BUTE — R48

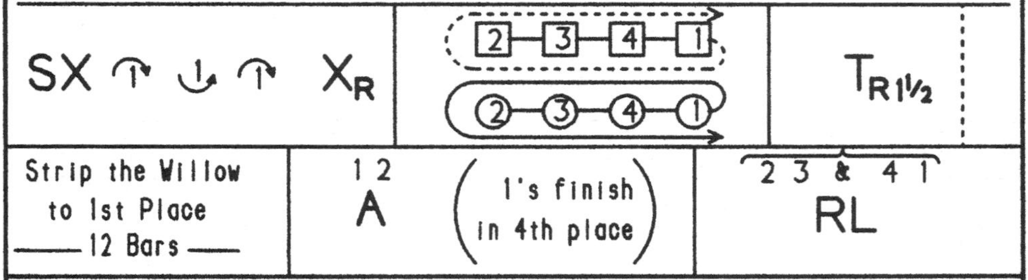

SX 1 1 1 X_R	2 3 4 1 / 2 3 4 1	$T_{R1\frac{1}{2}}$
Strip the Willow to 1st Place — 12 Bars	1 2 A (1's finish in 4th place)	2 3 & 4 1 RL

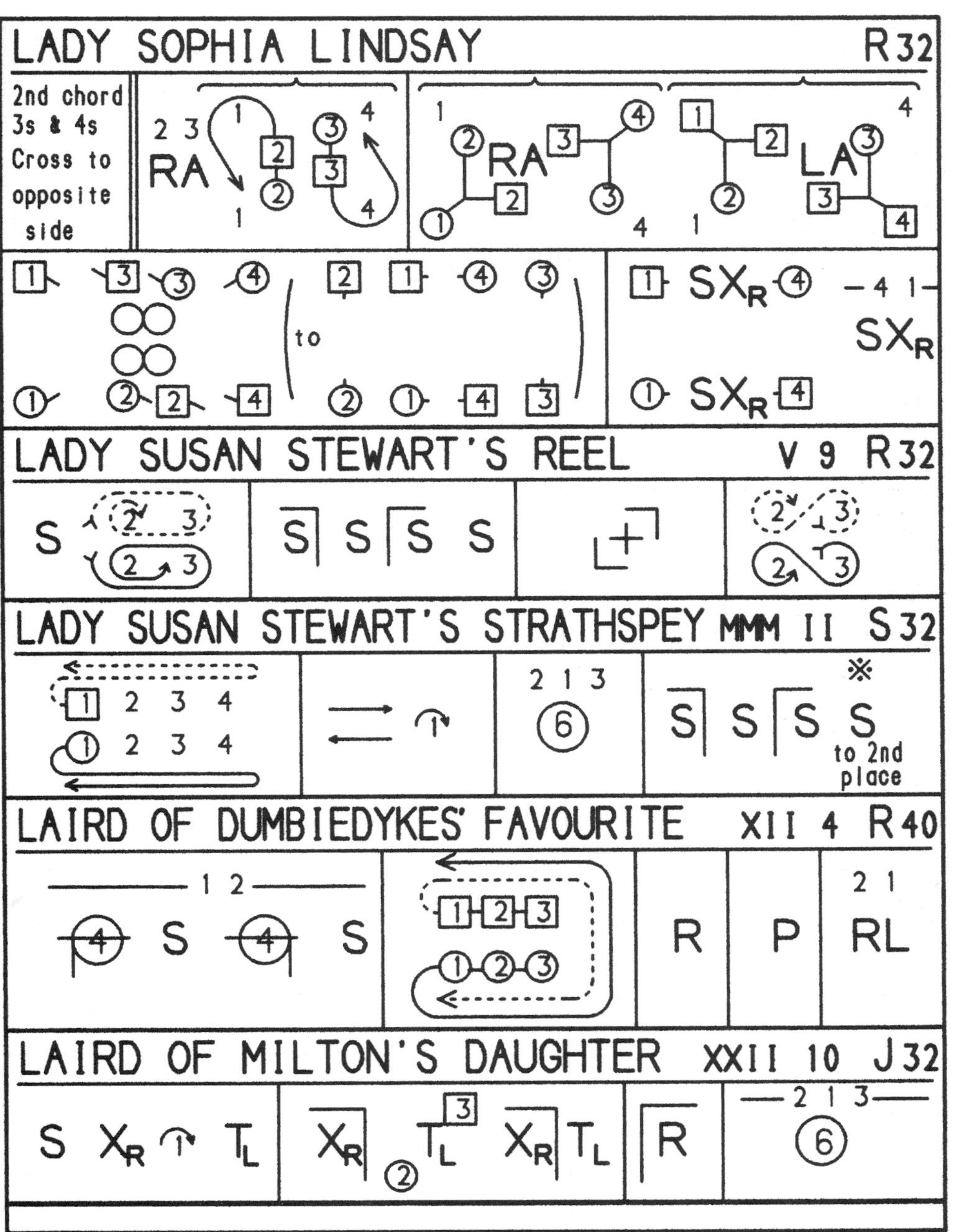
LADY SOPHIA LINDSAY R32
2nd chord 3s & 4s Cross to opposite side
RA
RA
LA
to
SXR
LADY SUSAN STEWART'S REEL V 9 R32
S
LADY SUSAN STEWART'S STRATHSPEY MMM II S32
to 2nd place
LAIRD OF DUMBIEDYKES' FAVOURITE XII 4 R40
S
R
P
RL
LAIRD OF MILTON'S DAUGHTER XXII 10 J32
S
R

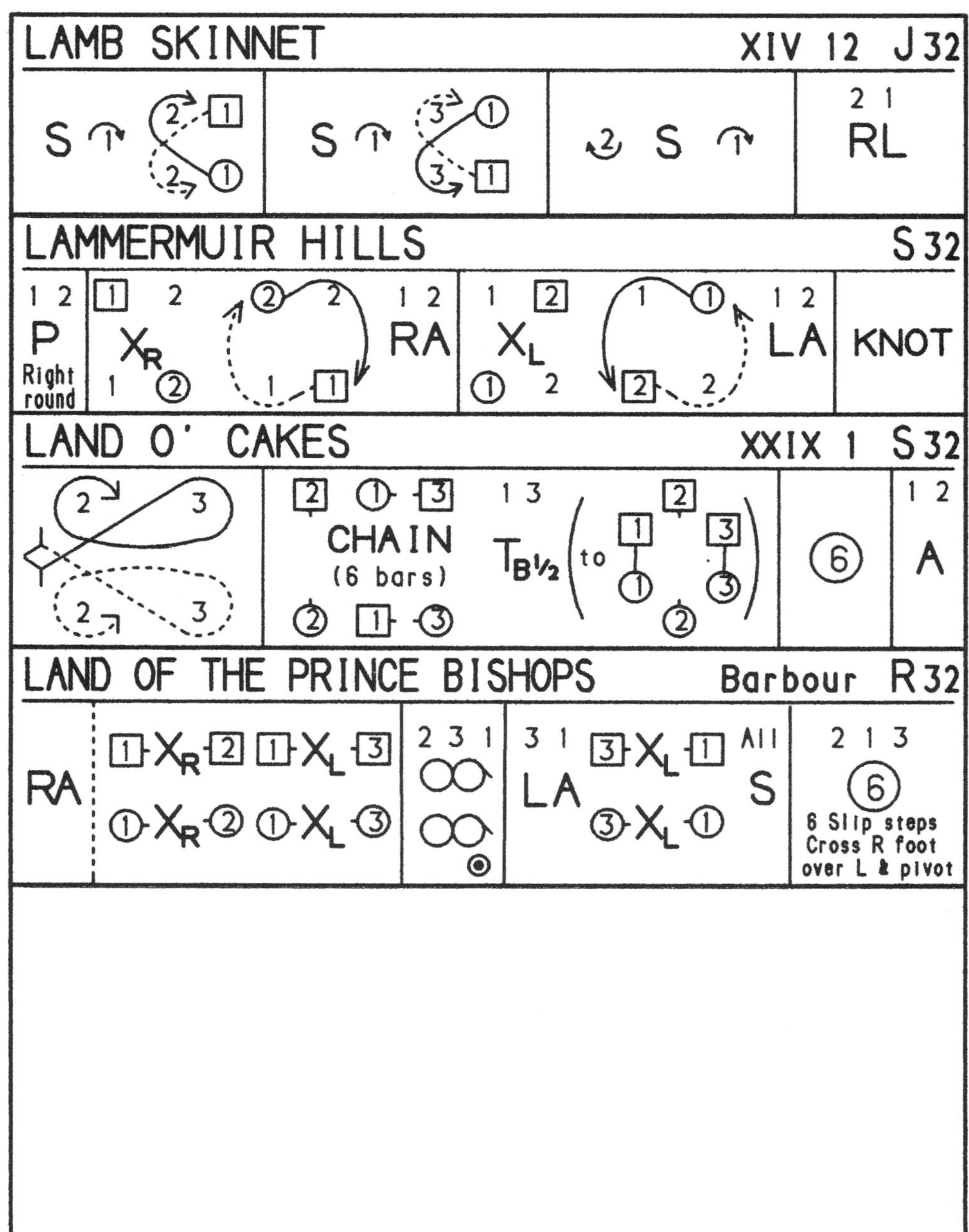
LAMB SKINNET
XIV 12 J32
S
S
S
2 1
RL
LAMMERMUIR HILLS
S32
1 2
P
Right round
RA
KNOT
LAND O' CAKES
XXIX 1 S32
CHAIN
(6 bars)
to
A
LAND OF THE PRINCE BISHOPS
Barbour R32
RA
2 3 1
3 1
LA
All
S
2 1 3
6 Slip steps
Cross R foot
over L & pivot

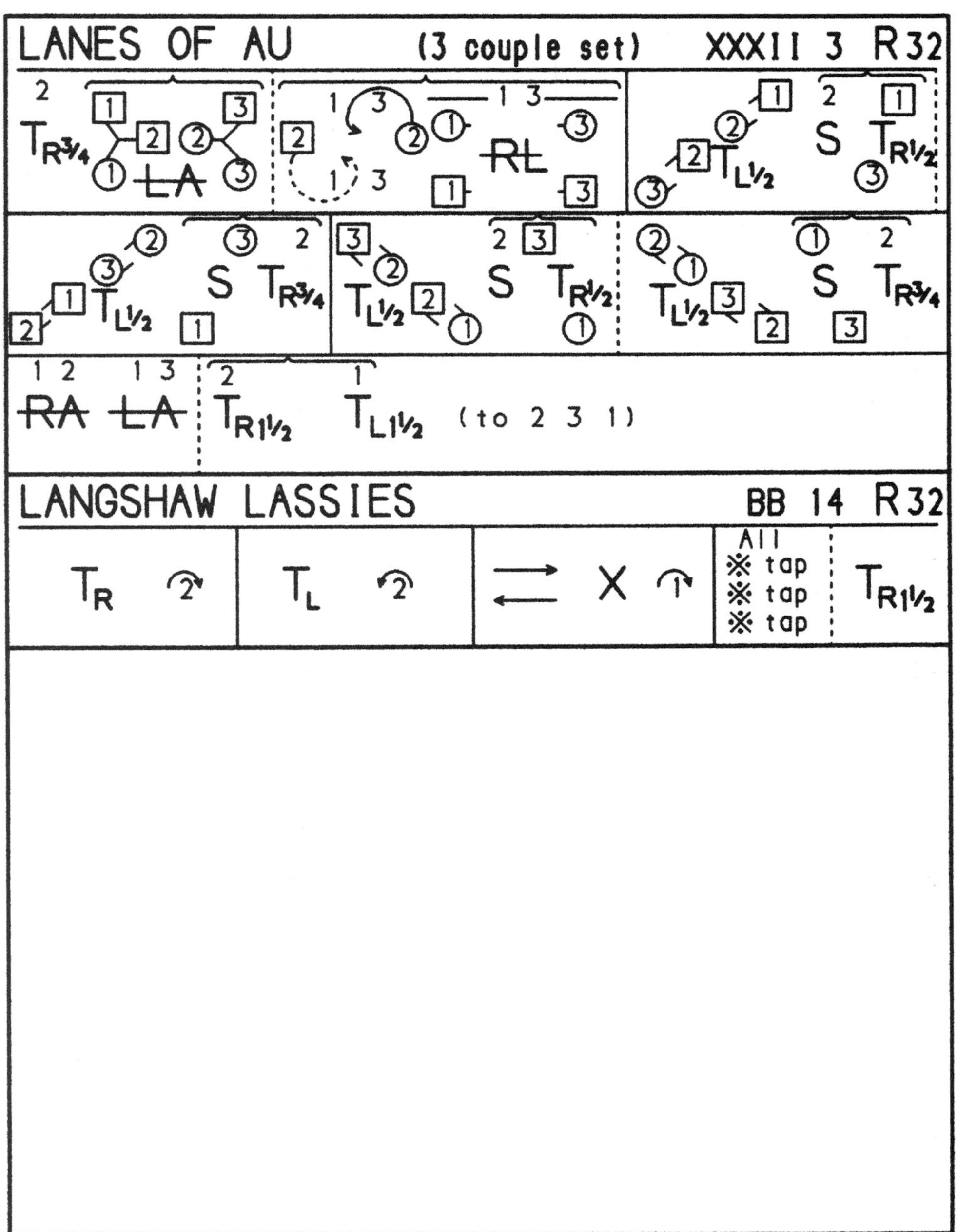
LANES OF AU
(3 couple set)
XXXII 3 R32
(to 2 3 1)
LANGSHAW LASSIES
BB 14 R32
All
tap
tap
tap

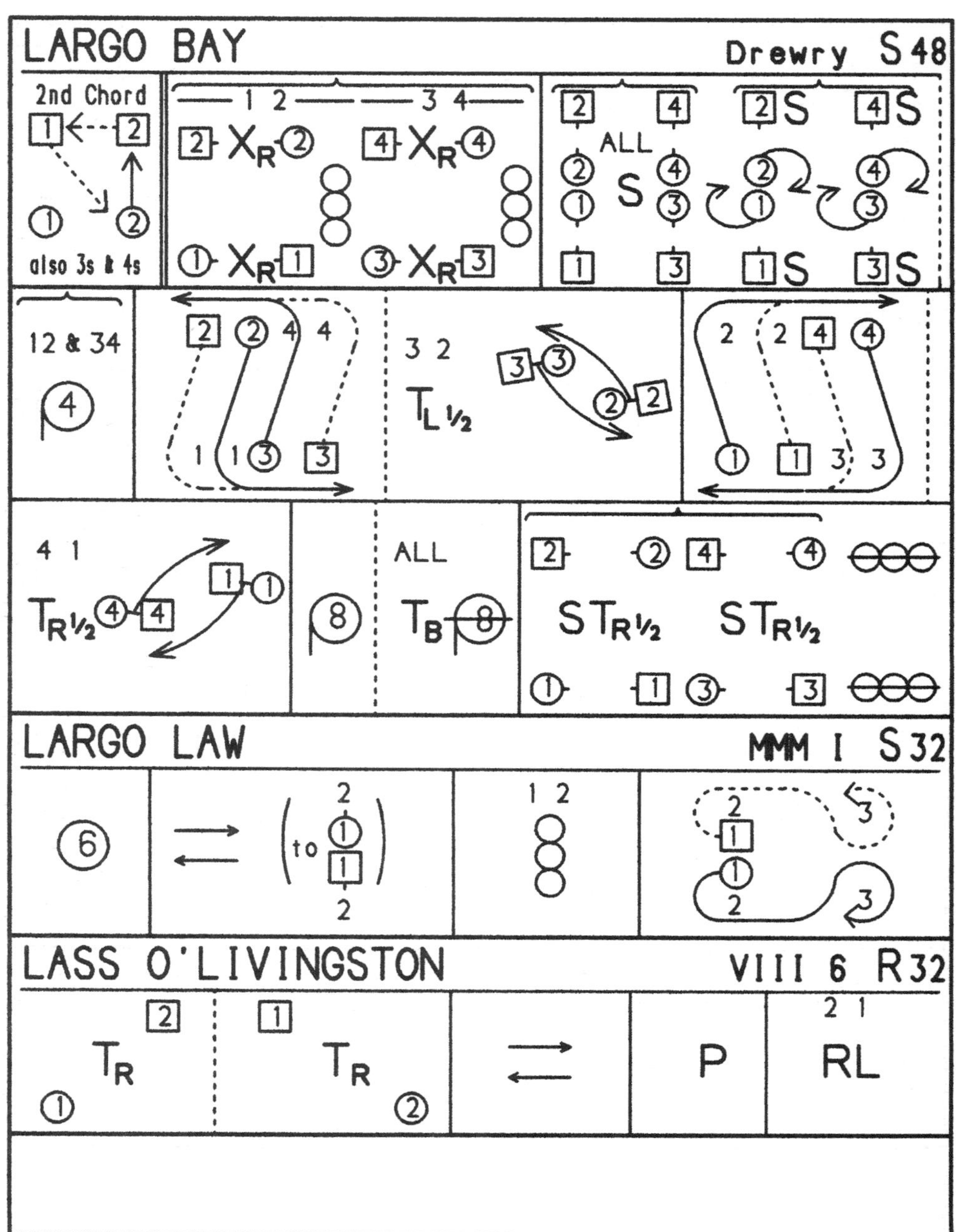
LARGO BAY
Drewry S 48
2nd Chord
also 3s & 4s
1 2
3 4
ALL
S
12 & 34
3 2
$T_{L\,1/2}$
4 1
$T_{R\,1/2}$
ALL
T_B
$ST_{R\,1/2}$
$ST_{R\,1/2}$
LARGO LAW
MMM I S 32
to
1 2
LASS O'LIVINGSTON
VIII 6 R 32
T_R
T_R
P
2 1
RL

LASS O'LOUDON — MMM II S32

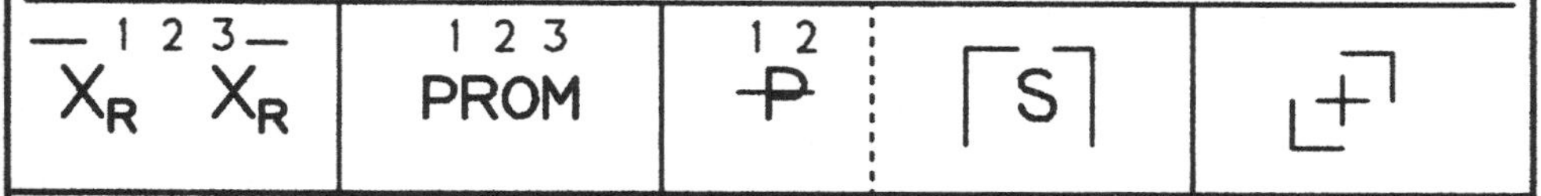

— 1 2 3 — X_R X_R	1 2 3 PROM	1 2 P ⁝ S	+

LASSIE COME AND DANCE WITH ME — J32

S T$_B$ 1 X_R	⊙	ST	⊙ 8 8 X_R

LASSIE WI'THE YELLOW COATIE — VIII 10 R32

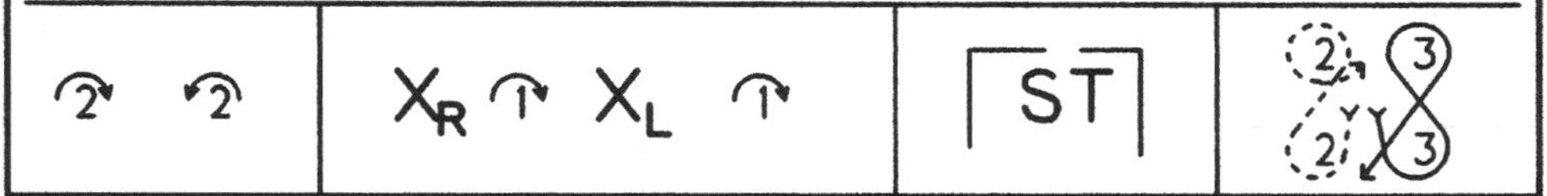

2 2	X_R 1 X_L 1	ST	2 3 2 3

LASSIE WI'THE YELLOW COATIE — BB 15 R32

1 2 RA S walk ⁝ RA S walk	R	walk chassé	A

LASSIES OF DUNSE — XVIII 5 J32

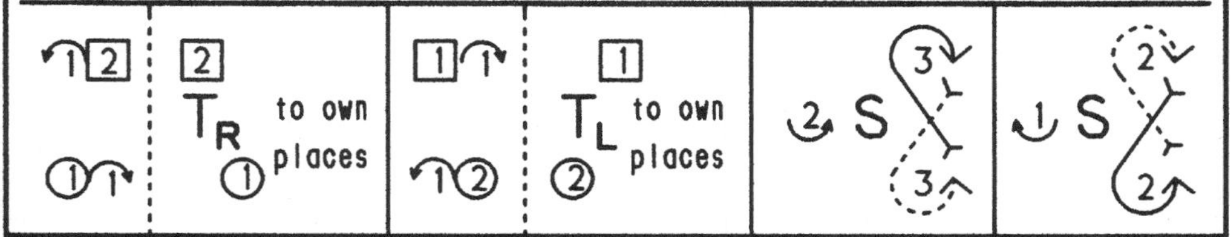

1 2 1 1 ⁝ 2 T_R to own places 1	1 1 1 2 ⁝ 1 T_L to own places 2	2 S 3 3	1 S 2 2

LASSIES O'MELROSE — BB 13 J32

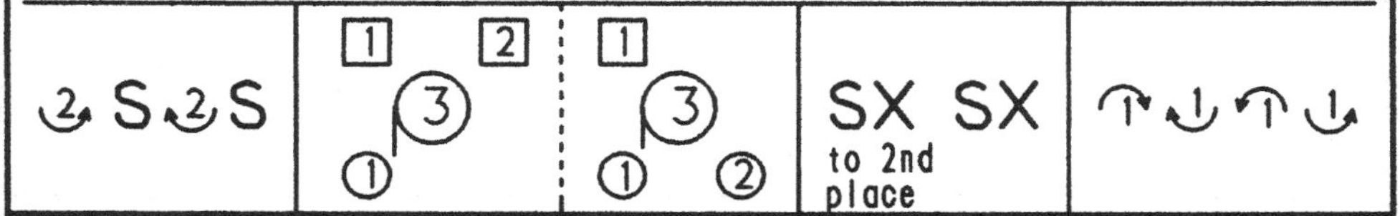

2 S 2 S	1 2 3 1 ⁝ 1 3 1 2	SX SX to 2nd place	1 1 1 1

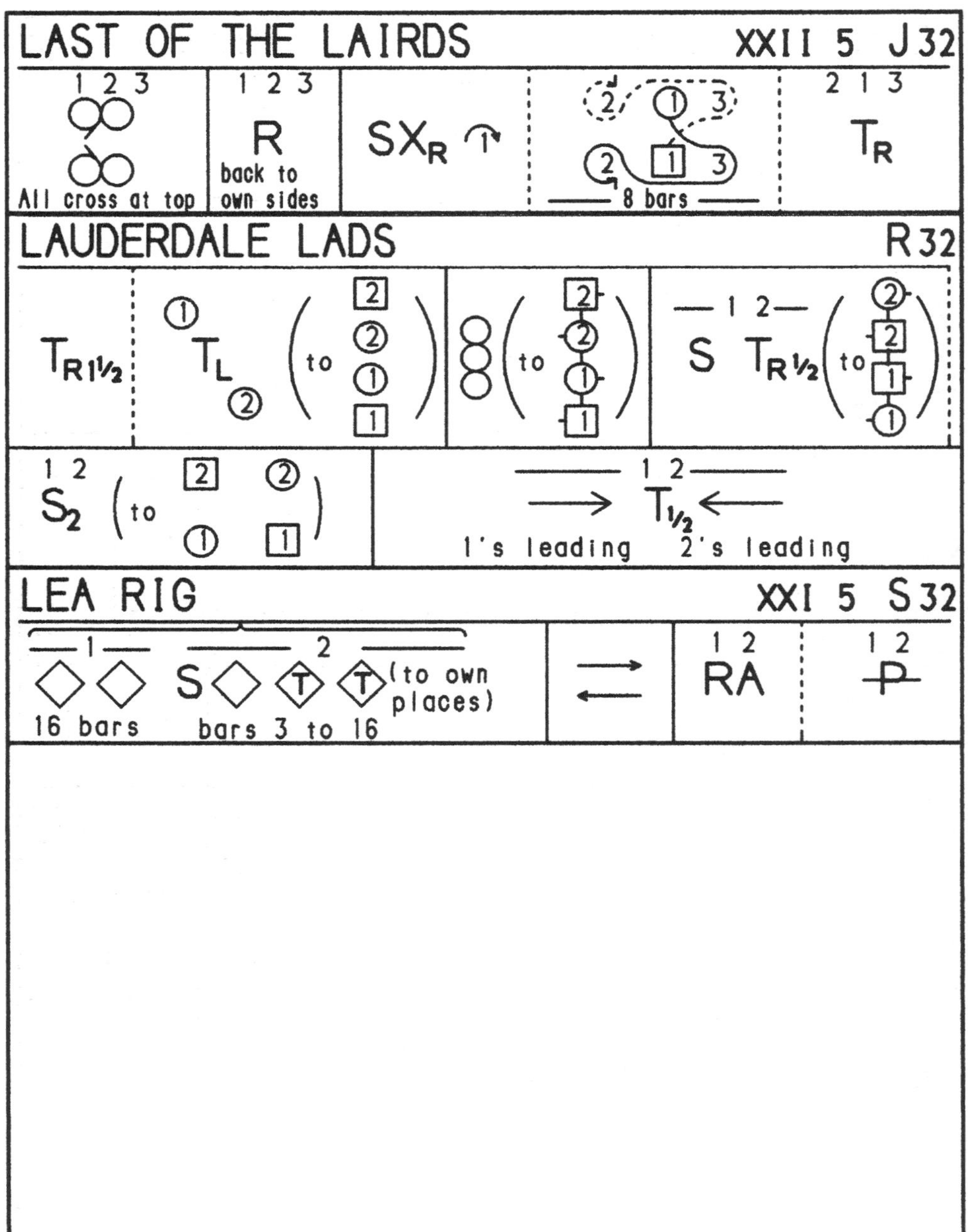

LAST OF THE LAIRDS
XXII 5 J32
1 2 3
All cross at top
1 2 3
R
back to own sides
SXR
8 bars
2 1 3
TR
LAUDERDALE LADS
R32
TR1½
TL
to
S TR½
1 2
S2
to
1 2
T½
1's leading
2's leading
LEA RIG
XXI 5 S32
1
2
S
(to own places)
16 bars
bars 3 to 16
1 2
RA
1 2
P

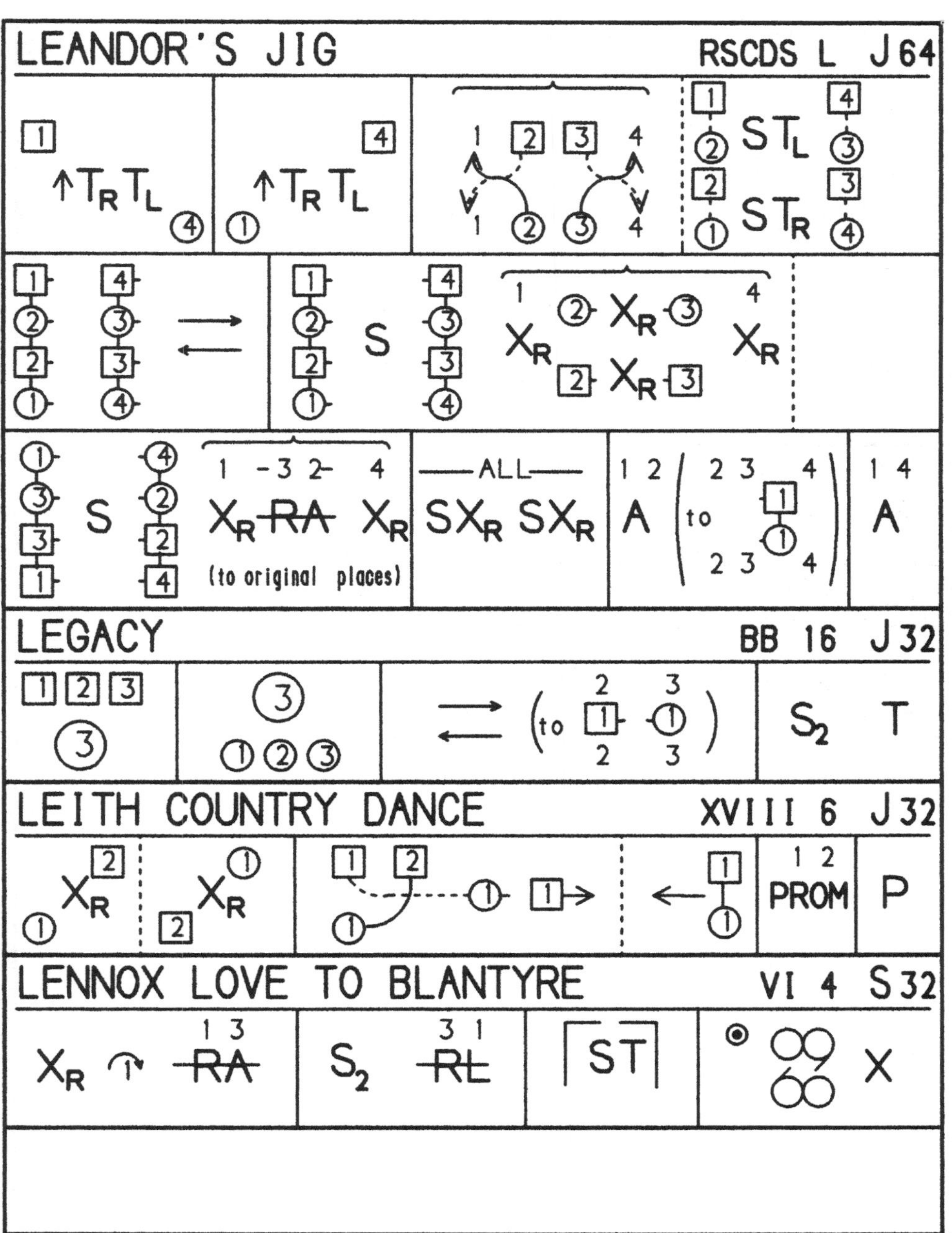
LEANDOR'S JIG
RSCDS L J64
ST
S
ALL
SXR SXR
A
(to original places)
LEGACY
BB 16 J32
S2 T
LEITH COUNTRY DANCE
XVIII 6 J32
PROM
P
LENNOX LOVE TO BLANTYRE
VI 4 S32
RA
RL
ST
X

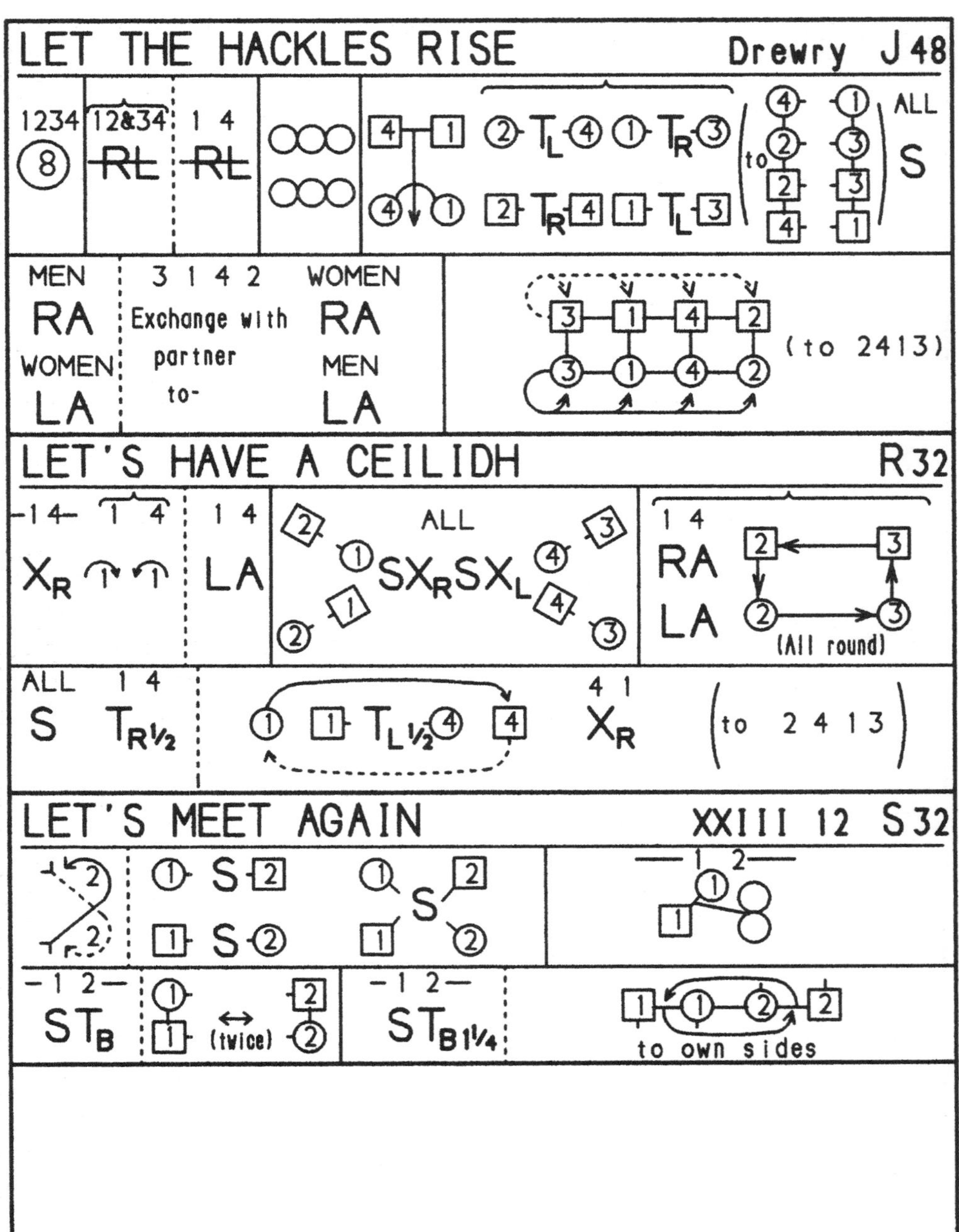
LET THE HACKLES RISE
Drewry J48
1234
8
12&34
RL
1 4
RL
4
1
2 TL 4 1 TR 3
2 TR 4 1 TL 3
to
ALL
S
MEN
RA
WOMEN
LA
3 1 4 2
Exchange with partner to-
WOMEN
RA
MEN
LA
3 1 4 2
(to 2413)
LET'S HAVE A CEILIDH
R32
1 4
XR
LA
ALL
SXRSXL
1 4
RA
LA
(All round)
ALL
S
1 4
TR½
1 TL½ 4
4 1
XR
(to 2 4 1 3)
LET'S MEET AGAIN
XXIII 12 S32
1 S 2
1 S 2
S
1 2
1 2
STB
(twice)
1 2
STB1¼
to own sides

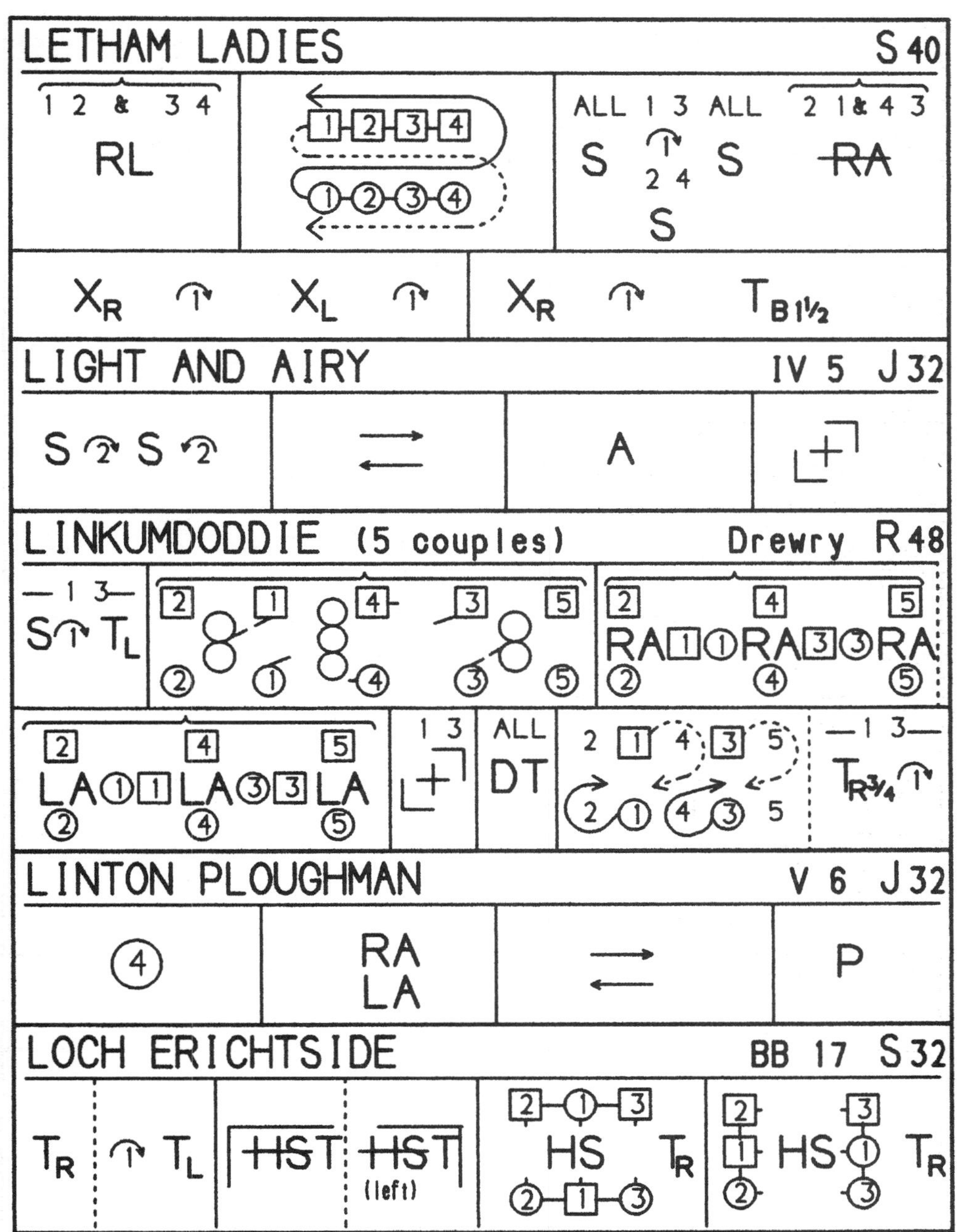
LETHAM LADIES
S 40
1 2 & 3 4
RL
ALL 1 3 ALL
2 1& 4 3
S S RA
S
XR XL XR TB1½
LIGHT AND AIRY
IV 5 J32
S S
A
LINKUMDODDIE (5 couples)
Drewry R48
1 3
S TL
RA RA RA
LA LA LA
1 3
ALL
DT
1 3
TR¾
LINTON PLOUGHMAN
V 6 J32
RA
LA
P
LOCH ERICHTSIDE
BB 17 S32
TR TL
HST HST
(left)
HS TR
HS TR

LOCH LEVEN CASTLE XXI 3 R32

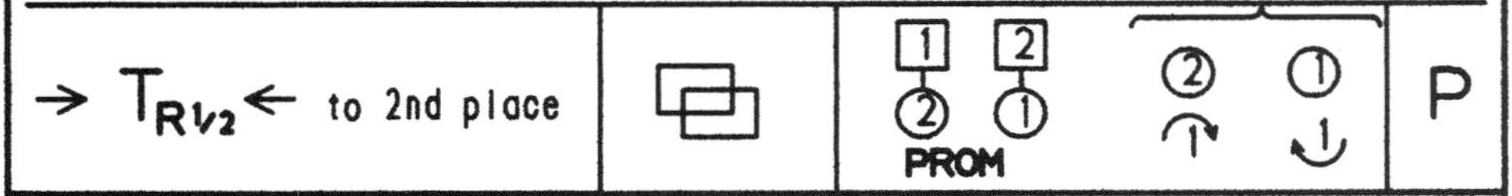

→ $T_{R\frac{1}{2}}$ ← to 2nd place | 1 2 / 2 1 PROM | 2 1 | P

LOCHALSH REEL Skye 2 R40

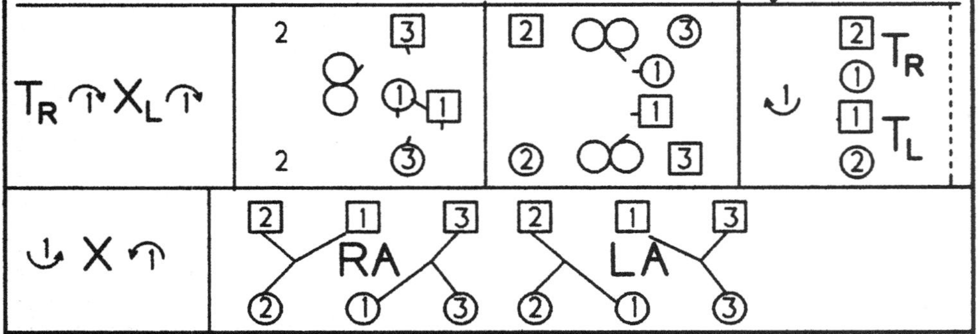

T_R X_L | 2 3 1 1 2 3 | 2 3 1 1 2 3 | 2 T_R 1 1 T_L 2

X | 2 1 3 RA 2 1 3 | 2 1 3 LA 2 1 3

LOCHIEL'S AWA' TO FRANCE XV 7 S48

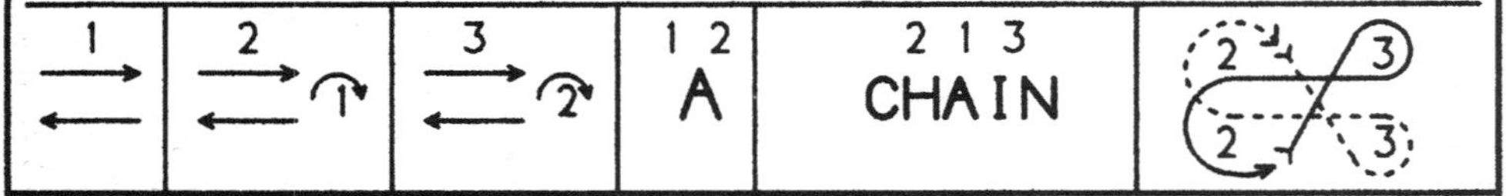

1 | 2 | 3 | 1 2 A | 2 1 3 CHAIN | 2 3 2 3

LOCHIEL'S RANT XIX 2 S32

2 1 ST_R | 1 T_L 1 | 1 ST_L 2 | 1 T_R 1 | T_B | 2 | S | $T_{1\frac{1}{2}}$

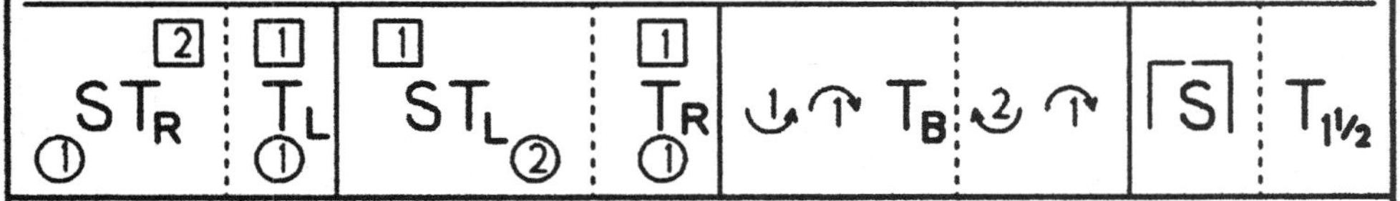

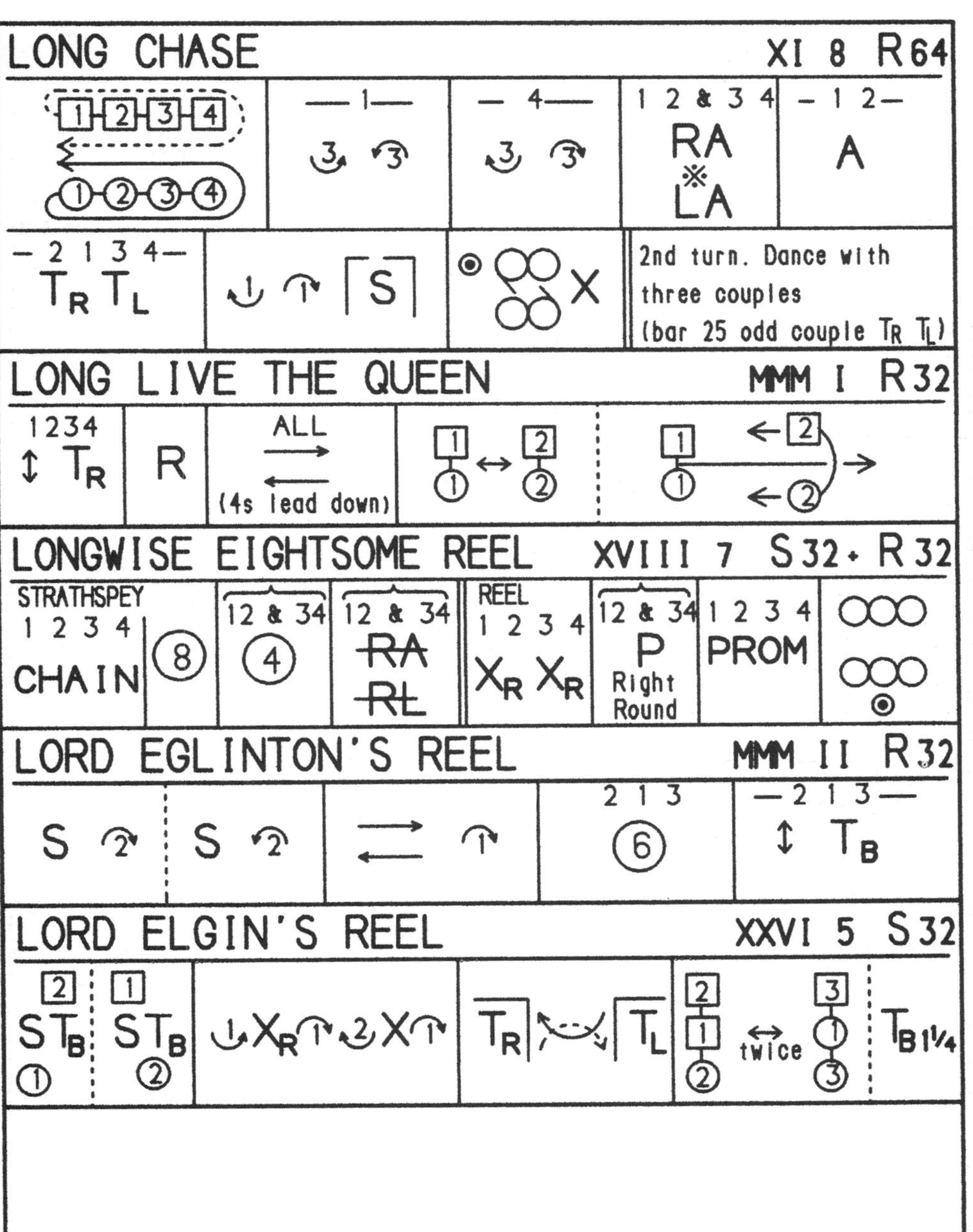
LONG CHASE
XI 8 R64
1 2 3 4
1 2 3 4
— 1 —
— 4 —
1 2 & 3 4
RA
LA
— 1 2 —
A
— 2 1 3 4 —
TR TL
S
X
2nd turn. Dance with
three couples
(bar 25 odd couple TR TL)
LONG LIVE THE QUEEN
MMM I R32
1234
TR
R
ALL
(4s lead down)
LONGWISE EIGHTSOME REEL
XVIII 7 S32 + R32
STRATHSPEY
1 2 3 4
CHAIN
8
12 & 34
4
12 & 34
RA
RL
REEL
1 2 3 4
XR XR
12 & 34
P
Right
Round
1 2 3 4
PROM
LORD EGLINTON'S REEL
MMM II R32
S
S
2 1 3
6
— 2 1 3 —
TB
LORD ELGIN'S REEL
XXVI 5 S32
STB
STB
XR
X
TR
TL
twice
TB 1¼

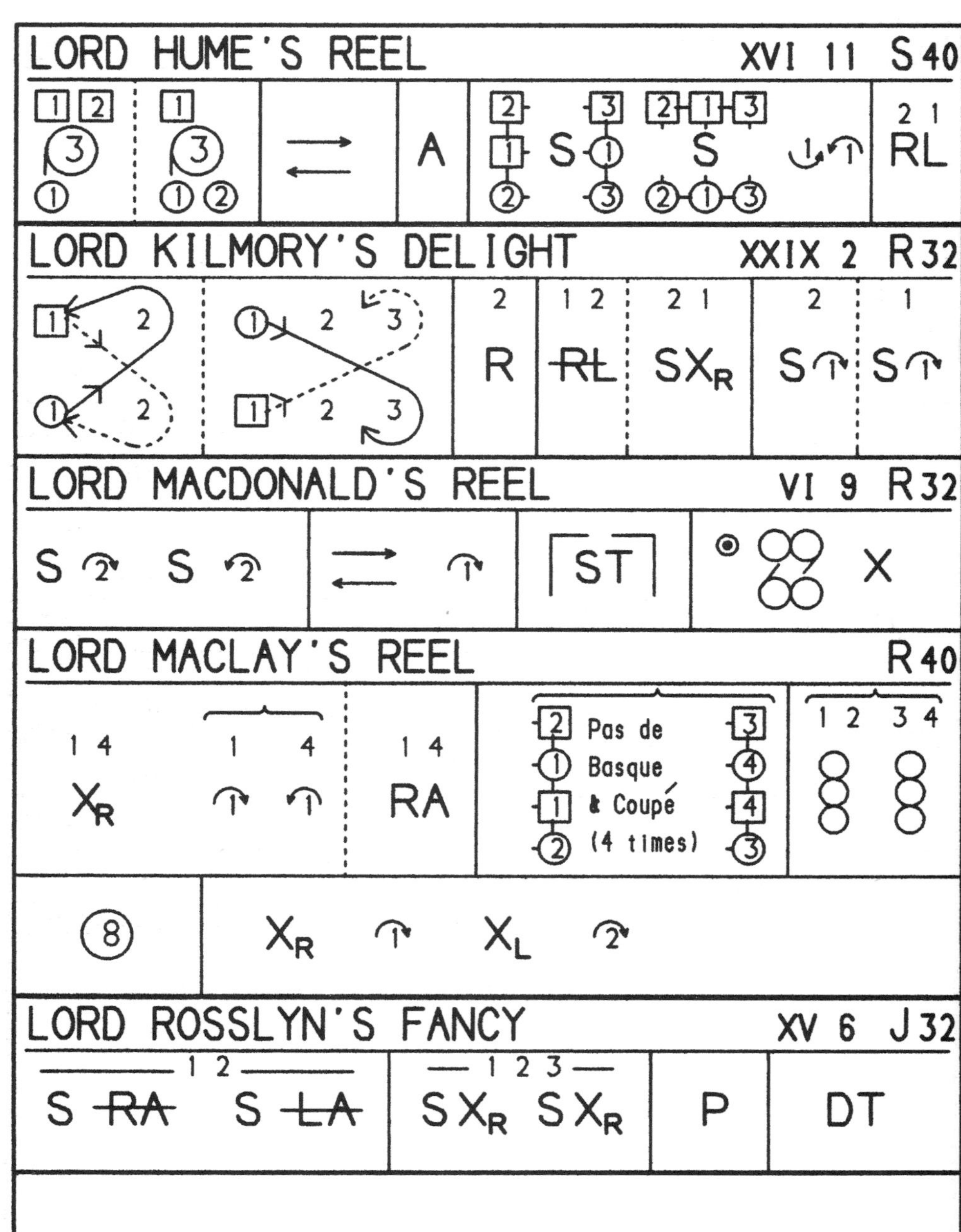
LORD HUME'S REEL
XVI 11 S40
Pas de Basque & Coupé (4 times)
LORD KILMORY'S DELIGHT
XXIX 2 R32
LORD MACDONALD'S REEL
VI 9 R32
LORD MACLAY'S REEL
R40
LORD ROSSLYN'S FANCY
XV 6 J32

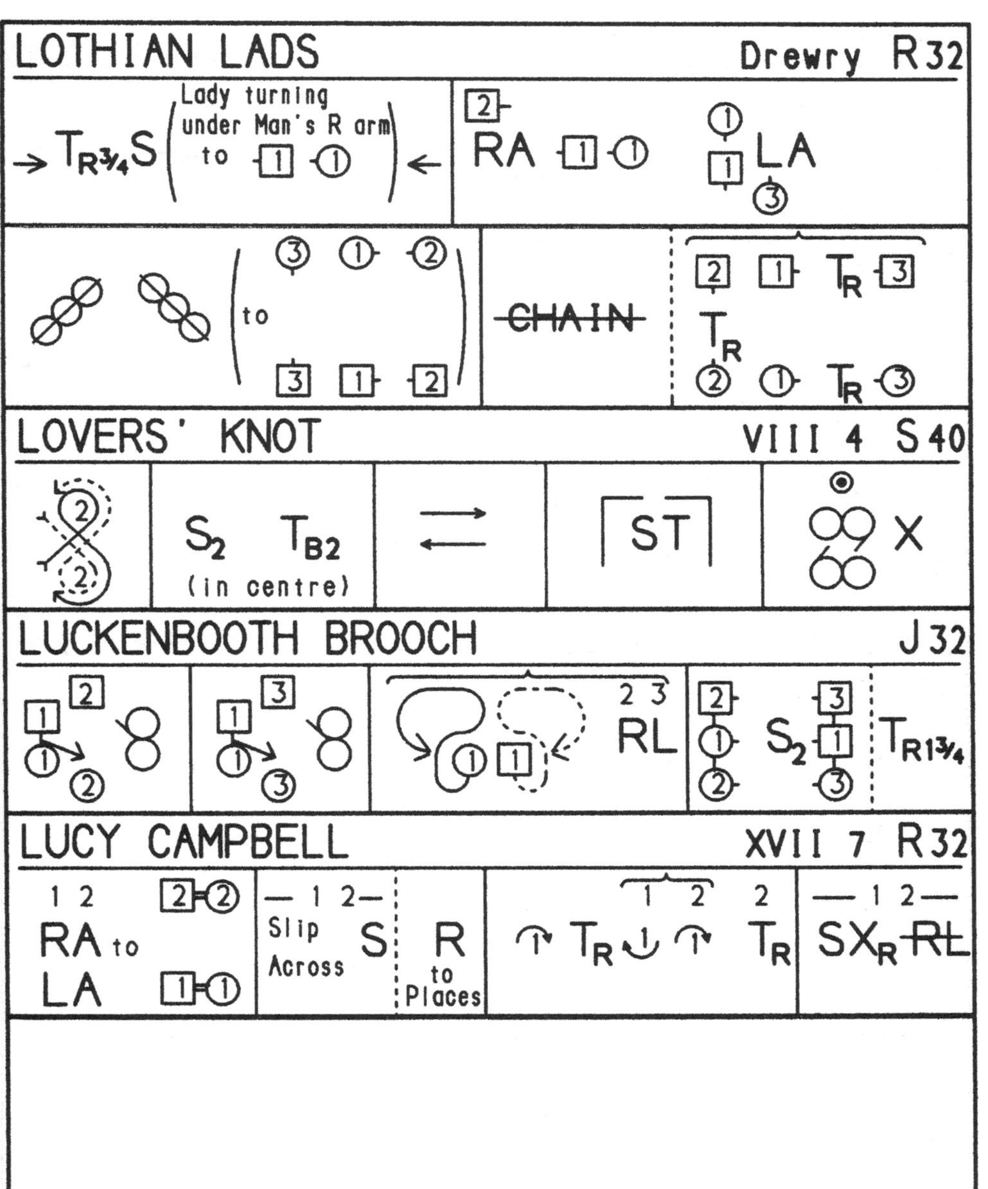
LOTHIAN LADS
Drewry R32
Lady turning under Man's R arm to
RA
LA
to
CHAIN
LOVERS' KNOT
VIII 4 S40
(in centre)
ST
X
LUCKENBOOTH BROOCH
J32
2 3
RL
LUCY CAMPBELL
XVII 7 R32
RA to LA
Slip Across
S
R to Places
SX
RL

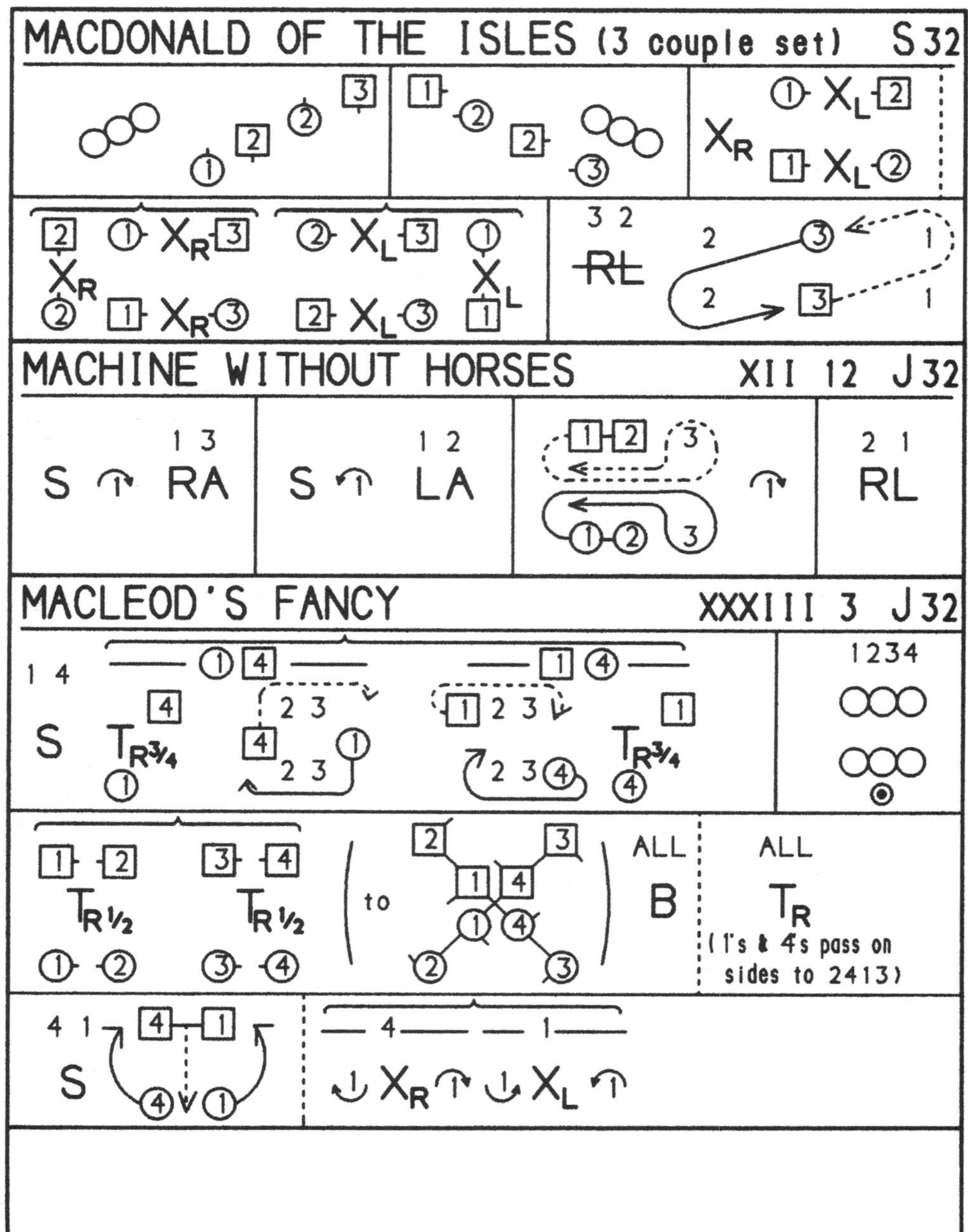
MACDONALD OF THE ISLES (3 couple set) S32
MACHINE WITHOUT HORSES XII 12 J32
MACLEOD'S FANCY XXXIII 3 J32
ALL
B
ALL
(1's & 4's pass on sides to 2413)

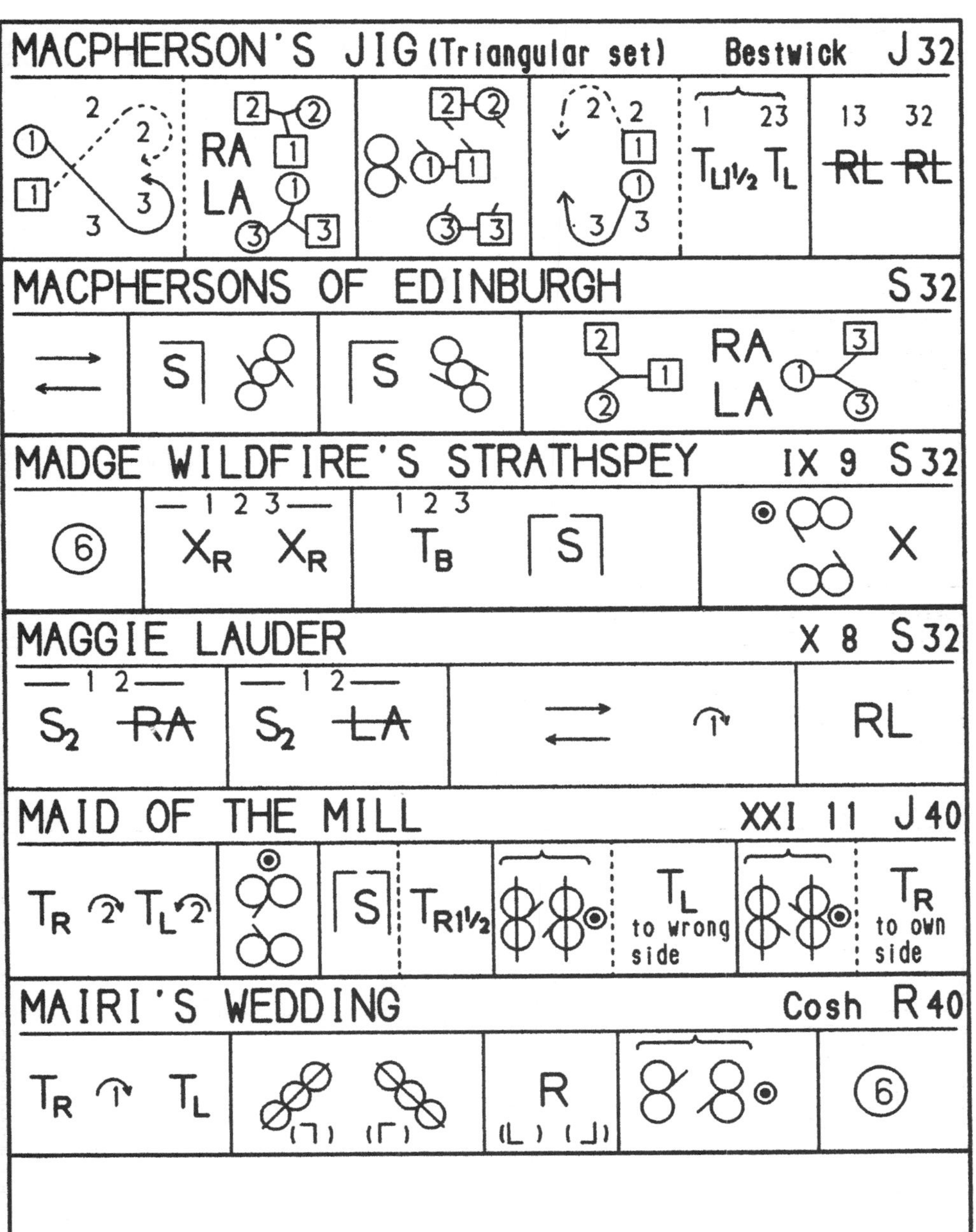
MACPHERSON'S JIG (Triangular set)
Bestwick J 32
RA
LA
MACPHERSONS OF EDINBURGH
S 32
RA
LA
MADGE WILDFIRE'S STRATHSPEY
IX 9 S 32
MAGGIE LAUDER
X 8 S 32
RL
MAID OF THE MILL
XXI 11 J 40
to wrong side
to own side
MAIRI'S WEDDING
Cosh R 40
R

MAIRRIT MAN'S FAVOURITE							XXIV 12 R32
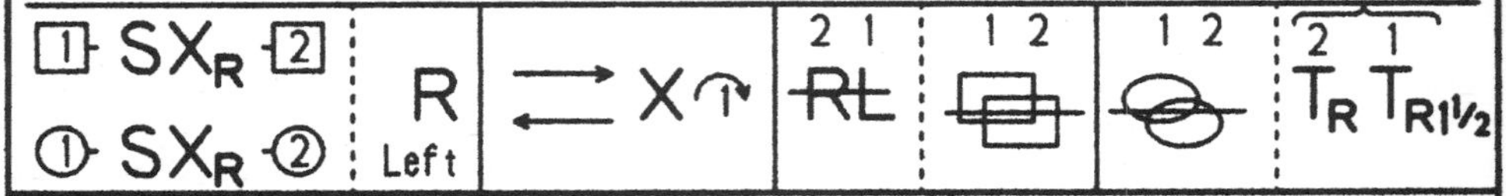 1 SXR 2 / 1 SXR 2	R Left	⇄ X	2 1 RL	1 2	1 2	2 1 T_R $T_{R1½}$	

MAJOR IAN STEWART						XXXV 4 J32
 1 2 $T_{R½}$ RA	2 1 T_R	2 1 3	S S S T	2 1 3 6 — 6 slip steps cross R foot over L & pivot	Chase anticlockwise to 2 1 3	

A MAN'S A MAN FOR A'THAT					XXX 5 S32
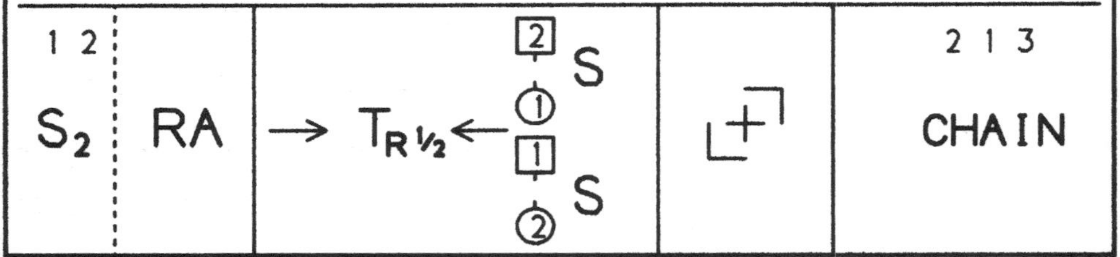 1 2 S_2	RA	→ $T_{R½}$ ← 2 1 S / 1 2 S		2 1 3 CHAIN	

MARCHIONESS OF BLANDFORD'S REEL						XXI 1 J48
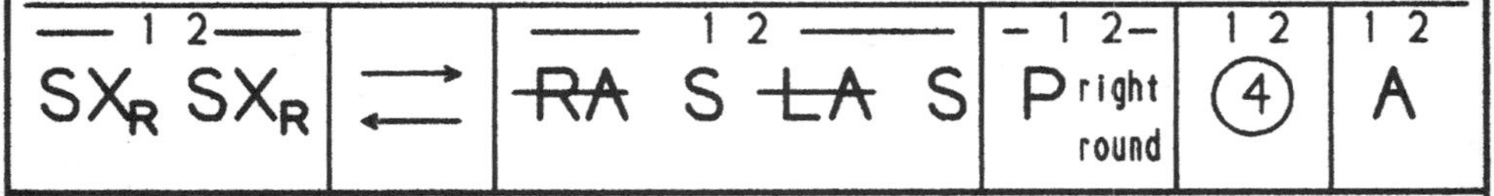 1 2 SXR SXR	⇄	1 2 RA S LA S	1 2 P right round	1 2 4	1 2 A	

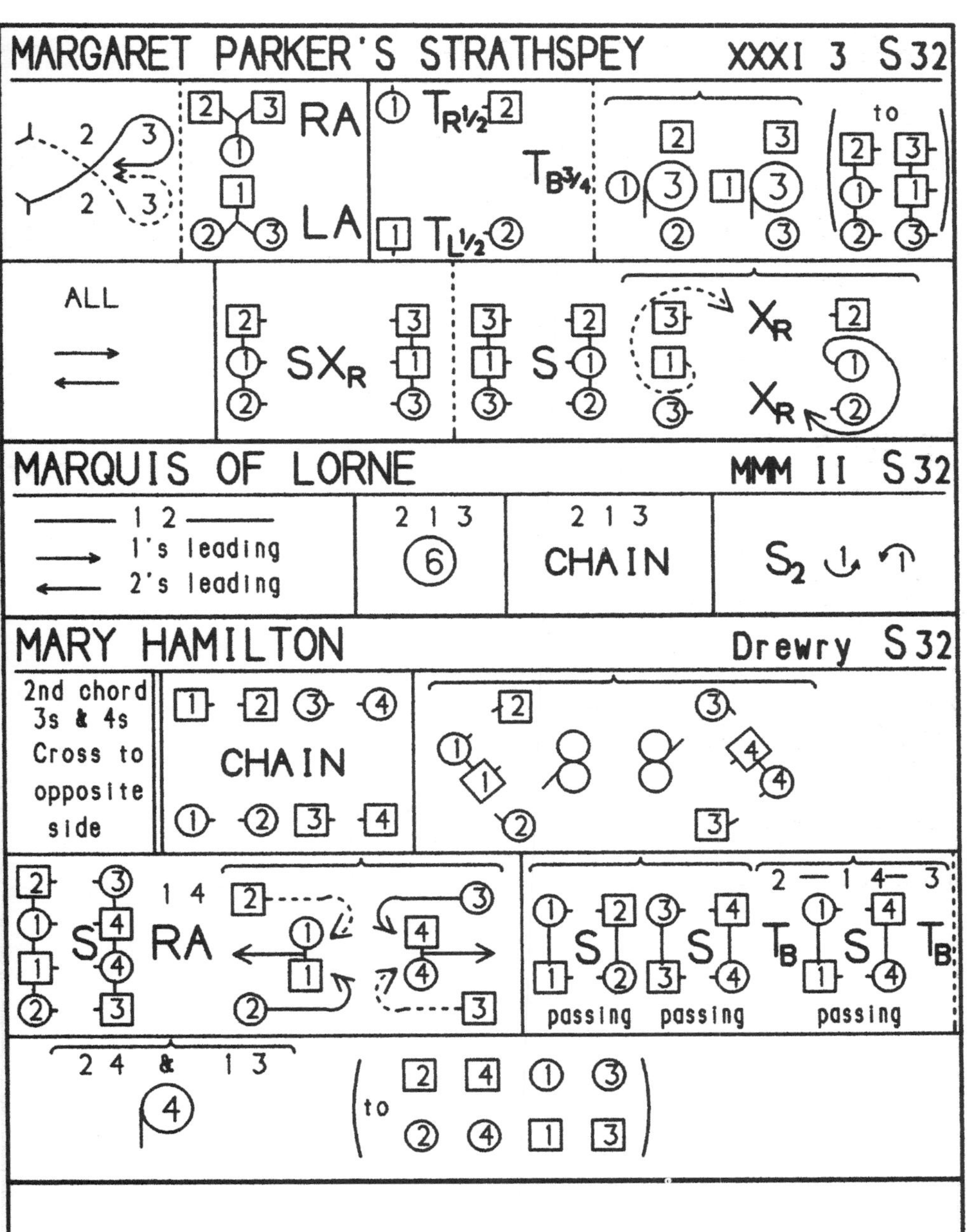
MARGARET PARKER'S STRATHSPEY
XXXI 3 S32
RA
LA
ALL
SXR
S
XR
to
MARQUIS OF LORNE
MMM II S32
1 2
1's leading
2's leading
2 1 3
6
2 1 3
CHAIN
S2
MARY HAMILTON
Drewry S32
2nd chord
3s & 4s
Cross to
opposite
side
CHAIN
1 4
RA
S
TB
passing
passing
passing
2 — 1 4 — 3
2 4 & 1 3
4
to

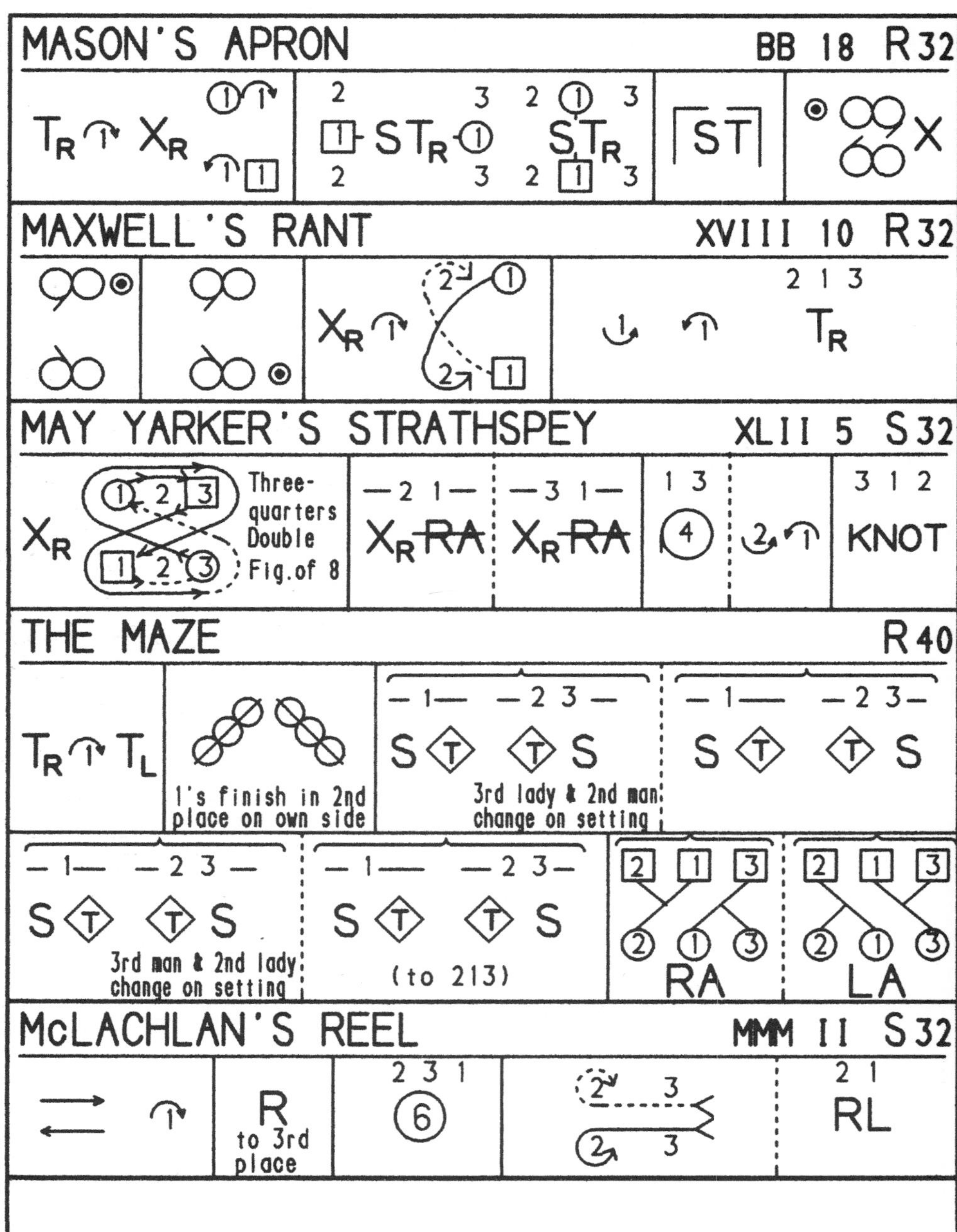

MASON'S APRON
BB 18 R32
MAXWELL'S RANT
XVIII 10 R32
MAY YARKER'S STRATHSPEY
XLII 5 S32
Three-quarters Double Fig.of 8
KNOT
THE MAZE
R40
1's finish in 2nd place on own side
3rd lady & 2nd man change on setting
3rd man & 2nd lady change on setting
(to 213)
RA
LA
McLACHLAN'S REEL
MMM II S32
R to 3rd place
RL

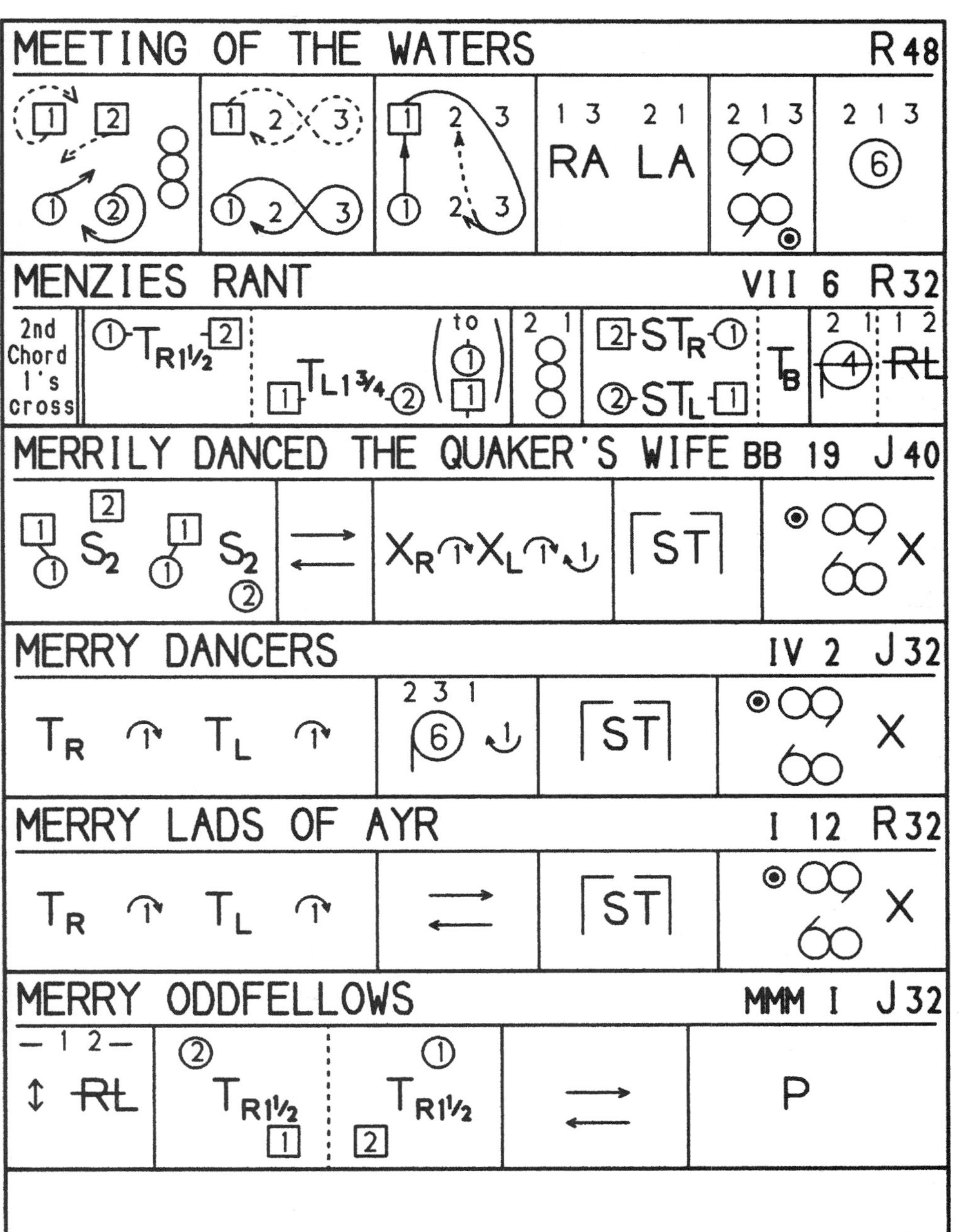
MEETING OF THE WATERS R48
RA LA
MENZIES RANT VII 6 R32
2nd Chord 1's cross
MERRILY DANCED THE QUAKER'S WIFE BB 19 J40
ST
MERRY DANCERS IV 2 J32
ST
MERRY LADS OF AYR I 12 R32
ST
MERRY ODDFELLOWS MMM I J32
P

MID LOTHIAN — VII 11 R40

1 2 3 4 / 1 2 3 4	⇄	P	$\llcorner + \urcorner$	— 2 1 — ④ RL

MIDDLETON MEDLEY — XXII 6 S16 + J16

STRATHSPEY

1 2 3 / 1 2 3	1 2 1 X_L 2 / T_R / 1 X_L 2	$S_{\uparrow}$ T_R T_L T_R

JIG

S ST_B	SST_B

MIDDLING THANK YOU — XV 8 J40

— 1 2 — S_2 RL	R	P	⇄ ↻	$\llcorner + \urcorner$

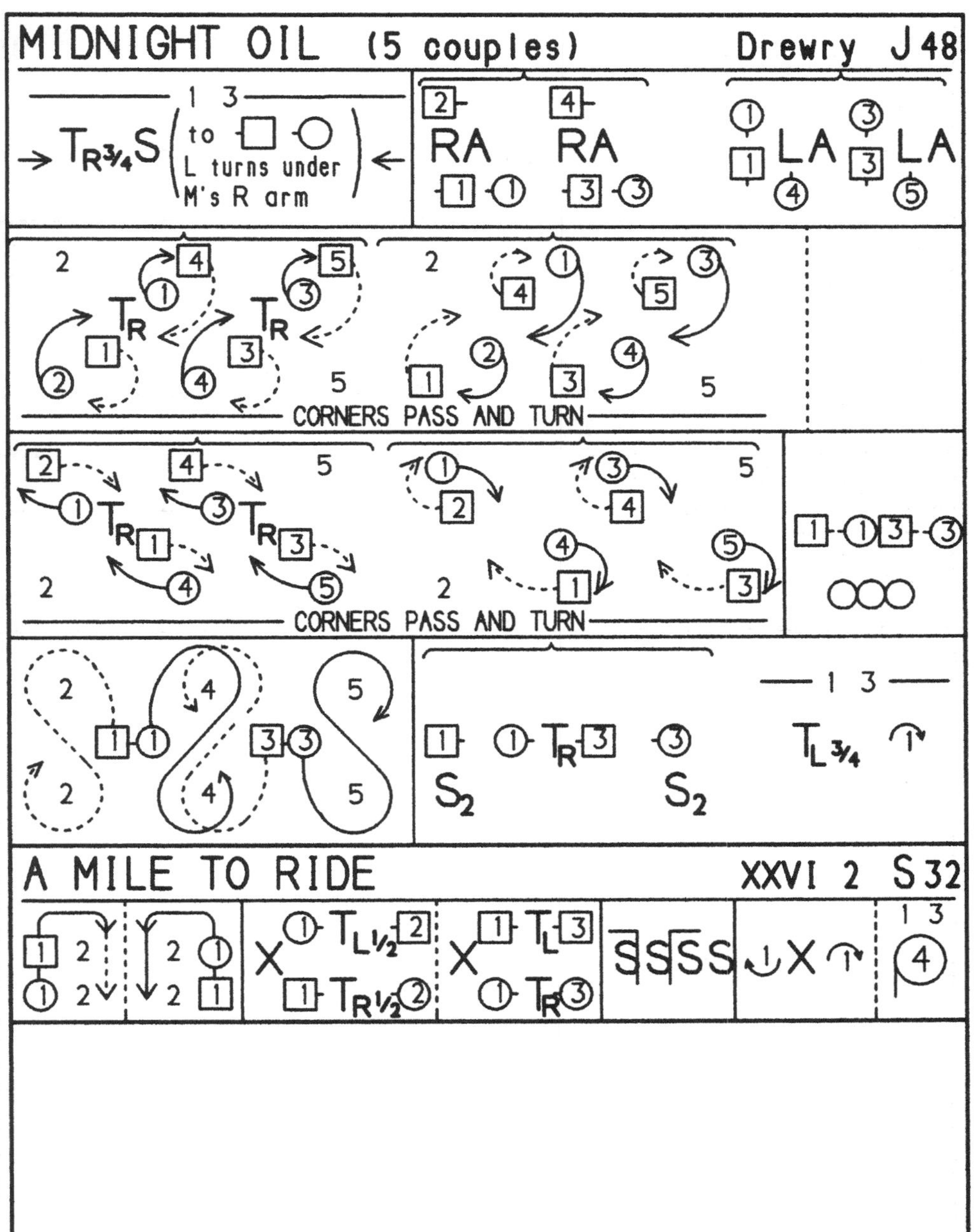
MIDNIGHT OIL (5 couples)
Drewry J 48
1 3
to
L turns under
M's R arm
RA RA
LA LA
CORNERS PASS AND TURN
CORNERS PASS AND TURN
A MILE TO RIDE
XXVI 2 S 32

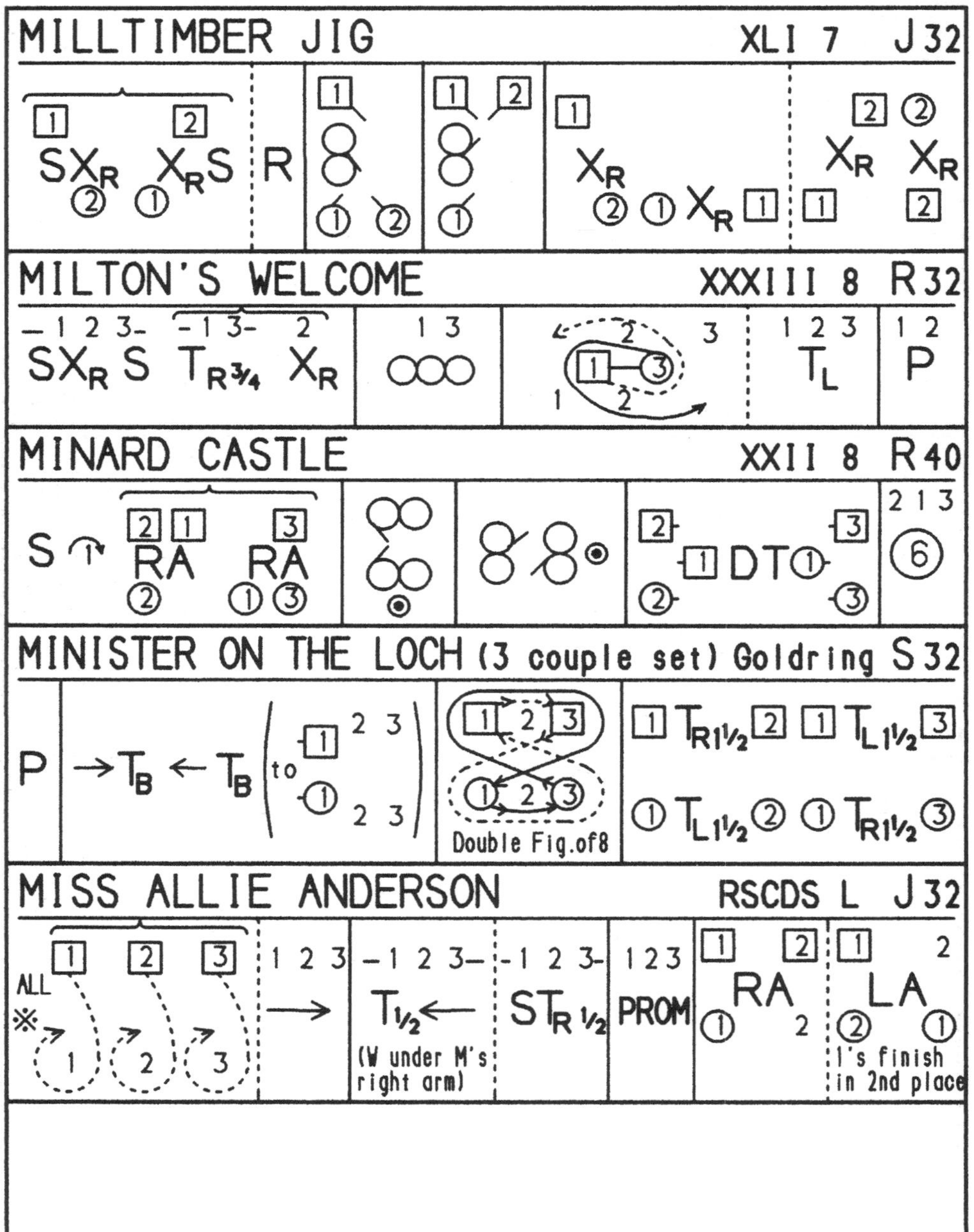

MILLTIMBER JIG
XLI 7 J32
MILTON'S WELCOME
XXXIII 8 R32
MINARD CASTLE
XXII 8 R40
MINISTER ON THE LOCH (3 couple set) Goldring S32
Double Fig.of8
MISS ALLIE ANDERSON
RSCDS L J32
ALL
PROM
(W under M's right arm)
1's finish in 2nd place

MISS BENNET'S JIG   XX 3 J32

1 2 T_B	MEN R	X_R X_L	S T_R

MISS BETTY BOYLE   Gr 17 R32

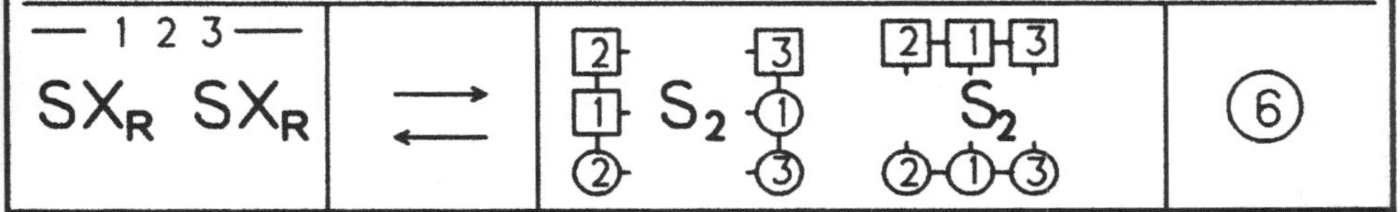

— 1 2 3 — SX_R SX_R	⇄	S_2 S_2	⑥

MISS BROWN'S REEL   XXV 5 R32

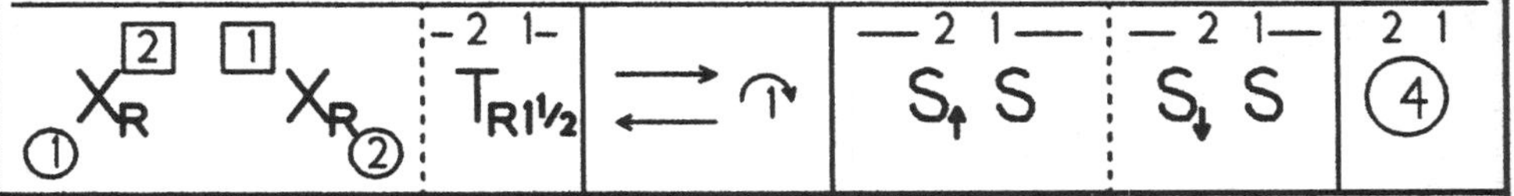

X_R X_R	– 2 1 – $T_{R1½}$	⇄	— 2 1 — S S	— 2 1 — S S	2 1 ④

MISS BURNS'S REEL   XX 5 R32

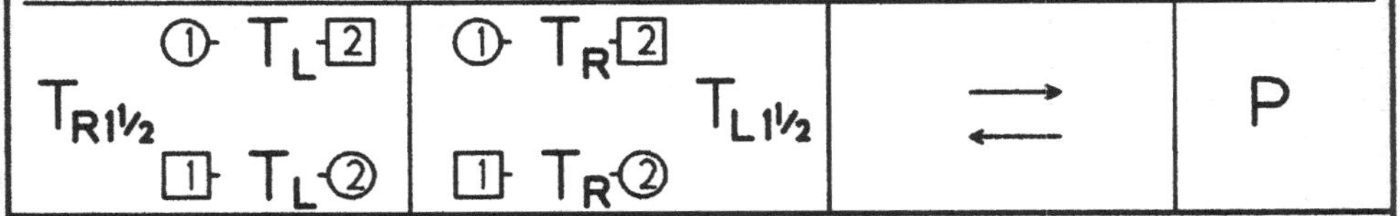

T_L $T_{R1½}$ T_L	T_R $T_{L1½}$ T_R	⇄	P

MISS CAHOON'S REEL   XIII 2 J48

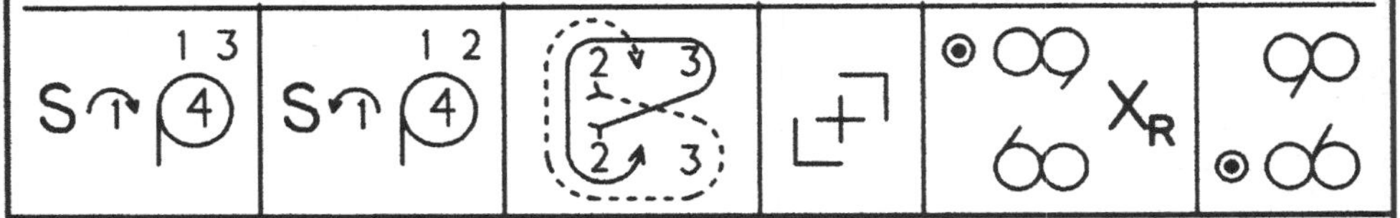

1 3 S ④	1 2 S ④	2 3 2 3		X_R	

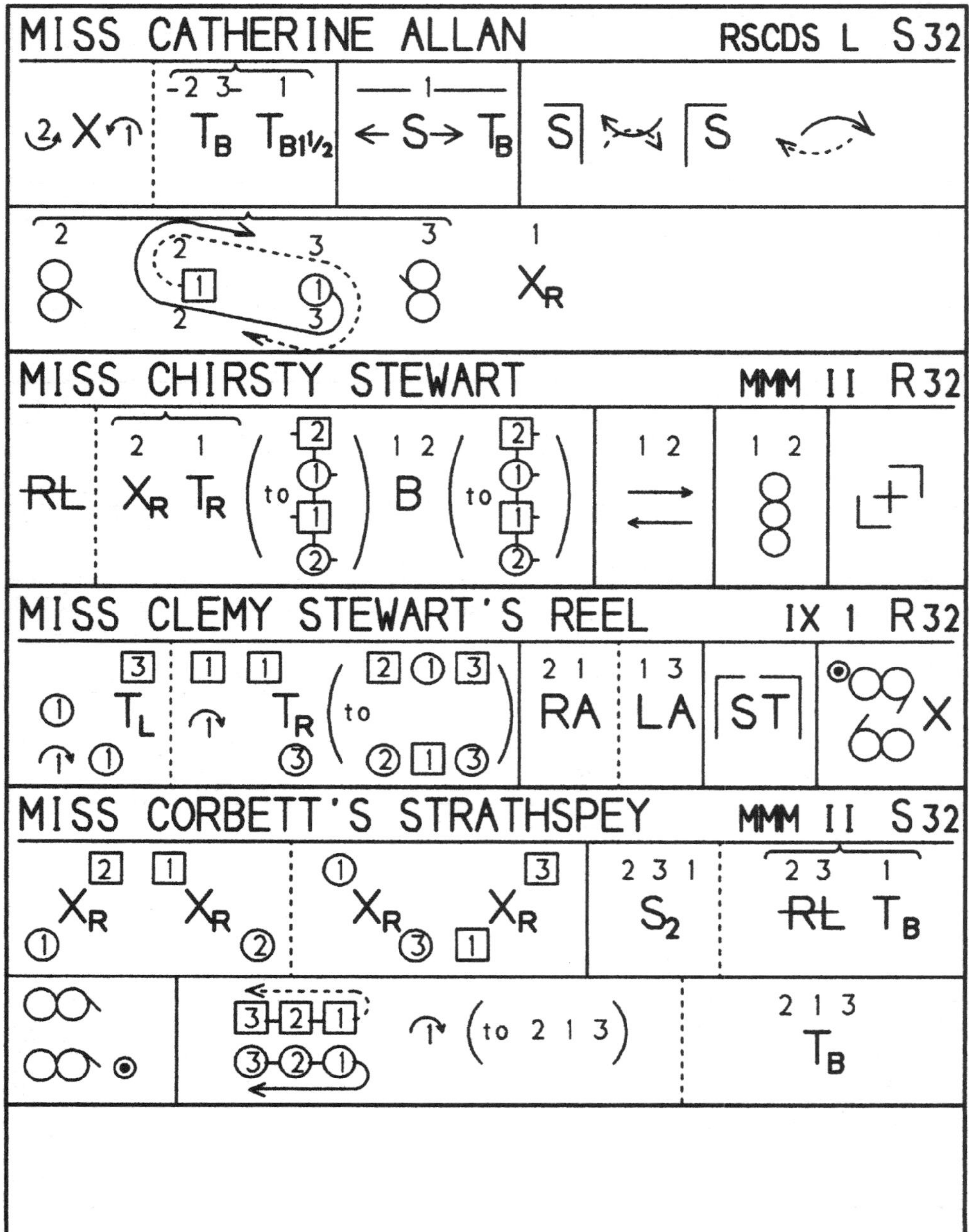
MISS CATHERINE ALLAN
RSCDS L S32
MISS CHIRSTY STEWART
MMM II R32
MISS CLEMY STEWART'S REEL
IX 1 R32
MISS CORBETT'S STRATHSPEY
MMM II S32

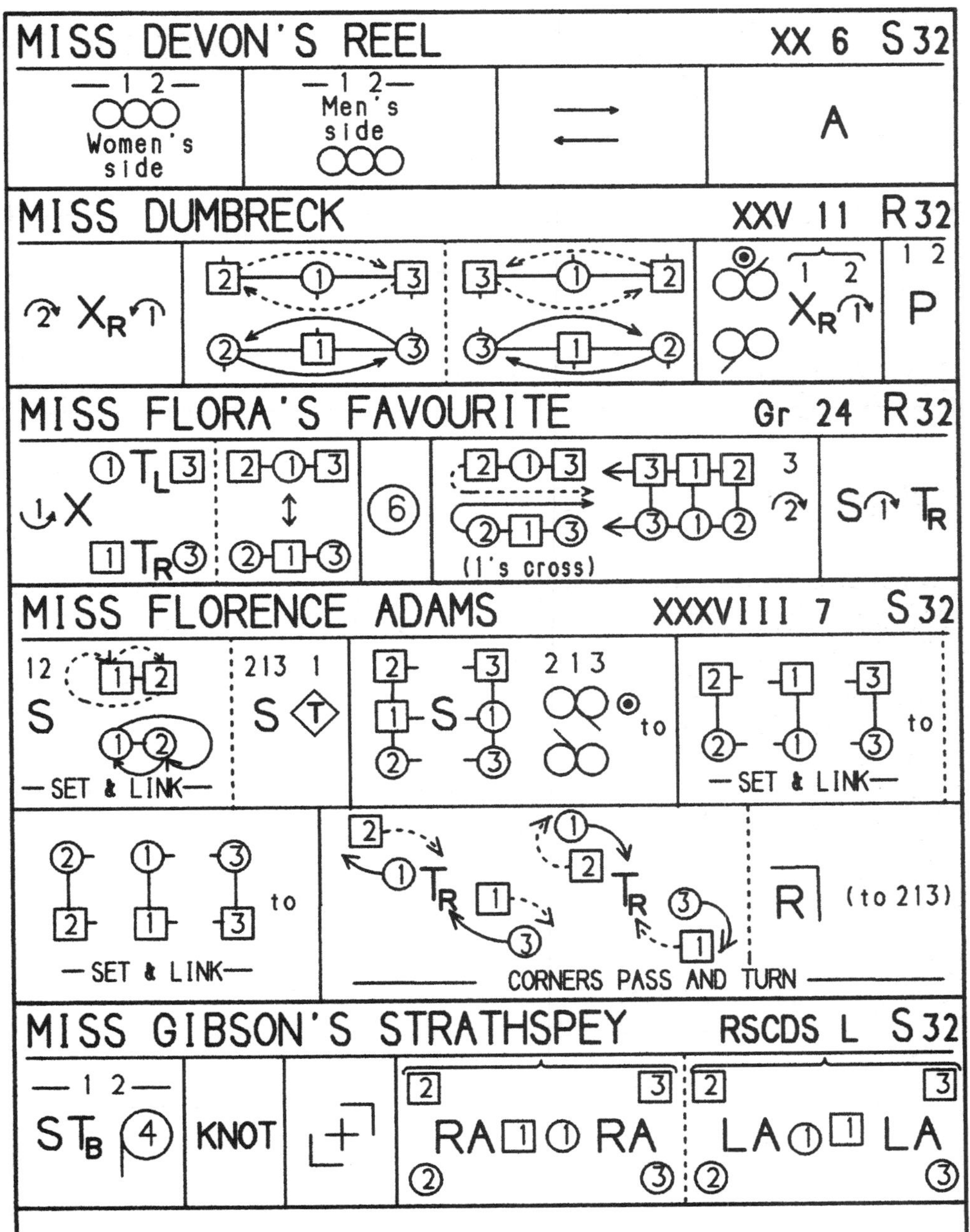
MISS DEVON'S REEL
XX 6 S32
Women's side
Men's side
A
MISS DUMBRECK
XXV 11 R32
P
MISS FLORA'S FAVOURITE
Gr 24 R32
(1's cross)
MISS FLORENCE ADAMS
XXXVIII 7 S32
— SET & LINK —
to
CORNERS PASS AND TURN
R
(to 213)
MISS GIBSON'S STRATHSPEY
RSCDS L S32
KNOT
RA
LA

MISS HADDEN'S REEL — XXIII 5 J32

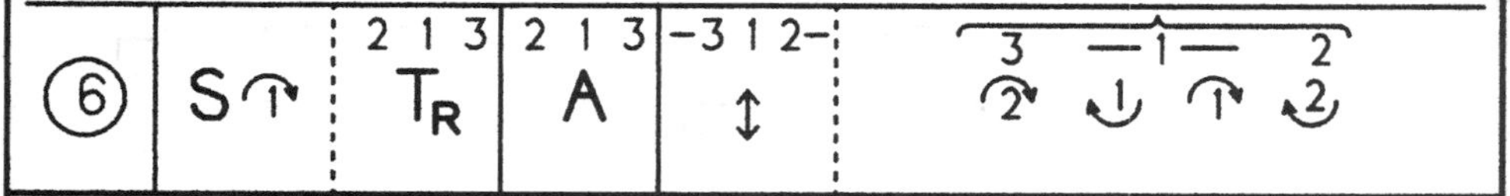

⑥	S ↷	2 1 3 T_R	2 1 3 A	–3 1 2– ↕	3 —1— 2

MISS HEYDEN — XVII 6 S40

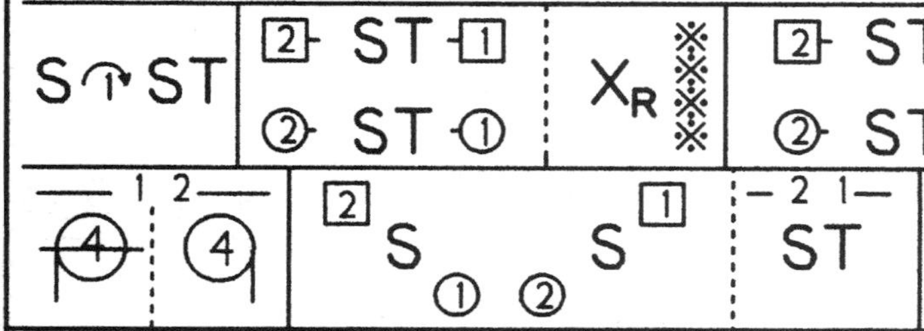

S ↷ ST	[2] ST [1] / ② ST ①	X_R	[2] $ST_{1½}$ ① / ② $ST_{1½}$ [1]	2 X_R

— 1 2 — ④ ④	[2] S ① ② S [1]	– 2 1 – ST	Note: bars 15/16 and 23/24 Lady claps on 1st beat Man claps on 3rd beat

MISS ISABELLA McLEOD — XXV 7 S32

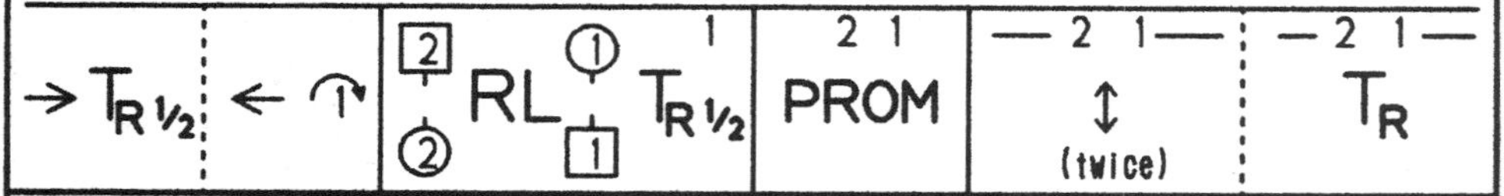

→ $T_{R½}$	← ↷	[2] ② RL ① [1] 1 $T_{R½}$	2 1 PROM	— 2 1 — ↕ (twice)	— 2 1 — T_R

MISS JANET LAING'S STRATHSPEY — XXII 11 S32

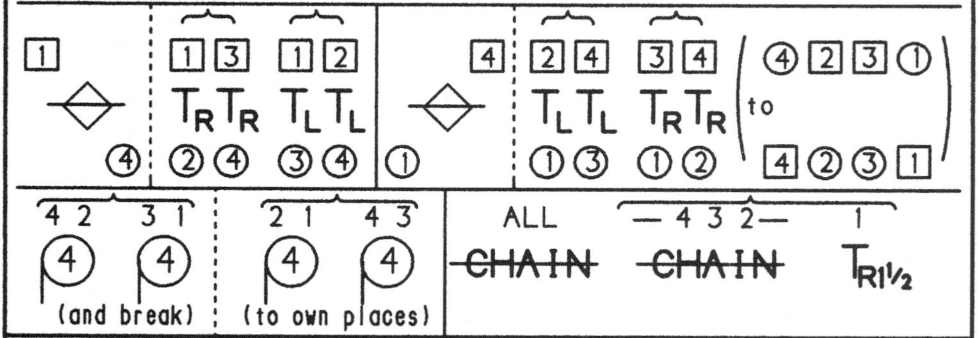

[1] ④	[1] [3] $T_R T_R$ ② ④	[1] [2] $T_L T_L$ ③ ④	[4] ①	[2] [4] $T_L T_L$ ① ③	[3] [4] $T_R T_R$ ① ②	④ [2] [3] ① to [4] ② ③ [1]

4 2 3 1 ④ ④ (and break)	2 1 4 3 ④ ④ (to own places)	ALL CHAIN	— 4 3 2 — CHAIN	1 $T_{R1½}$

MISS JARVIS'S REEL — R40

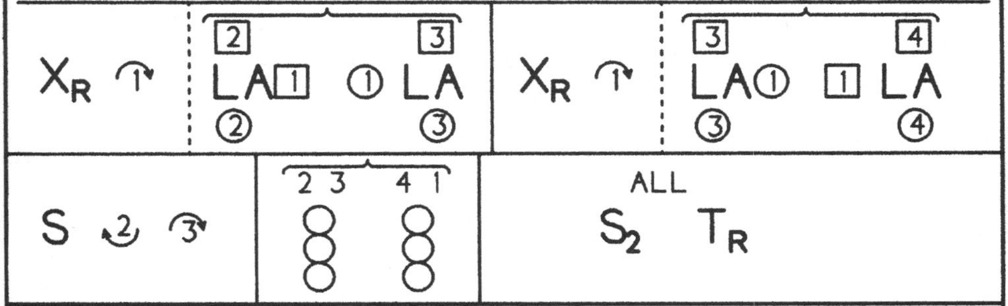

X_R ↻1 | 2 LA 1 / 1 LA 3 | X_R ↻1 | 3 LA 1 / 1 LA 4

S ↺2 ↻3 | 2 3 4 1 (reels) | ALL S_2 T_R

MISS JEANNIE CARMICHAEL — S32 + R32

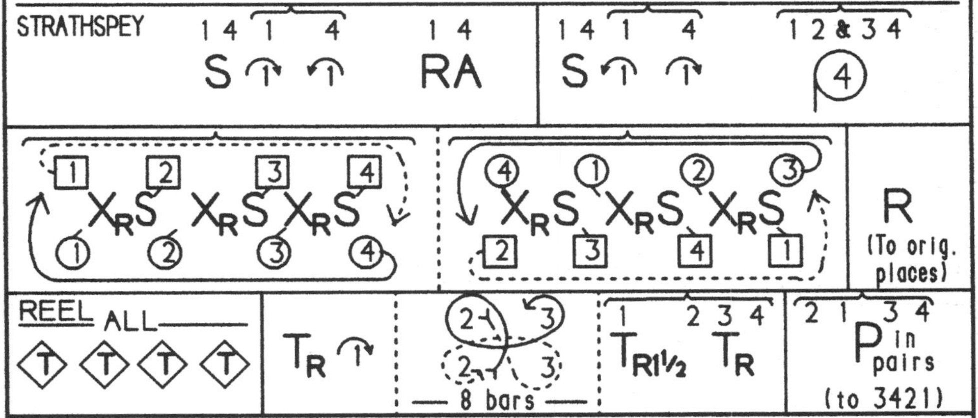

STRATHSPEY

1 4 S ↻1 ↺4 1 4 RA | 1 4 S ↺1 ↻4 | 1 2 & 3 4 (4)

1 X_RS 2 X_RS 3 X_RS 4 | 4 X_RS 1 X_RS 2 X_RS 3 | R (To orig. places)

REEL ALL T T T T | T_R ↻1 | 2 3 — 8 bars — | 1 $T_{R1½}$ 2 3 4 T_R | 2 1 3 4 P in pairs (to 3421)

MISS JESSIE DALRYMPLE'S REEL — XX 9 R32

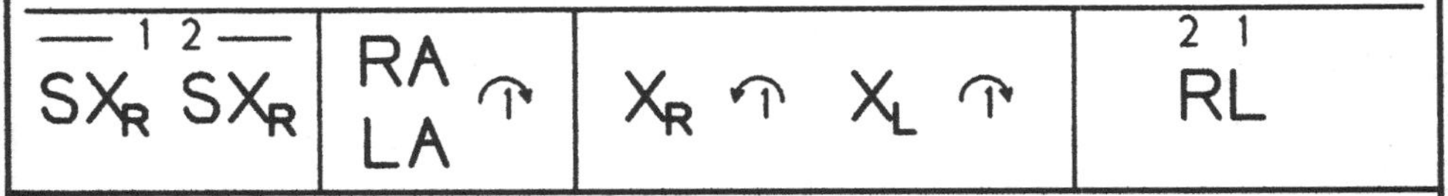

— 1 2 — SX_R SX_R | RA LA ↻1 | X_R ↺1 X_L ↻1 | 2 1 RL

MISS JOHNSTONE OF ARDROSSAN (5 couples) — R32

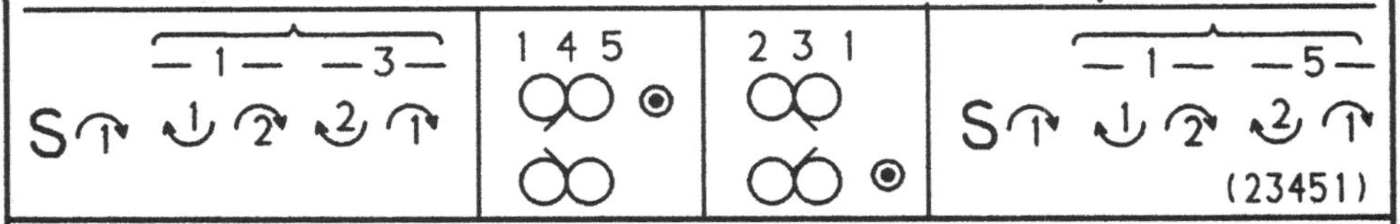

S ↻1 —1— ↺1 ↻2 —3— ↺2 ↻1 | 1 4 5 | 2 3 1 | S ↻1 —1— ↺1 ↻2 —5— ↺2 ↻1 (23451)

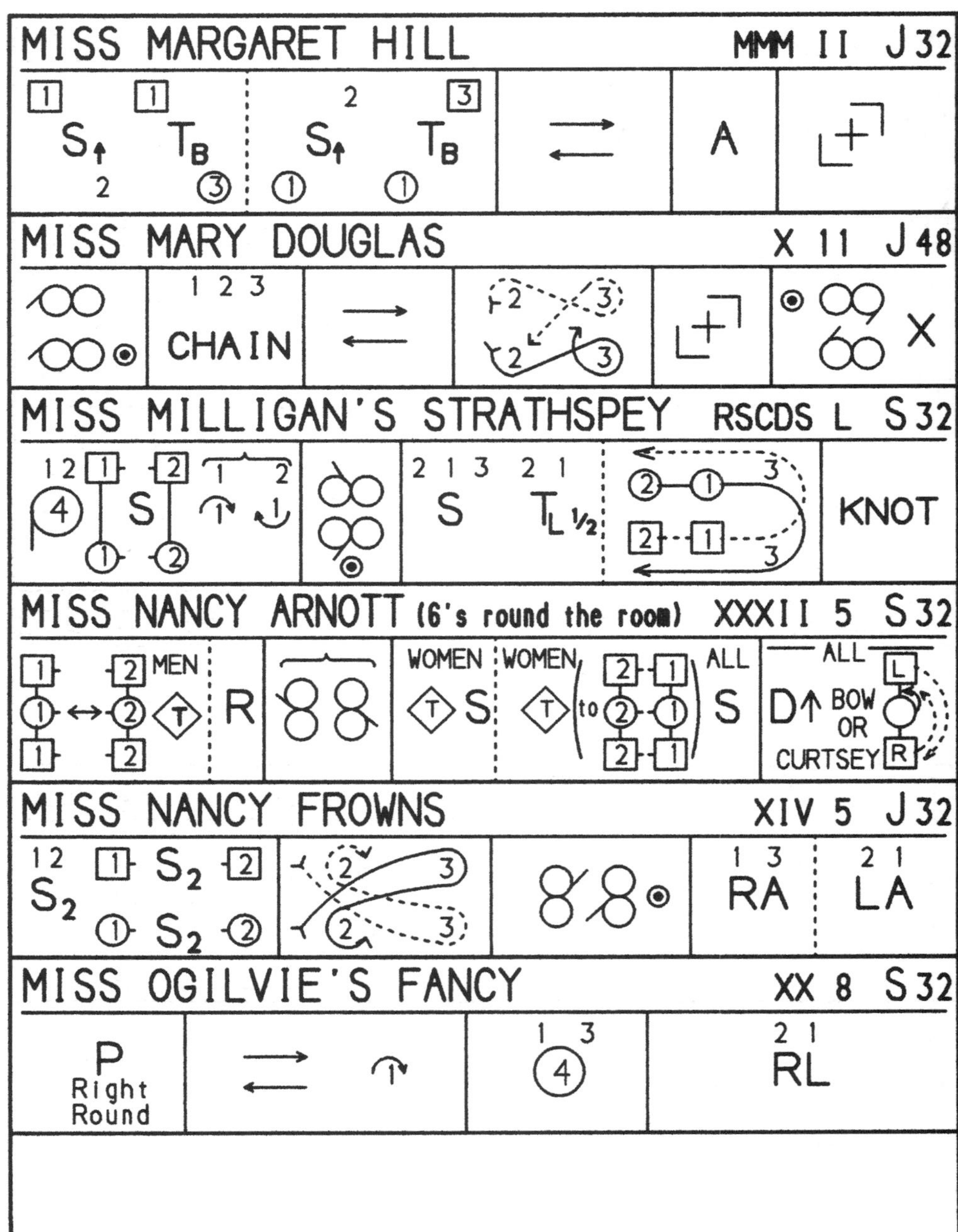

MISS MARGARET HILL
MMM II J32
MISS MARY DOUGLAS
X 11 J48
CHAIN
MISS MILLIGAN'S STRATHSPEY
RSCDS L S32
KNOT
MISS NANCY ARNOTT (6's round the room)
XXXII 5 S32
MEN
WOMEN
ALL
BOW OR CURTSEY
MISS NANCY FROWNS
XIV 5 J32
RA
LA
MISS OGILVIE'S FANCY
XX 8 S32
P Right Round
RL

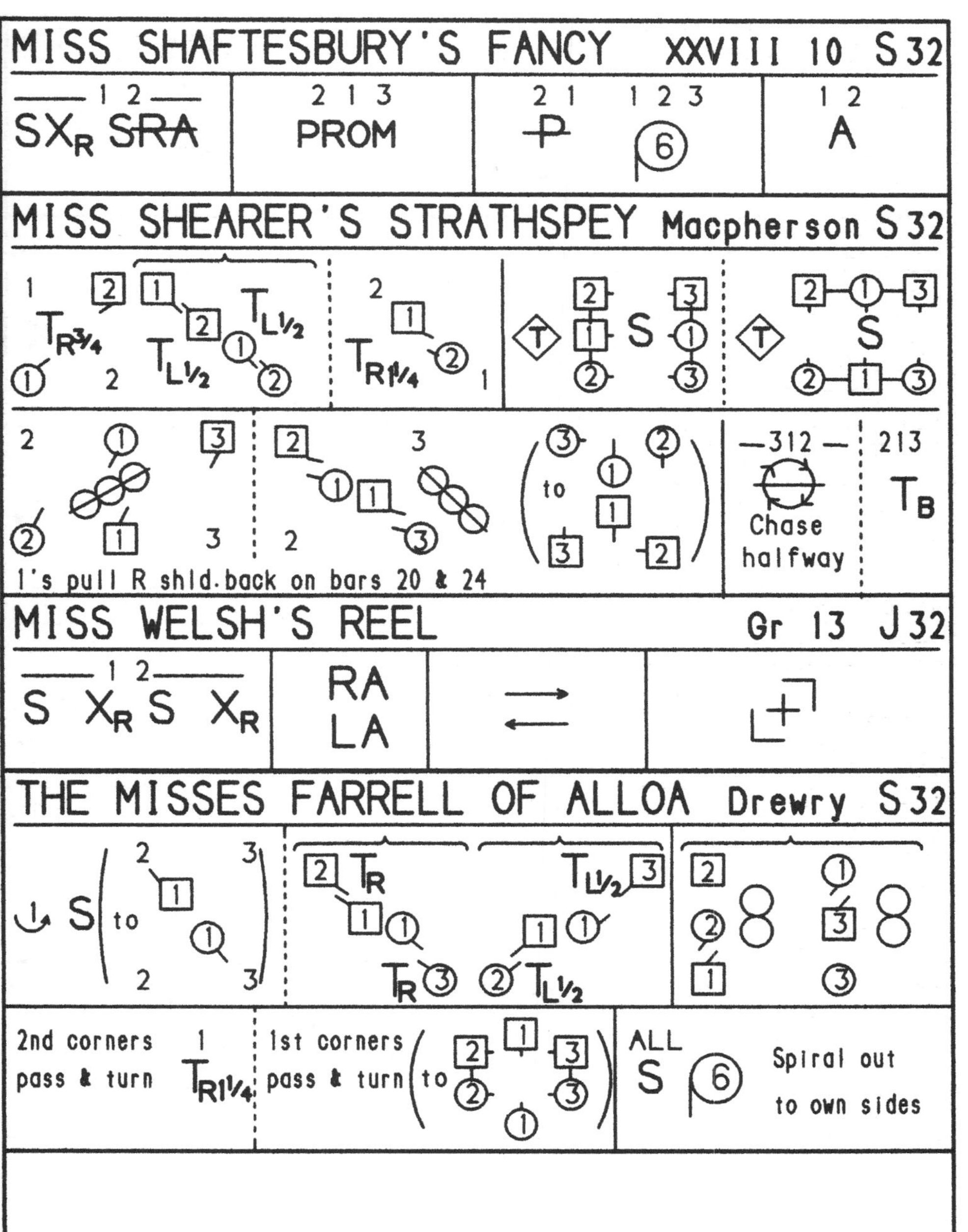
MISS SHAFTESBURY'S FANCY XXVIII 10 S32
1 2
SXR SRA
2 1 3
PROM
2 1
P
1 2 3
6
1 2
A
MISS SHEARER'S STRATHSPEY Macpherson S32
TR¾
TL½
TL½
TR1¼
T
S
T
S
1's pull R shld. back on bars 20 & 24
to
312
Chase halfway
213
TB
MISS WELSH'S REEL Gr 13 J32
1 2
S XR S XR
RA
LA
THE MISSES FARRELL OF ALLOA Drewry S32
S
to
TR
TL½
TR
TL½
2nd corners pass & turn
1
TR1¼
1st corners pass & turn
to
ALL
S
6
Spiral out to own sides

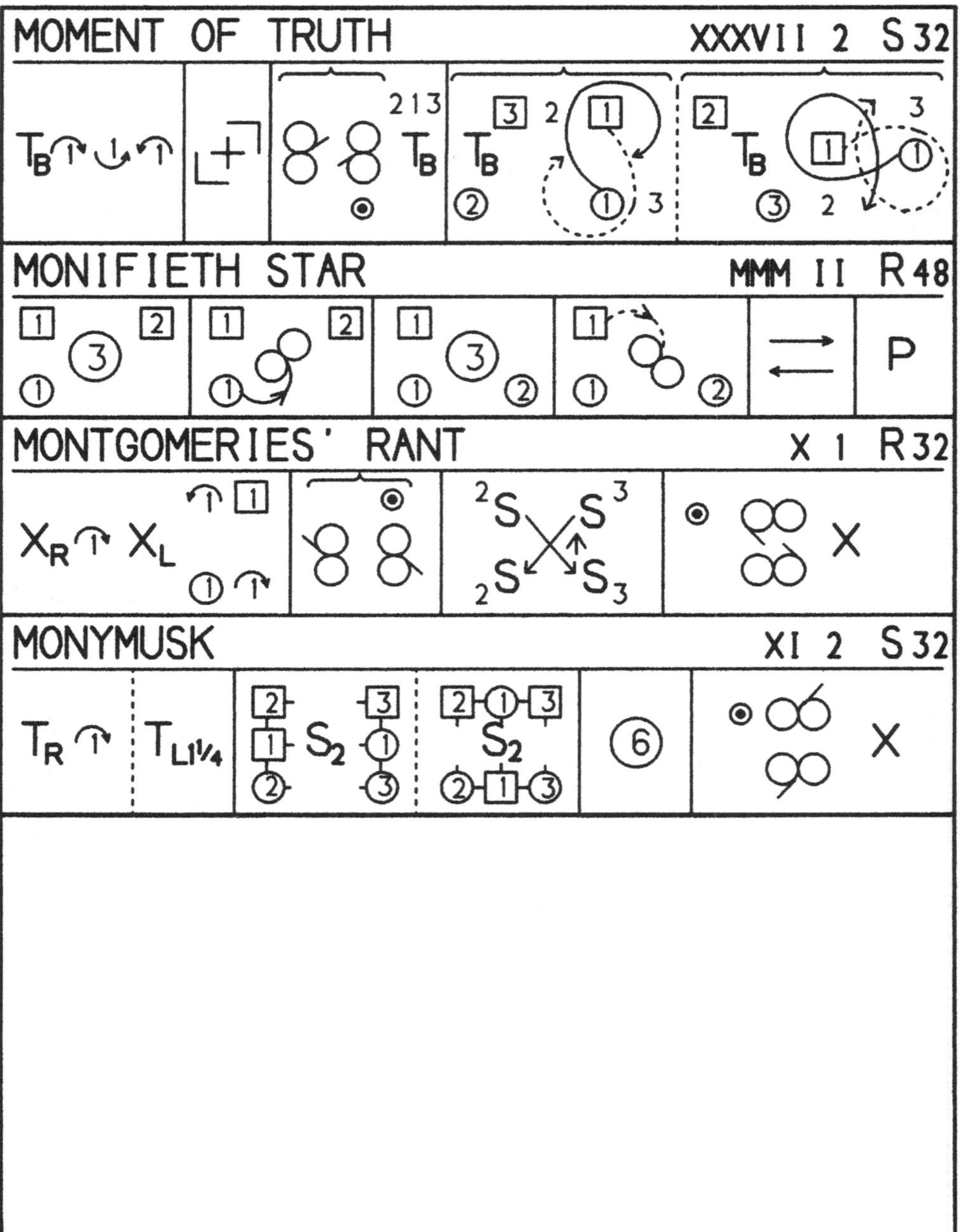

MOMENT OF TRUTH
XXXVII 2 S 32
MONIFIETH STAR
MMM II R 48
MONTGOMERIES' RANT
X 1 R 32
MONYMUSK
XI 2 S 32

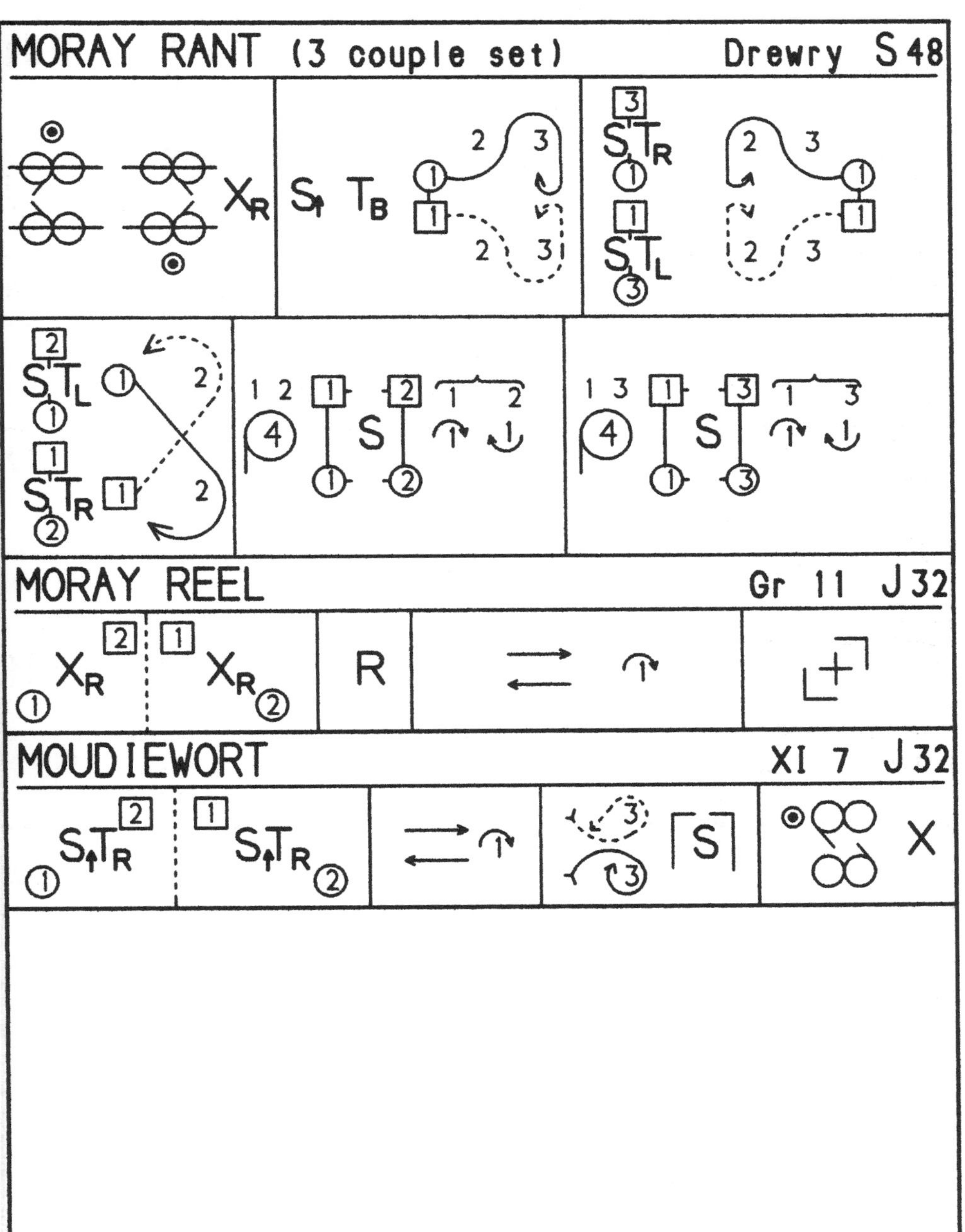
MORAY RANT (3 couple set)
Drewry S 48
MORAY REEL
Gr 11 J 32
MOUDIEWORT
XI 7 J 32

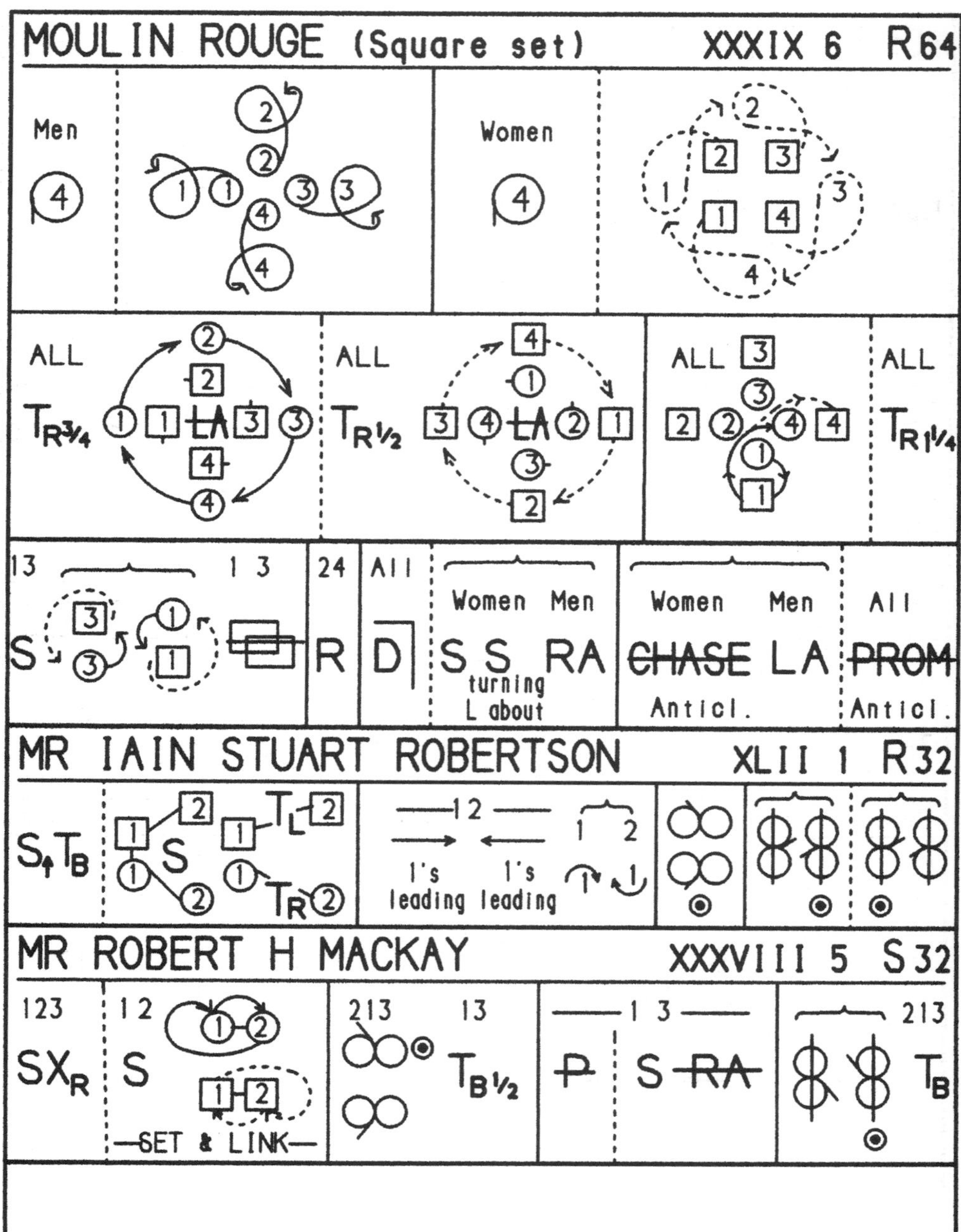
MOULIN ROUGE (Square set)
XXXIX 6 R64
Men
Women
ALL
ALL
ALL
ALL
LA
LA
13
1 3
24
All
Women Men
S S RA
turning
L about
Women Men
CHASE LA
Anticl.
All
PROM
Anticl.
MR IAIN STUART ROBERTSON
XLII 1 R32
S
1's leading
1's leading
MR ROBERT H MACKAY
XXXVIII 5 S32
123
SX
12
S
SET & LINK
213
13
1 3
S RA
213

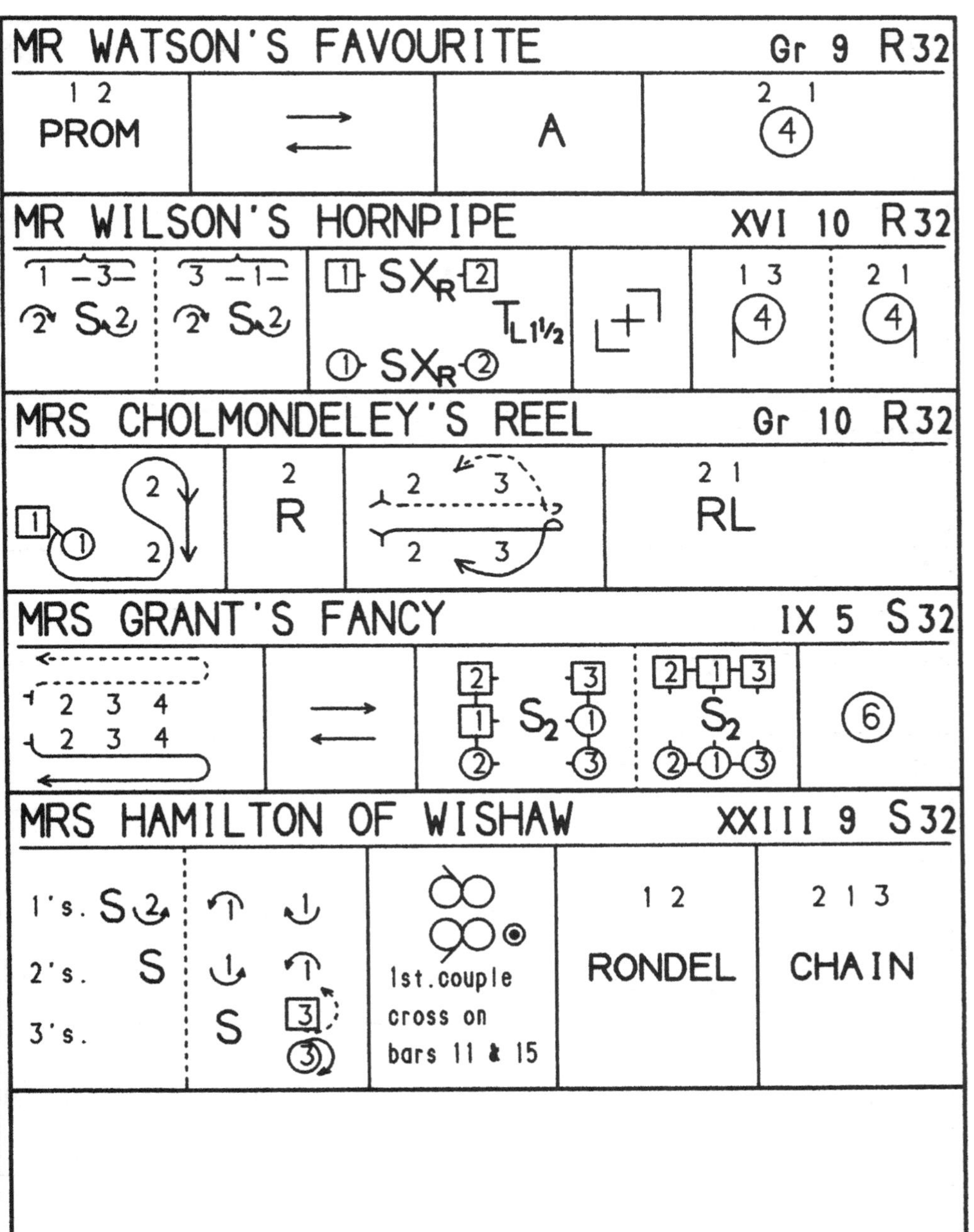
MR WATSON'S FAVOURITE Gr 9 R32
1 2
PROM
A
2 1
4
MR WILSON'S HORNPIPE XVI 10 R32
1 3
2 1
MRS CHOLMONDELEY'S REEL Gr 10 R32
2
R
2 1
RL
MRS GRANT'S FANCY IX 5 S32
2 3 4
2 3 4
6
MRS HAMILTON OF WISHAW XXIII 9 S32
1's.
2's.
3's.
1st.couple
cross on
bars 11 & 15
1 2
RONDEL
2 1 3
CHAIN

MRS HEPBURN BELCHES — R48

— 1 2 3 — S_2 X	— 1 2 3 — S_2 X	1 2 (reel of three)	1 3 (reel of three)	1 3 RA LA	2 1 RL

MRS MACLEOD — VI 11 R32

RA LA	⟶ ⟵	ST	 ⊙ X

MRS MACPHERSON OF INVERAN — Drewry R32

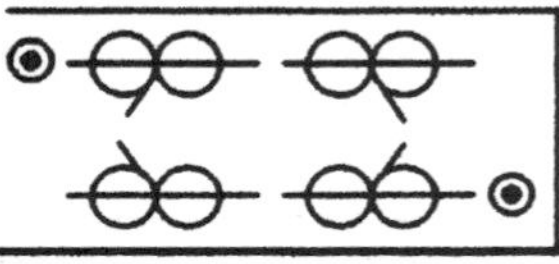 ⊙ ⊙	$T_{R1½}$ 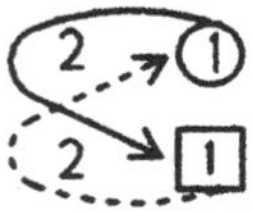	2 → 1, 2 → 1	CHAIN	6

MRS MILNE OF KINNEFF (Square) — RSCDS L32 2 S32

1 3 ↑ ; 2 2 ; 1 T_R 3 ; 1 T_R 3 ; 4 4	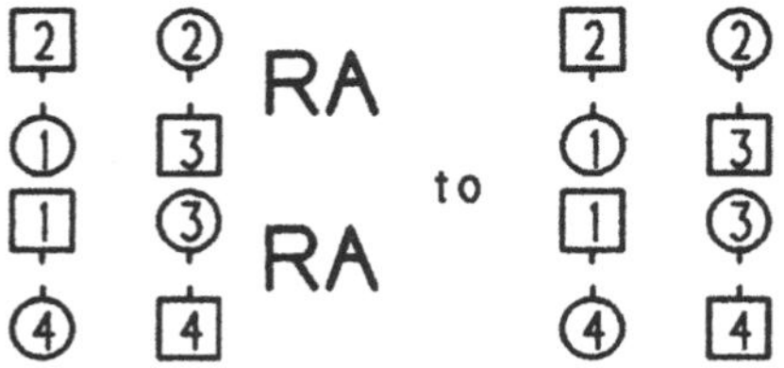 2 2 / 1 3 / 1 3 / 4 4 RA RA to 2 2 / 1 3 / 1 3 / 4 4	(reels of three)

ALL S ; 2 1 3 ; 1 4 3 4 ; ALL T_B	8	ALL $T_{R¾}$ ALL PROM (1 place clock.)

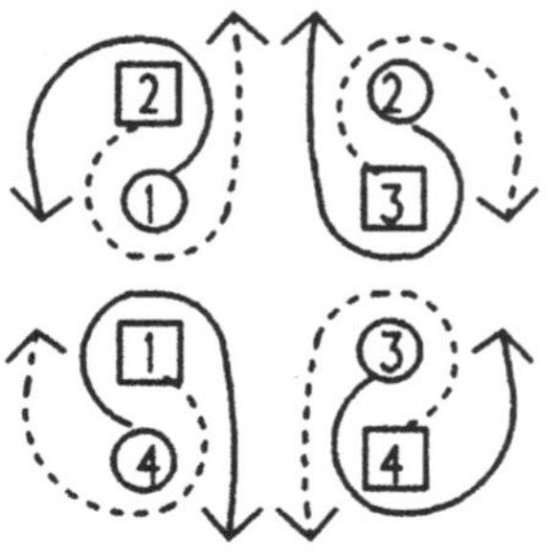

Repeat from new positions

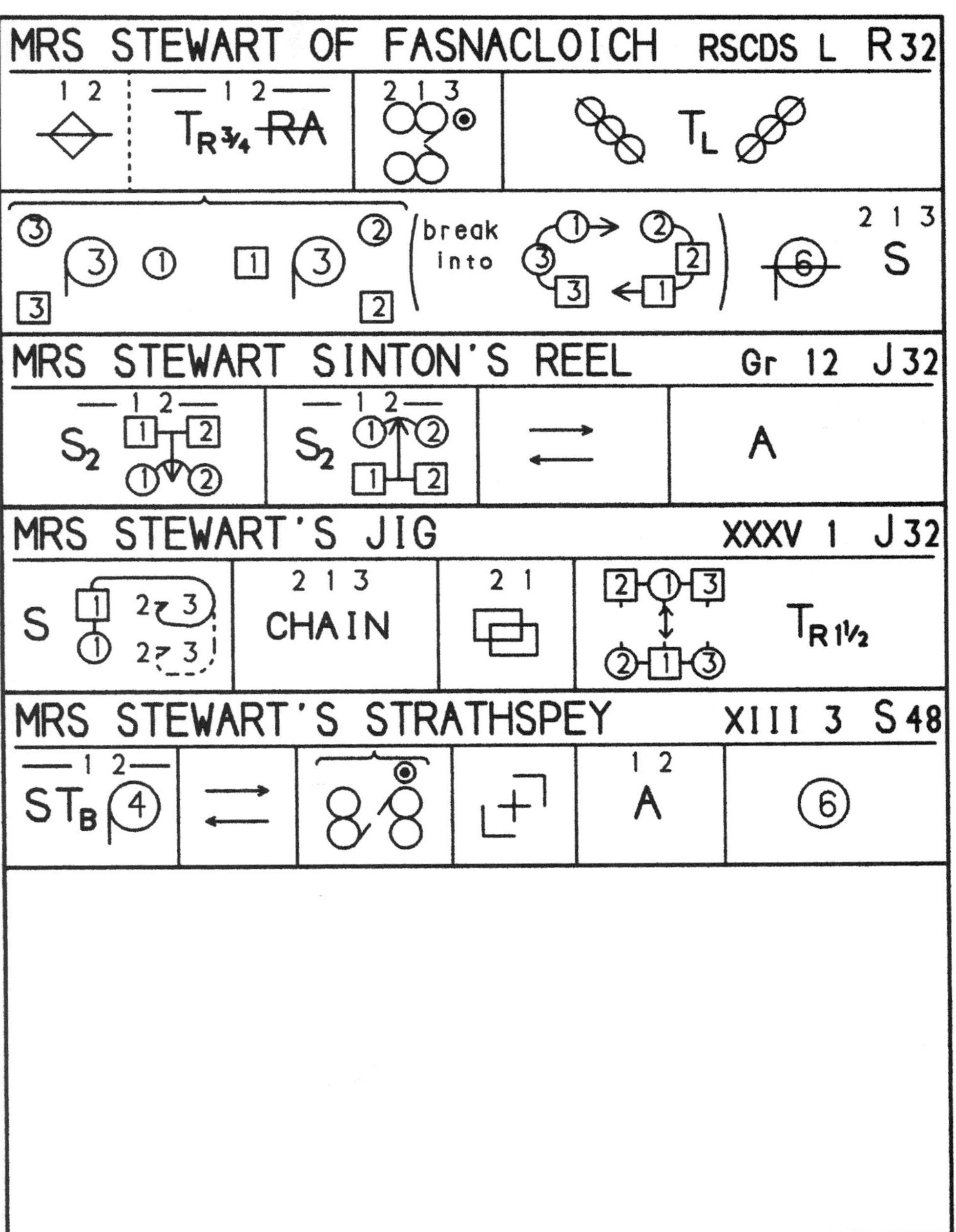
MRS STEWART OF FASNACLOICH RSCDS L R32
break into
MRS STEWART SINTON'S REEL Gr 12 J32
MRS STEWART'S JIG XXXV 1 J32
CHAIN
MRS STEWART'S STRATHSPEY XIII 3 S48

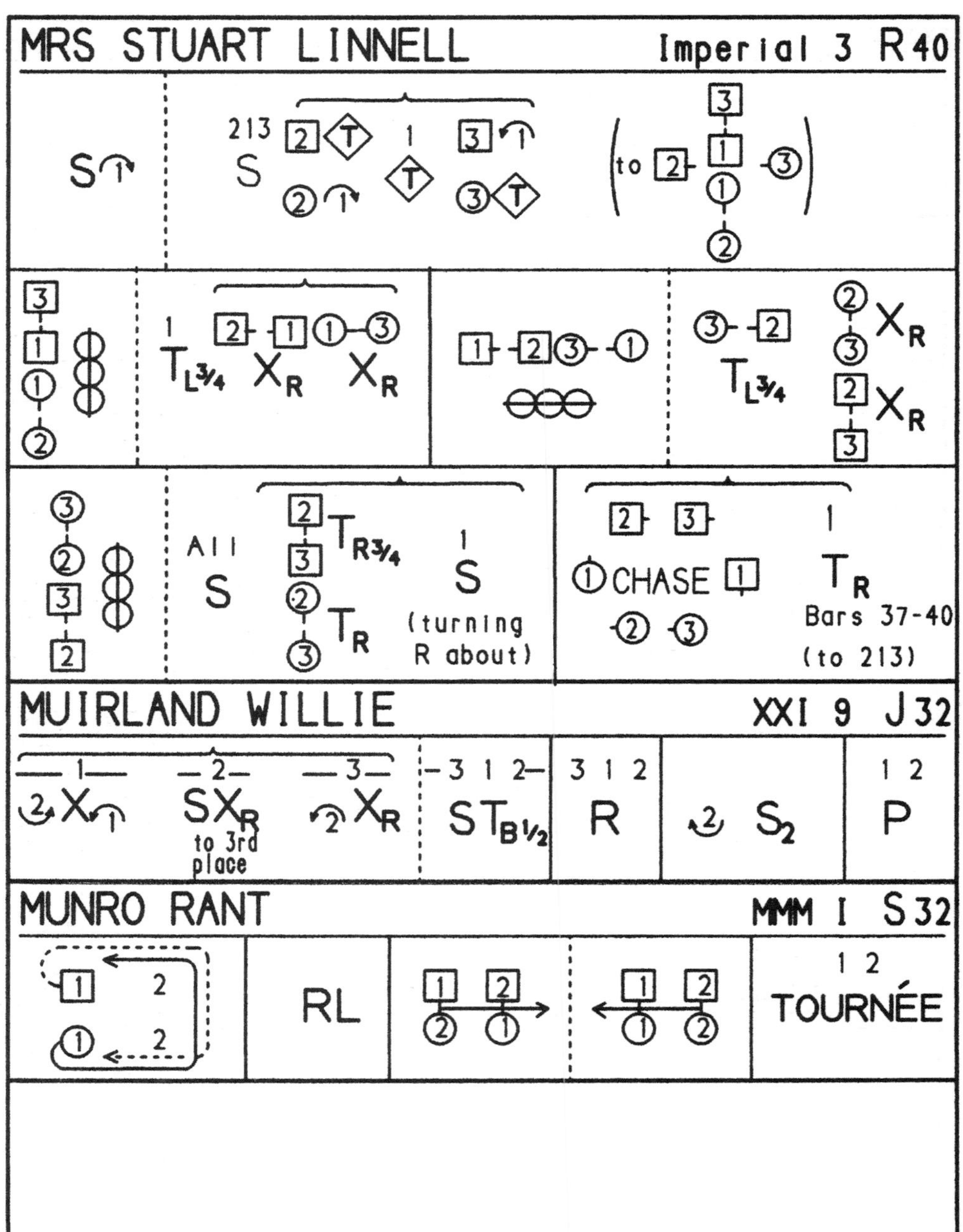
MRS STUART LINNELL
Imperial 3 R40
213
S
1
to
1
All
S
1
S
(turning
R about)
CHASE
1
Bars 37-40
(to 213)
MUIRLAND WILLIE
XXI 9 J32
1
2
3
SX
to 3rd
place
3 1 2
3 1 2
R
1 2
P
MUNRO RANT
MMM I S32
2
2
RL
1 2
TOURNÉE

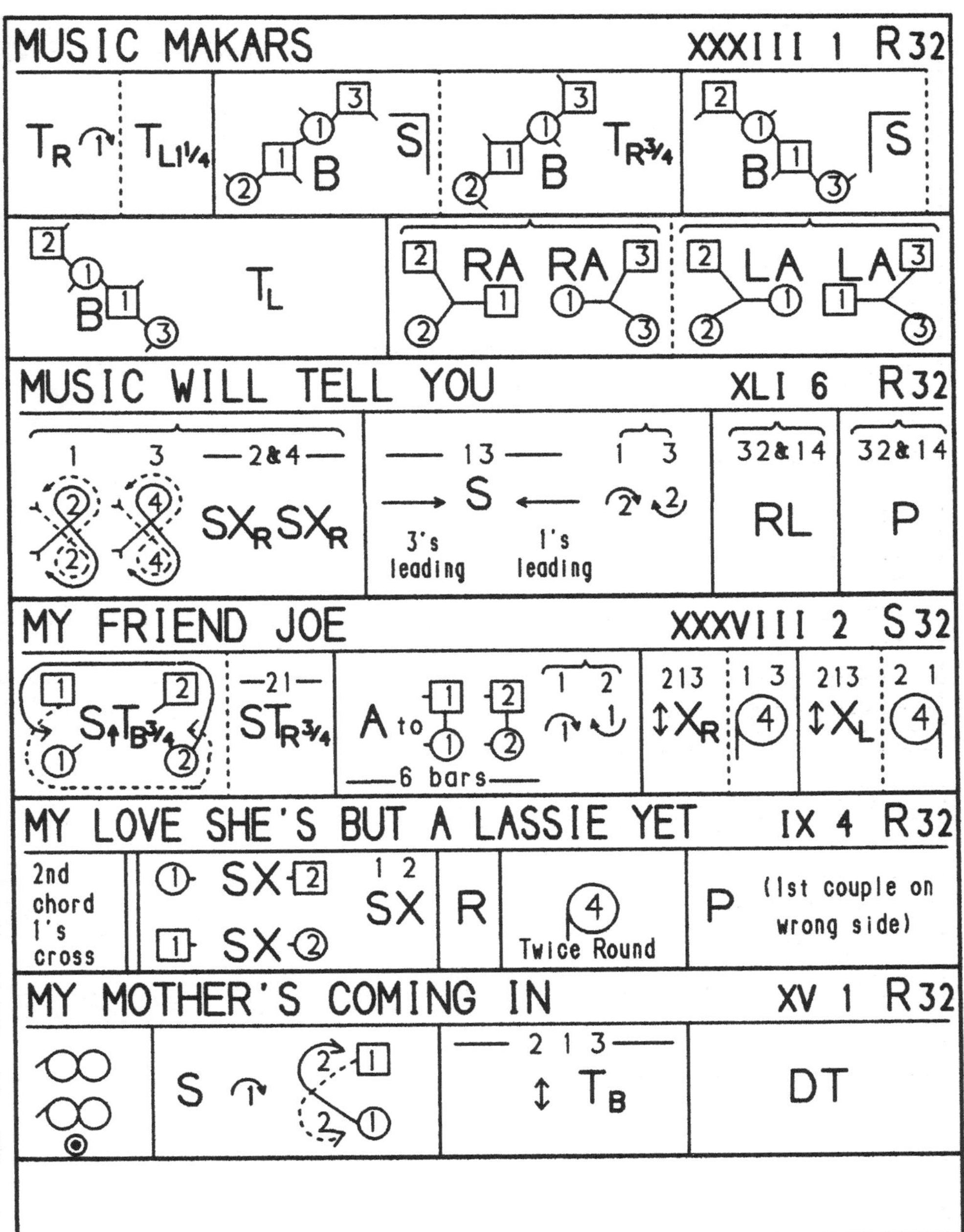
MUSIC MAKARS
XXXIII 1 R32
TR
TL1¼
B
S
B
TR¾
B
S
B
TL
RA RA
LA LA
MUSIC WILL TELL YOU
XLI 6 R32
1 3 —2&4—
SXR SXR
—13—
S
3's leading
1's leading
1 3
32&14
RL
32&14
P
MY FRIEND JOE
XXXVIII 2 S32
S↑TB¾
—21—
STR¾
A to
—6 bars—
1 2
213
↕XR
1 3
213
↕XL
2 1
MY LOVE SHE'S BUT A LASSIE YET
IX 4 R32
2nd chord 1's cross
SX
SX
1 2
SX
R
Twice Round
P
(1st couple on wrong side)
MY MOTHER'S COMING IN
XV 1 R32
S
—2 1 3—
↕ TB
DT

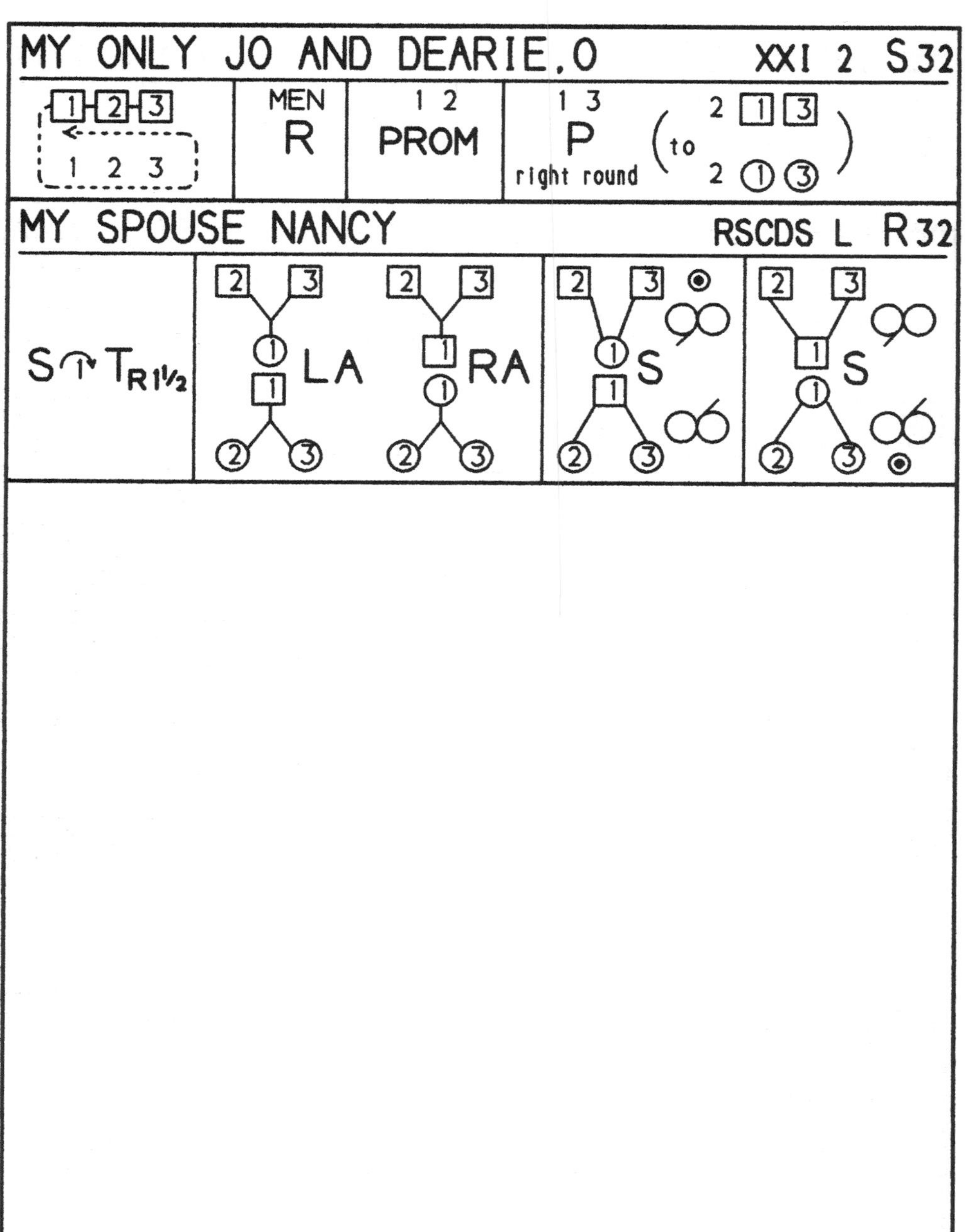
MY ONLY JO AND DEARIE, O
XXI 2 S32
1 2 3
1 2 3
MEN
R
1 2
PROM
1 3
P
right round
to
2 1 3
2 1 3
MY SPOUSE NANCY
RSCDS L R32
S T R 1½
2 3
1
1
2 3
LA
RA
S
S

NEIDPATH CASTLE (3 couple set) XXII 9 S32

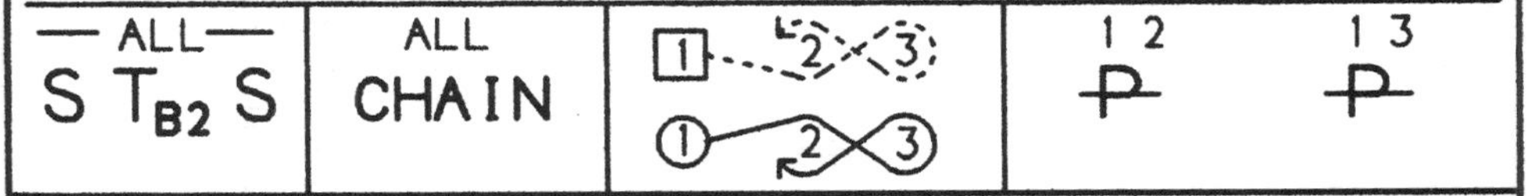

— ALL — S T B2 S	ALL CHAIN	1 2 3	1 2 P 1 3 P

NETHER BOW HAS VANISHED XIII 7 S48

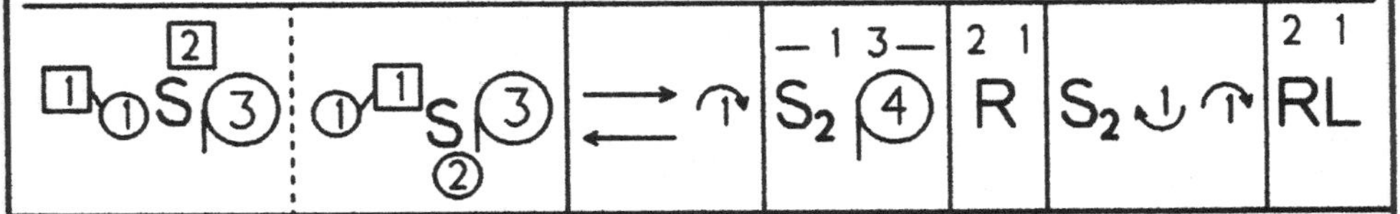

2 1 1 S 3	1 1 S 2 3	⇄	— 1 3 — S2 4	2 1 R	S2	2 1 RL

NEW ASHLUDIE RANT J32

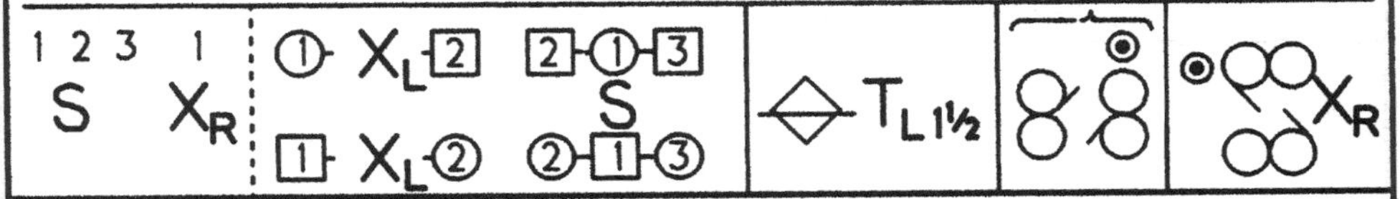

1 2 3 S 1 XR	1 XL 2 1 XL 2 2 1 3 S 2 1 3	T L 1½		XR

NEW HIGHLAND LADDIE MMM II R32

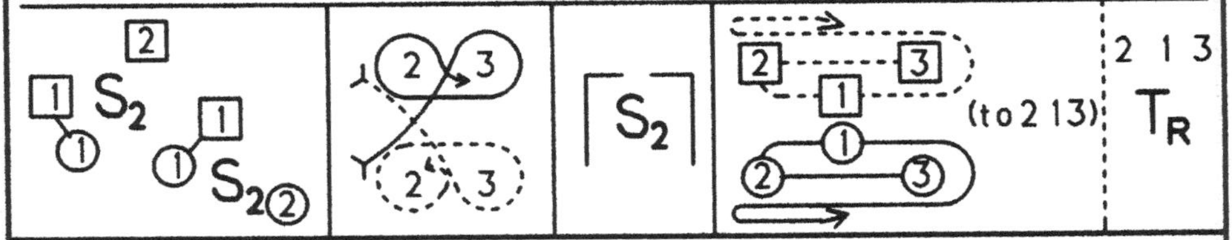

2 1 S2 1 1 1 S2 2	2 3 2 3	S2	2 3 1 1 2 3 (to 2 1 3)	2 1 3 TR

NEW PARK XIX 11 S32

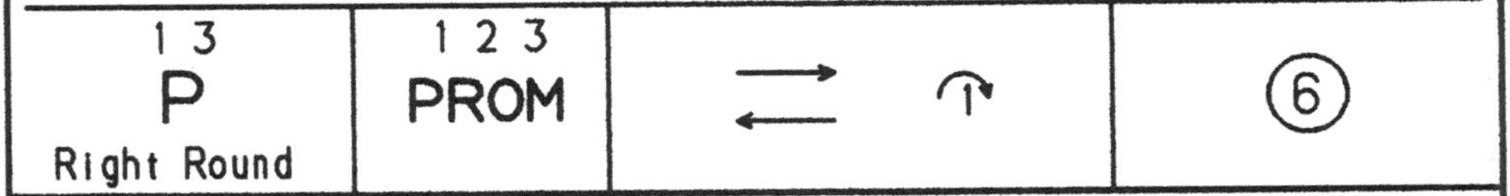

1 3 P Right Round	1 2 3 PROM	⇄	6

NEW RIGGED SHIP IX 7 J48

4		⇄	XR XL 2 — 12 bars —	S	X

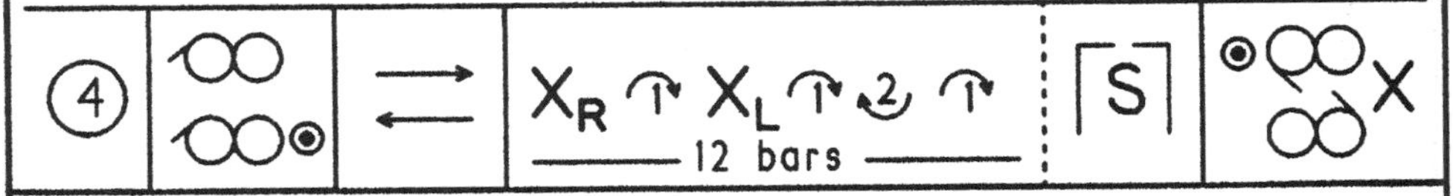

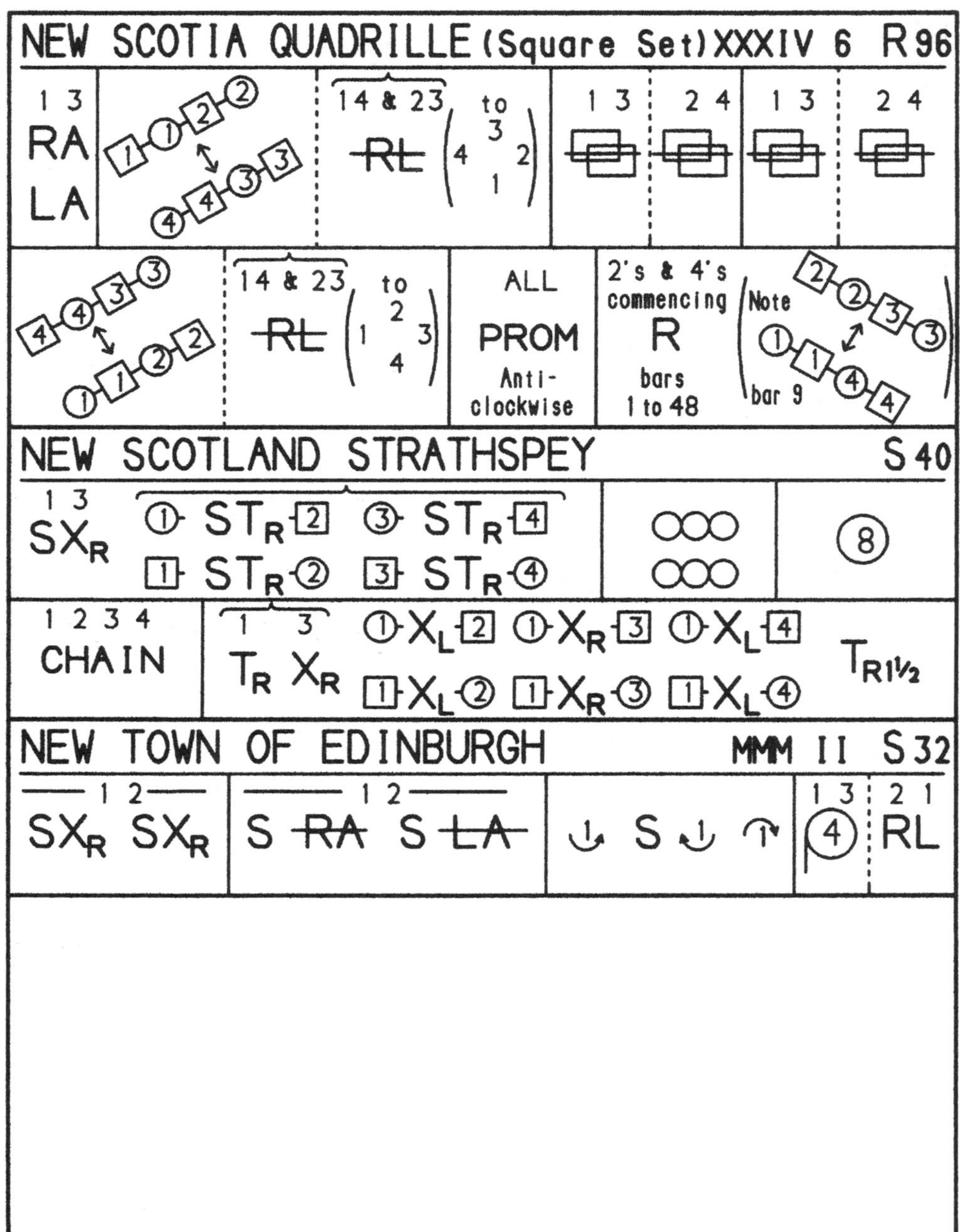

NEW SCOTIA QUADRILLE (Square Set) XXXIV 6 R96
1 3
RA
LA
14 & 23
RL
to
3
4 2
1
1 3
2 4
1 3
2 4
14 & 23
RL
to
2
1 3
4
ALL
PROM
Anti-clockwise
2's & 4's commencing
R
bars 1 to 48
Note
bar 9
NEW SCOTLAND STRATHSPEY S40
1 3
SXR
ST R
ST R
ST R
ST R
8
1 2 3 4
CHAIN
1 3
TR XR
XL XR XL
XL XR XL
TR1½
NEW TOWN OF EDINBURGH MMM II S32
1 2
SXR SXR
1 2
S RA S LA
S
1 3
4
2 1
RL

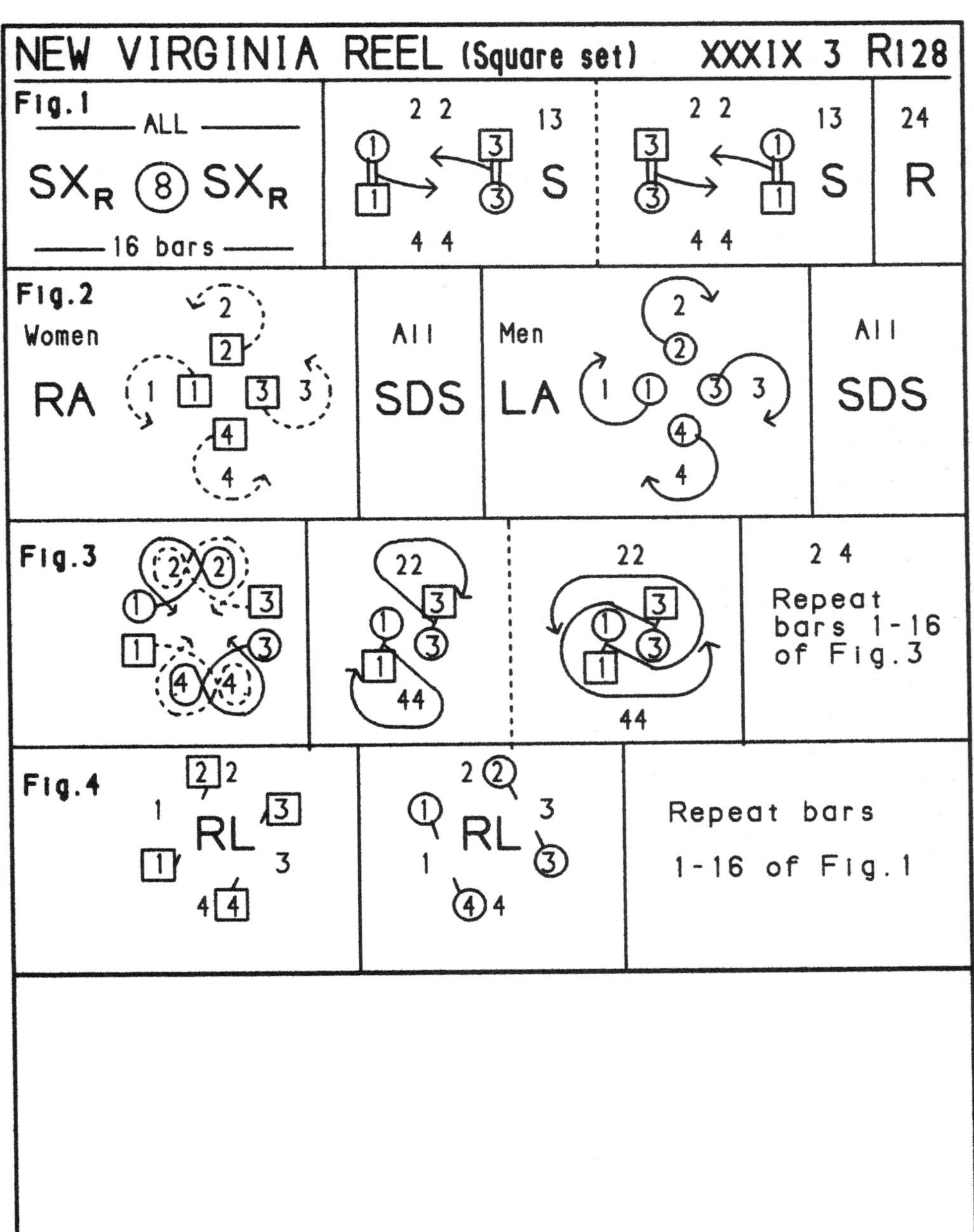
NEW VIRGINIA REEL (Square set) XXXIX 3 R128
Fig.1
ALL
SXR 8 SXR
16 bars
2 2
13
S
4 4
2 2
13
S
4 4
24
R
Fig.2
Women
RA
All
SDS
Men
LA
All
SDS
Fig.3
22
44
22
44
2 4
Repeat bars 1-16 of Fig.3
Fig.4
RL
RL
Repeat bars
1-16 of Fig.1

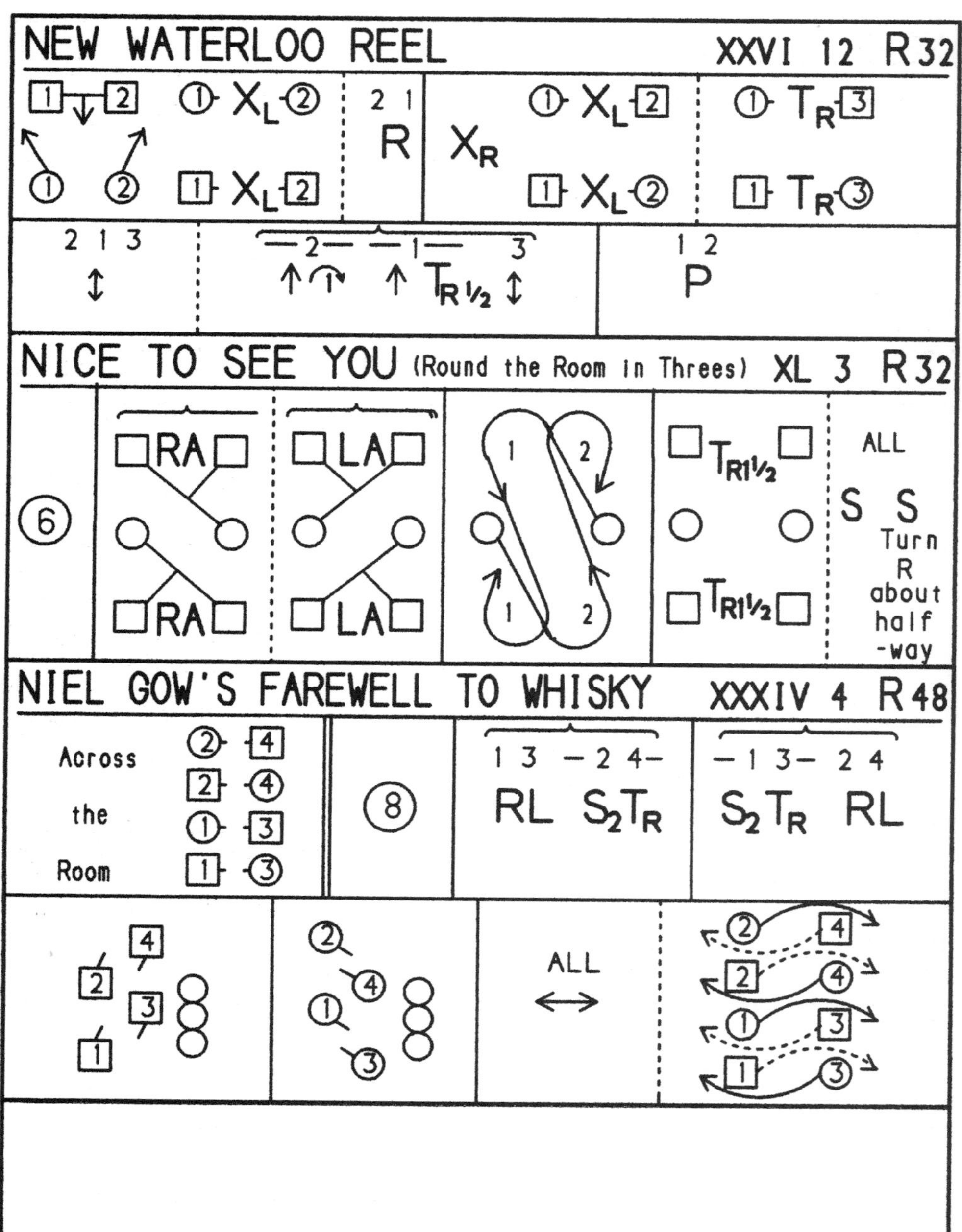

NEW WATERLOO REEL
XXVI 12 R32
1 X L 2
2 1
R
X R
1 X L 2
1 T R 3
1 X L 2
1 X L 2
1 T R 3
2 1 3
2 1 3
T R ½
1 2
P
NICE TO SEE YOU (Round the Room in Threes)
XL 3 R32
6
RA
RA
LA
LA
1 2
1 2
T R1½
T R1½
ALL
S S
Turn
R
about
half
-way
NIEL GOW'S FAREWELL TO WHISKY
XXXIV 4 R48
Across
the
Room
2 4
2 4
1 3
1 3
8
1 3 2 4
RL S2TR
1 3 2 4
S2TR RL
ALL

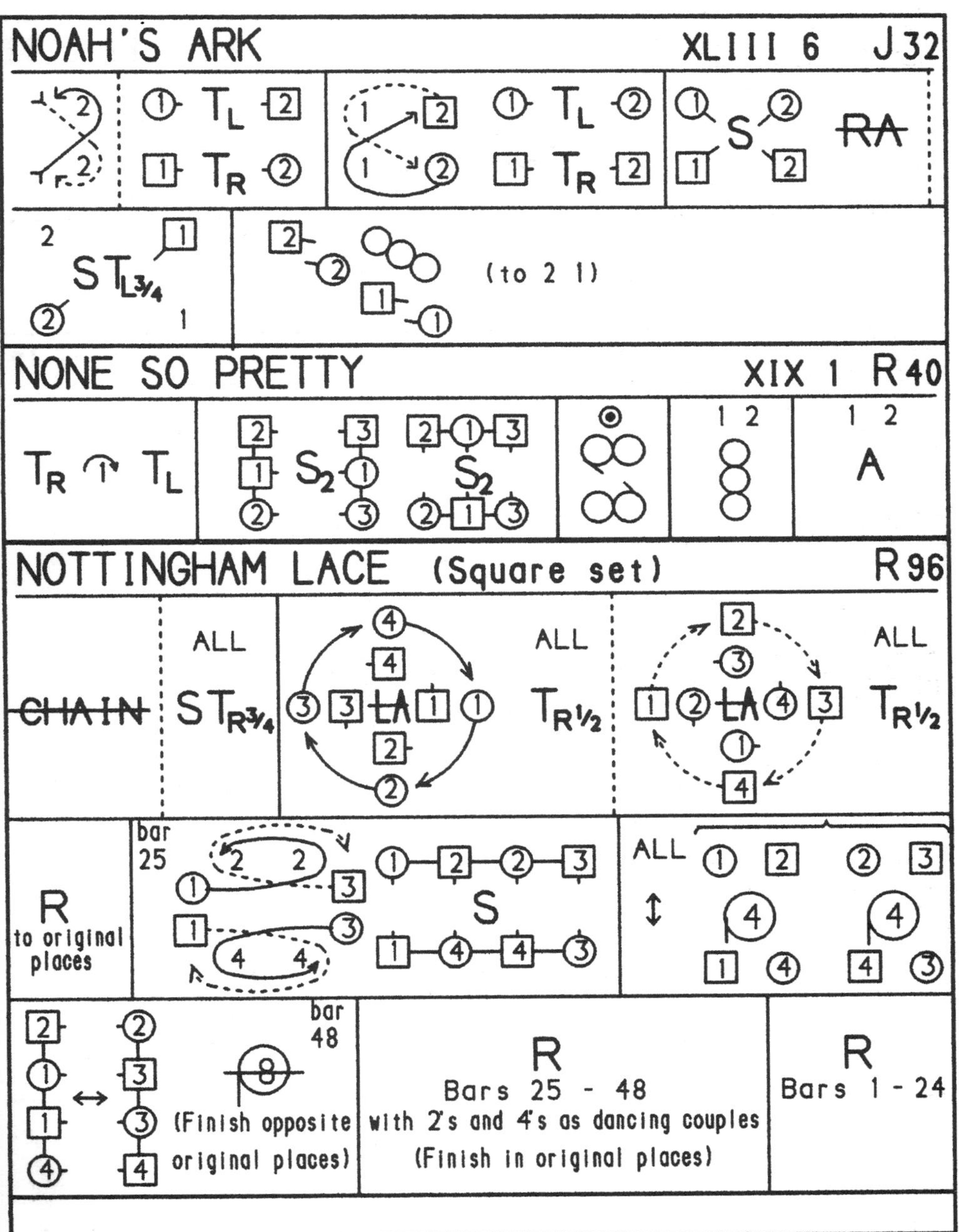
NOAH'S ARK
XLIII 6 J32
TL
TR
TL
TR
S
RA
2
STL3/4
1
(to 2 1)
NONE SO PRETTY
XIX 1 R40
TR TL
S2
S2
1 2
1 2
A
NOTTINGHAM LACE (Square set)
R96
CHAIN
ALL
STR3/4
LA
ALL
TR1/2
LA
ALL
TR1/2
R
to original places
bar 25
S
ALL
bar 48
(Finish opposite original places)
R
Bars 25 - 48
with 2's and 4's as dancing couples
(Finish in original places)
R
Bars 1 - 24

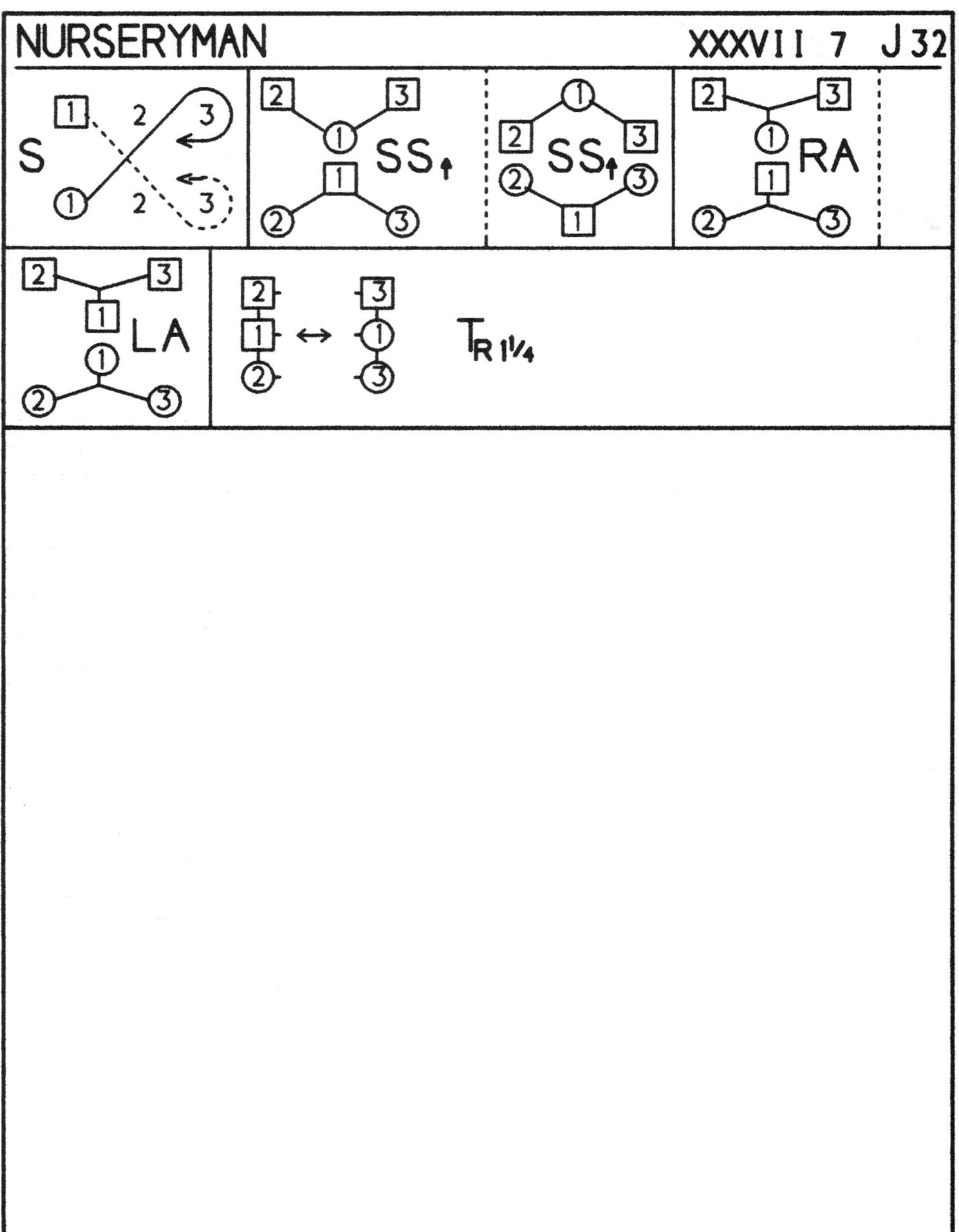
NURSERYMAN
XXXVII 7 J 32
S
SS
SS
RA
LA
$T_{R\ 1\frac{1}{4}}$

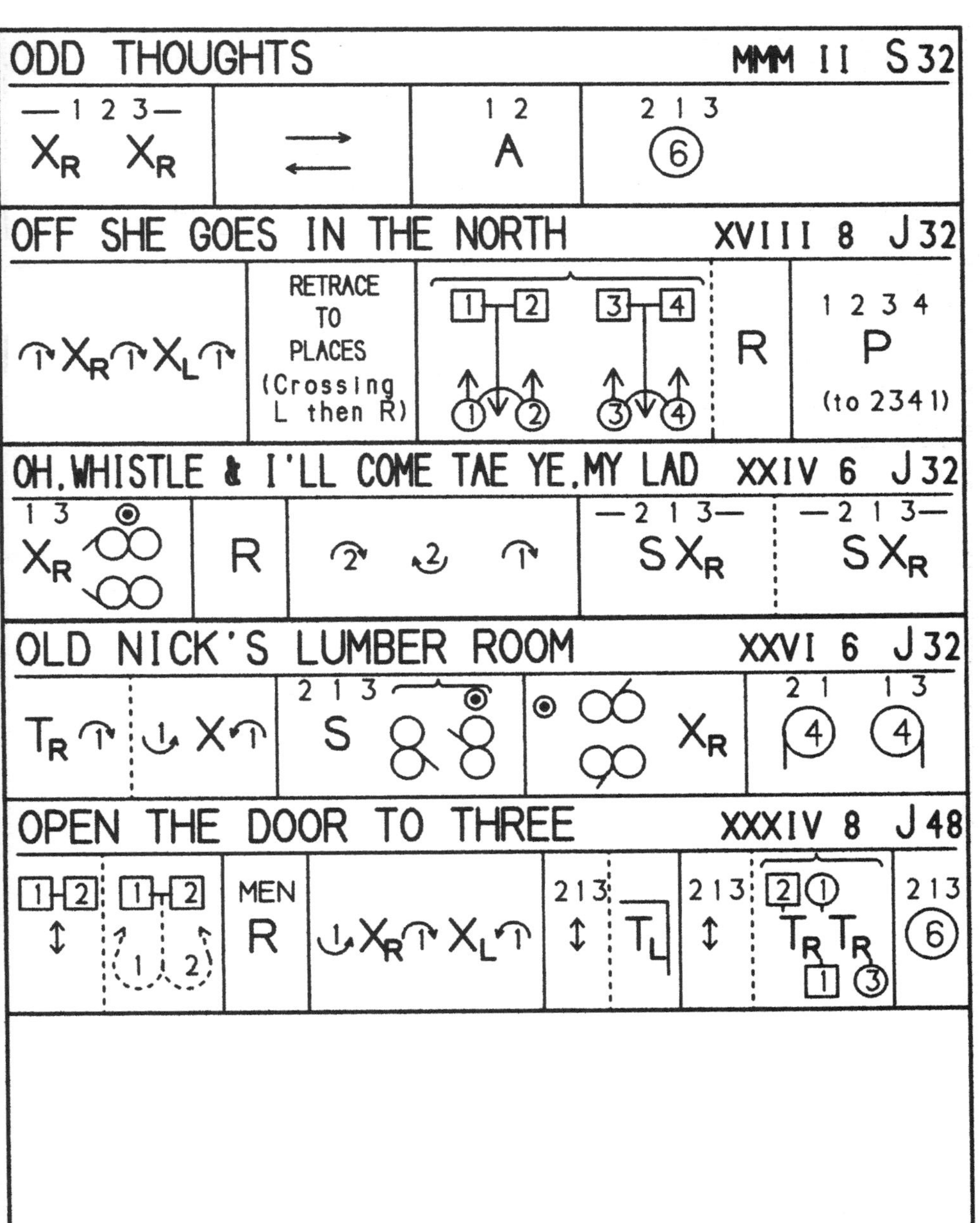
ODD THOUGHTS
MMM II S32
XR XR
A
OFF SHE GOES IN THE NORTH
XVIII 8 J32
RETRACE TO PLACES (Crossing L then R)
R
P
(to 2341)
OH, WHISTLE & I'LL COME TAE YE, MY LAD
XXIV 6 J32
XR
R
SXR
SXR
OLD NICK'S LUMBER ROOM
XXVI 6 J32
TR
X
S
XR
OPEN THE DOOR TO THREE
XXXIV 8 J48
MEN
R
XR XL
TL
TR TR

ORIEL STRATHSPEY — XXXII 2 S32

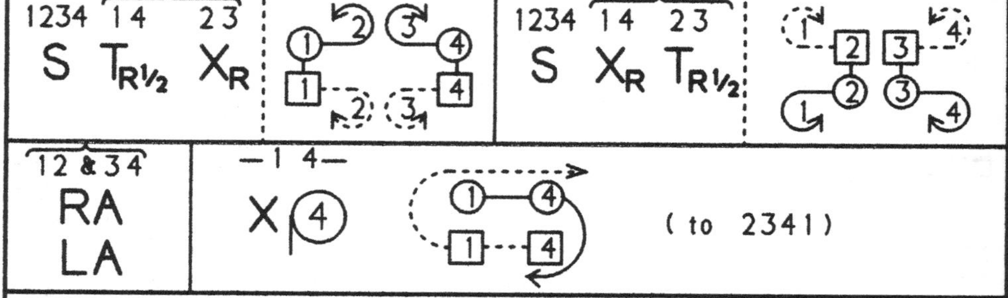

1234 14 23 S $T_{R1/2}$ X_R	1234 14 23 S X_R $T_{R1/2}$
12 & 34 RA LA	—1 4— X ④ (to 2341)

OVER THE WATER TO CHARLIE — XXXIV 5 J32

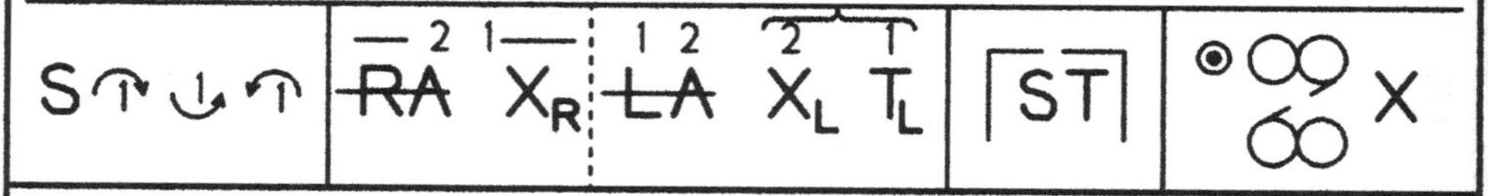

S	—2 1— RA X_R 1 2 LA	2 1 X_L T_L	ST	X

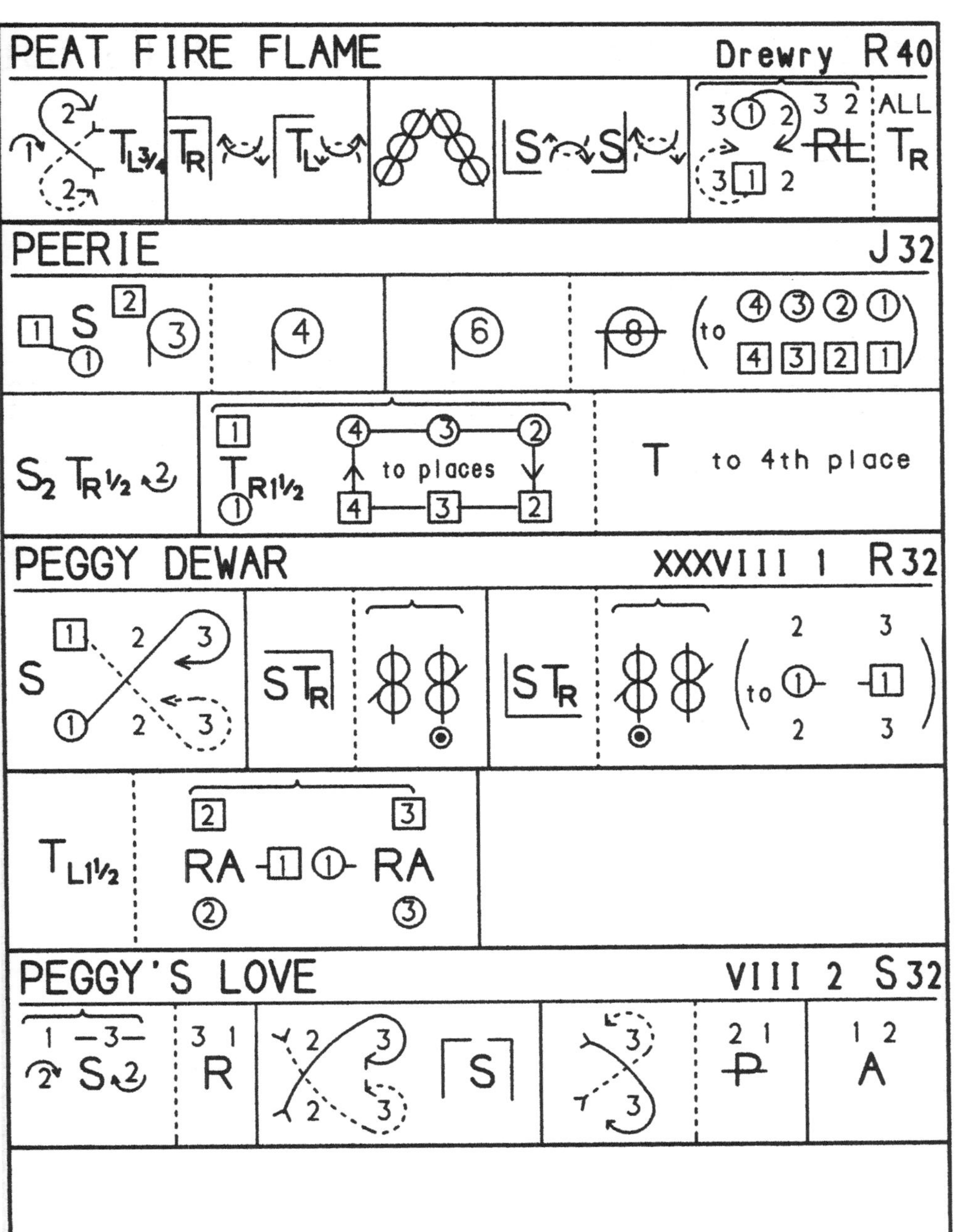
PEAT FIRE FLAME
Drewry R40
ALL
PEERIE
J32
to places
to 4th place
PEGGY DEWAR
XXXVIII 1 R32
PEGGY'S LOVE
VIII 2 S32

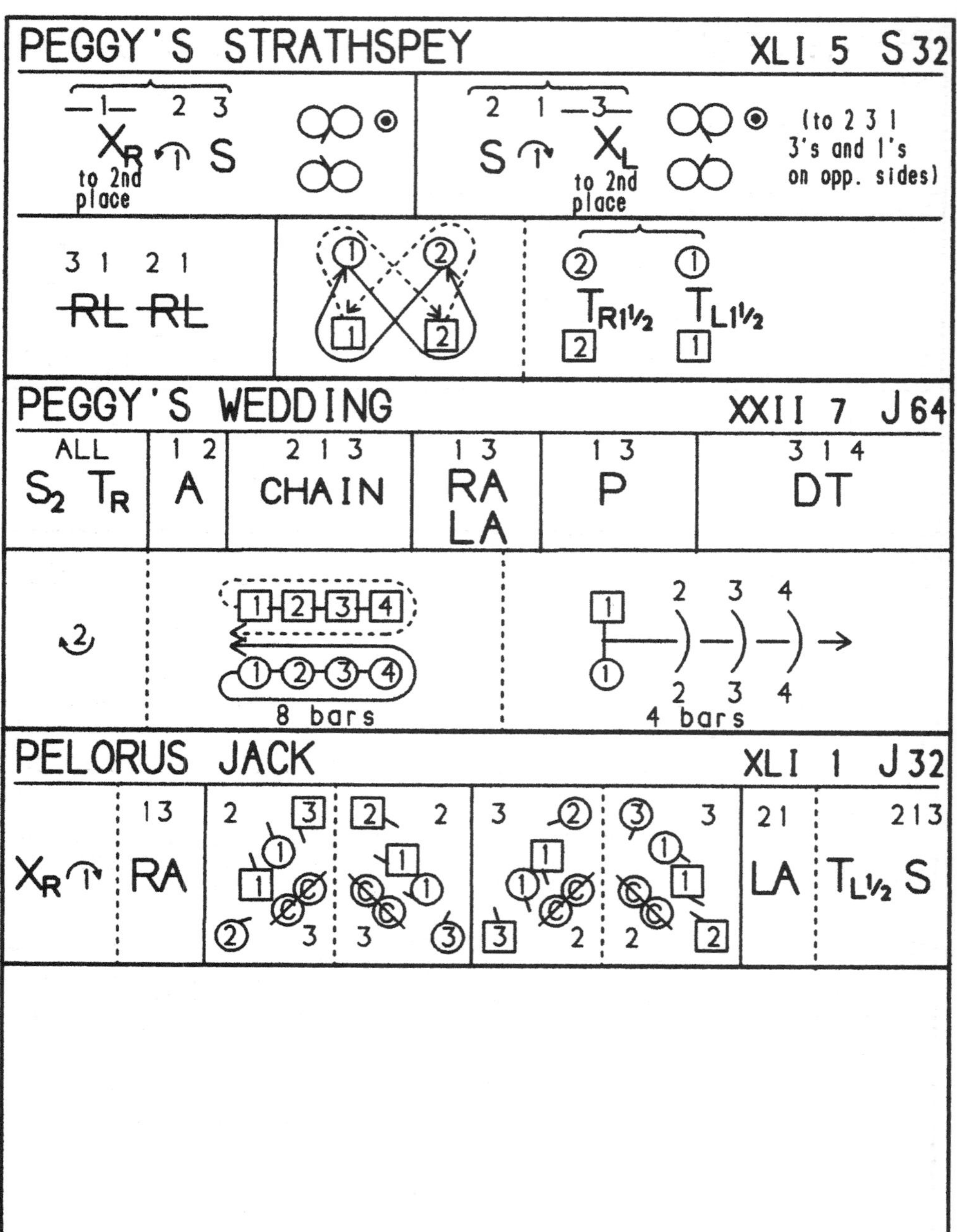
PEGGY'S STRATHSPEY
XLI 5 S32
1 2 3
XR 1 S
to 2nd place
2 1 3
S 1 XL
to 2nd place
(to 2 3 1 3's and 1's on opp. sides)
3 1 2 1
RL RL
1 2
1 2
2 1
TR1½ TL1½
2 1
PEGGY'S WEDDING
XXII 7 J64
ALL
S2 TR
1 2
A
2 1 3
CHAIN
1 3
RA
LA
1 3
P
3 1 4
DT
2
1 2 3 4
1 2 3 4
8 bars
1
2 3 4
1
2 3 4
4 bars
PELORUS JACK
XLI 1 J32
XR 1
13
RA
LA
21
213
TL½ S

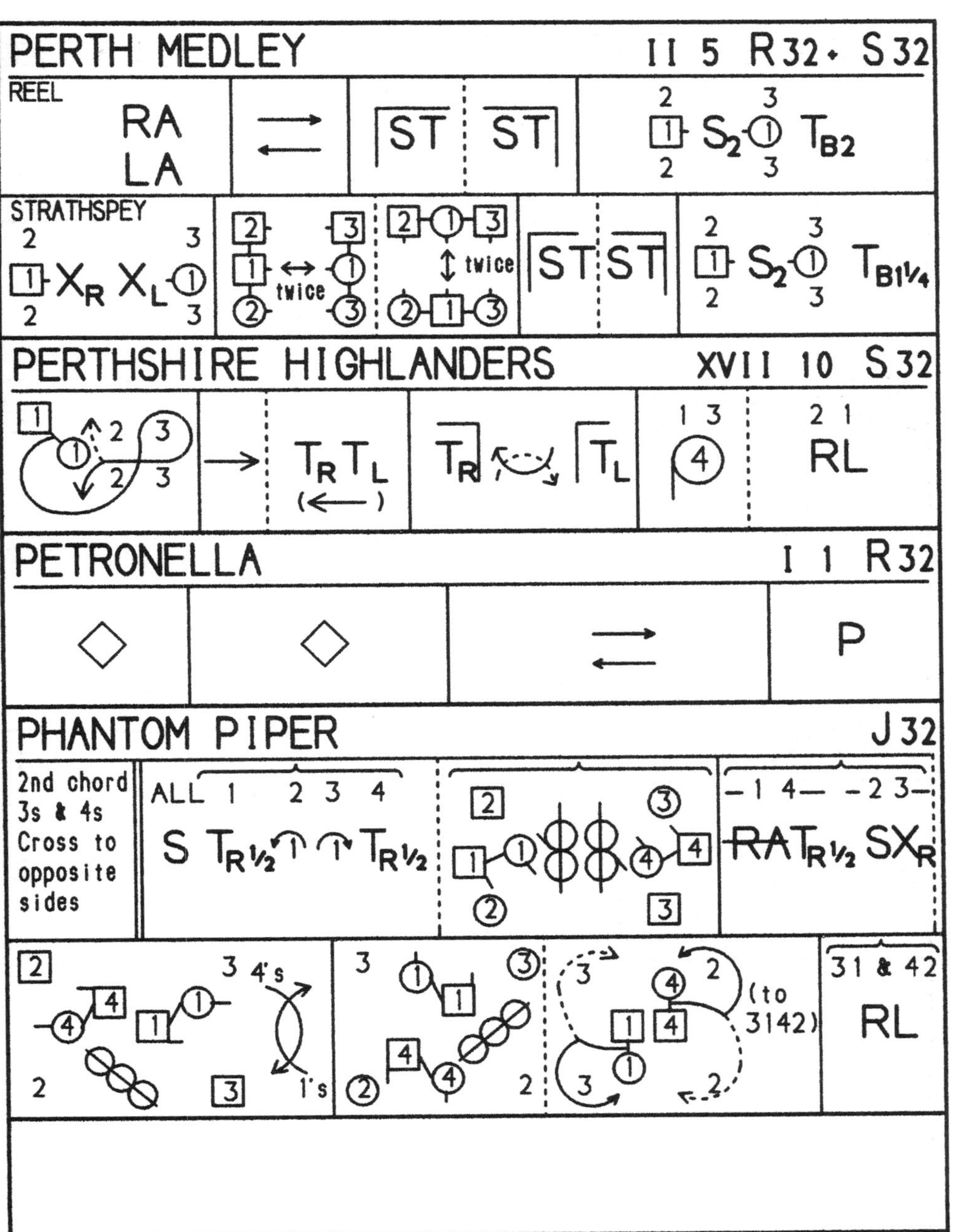
PERTH MEDLEY
II 5 R32 + S32
REEL
RA
LA
ST ST
STRATHSPEY
twice
ST ST
PERTHSHIRE HIGHLANDERS
XVII 10 S32
RL
PETRONELLA
I 1 R32
P
PHANTOM PIPER
J32
2nd chord 3s & 4s Cross to opposite sides
ALL 1 2 3 4
S
-1 4- -2 3-
RAT
SX
4's
1's
(to 3142)
31 & 42
RL

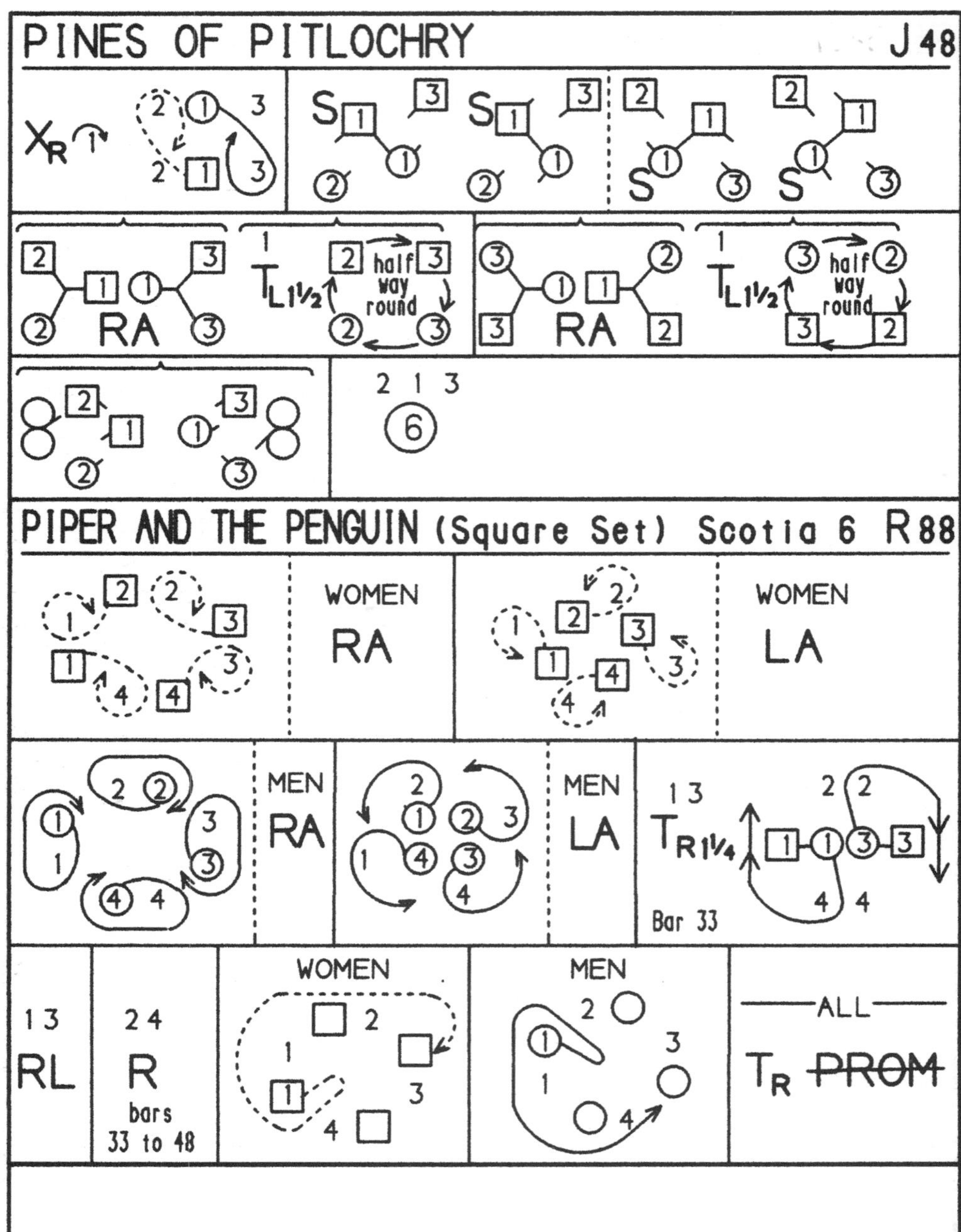

PINES OF PITLOCHRY J48
XR
S
S
S
S
RA
TL1½
half way round
RA
TL1½
half way round
2 1 3
6
PIPER AND THE PENGUIN (Square Set) Scotia 6 R88
WOMEN
RA
WOMEN
LA
MEN
RA
MEN
LA
TR1¼
Bar 33
1 3
RL
2 4
R
bars 33 to 48
WOMEN
MEN
ALL
TR PROM

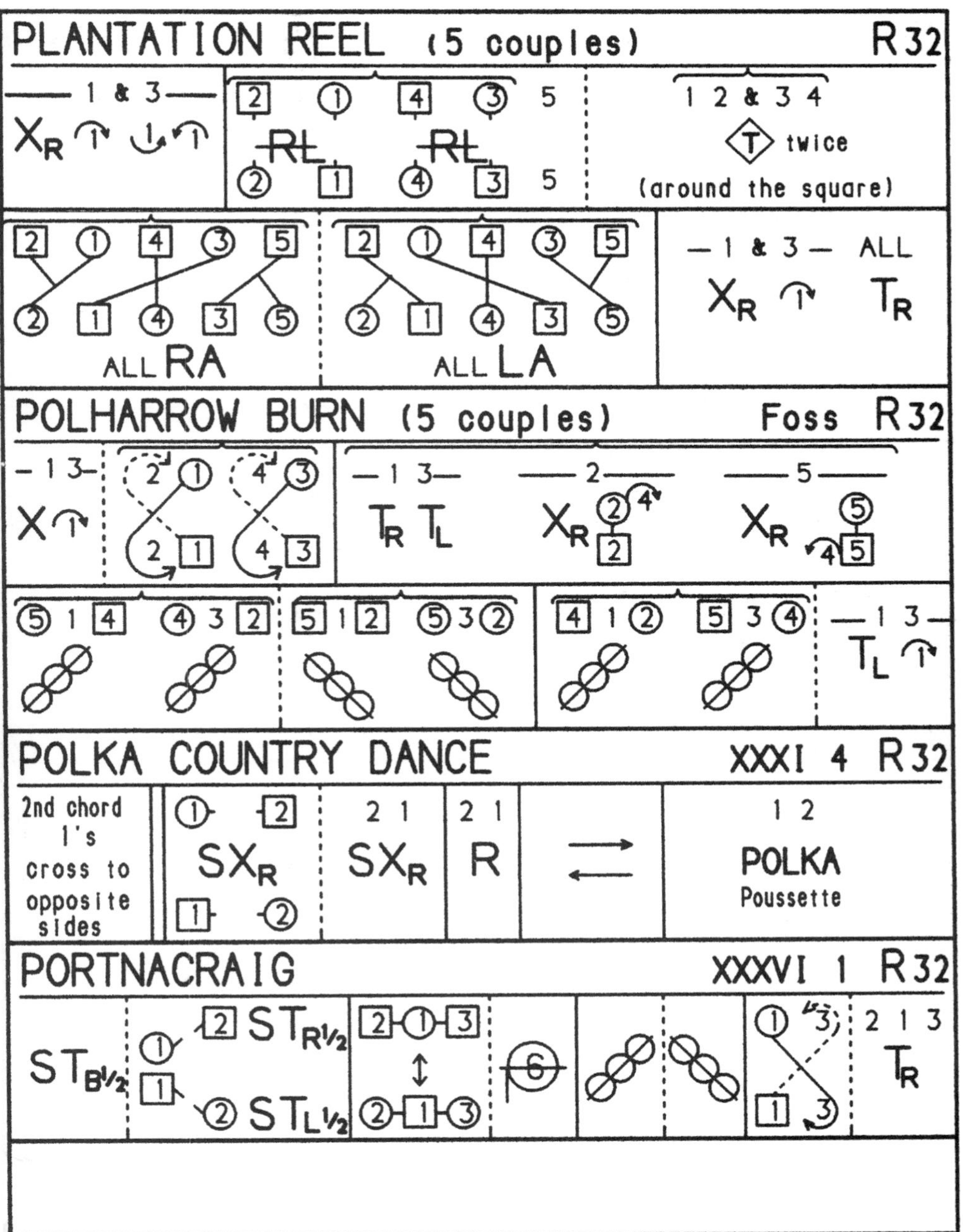
PLANTATION REEL (5 couples) R32
1 & 3
RL RL
1 2 & 3 4
twice
(around the square)
ALL RA
ALL LA
1 & 3 ALL
POLHARROW BURN (5 couples) Foss R32
1 3
2
5
POLKA COUNTRY DANCE XXXI 4 R32
2nd chord 1's cross to opposite sides
SX
2 1
R
1 2
POLKA
Poussette
PORTNACRAIG XXXVI 1 R32
ST
2 1 3

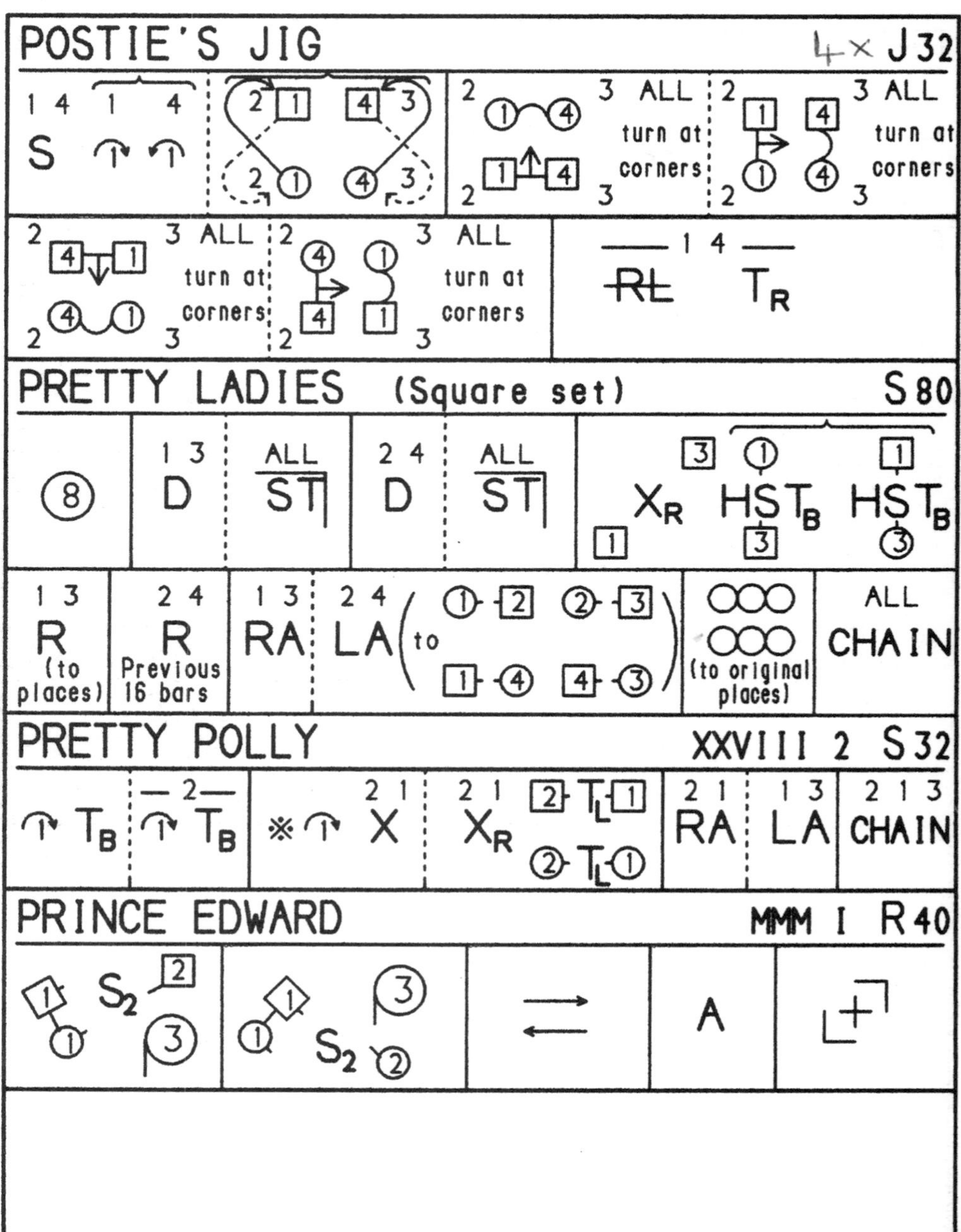
POSTIE'S JIG
4× J32
1 4 1 4
S
2 1 4 3
2 1 4 3
2 3 ALL
turn at corners
2 3
2 3 ALL
turn at corners
2 3
2 3 ALL
turn at corners
2 3
2 3 ALL
turn at corners
2 3
1 4
RL TR
PRETTY LADIES (Square set)
S80
8
1 3 D
ALL ST
2 4 D
ALL ST
XR HST B HST B
1 3
R
(to places)
2 4
R
Previous 16 bars
1 3 RA
2 4 LA
to
(to original places)
ALL
CHAIN
PRETTY POLLY
XXVIII 2 S32
TB
2
TB
2 1 X
2 1 XR
TL
TL
2 1 RA
1 3 LA
2 1 3 CHAIN
PRINCE EDWARD
MMM I R40
S2
S2
A

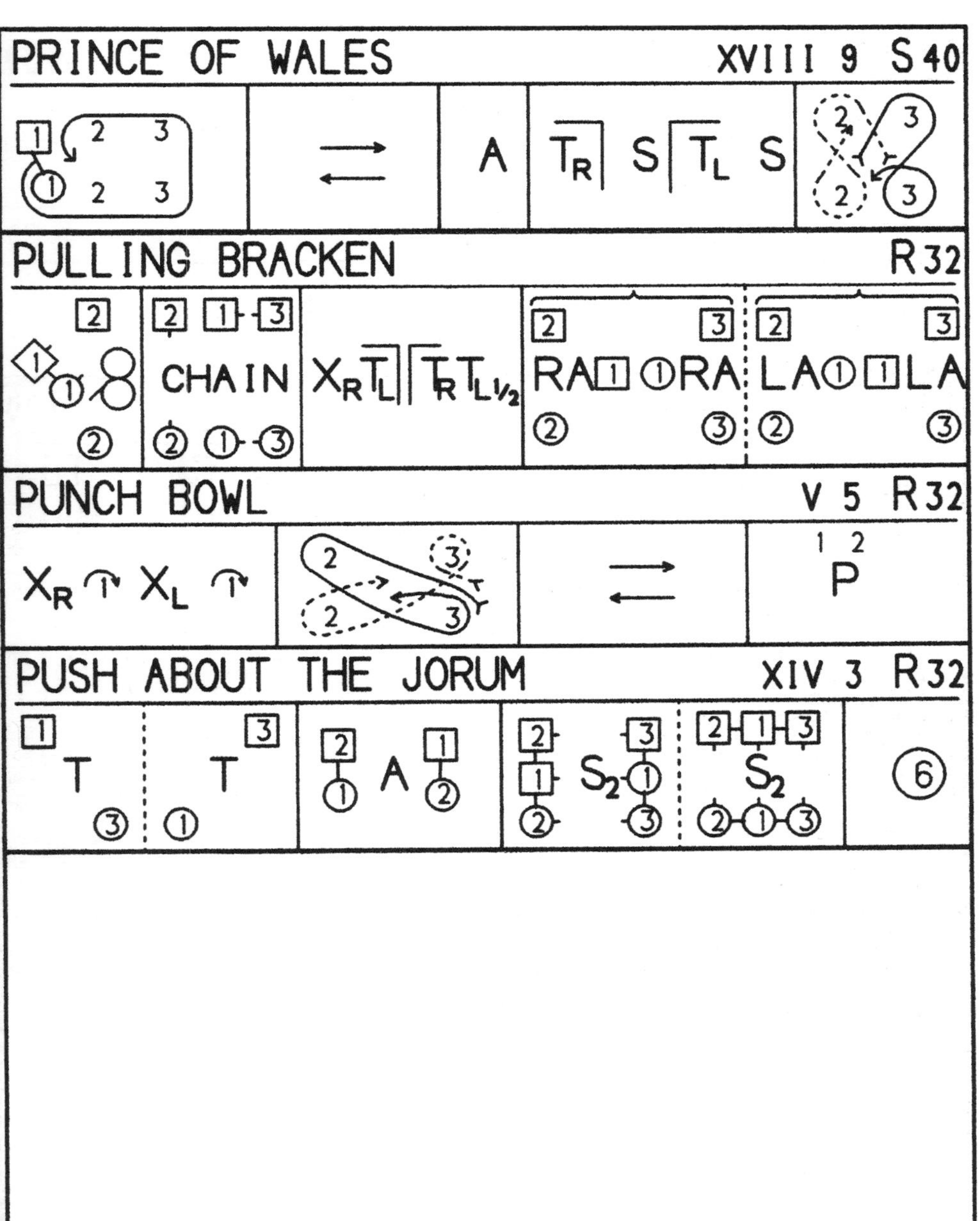
PRINCE OF WALES
XVIII 9 S40
A
S
S
PULLING BRACKEN
R32
CHAIN
PUNCH BOWL
V 5 R32
P
PUSH ABOUT THE JORUM
XIV 3 R32
T
T
A

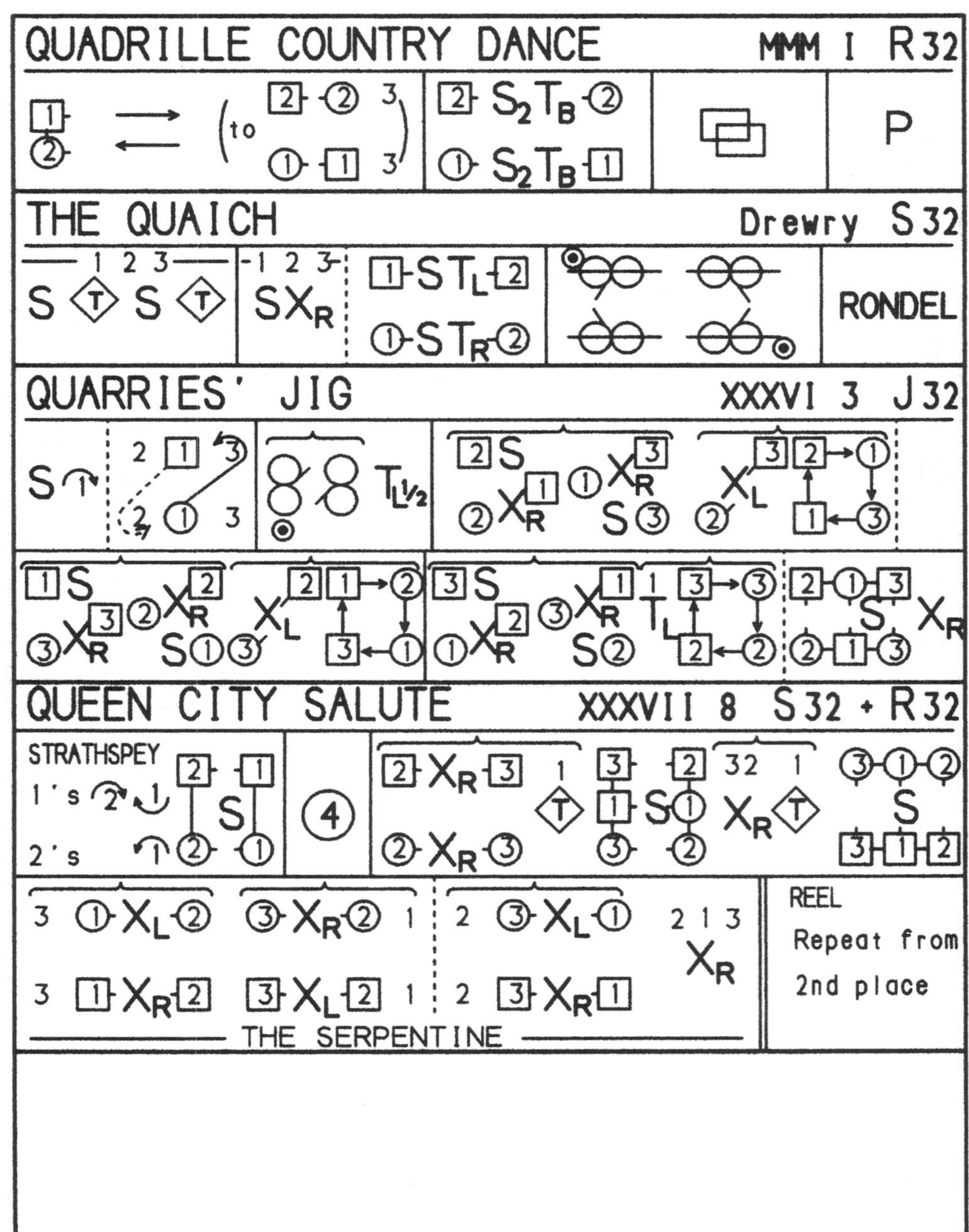
QUADRILLE COUNTRY DANCE
MMM I R32
to
P
THE QUAICH
Drewry S32
RONDEL
QUARRIES' JIG
XXXVI 3 J32
QUEEN CITY SALUTE
XXXVII 8 S32 + R32
STRATHSPEY
1's
2's
REEL
Repeat from
2nd place
THE SERPENTINE

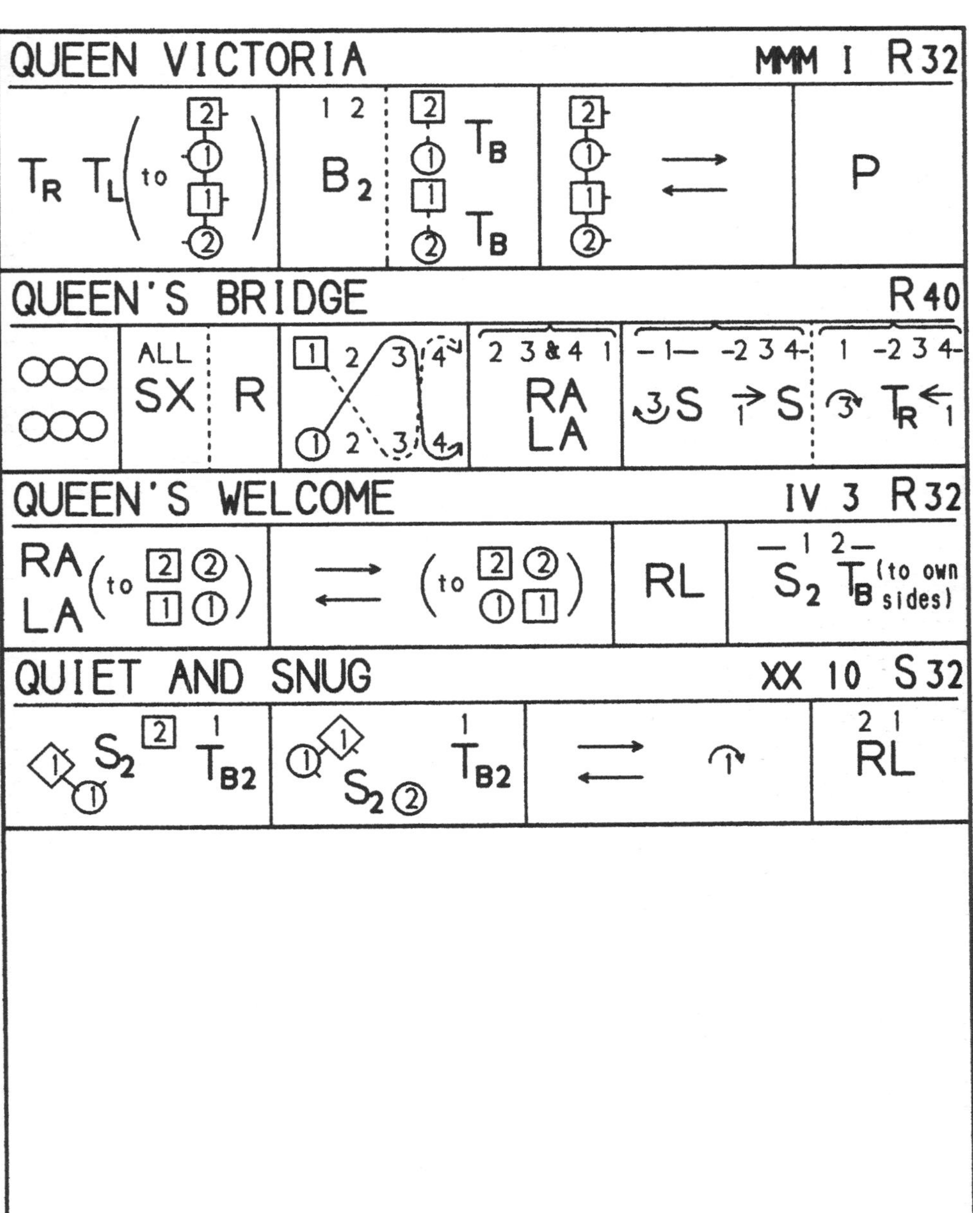
QUEEN VICTORIA
MMM I R32
QUEEN'S BRIDGE
R40
QUEEN'S WELCOME
IV 3 R32
QUIET AND SNUG
XX 10 S32

RAKES OF GLASGOW
XI 11 S 32

RL	⇄	A	(6)

RAKISH HIGHLANDMAN
XIX 6 J 40

	⇄	A	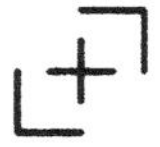	DT

RAY MILBOURNE
R 32

2nd chord 2s & 4s cross to opposite sides	— 1 — — 4 — X_R X_R	2 (1) [4] 3 / 2 [1] (4) 3	1 4 RL (2) [4] (1) [3] / [2] (4) [1] (3)
3 1 & 4 2	(8)		

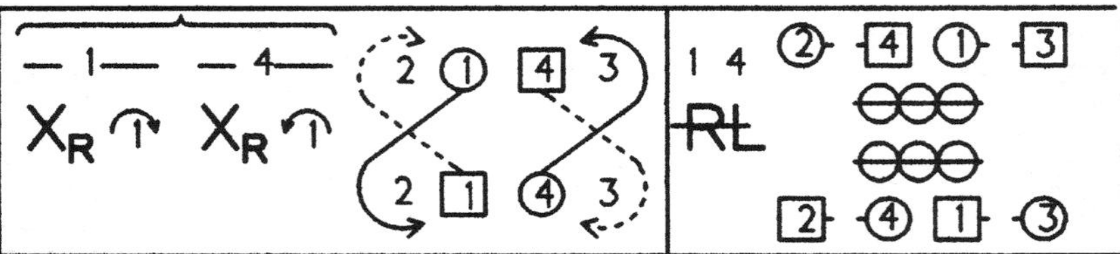

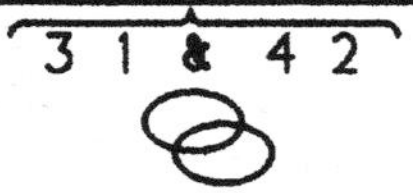

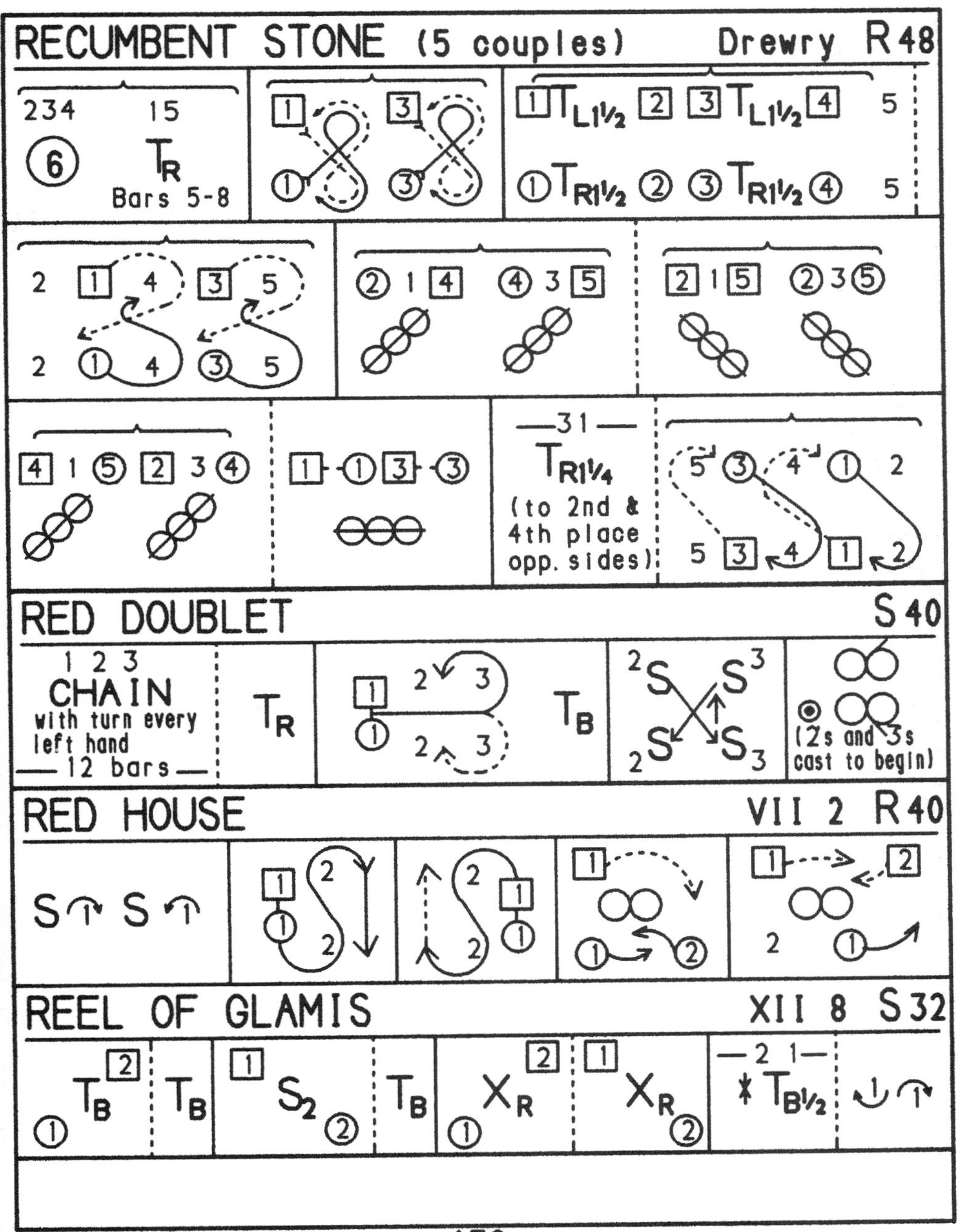

RECUMBENT STONE (5 couples)
Drewry
R48
234
15
6
T_R
Bars 5-8
$T_{L1½}$
$T_{R1½}$
31
$T_{R1¼}$
(to 2nd & 4th place opp. sides)
RED DOUBLET
S40
1 2 3
CHAIN
with turn every left hand
12 bars
T_R
T_B
(2s and 3s cast to begin)
RED HOUSE
VII 2
R40
REEL OF GLAMIS
XII 8
S32
T_B
S_2
X_R
$T_{B1½}$

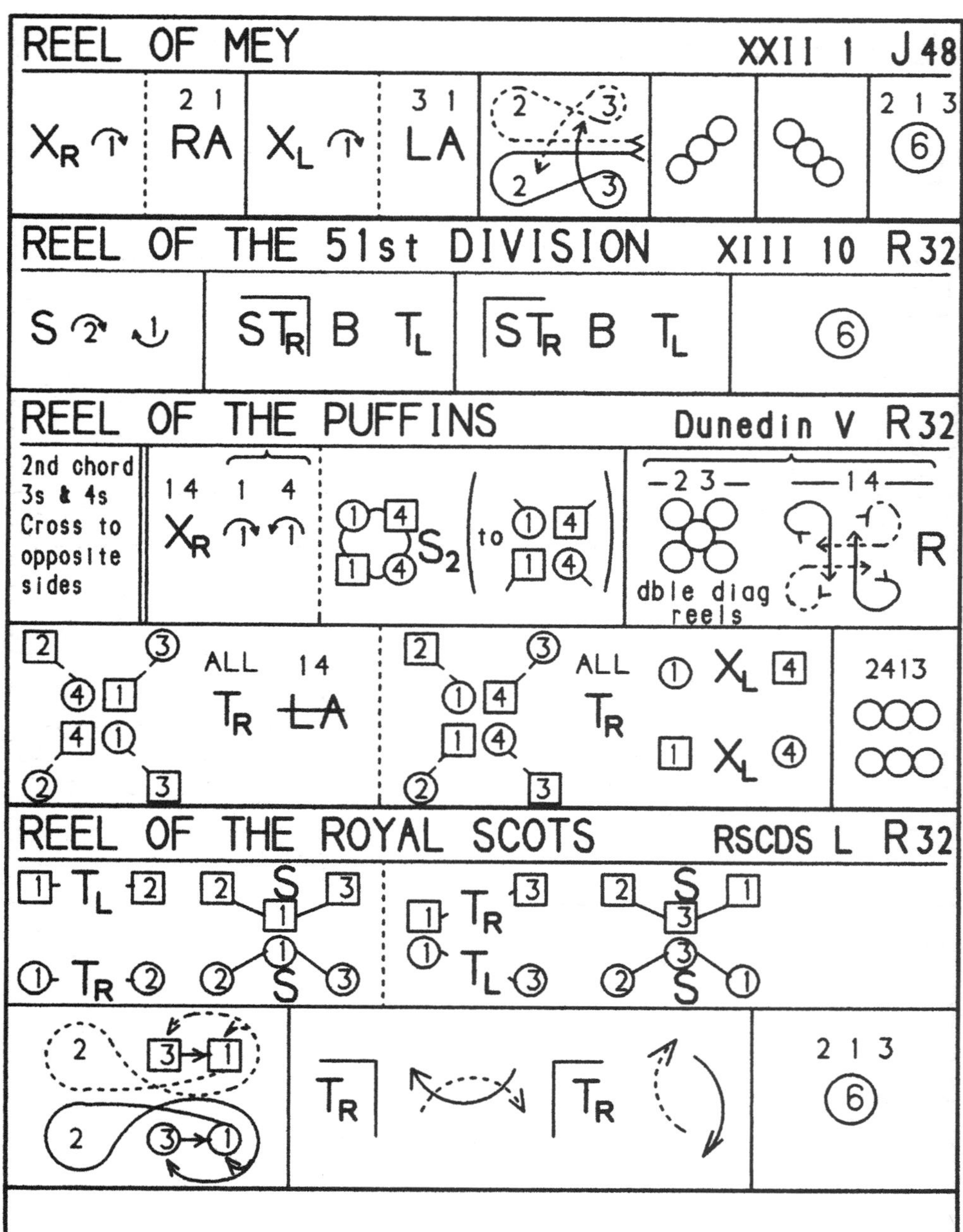
REEL OF MEY
XXII 1 J48
REEL OF THE 51st DIVISION
XIII 10 R32
REEL OF THE PUFFINS
Dunedin V R32
2nd chord
3s & 4s
Cross to
opposite
sides
dble diag
reels
ALL
REEL OF THE ROYAL SCOTS
RSCDS L R32

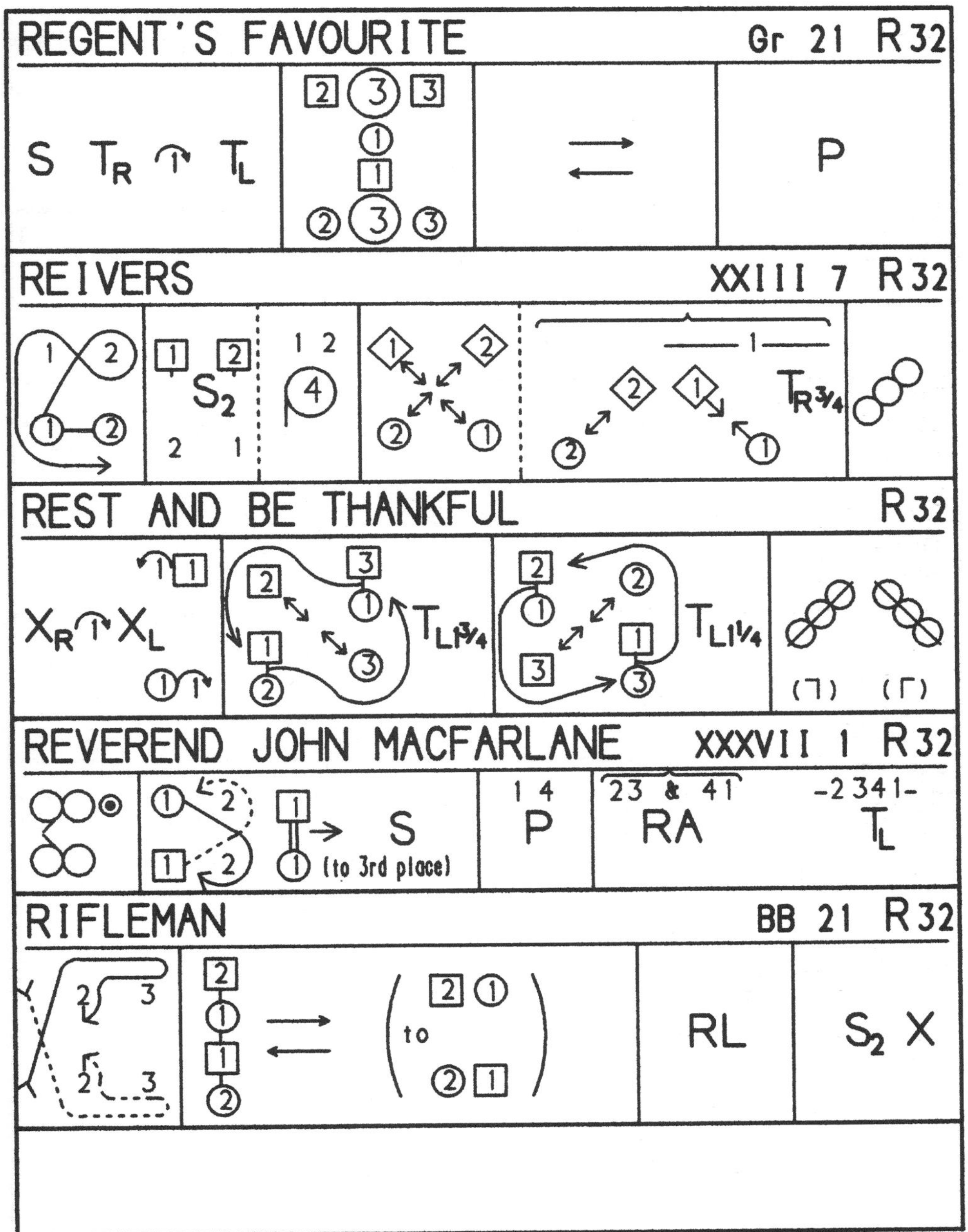
REGENT'S FAVOURITE
Gr 21 R32
S
P
REIVERS
XXIII 7 R32
S_2
REST AND BE THANKFUL
R32
REVEREND JOHN MACFARLANE
XXXVII 1 R32
S
(to 3rd place)
P
23 & 41
RA
-2341-
RIFLEMAN
BB 21 R32
to
RL
S_2 X

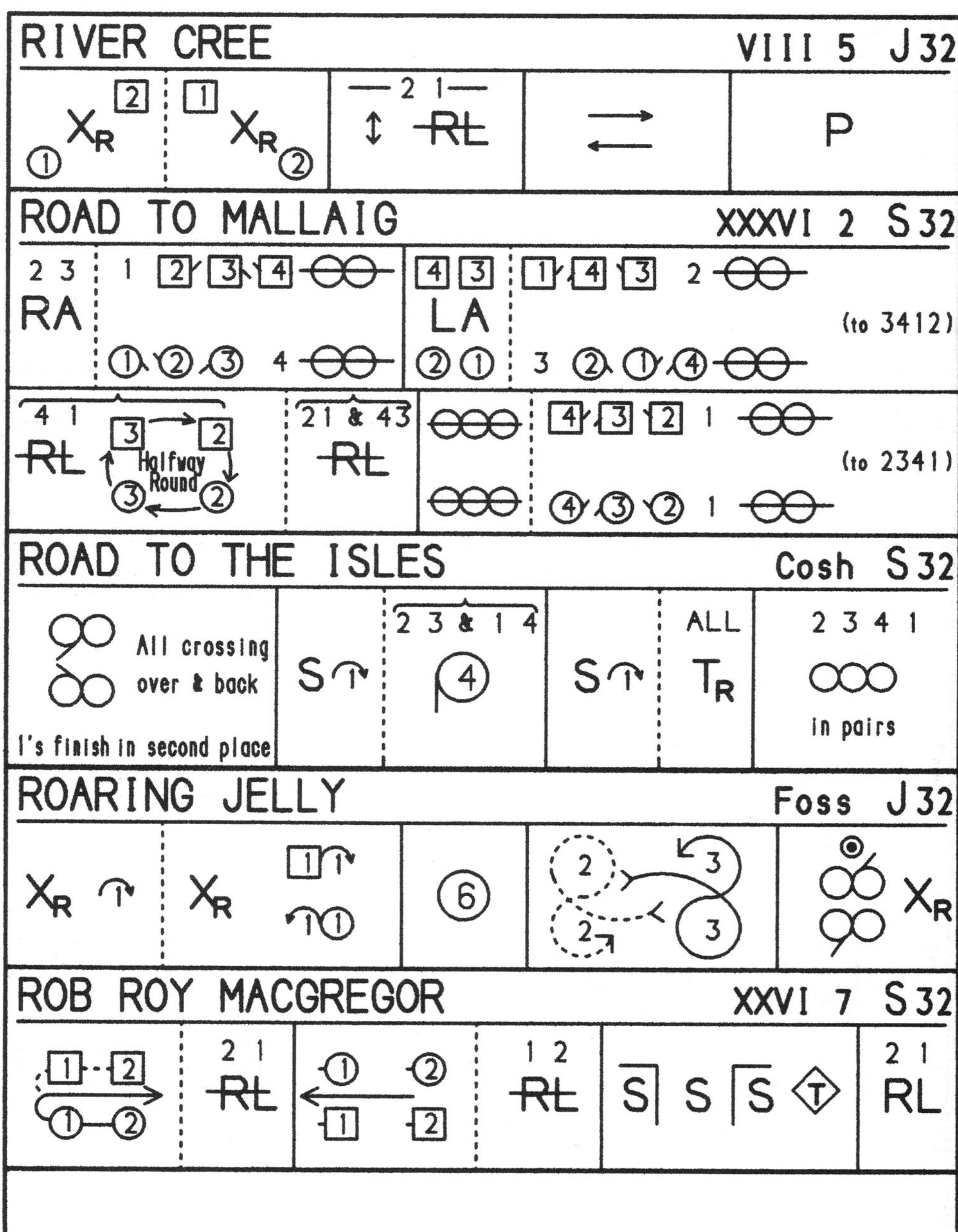
RIVER CREE
VIII 5 J32
X_R
X_R
2 1
RL
P
ROAD TO MALLAIG
XXXVI 2 S32
2 3
RA
LA
(to 3412)
4 1
RL
Halfway Round
21 & 43
RL
(to 2341)
ROAD TO THE ISLES
Cosh S32
All crossing over & back
1's finish in second place
S
2 3 & 1 4
S
ALL
T_R
2 3 4 1
in pairs
ROARING JELLY
Foss J32
X_R
X_R
X_R
ROB ROY MACGREGOR
XXVI 7 S32
2 1
RL
1 2
RL
S S S
2 1
RL

ROBERTSON RANT (Square set) XXXIX 8 S80

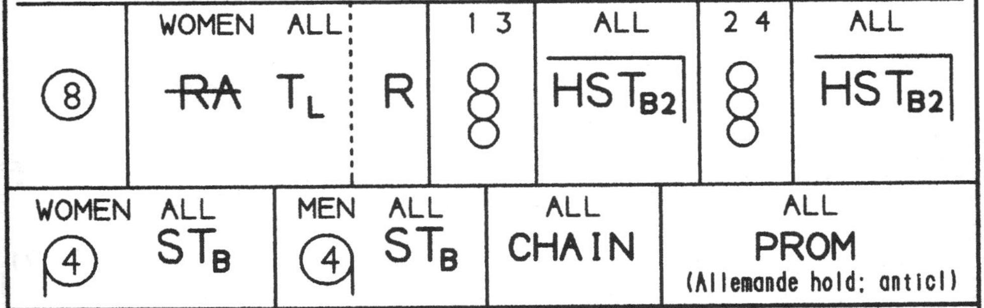

	WOMEN ALL		1 3	ALL	2 4	ALL
⑧	RA T_L	R	8	HST_{B2}	8	HST_{B2}

WOMEN ALL	MEN ALL	ALL	ALL
④ ST_B	④ ST_B	CHAIN	PROM (Allemande hold; anticl)

ROCK AND THE WEE PICKLE TOW III 7 J32

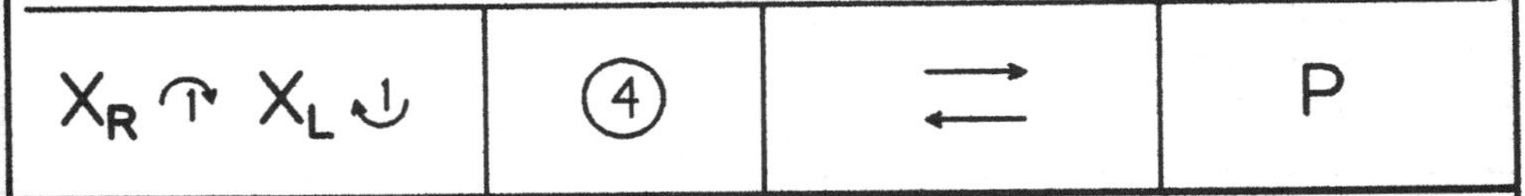

X_R 1 X_L 1	④	⇄	P

ROCKS OF GIBRALTAR BB 22 R32

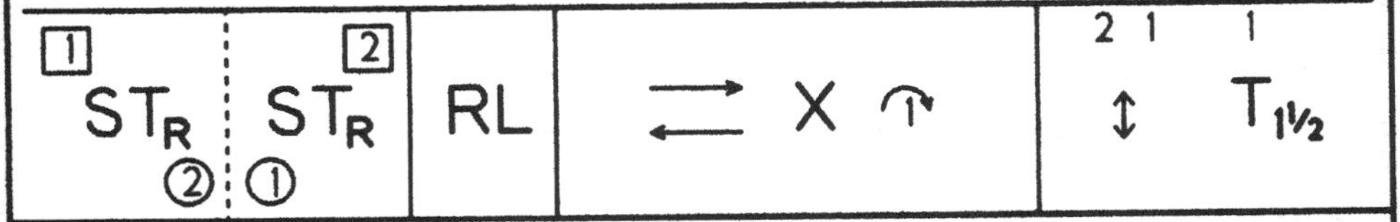

1 | 2			2 1 1
ST_R ② | ST_R ①	RL	⇄ X 1	↕ $T_{1½}$

RORY O'MORE I 9 J32

1 2 ↕ 1 2 ↑ ↑ ① ↓ ② 1's turn under to 2nd place	2 1 ↕ ② ① ↑ ↑ 2 ↓ 1 1's turn under to 1st place	⇄	P

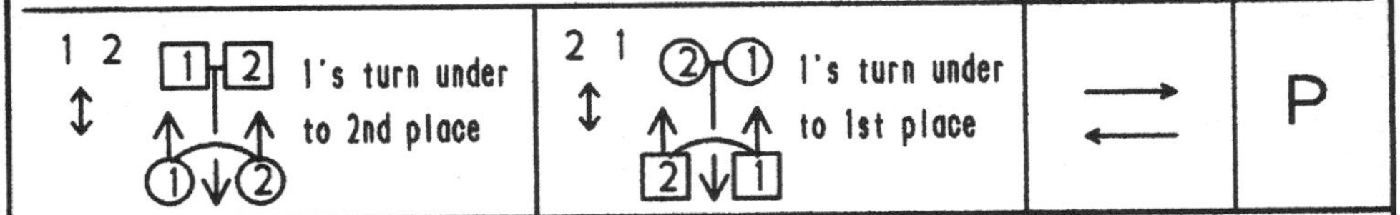

ROSE OF THE NORTH S32

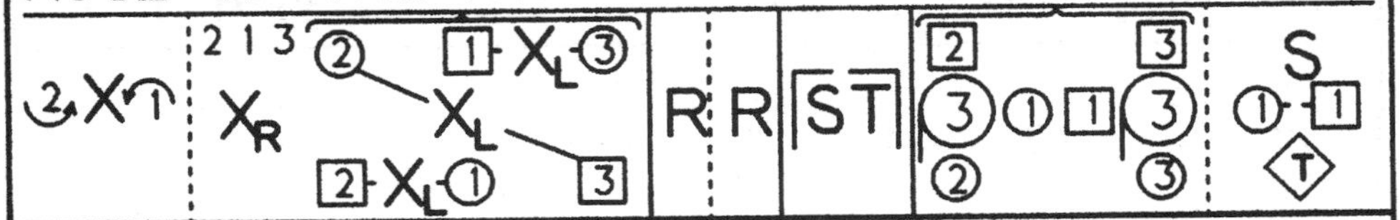

2 X 1	2 1 3 X_R ② 1 X_L ③ X_L 2 X_L ① 3	R | R	ST	2 3 ③ ① 1 ③ ② ③	S ① 1 T

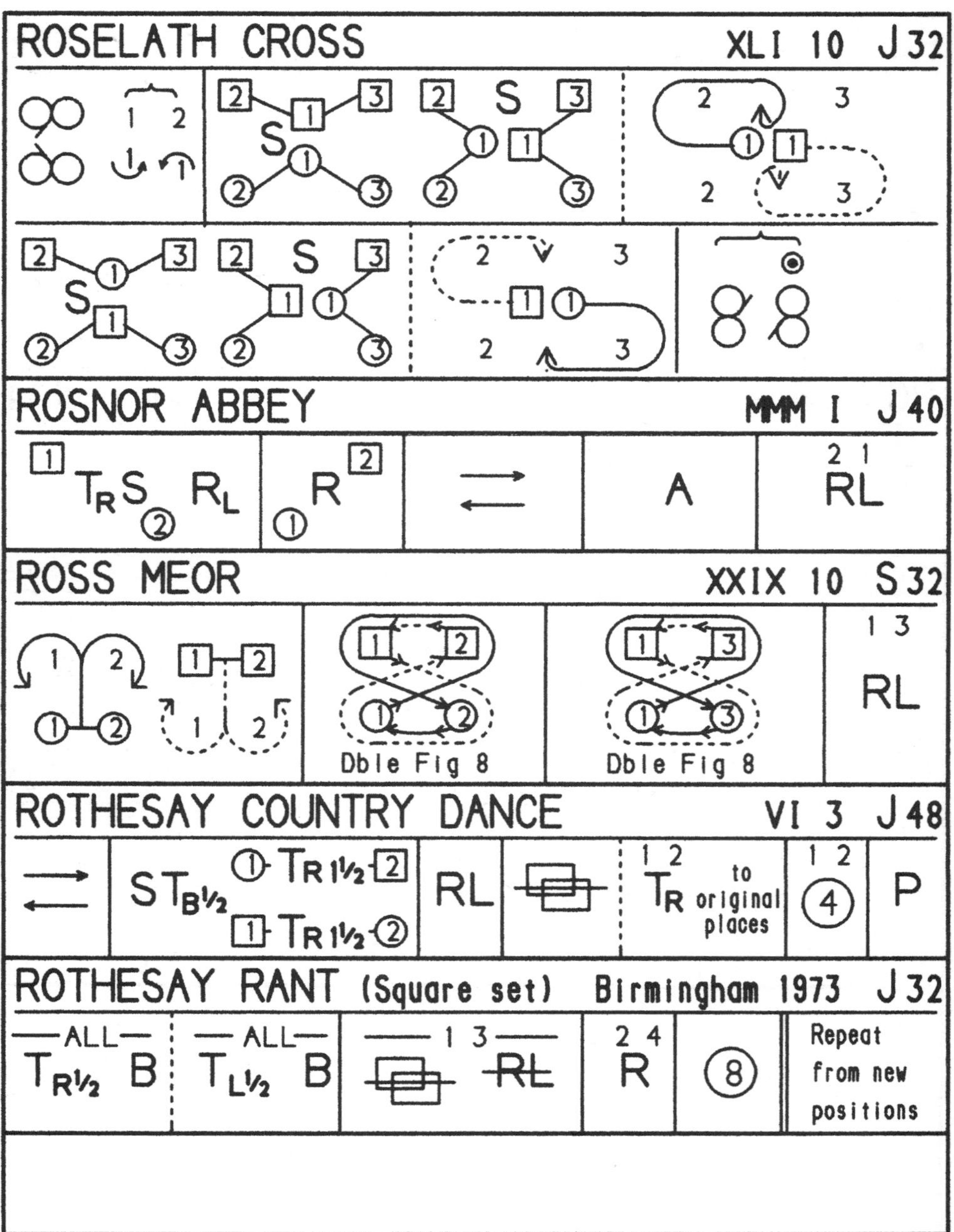
ROSELATH CROSS
XLI 10 J32
ROSNOR ABBEY
MMM I J40
A
RL
ROSS MEOR
XXIX 10 S32
Dble Fig 8
Dble Fig 8
RL
ROTHESAY COUNTRY DANCE
VI 3 J48
RL
to original places
P
ROTHESAY RANT (Square set)
Birmingham 1973 J32
ALL
ALL
Repeat from new positions

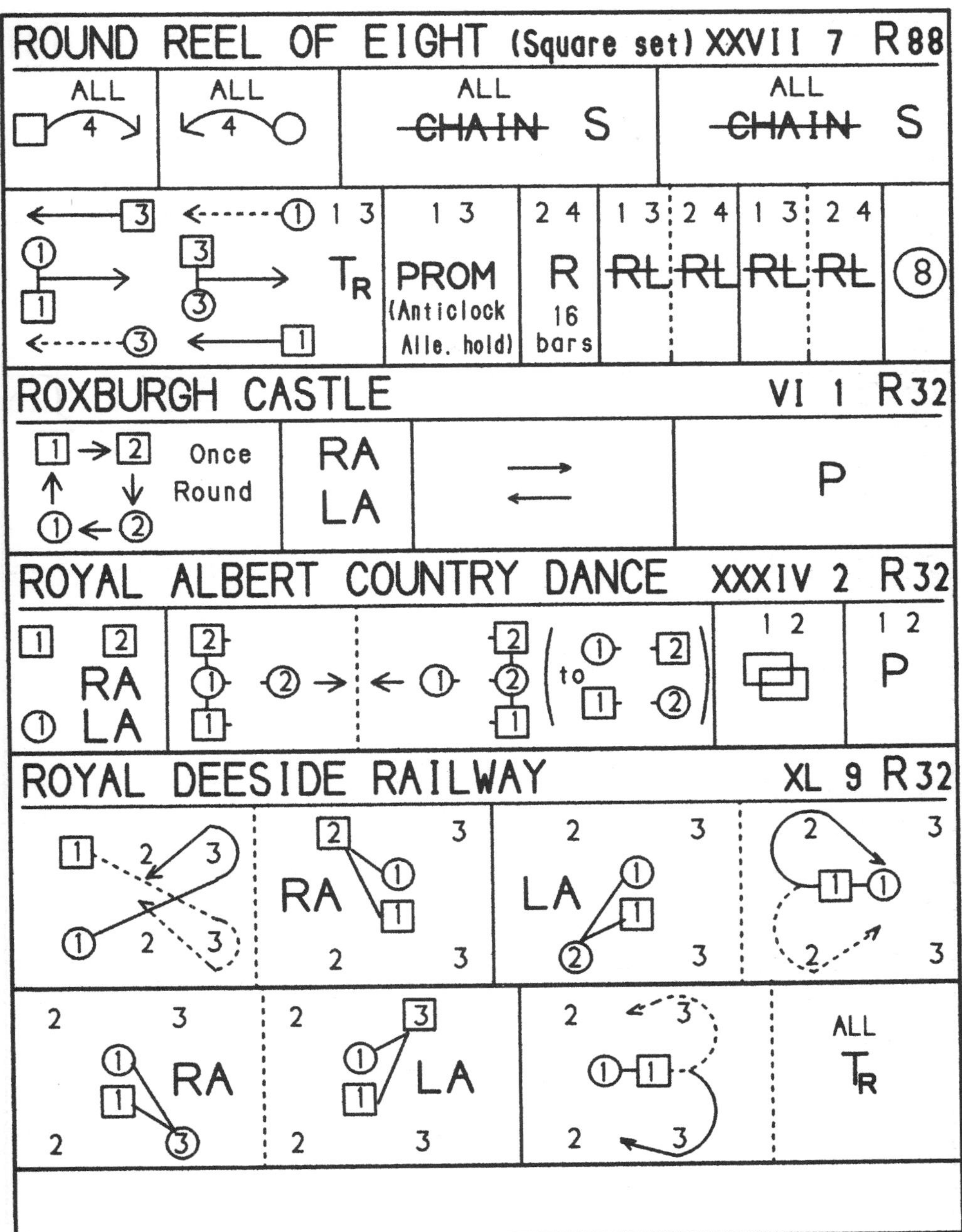
ROUND REEL OF EIGHT (Square set) XXVII 7 R88
ALL
4
ALL
4
ALL
CHAIN S
ALL
CHAIN S
3
1
1 3
1
3
TR
3
1
PROM
(Anticlock
Alle. hold)
2 4
R
16
bars
1 3 2 4 1 3 2 4
RL RL RL RL
8
ROXBURGH CASTLE VI 1 R32
1 2
Once
Round
1 2
RA
LA
P
ROYAL ALBERT COUNTRY DANCE XXXIV 2 R32
1 2
RA
1 LA
2
1
1
2
1
2
2
1
to
1 2
1 2
1 2
1 2
P
ROYAL DEESIDE RAILWAY XL 9 R32
RA
LA
ALL
TR

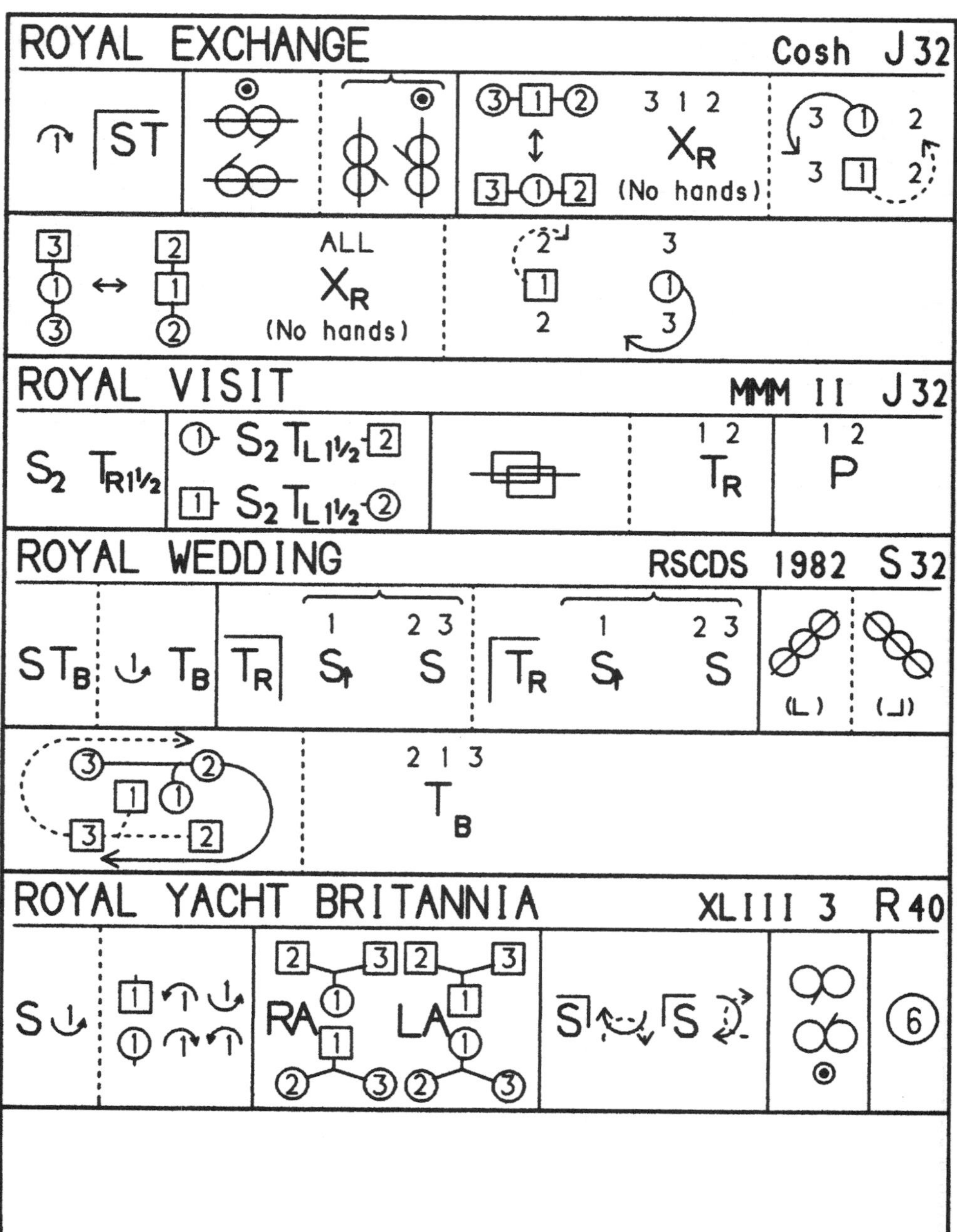
ROYAL EXCHANGE
Cosh J32
ST
3 1 2
(No hands)
ALL
(No hands)
ROYAL VISIT
MMM II J32
1 2
1 2
P
ROYAL WEDDING
RSCDS 1982 S32
1 2 3
1 2 3
(L)
2 1 3
ROYAL YACHT BRITANNIA
XLIII 3 R40
RA
LA

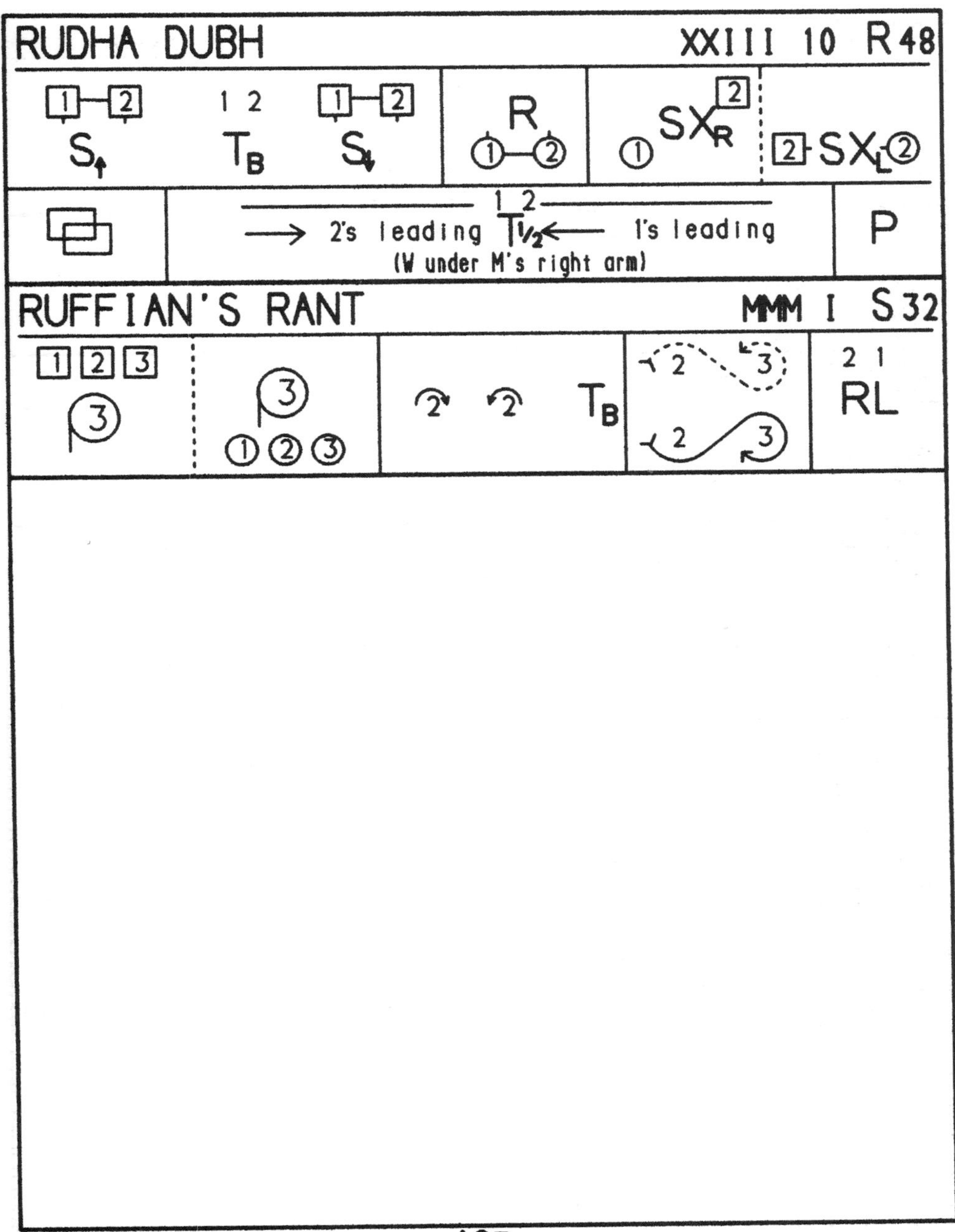
RUDHA DUBH
XXIII 10 R48
1 2
S
T B
S
R
1 2
SX R
2 SX L 2
1 2
2's leading T 1/2 1's leading
(W under M's right arm)
P
RUFFIAN'S RANT
MMM I S32
1 2 3
3
3
1 2 3
2 2
T B
2 3
2 3
2 1
RL

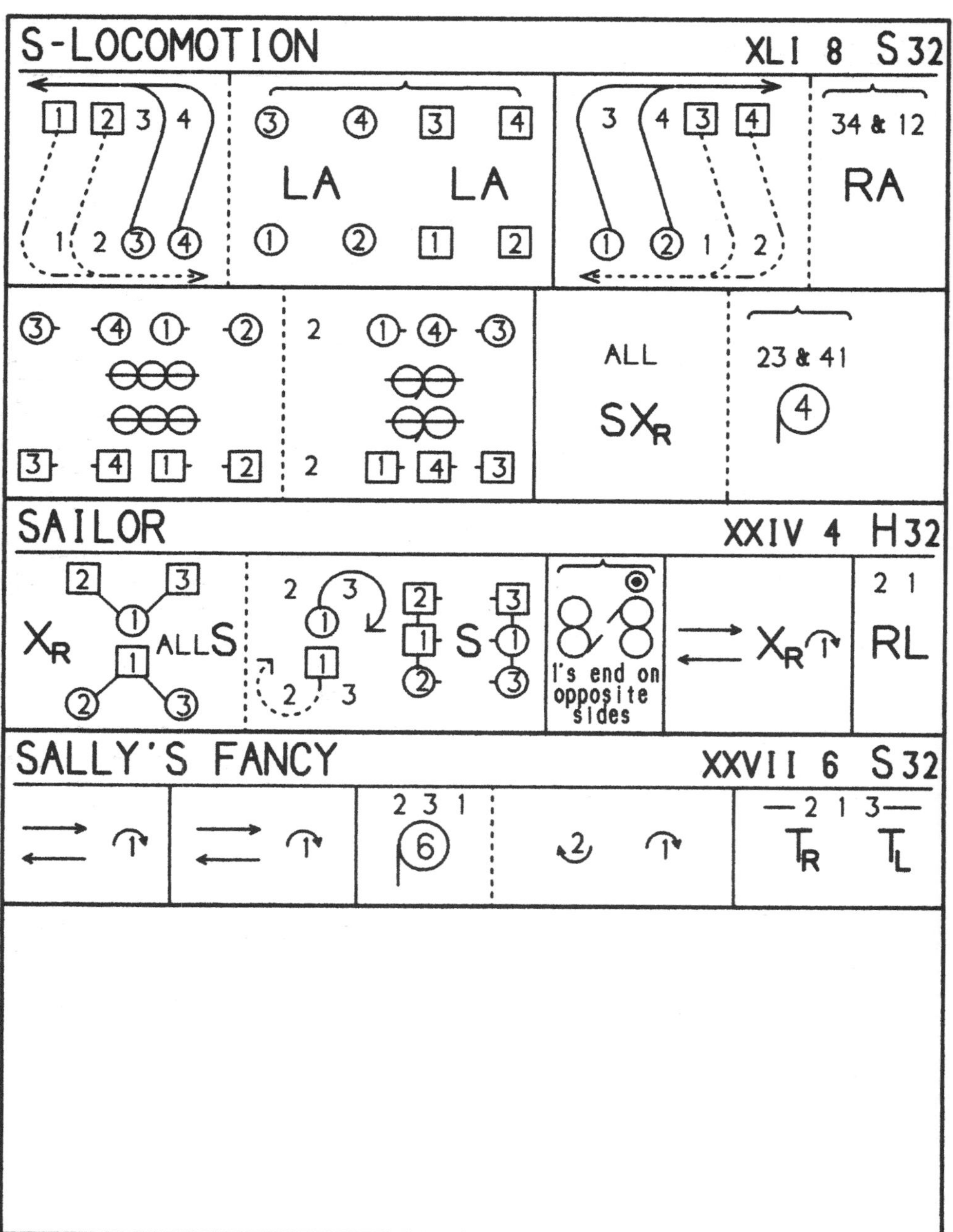
S-LOCOMOTION
XLI 8 S32
34 & 12
LA
LA
RA
ALL
SX
R
23 & 41
SAILOR
XXIV 4 H32
X
R
ALL
S
S
1's end on opposite sides
X
R
2 1
RL
SALLY'S FANCY
XXVII 6 S32
2 3 1
2 1 3
T
R
T
L

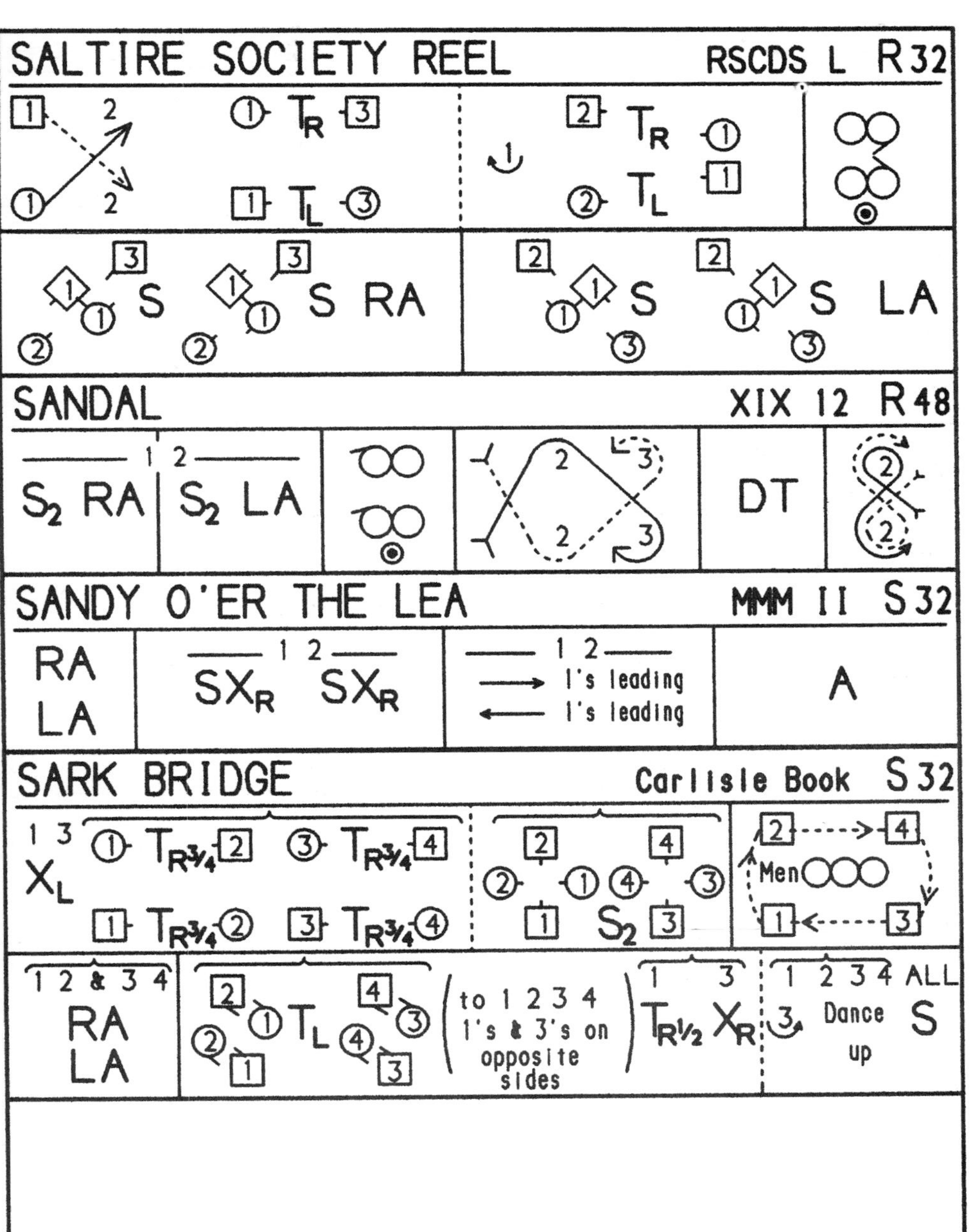
SALTIRE SOCIETY REEL
RSCDS L R32
TR
TL
S
S RA
S LA
SANDAL
XIX 12 R48
S2 RA
S2 LA
DT
SANDY O'ER THE LEA
MMM II S32
RA
LA
SXR SXR
1's leading
1's leading
A
SARK BRIDGE
Carlisle Book S32
XL
TR3/4
S2
Men
1 2 & 3 4
RA
LA
TL
to 1 2 3 4
1's & 3's on
opposite
sides
TR1/2 XR
1 2 3 4 ALL
Dance
up
S

SAUCHIE HAUGH

RSCDS L S 32

⇄	1 2 RONDEL	—— 2 1 —— ↕ T_B (4) (1 step)	2 1 P (Right Round)

SAW YE MY WEE THING

XXV 9 J 32

SX_R 	(2) (2)	—— 2 —— SX_R	(1) (1)	—— 1 2 —— → 1's leading ← 2's leading	2 1 RL

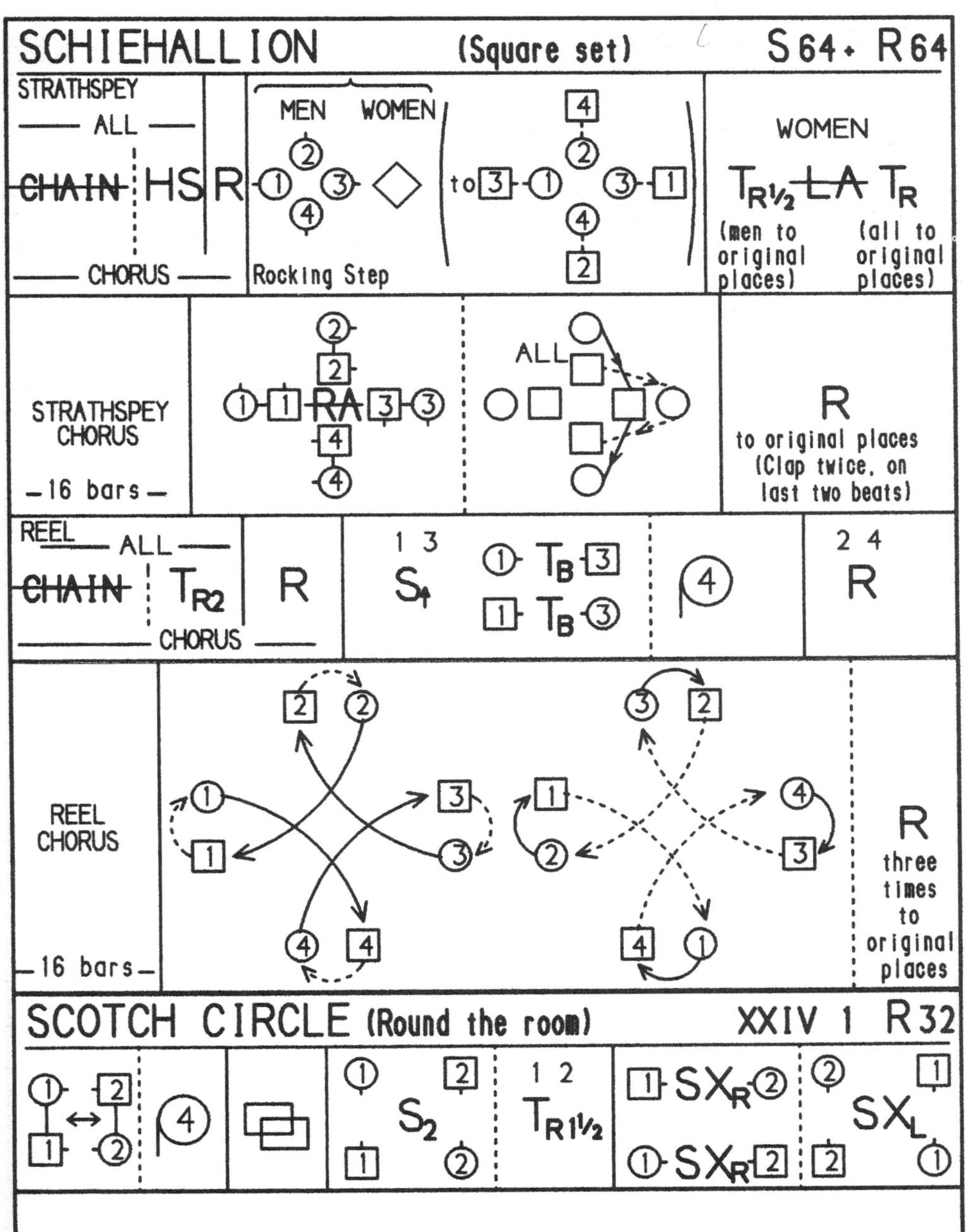
SCHIEHALLION
(Square set)
S64 + R64
STRATHSPEY
ALL
CHAIN
HS
R
CHORUS
MEN
WOMEN
Rocking Step
to
WOMEN
(men to original places)
(all to original places)
STRATHSPEY CHORUS
16 bars
RA
ALL
R
to original places
(Clap twice, on last two beats)
REEL
ALL
CHAIN
CHORUS
R
1 3
2 4
REEL CHORUS
16 bars
R
three times to original places
SCOTCH CIRCLE (Round the room)
XXIV 1
R32
1 2

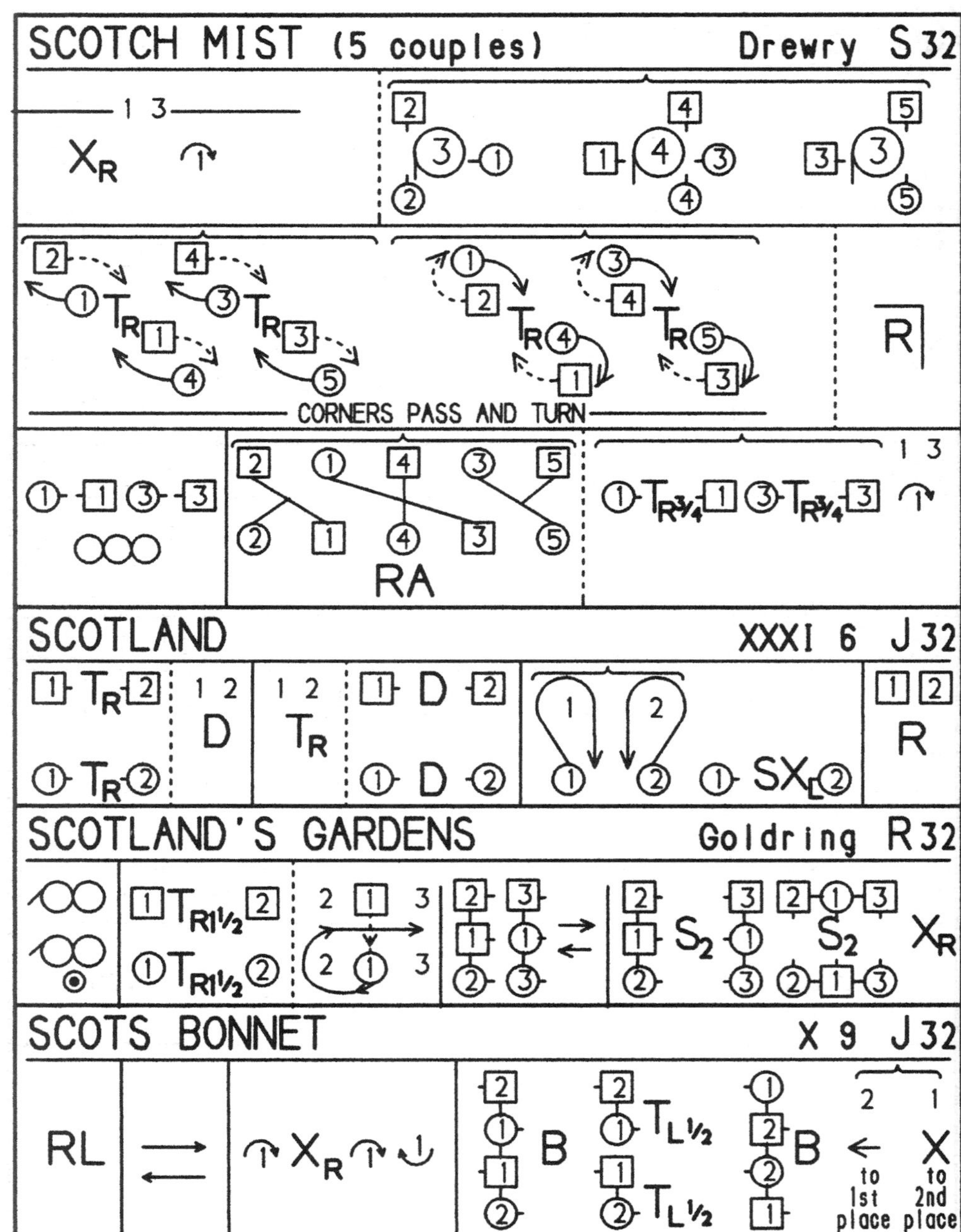
SCOTCH MIST (5 couples) Drewry S 32
CORNERS PASS AND TURN
SCOTLAND XXXI 6 J 32
SCOTLAND'S GARDENS Goldring R 32
SCOTS BONNET X 9 J 32
to 1st place
to 2nd place

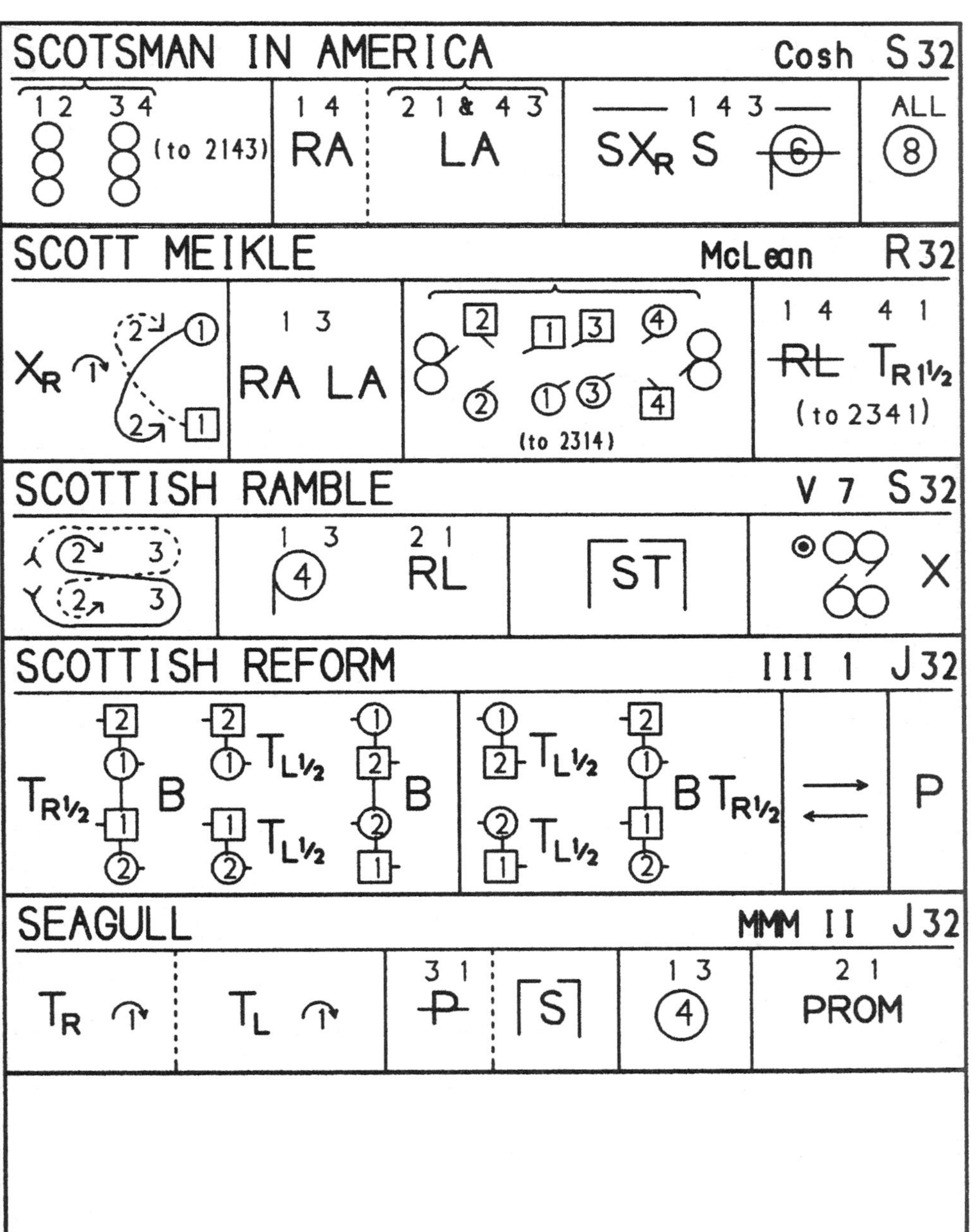
SCOTSMAN IN AMERICA
Cosh S32
1 2 3 4
(to 2143)
1 4
RA
2 1 & 4 3
LA
1 4 3
SX R S
6
ALL
8
SCOTT MEIKLE
McLean R32
X R
1 3
RA LA
(to 2314)
1 4 4 1
RL T R1½
(to 2341)
SCOTTISH RAMBLE
V 7 S32
1 3
4
2 1
RL
ST
X
SCOTTISH REFORM
III 1 J32
T R½
B
T L½
B
T L½
B T R½
P
SEAGULL
MMM II J32
T R
T L
3 1
P
S
1 3
4
2 1
PROM

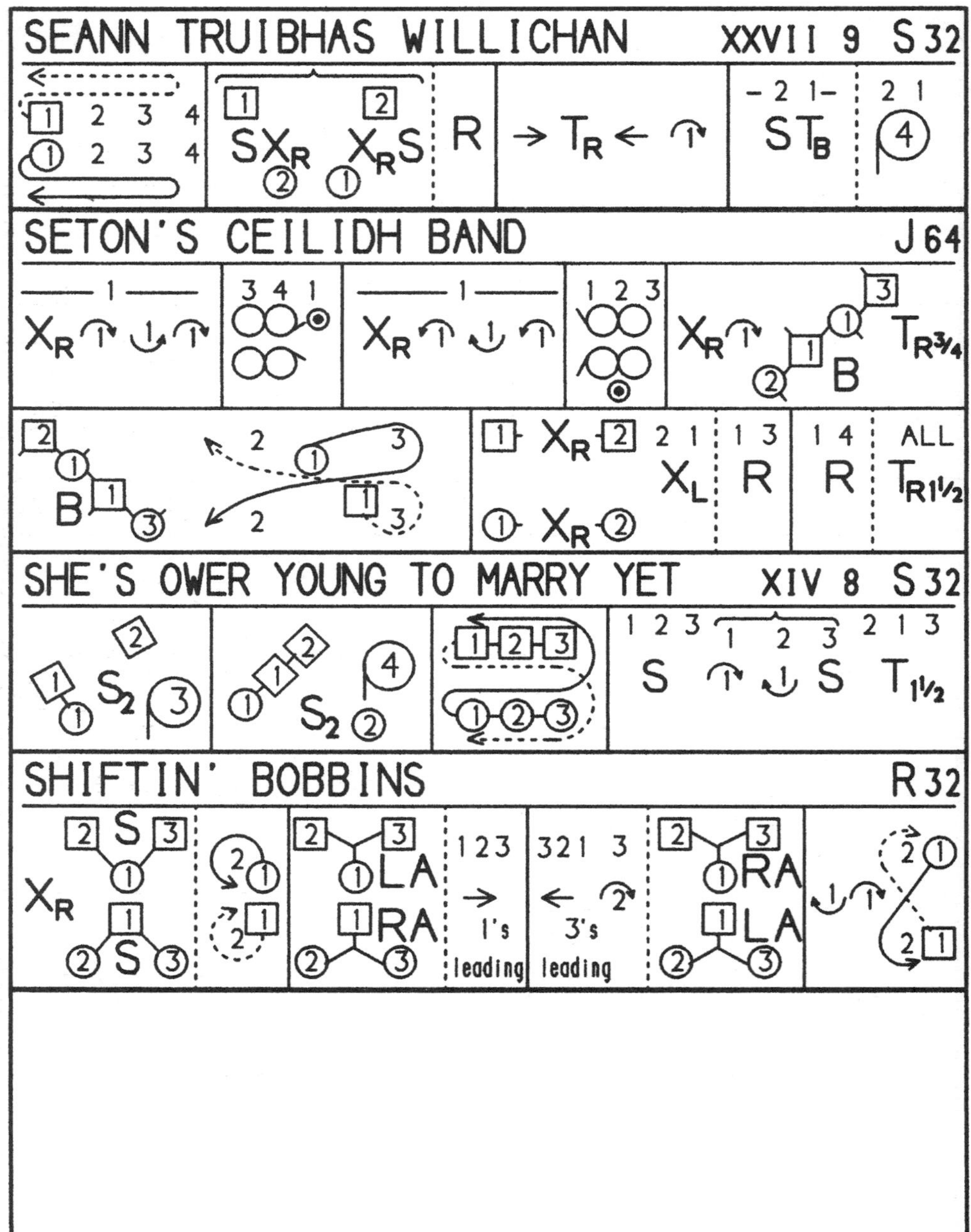
SEANN TRUIBHAS WILLICHAN XXVII 9 S32
SETON'S CEILIDH BAND J64
SHE'S OWER YOUNG TO MARRY YET XIV 8 S32
SHIFTIN' BOBBINS R32
1's leading
3's leading

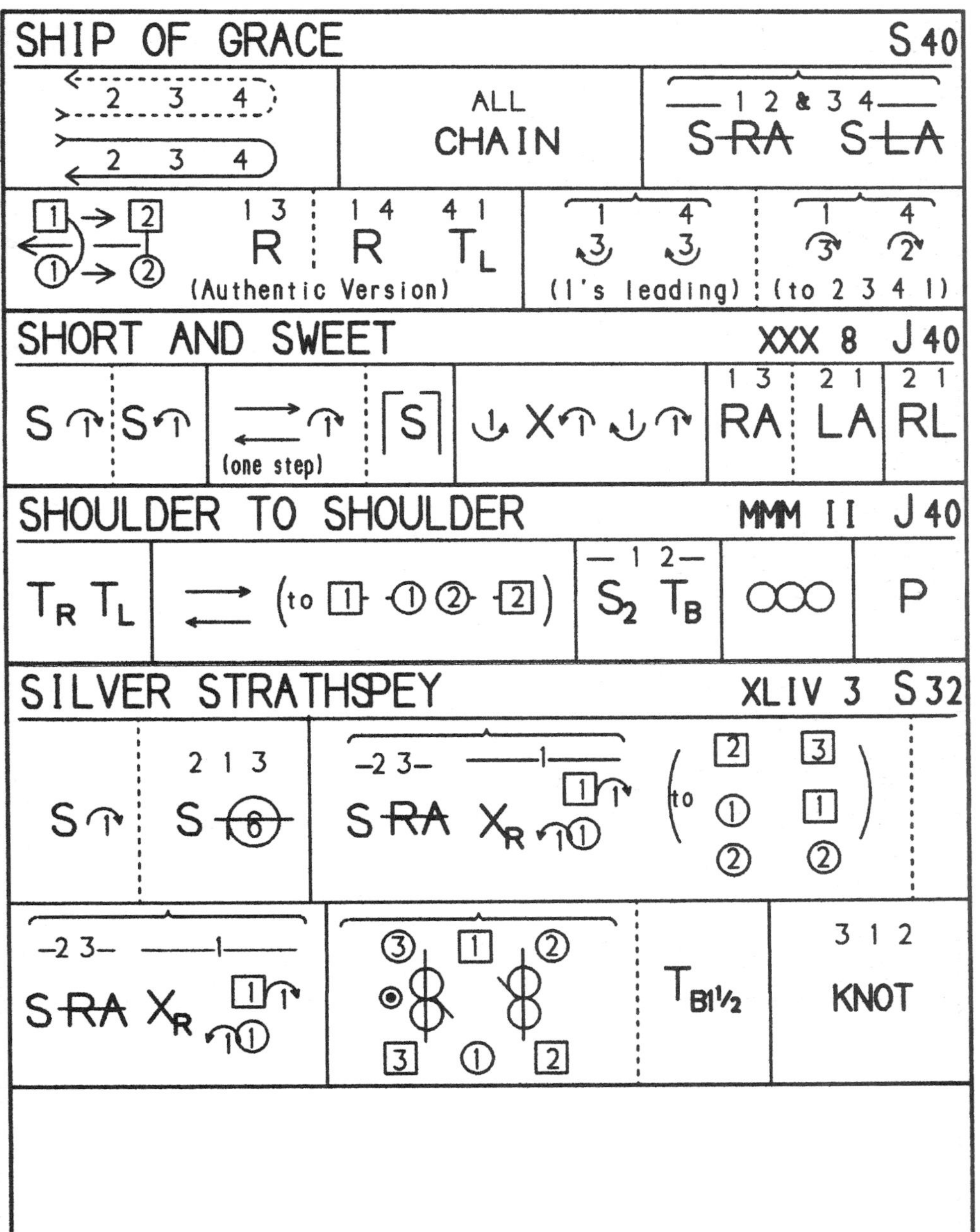
SHIP OF GRACE
S 40
2 3 4
2 3 4
ALL
CHAIN
1 2 & 3 4
S RA S LA
1 3
R
1 4
R
4 1
T_L
(Authentic Version)
(1's leading)
(to 2 3 4 1)
SHORT AND SWEET
XXX 8 J 40
(one step)
1 3
RA
2 1
LA
2 1
RL
SHOULDER TO SHOULDER
MMM II J 40
T_R T_L
1 2
S_2 T_B
P
SILVER STRATHSPEY
XLIV 3 S 32
2 1 3
S RA
to
S RA
$T_{B1½}$
3 1 2
KNOT

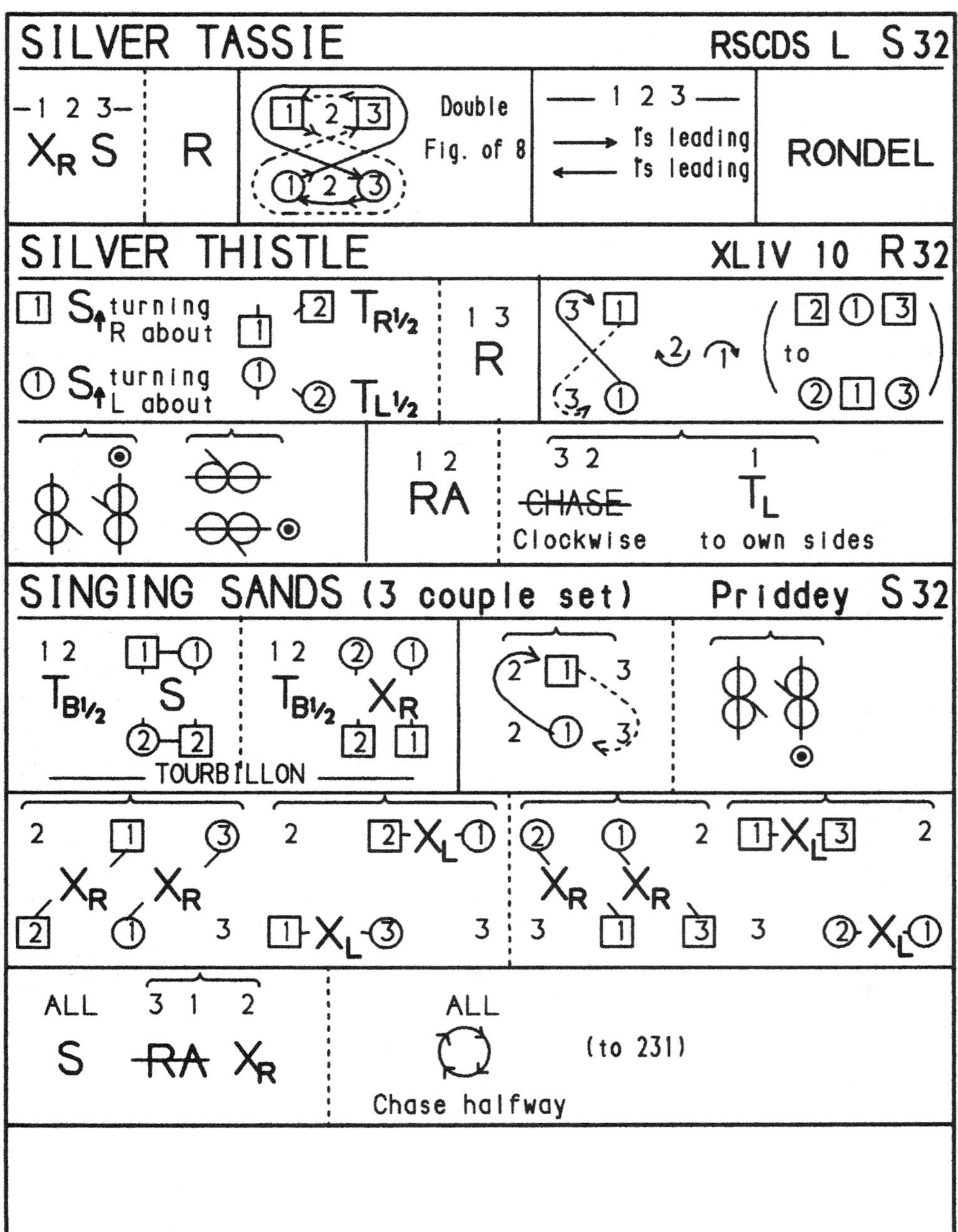
SILVER TASSIE
RSCDS L S32
1 2 3
XR S
R
Double Fig. of 8
1 2 3
1's leading
1's leading
RONDEL
SILVER THISTLE
XLIV 10 R32
S turning R about
T R½
S turning L about
T L½
1 3
R
to
1 2
RA
3 2
CHASE
Clockwise
1
TL
to own sides
SINGING SANDS (3 couple set)
Priddey S32
1 2
TB½
S
1 2
TB½
XR
TOURBILLON
XR XR
XL
ALL
3 1 2
S RA XR
ALL
(to 231)
Chase halfway

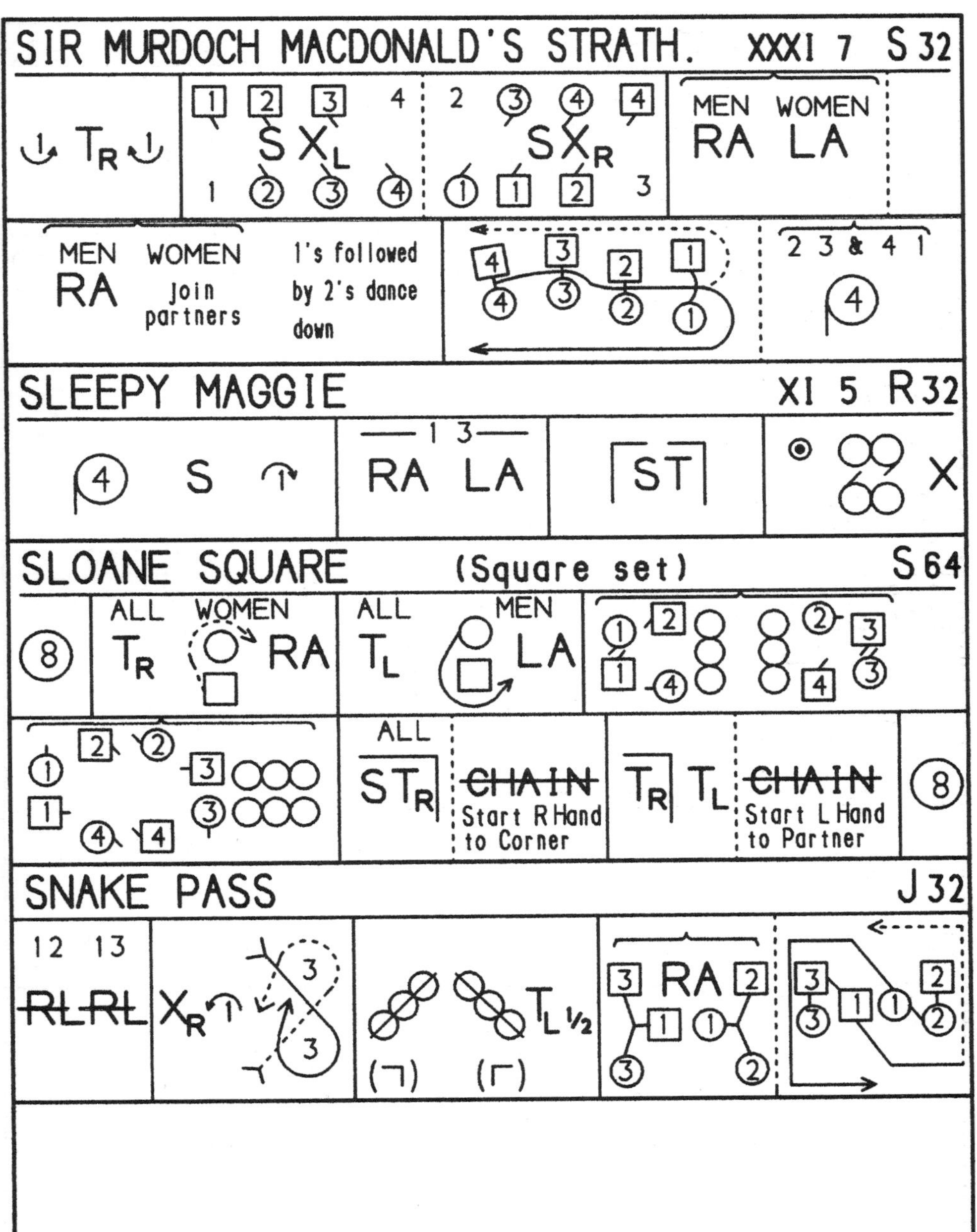
SIR MURDOCH MACDONALD'S STRATH. XXXI 7 S 32
1 2 3 4
S X L
1 2 3 4
2 3 4 4
S X R
1 1 2 3
MEN WOMEN
RA LA
MEN WOMEN
RA
join partners
1's followed by 2's dance down
4 3 2 1
4 3 2 1
2 3 & 4 1
4
SLEEPY MAGGIE XI 5 R 32
4 S 1
1 3
RA LA
ST
X
SLOANE SQUARE (Square set) S 64
8
ALL WOMEN
T R RA
ALL MEN
T L LA
1 2 3 4
2 3 4 1
ALL
ST R
CHAIN
Start R Hand to Corner
T R T L
CHAIN
Start L Hand to Partner
8
SNAKE PASS J 32
12 13
RLRL
X R 1
3
3
T L ½
RA
3 2
1 1
3 2
3 1 1 2
3 2

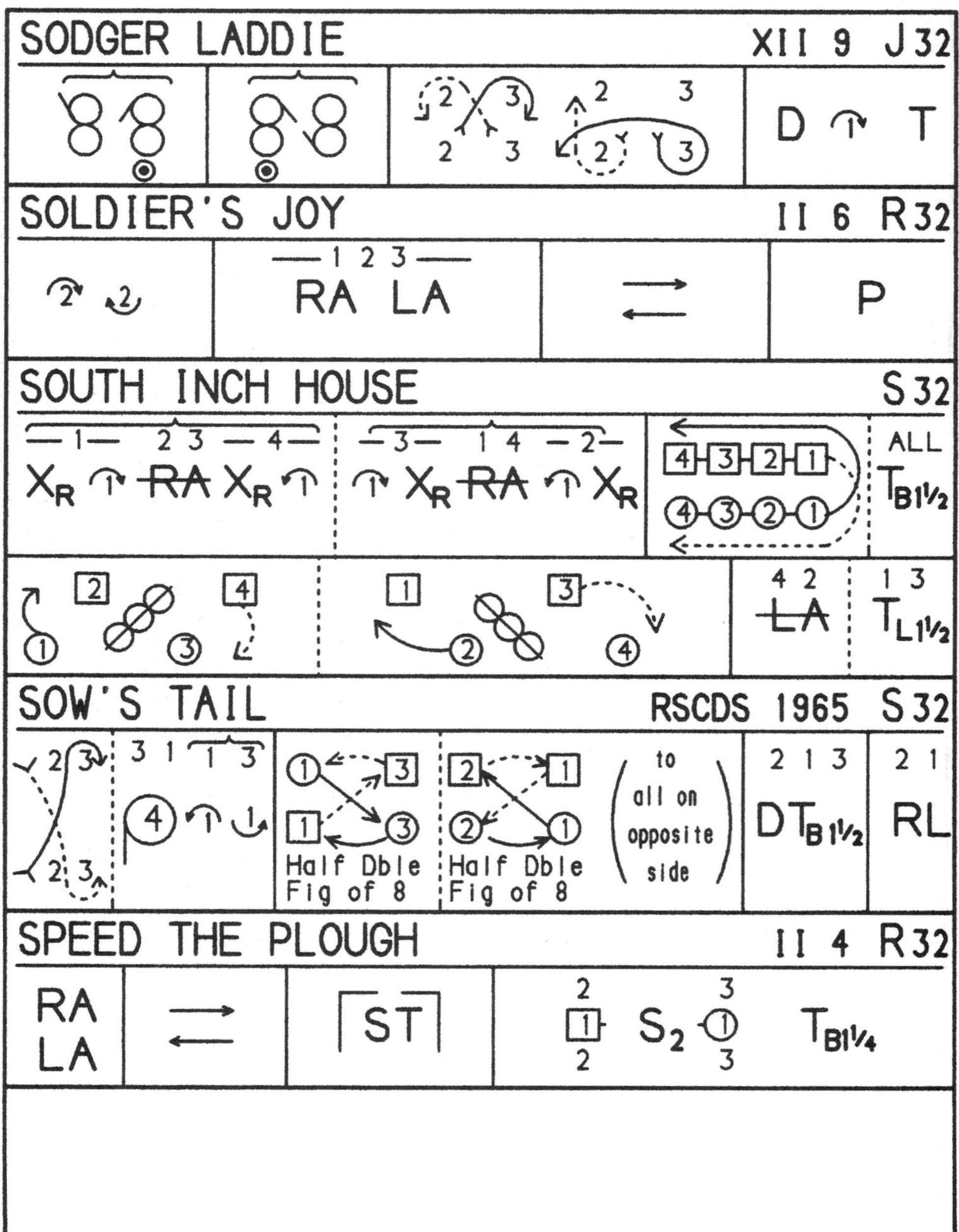

SODGER LADDIE
XII 9 J32
2 3
2 3
2 3
2 3
D T
SOLDIER'S JOY
II 6 R32
2 2
1 2 3
RA LA
P
SOUTH INCH HOUSE
S32
1 2 3 4
XR 1 RA XR 1
3 1 4 2
1 XR RA 1 XR
4 3 2 1
4 3 2 1
ALL
TB1½
2 4
1
3
1 3
2 4
4 2
LA
1 3
TL1½
SOW'S TAIL
RSCDS 1965 S32
2 3
2 3
3 1 1 3
4 1 1
1 3
1 3
Half Dble
Fig of 8
2 1
2 1
Half Dble
Fig of 8
to
all on
opposite
side
2 1 3
DTB1½
2 1
RL
SPEED THE PLOUGH
II 4 R32
RA
LA
ST
2 3
1 S2 1
2 3
TB1¼

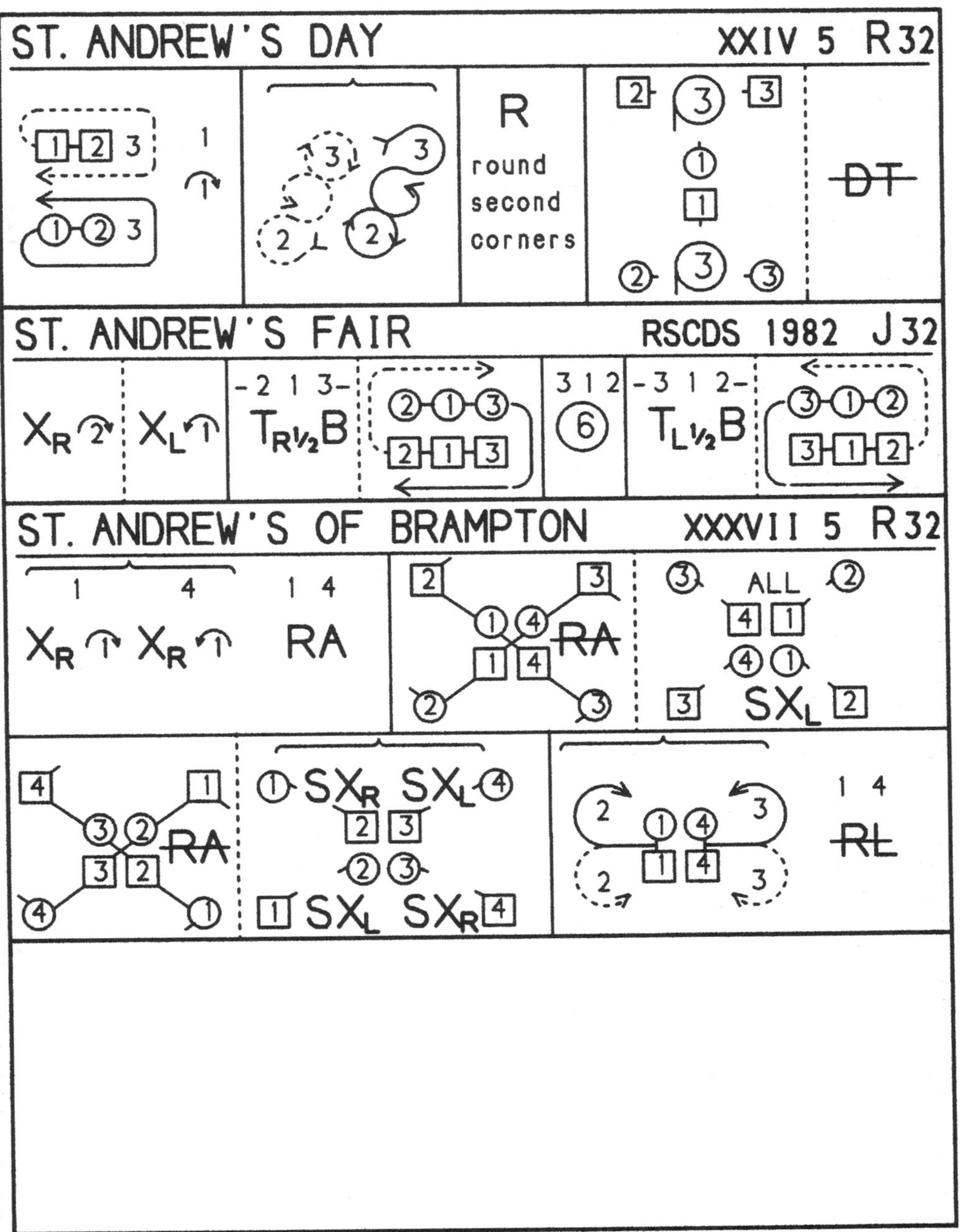
ST. ANDREW'S DAY
XXIV 5 R32
R
round
second
corners
DT
ST. ANDREW'S FAIR
RSCDS 1982 J32
-2 1 3-
T R½ B
3 1 2
-3 1 2-
T L½ B
ST. ANDREW'S OF BRAMPTON
XXXVII 5 R32
RA
ALL
SX L
SX R SX L
SX L SX R
1 4
RL

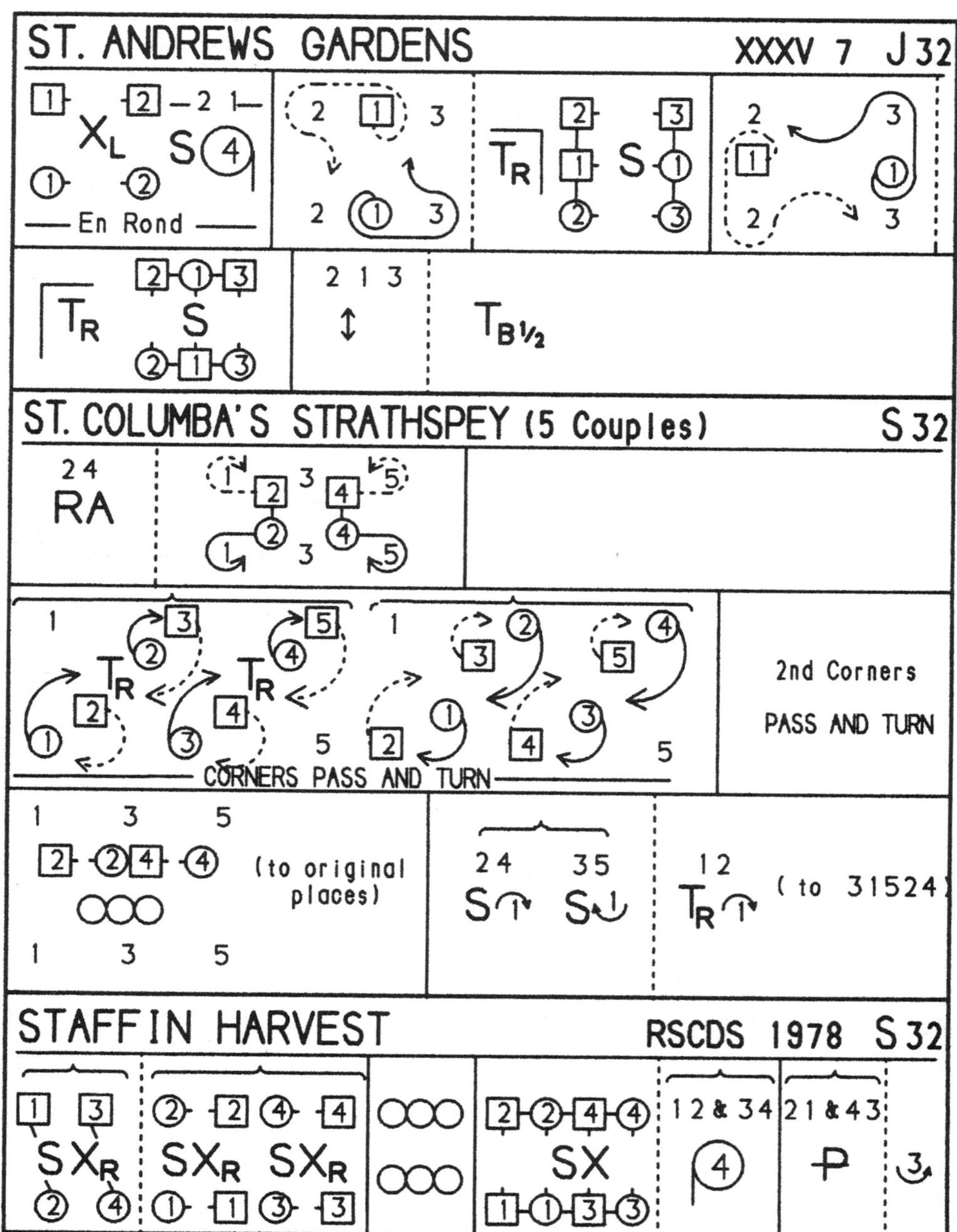
ST. ANDREWS GARDENS
XXXV 7 J32
En Rond
2nd Corners
PASS AND TURN
ST. COLUMBA'S STRATHSPEY (5 Couples)
S32
CORNERS PASS AND TURN
(to original places)
(to 31524)
STAFFIN HARVEST
RSCDS 1978 S32

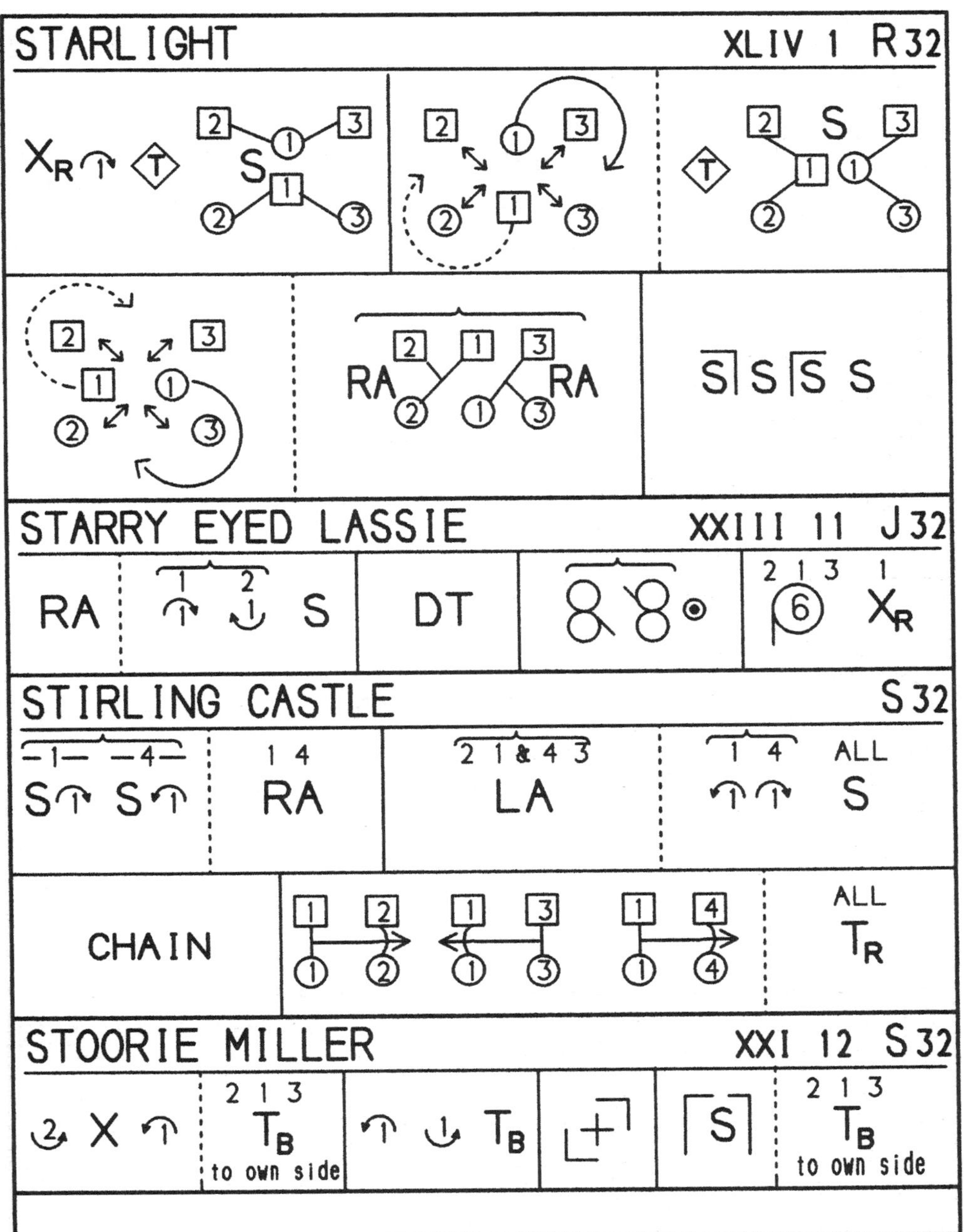
STARLIGHT
XLIV 1 R32
STARRY EYED LASSIE
XXIII 11 J32
RA
S
DT
STIRLING CASTLE
S32
RA
LA
ALL
S
CHAIN
ALL
STOORIE MILLER
XXI 12 S32
to own side
to own side

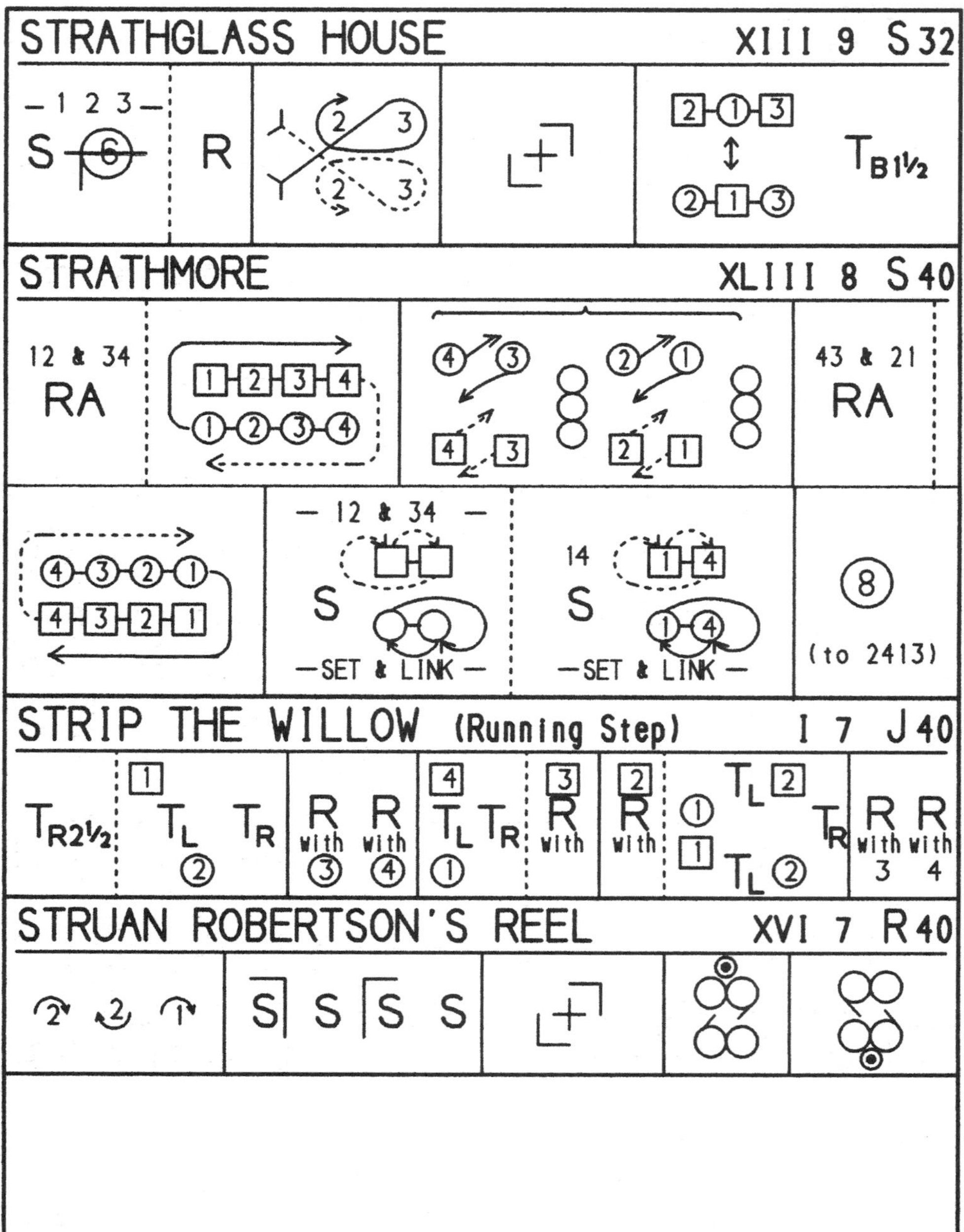
STRATHGLASS HOUSE
XIII 9 S32
— 1 2 3 —
S 6
R
T B1½
STRATHMORE
XLIII 8 S40
12 & 34
RA
43 & 21
RA
— 12 & 34 —
S
— SET & LINK —
14
S
— SET & LINK —
8
(to 2413)
STRIP THE WILLOW (Running Step)
I 7 J40
T R2½
T L
T R
R with
R with
T L
T R
R with
R with
T L
T R
T L
R with 3
R with 4
STRUAN ROBERTSON'S REEL
XVI 7 R40
S S S S

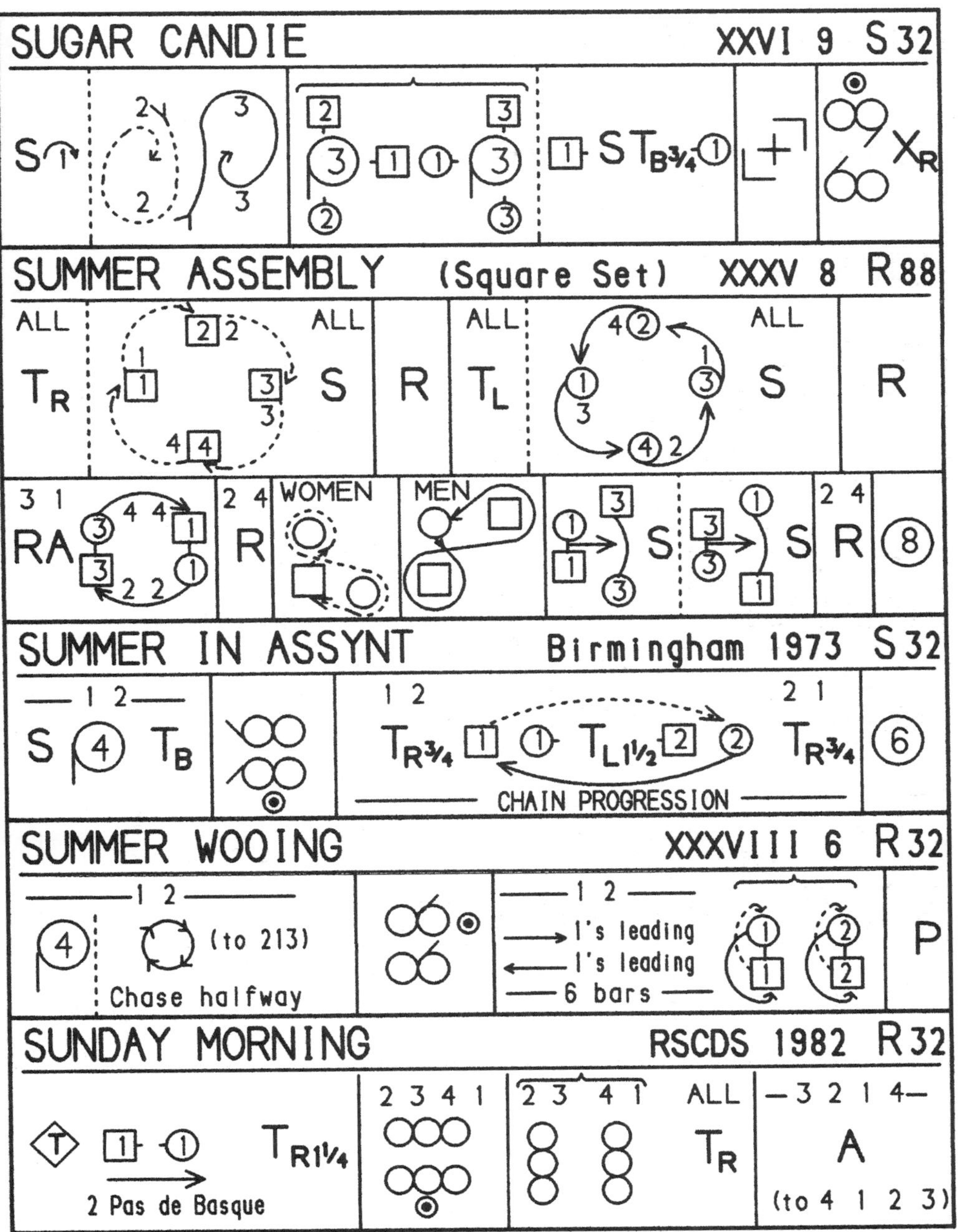
SUGAR CANDIE
XXVI 9 S32
S
2
3
2
3
2
3
1
1
2
3
ST
ALL
XR
SUMMER ASSEMBLY (Square Set)
XXXV 8 R88
ALL
TR
2 2
1
1
3
3
4 4
ALL
S
R
ALL
TL
4 2
1
3
1
3
4 2
ALL
S
R
3 1
RA
3
4 4
1
3
2 2
1
2 4
R
WOMEN
MEN
1
3
1
3
S
3
1
3
1
S
2 4
R
8
SUMMER IN ASSYNT
Birmingham 1973 S32
1 2
S
4
TB
1 2
1
1
2
2
2 1
CHAIN PROGRESSION
6
SUMMER WOOING
XXXVIII 6 R32
1 2
4
(to 213)
Chase halfway
1 2
1's leading
1's leading
6 bars
1
1
2
2
P
SUNDAY MORNING
RSCDS 1982 R32
T
1
1
2 Pas de Basque
2 3 4 1
2 3 4 1
ALL
TR
3 2 1 4
A
(to 4 1 2 3)

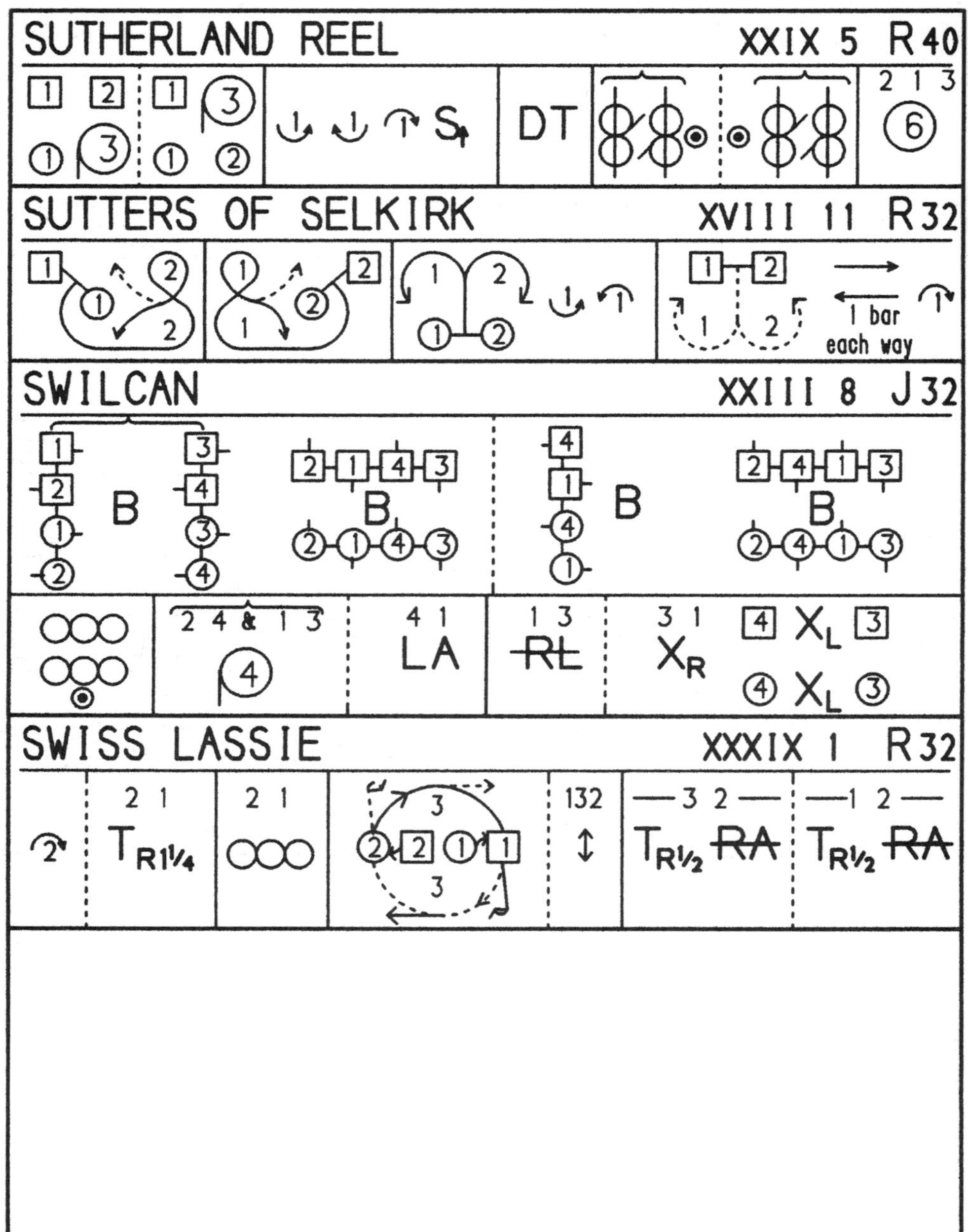
SUTHERLAND REEL
XXIX 5 R40
DT
SUTTERS OF SELKIRK
XVIII 11 R32
1 bar each way
SWILCAN
XXIII 8 J32
B
2 4 & 1 3
4 1
LA
1 3
RL
3 1
X_R
X_L
SWISS LASSIE
XXXIX 1 R32
2 1
$T_{R1\frac{1}{4}}$
132
— 3 2 —
$T_{R\frac{1}{2}}$
RA
— 1 2 —

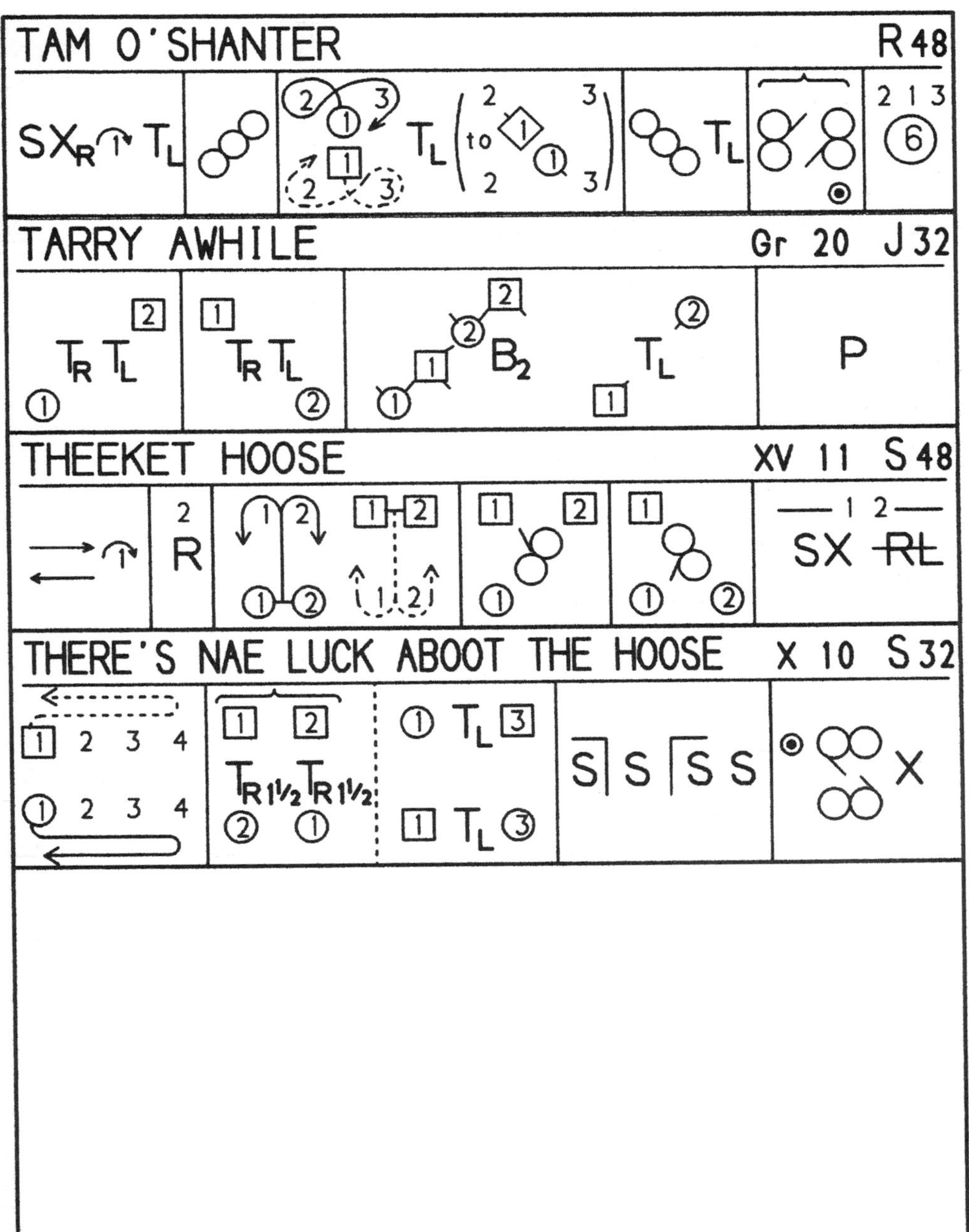
TAM O'SHANTER
R 48
TARRY AWHILE
Gr 20 J 32
THEEKET HOOSE
XV 11 S 48
THERE'S NAE LUCK ABOOT THE HOOSE
X 10 S 32

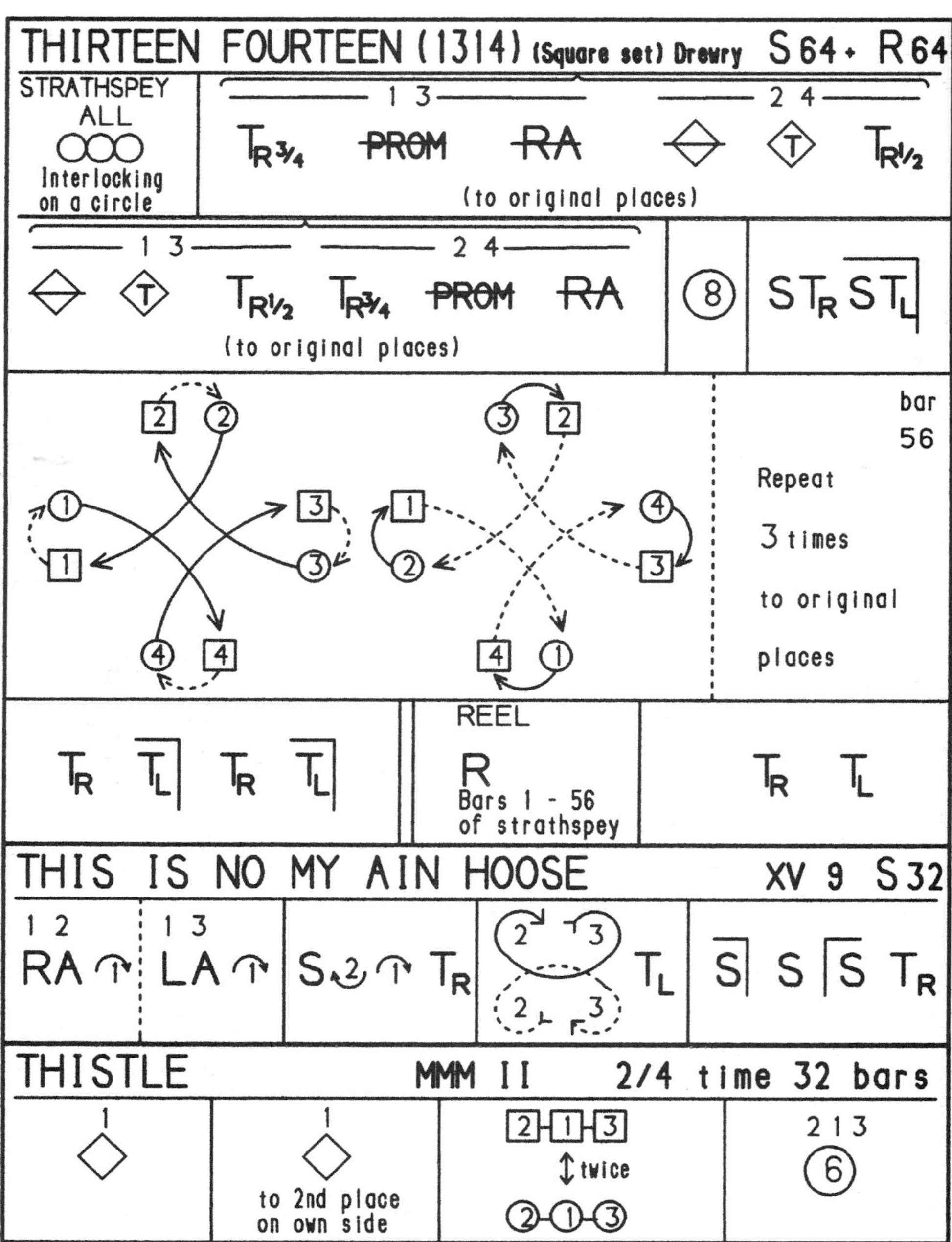
THIRTEEN FOURTEEN (1314) (Square set) Drewry S 64 + R 64
STRATHSPEY
ALL
Interlocking on a circle
1 3
2 4
PROM
RA
(to original places)
T
1 3
2 4
PROM
RA
(to original places)
8
bar 56
Repeat 3 times to original places
REEL
R
Bars 1 - 56 of strathspey
THIS IS NO MY AIN HOOSE XV 9 S 32
1 2
RA
1 3
LA
THISTLE MMM II 2/4 time 32 bars
1
1
to 2nd place on own side
twice
2 1 3
6

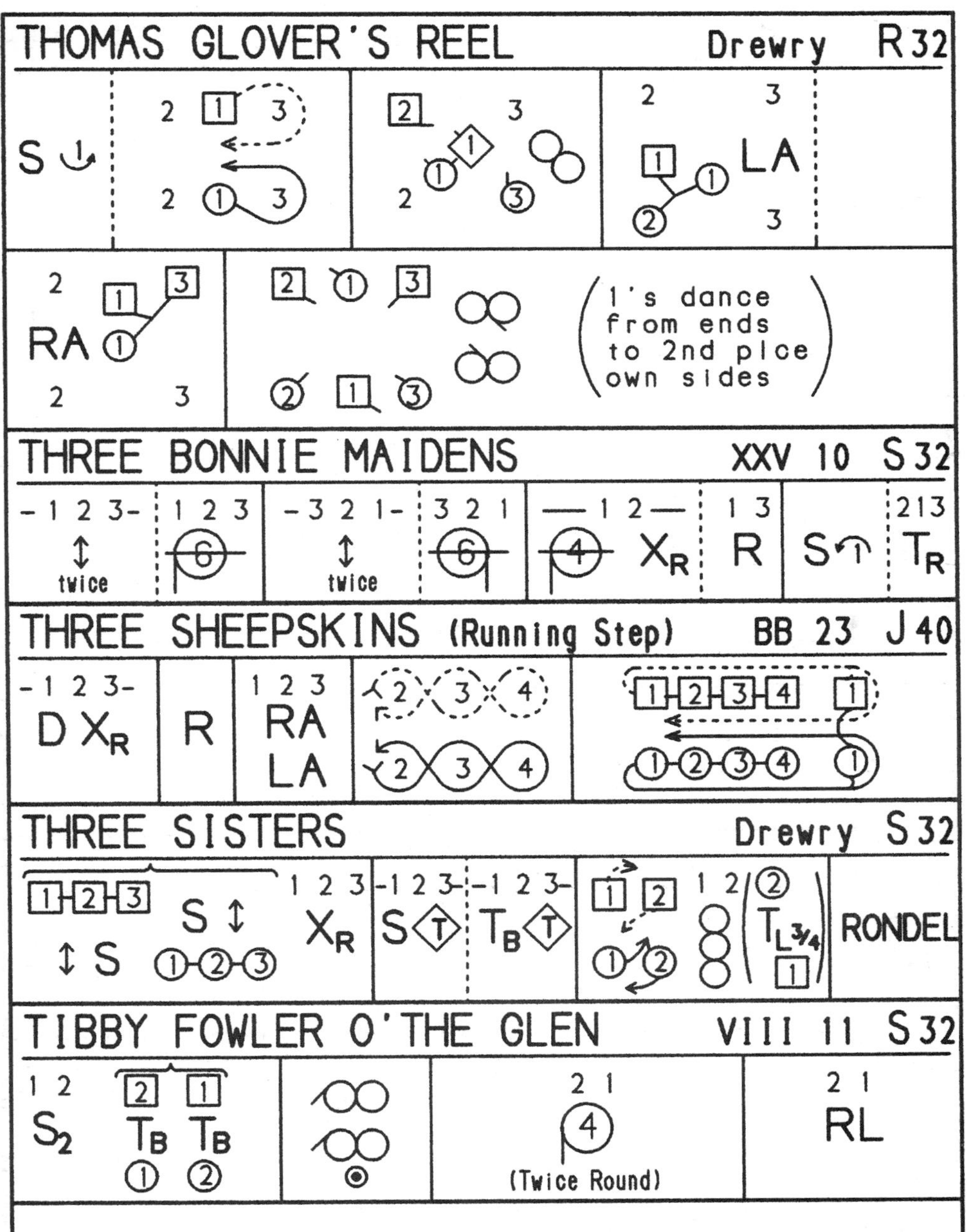
THOMAS GLOVER'S REEL
Drewry R32
S
2 1 3
2 1 3
2 3
1
2 1 3
2 3
1 LA
1 2
3
2
RA
1 3
1
2 3
2 1 3
2 1 3
1's dance
from ends
to 2nd plce
own sides
THREE BONNIE MAIDENS
XXV 10 S32
-1 2 3-
twice
1 2 3
6
-3 2 1-
twice
3 2 1
6
—1 2—
4
XR
1 3
R
S
213
TR
THREE SHEEPSKINS (Running Step)
BB 23 J40
-1 2 3-
D XR
R
1 2 3
RA
LA
2 3 4
2 3 4
1 2 3 4 1
1 2 3 4 1
THREE SISTERS
Drewry S32
1 2 3
S
S
1 2 3
1 2 3
XR
-1 2 3-
S T
-1 2 3-
TB T
1 2
1 2
1 2
2
TL3/4
1
RONDEL
TIBBY FOWLER O'THE GLEN
VIII 11 S32
1 2
S2
2 1
TB TB
1 2
2 1
4
(Twice Round)
2 1
RL

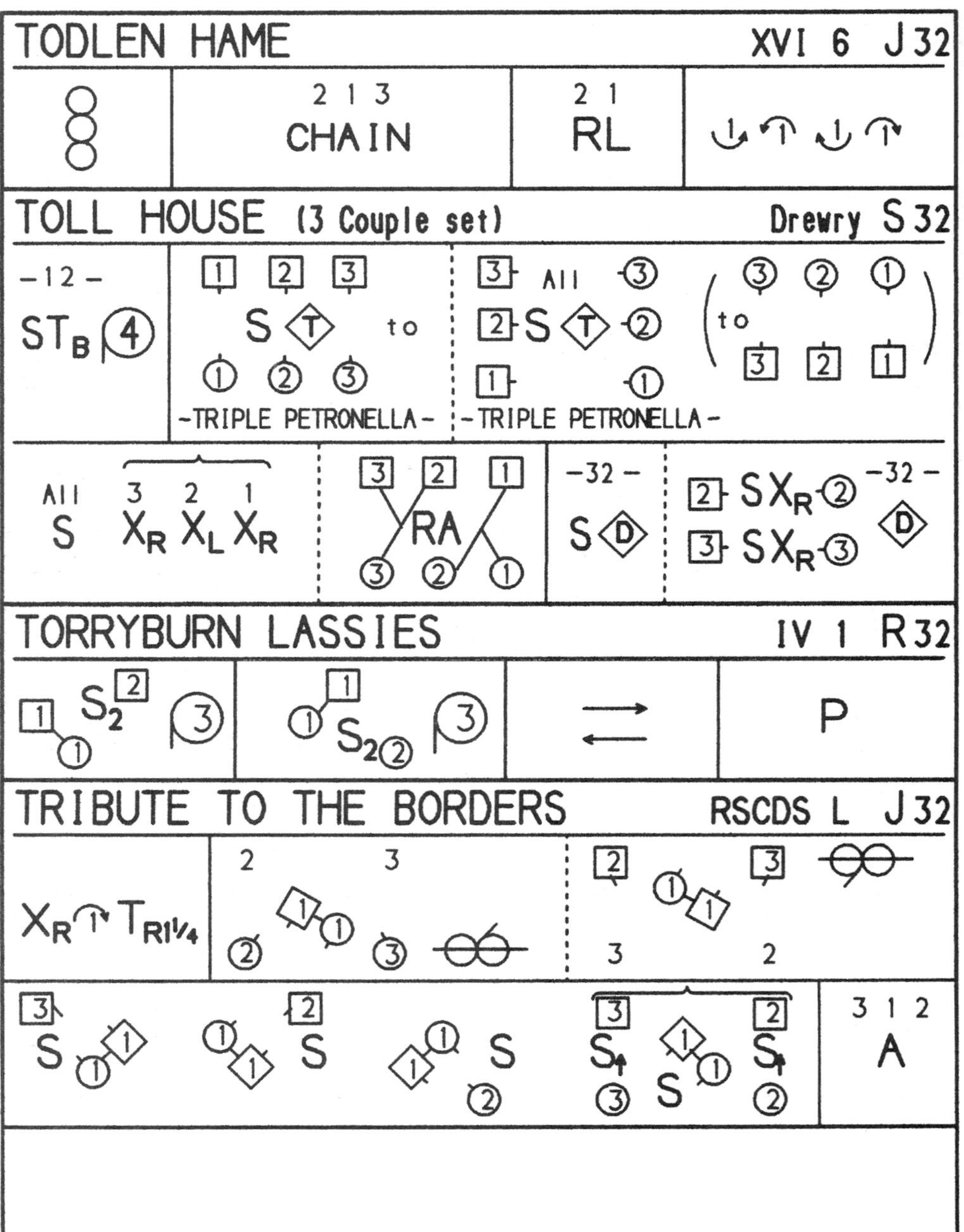
TODLEN HAME
XVI 6 J32
2 1 3
CHAIN
2 1
RL
TOLL HOUSE (3 Couple set)
Drewry S32
-12-
ST_B 4
S T to
-TRIPLE PETRONELLA-
All
S T
-TRIPLE PETRONELLA-
to
All
3 2 1
S X_R X_L X_R
RA
-32-
S D
S X_R
S X_R
-32-
D
TORRYBURN LASSIES
IV 1 R32
S_2
S_2
P
TRIBUTE TO THE BORDERS
RSCDS L J32
X_R T_R1¼
2 3
3 2
S
S
S
S
S
S
3 1 2
A

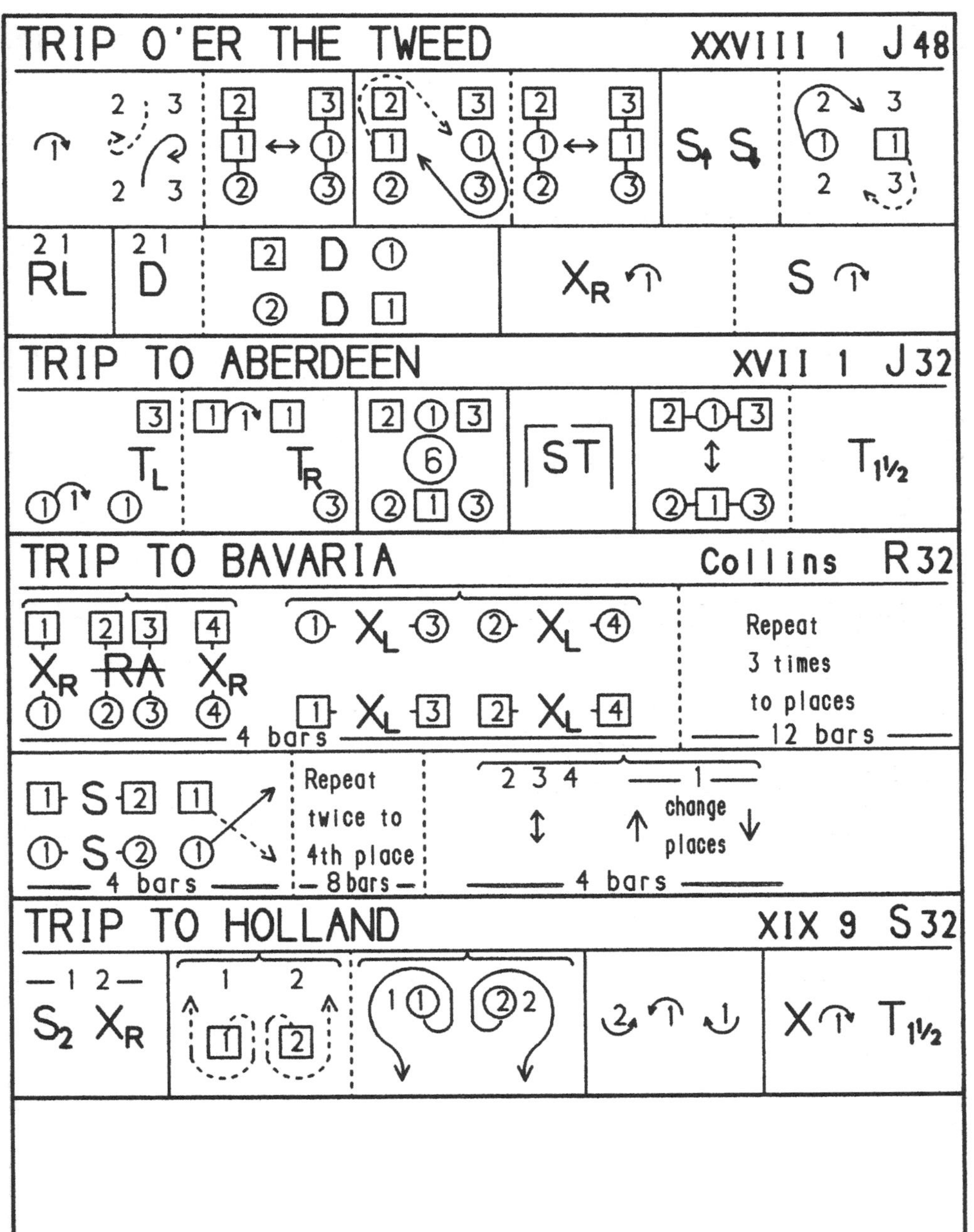

TRIP O'ER THE TWEED
XXVIII 1 J48
RL
D
S
TRIP TO ABERDEEN
XVII 1 J32
ST
TRIP TO BAVARIA
Collins R32
RA
Repeat
3 times
to places
12 bars
4 bars
Repeat
twice to
4th place
8 bars
change
places
4 bars
TRIP TO HOLLAND
XIX 9 S32

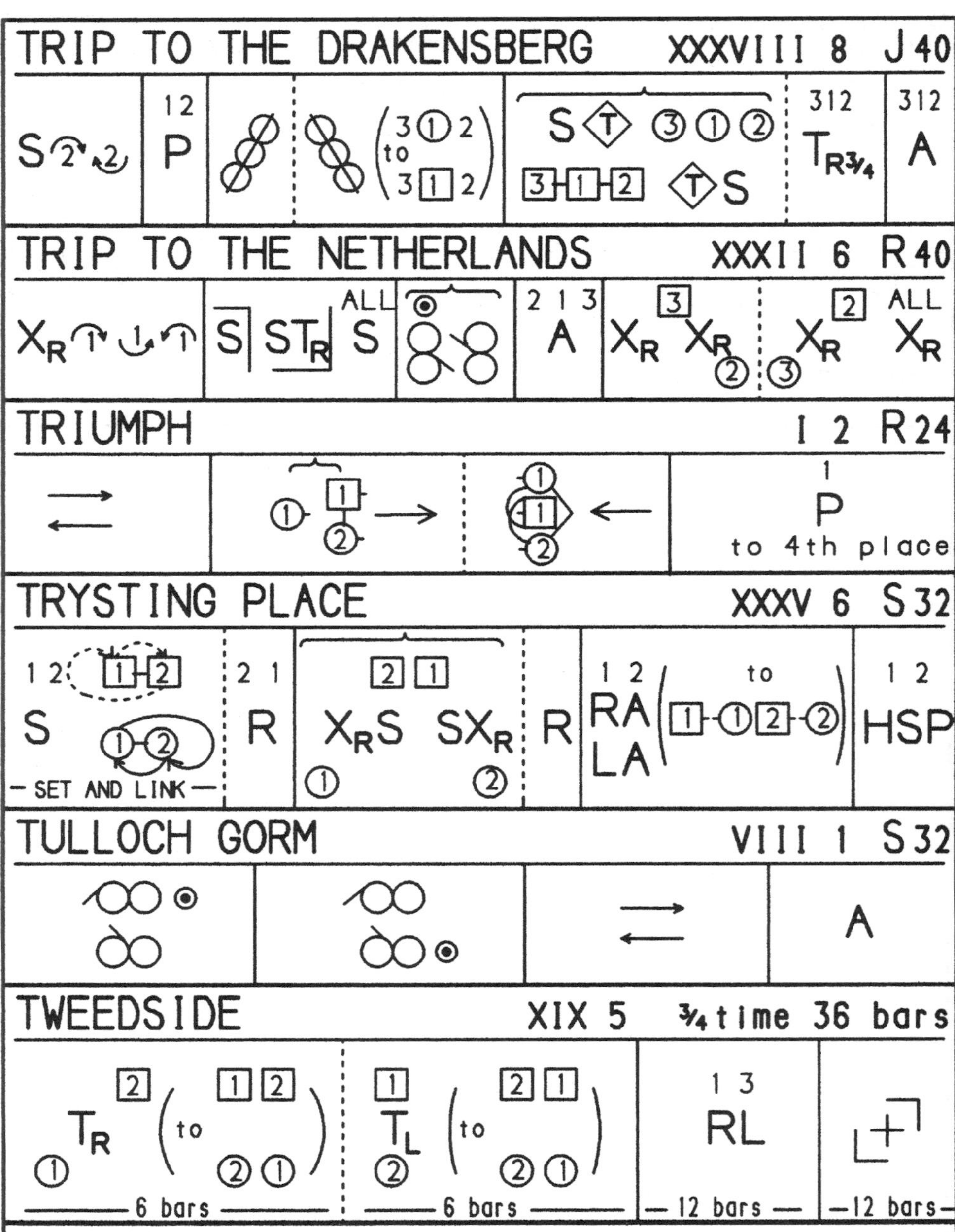
TRIP TO THE DRAKENSBERG
XXXVIII 8 J40
TRIP TO THE NETHERLANDS
XXXII 6 R40
TRIUMPH
I 2 R24
to 4th place
TRYSTING PLACE
XXXV 6 S32
– SET AND LINK –
TULLOCH GORM
VIII 1 S32
TWEEDSIDE
XIX 5 ¾ time 36 bars
6 bars
6 bars
12 bars
12 bars

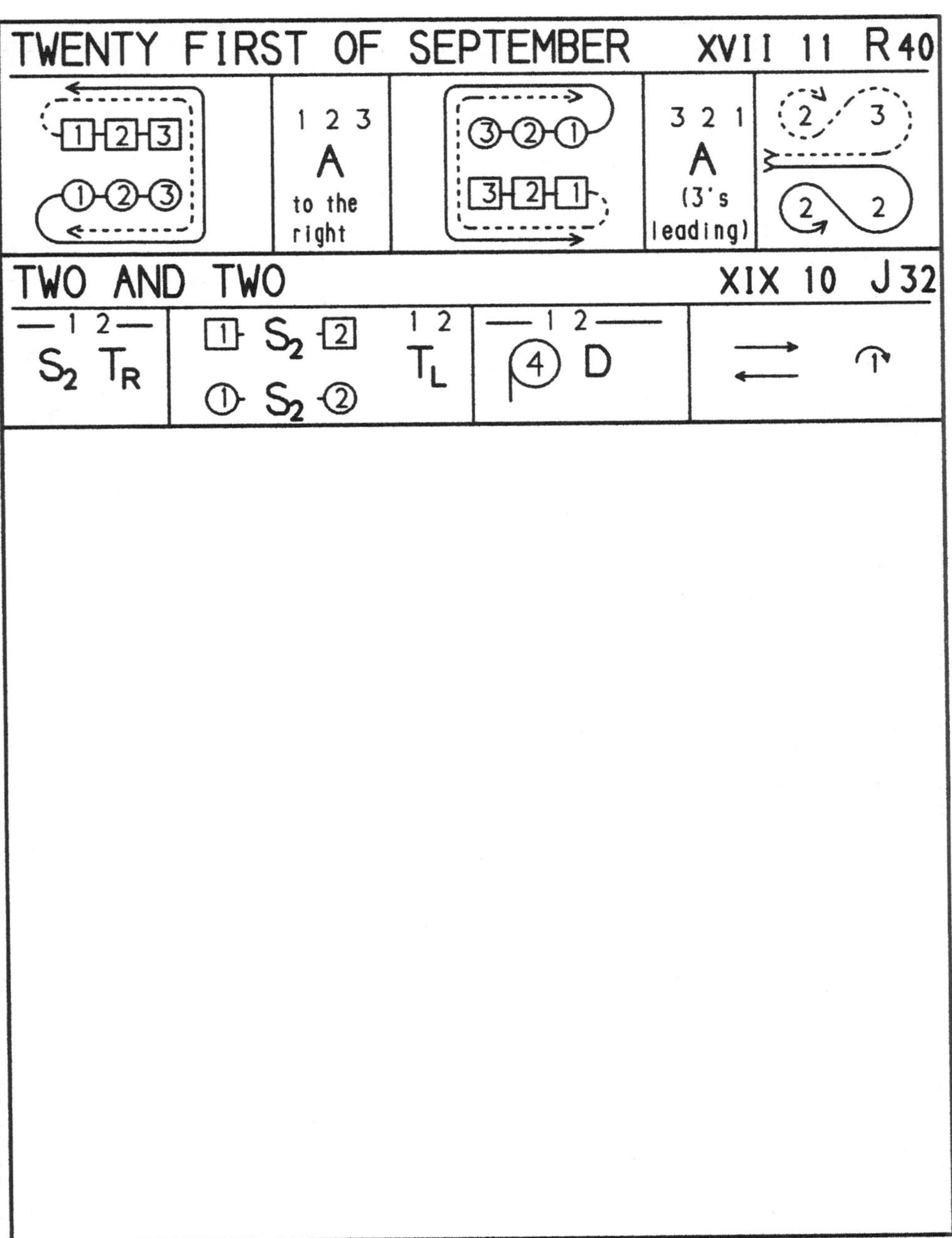
TWENTY FIRST OF SEPTEMBER XVII 11 R40
1 2 3
A
to the right
3 2 1
A
(3's leading)
TWO AND TWO XIX 10 J32
1 2
S2 TR
S2
S2
1 2
TL
1 2
4 D

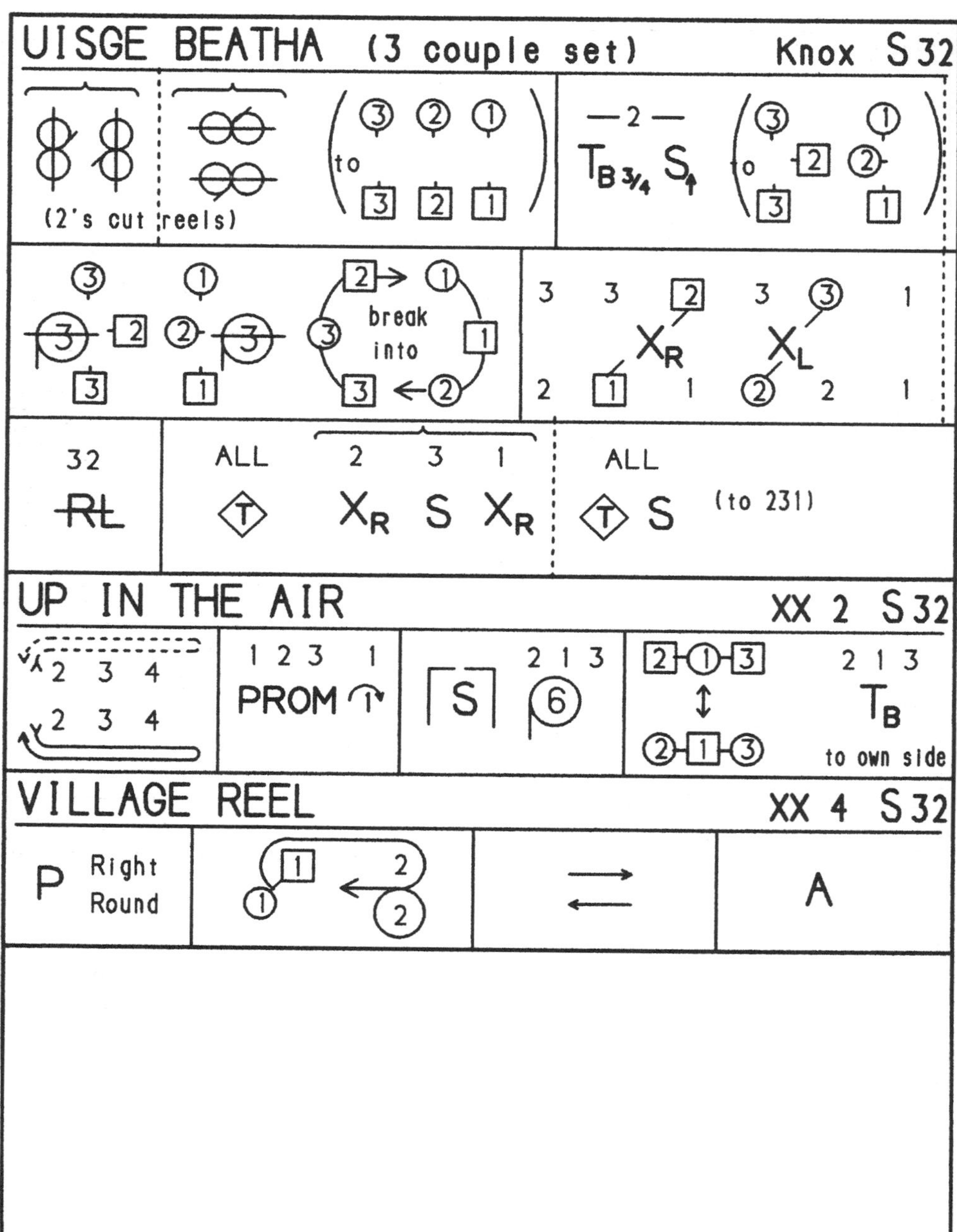

UISGE BEATHA (3 couple set)
Knox S32
(2's cut reels)
to
— 2 —
to
break
into
32
ALL
2 3 1
ALL
(to 231)
UP IN THE AIR
XX 2 S32
PROM
to own side
VILLAGE REEL
XX 4 S32
Right
Round

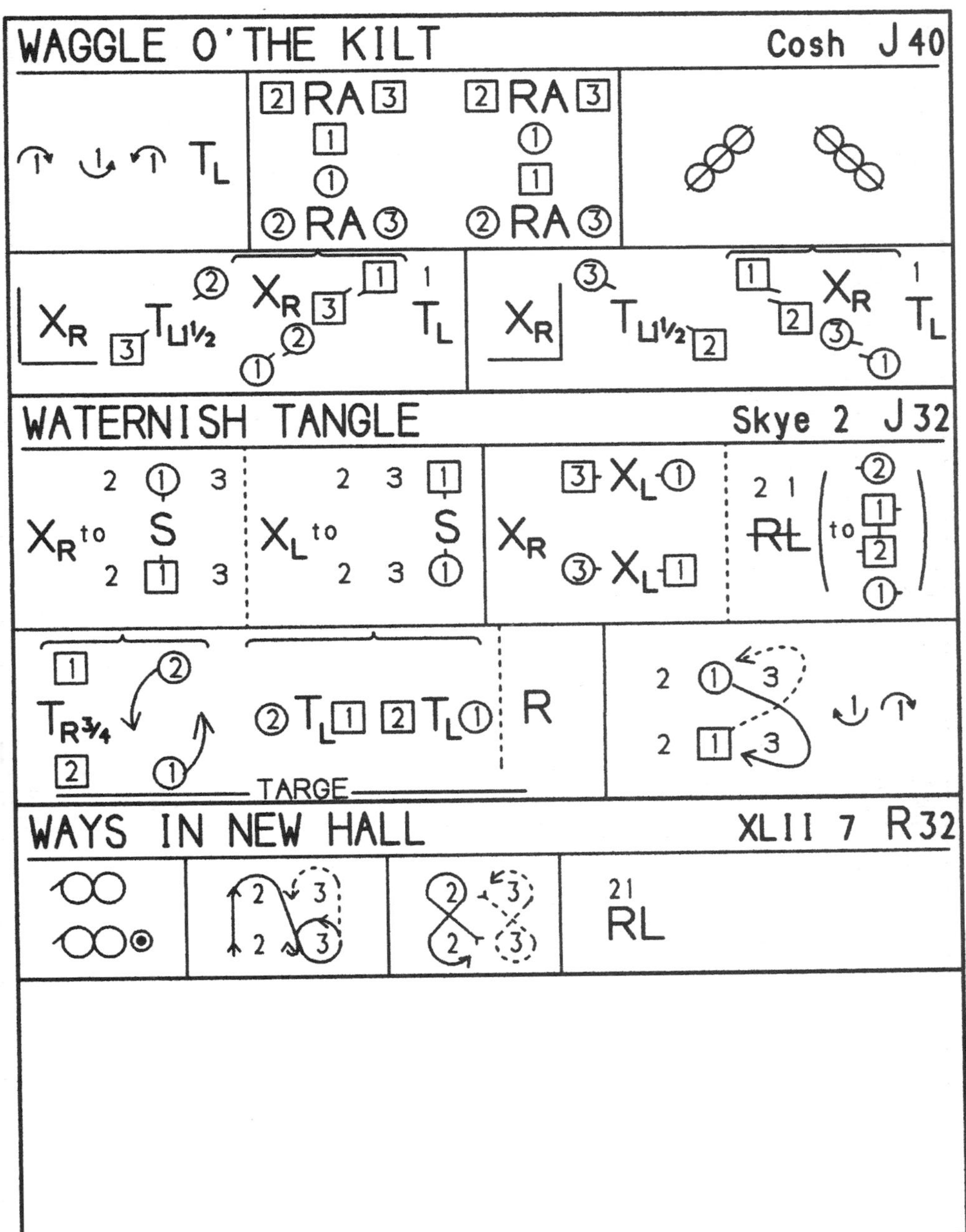
WAGGLE O'THE KILT
Cosh J40
RA
RA
RA
RA
X_R
$T_{L1½}$
X_R
T_L
X_R
$T_{L1½}$
X_R
T_L
WATERNISH TANGLE
Skye 2 J32
X_R to
S
X_L to
S
X_R
X_L
X_L
RL
to
$T_{R¾}$
T_L
T_L
R
TARGE
WAYS IN NEW HALL
XLII 7 R32
RL

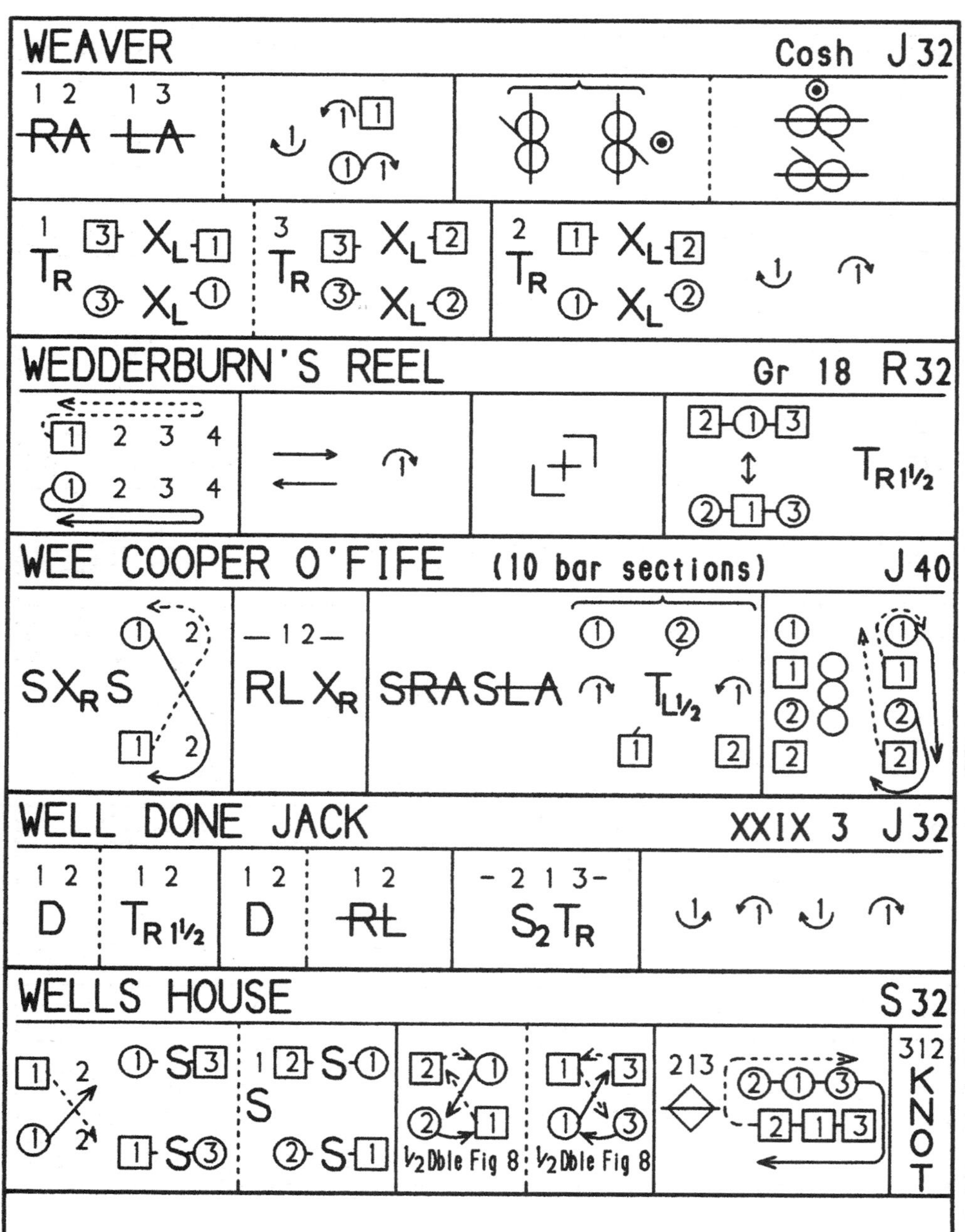
WEAVER
Cosh J32
WEDDERBURN'S REEL
Gr 18 R32
WEE COOPER O'FIFE (10 bar sections)
J40
SXRS
RL XR
SRASLA
WELL DONE JACK
XXIX 3 J32
D
D
RL
S2TR
WELLS HOUSE
S32
½ Dble Fig 8
½ Dble Fig 8
KNOT

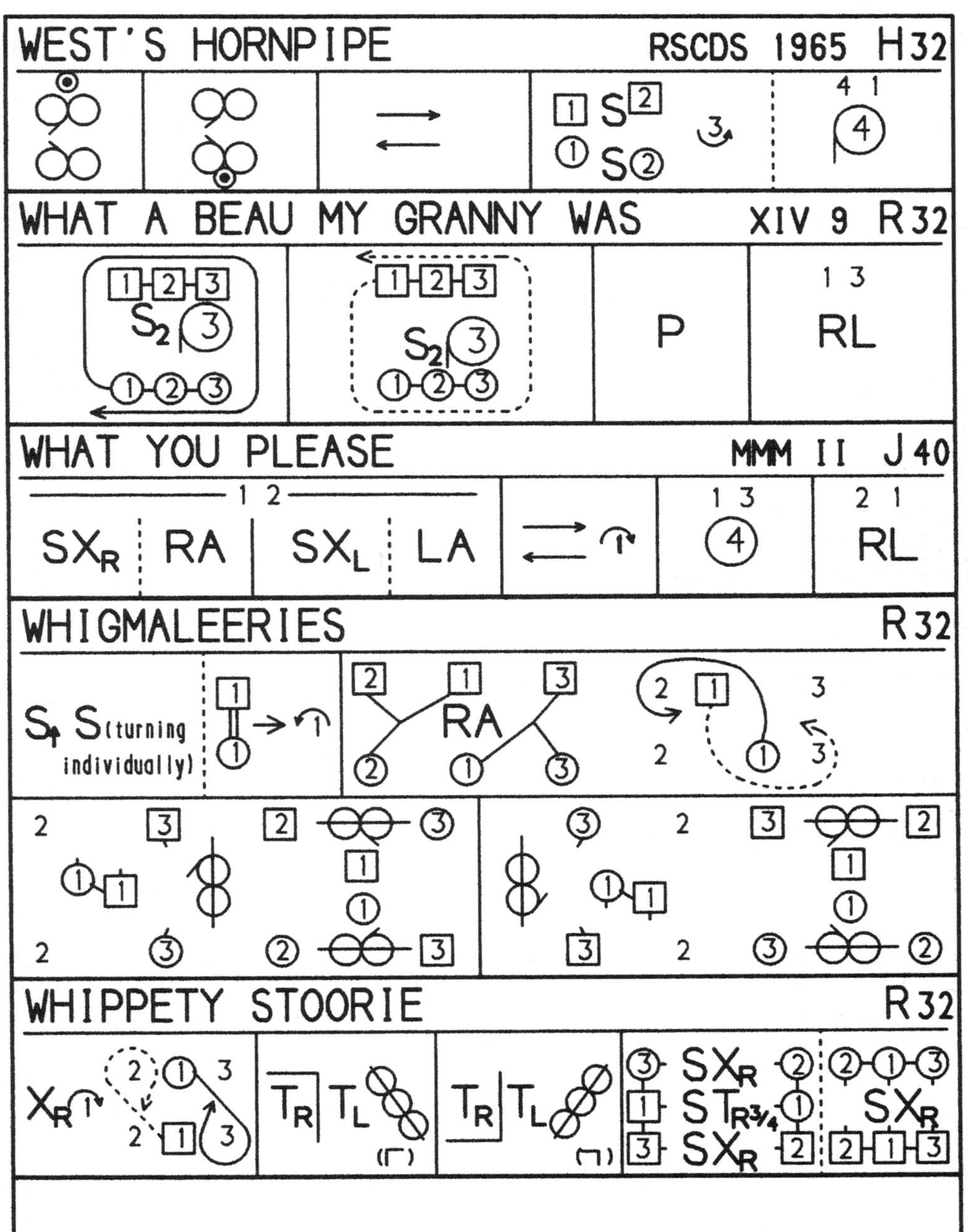
WEST'S HORNPIPE
RSCDS 1965 H32
S
S
4 1
4
WHAT A BEAU MY GRANNY WAS
XIV 9 R32
S2
S2
P
1 3
RL
WHAT YOU PLEASE
MMM II J40
1 2
SXR
RA
SXL
LA
1 3
4
2 1
RL
WHIGMALEERIES
R32
S S (turning individually)
RA
WHIPPETY STOORIE
R32
XR
TR
TL
SXR
STR3/4
SX

WHISTLING WIND XXXVI 5 R32

S ↷ S↑ | DT

3 1 2 3 3-XL-1 | 3 1 3 1-XL-2 3

XR XR | XR XR

3 1 2 1-XL-2 2 | 2 1 2 2 3-XL-1

WHITE COCKADE V 11 R32

1 2 3 SXR SXR | ⇄ | ↷ 1 3 (4) | 2 1 RL

WHITE HEATHER JIG Cosh J40

TR ↷ TL1½ | 1 2 | 1 3 | TL ↷ TR

WHITE ROSE OF SCOTLAND S32

1 ↷ S ↷ XR ↶ 1 | (┐) (┌) | R (└)(┘) | 2 3 2 3 3 1 1 3 3 1 1 3 2 3 2 3

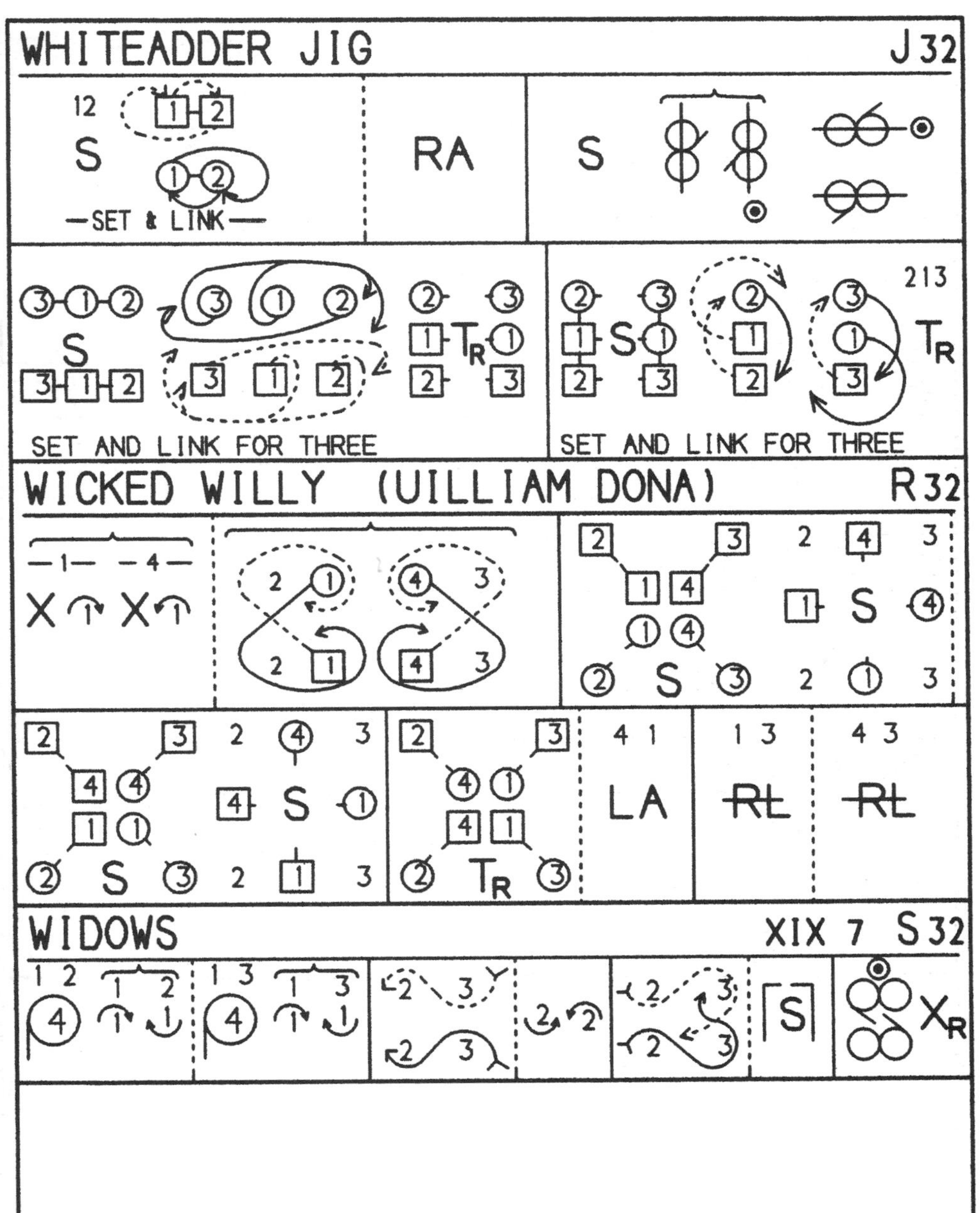

WHITEADDER JIG
J 32
12
S
RA
S
—SET & LINK—
S
SET AND LINK FOR THREE
T_R
213
S
T_R
SET AND LINK FOR THREE
WICKED WILLY (UILLIAM DONA)
R 32
—1— —4—
X X
S
S
S
S
T_R
4 1
LA
1 3
RL
4 3
RL
WIDOWS
XIX 7 S 32
1 2
1 3
S
X_R

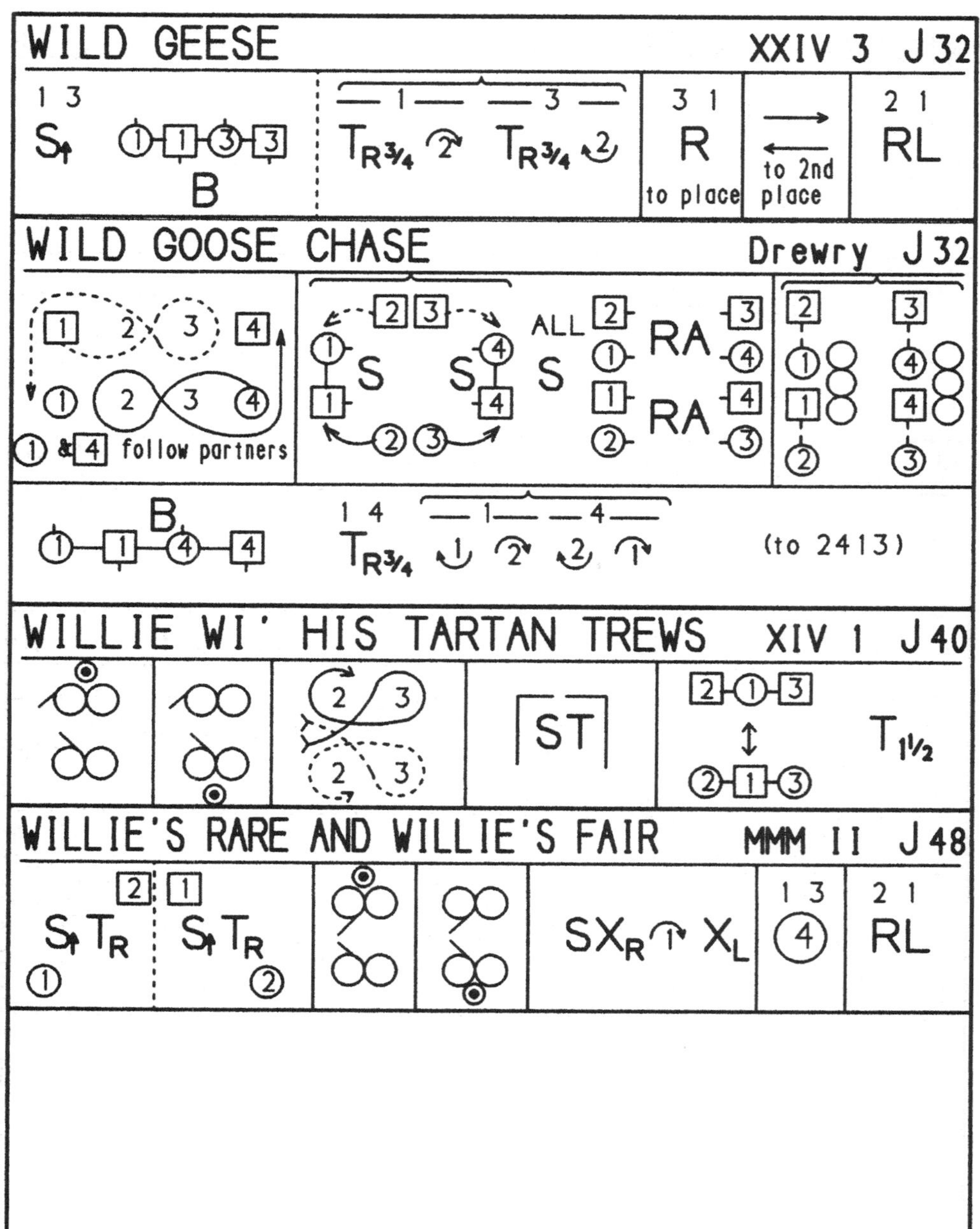

WILD GEESE
XXIV 3 J32
1 3
B
1
3
3 1
R
to place
to 2nd place
2 1
RL
WILD GOOSE CHASE
Drewry J32
1 & 4 follow partners
ALL
S
RA
RA
B
1 4
1
4
(to 2413)
WILLIE WI' HIS TARTAN TREWS
XIV 1 J40
ST
WILLIE'S RARE AND WILLIE'S FAIR
MMM II J48
1 3
2 1
RL

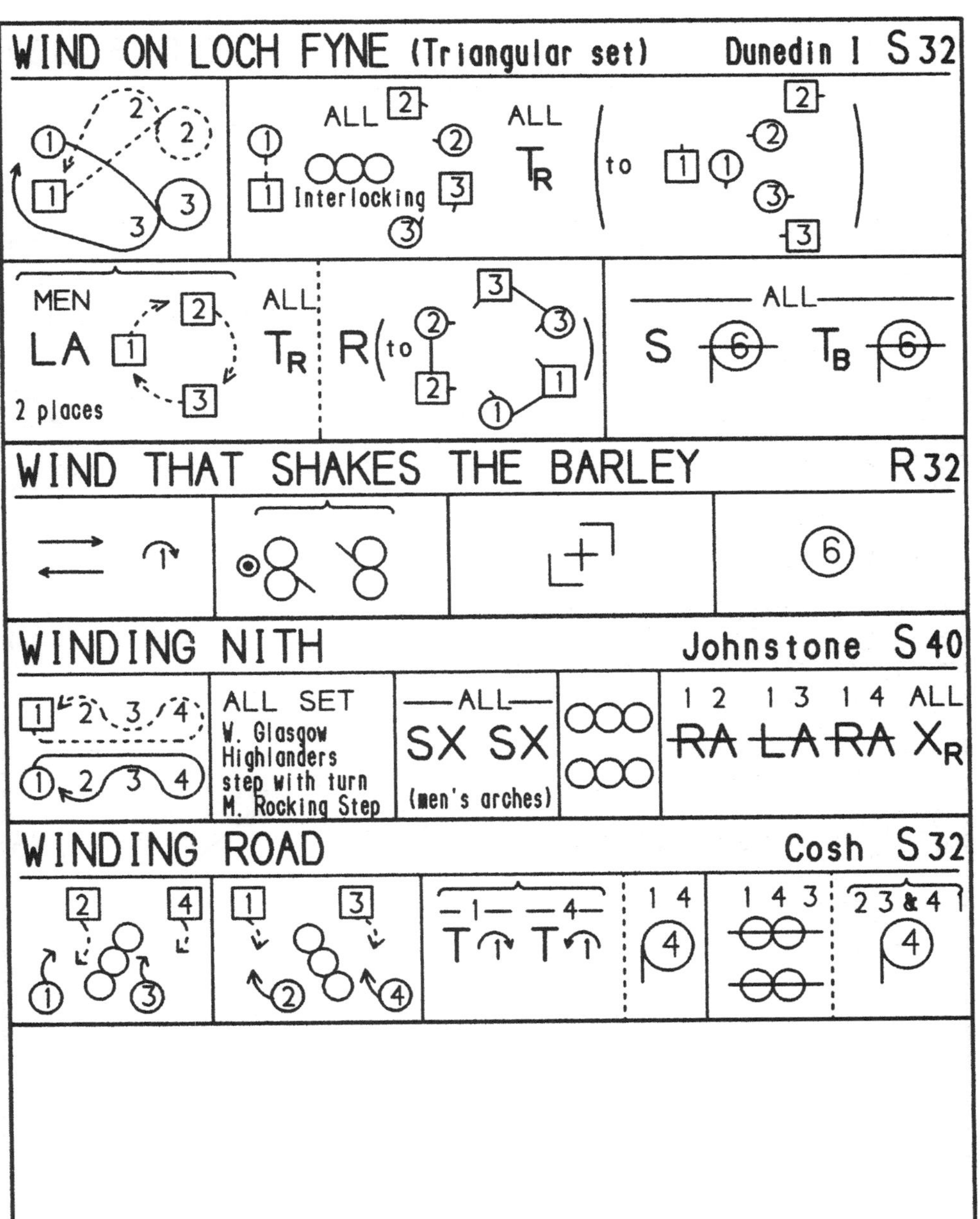
WIND ON LOCH FYNE (Triangular set)
Dunedin 1 S32
ALL
Interlocking
ALL
T_R
to
MEN
LA
2 places
ALL
T_R
R (to
ALL
S
T_B
WIND THAT SHAKES THE BARLEY
R32
WINDING NITH
Johnstone S40
ALL SET
W. Glasgow Highlanders step with turn
M. Rocking Step
ALL
SX SX
(men's arches)
1 2 1 3 1 4 ALL
RA LA RA X_R
WINDING ROAD
Cosh S32
T T
1 4
1 4 3
2 3 & 4

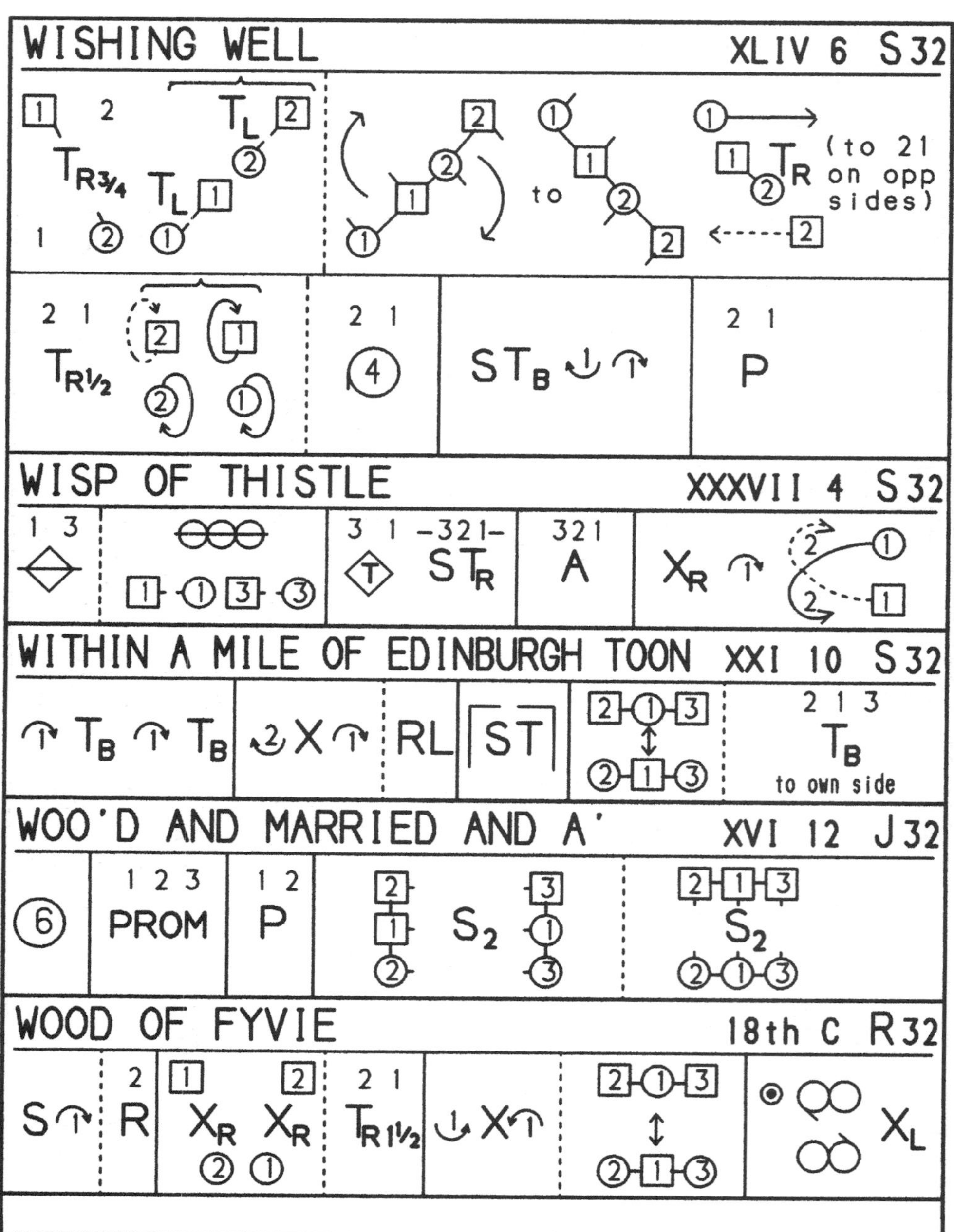
WISHING WELL
XLIV 6 S32
(to 21 on opp sides)
to
WISP OF THISTLE
XXXVII 4 S32
WITHIN A MILE OF EDINBURGH TOON
XXI 10 S32
to own side
WOO'D AND MARRIED AND A'
XVI 12 J32
PROM
WOOD OF FYVIE
18th C R32

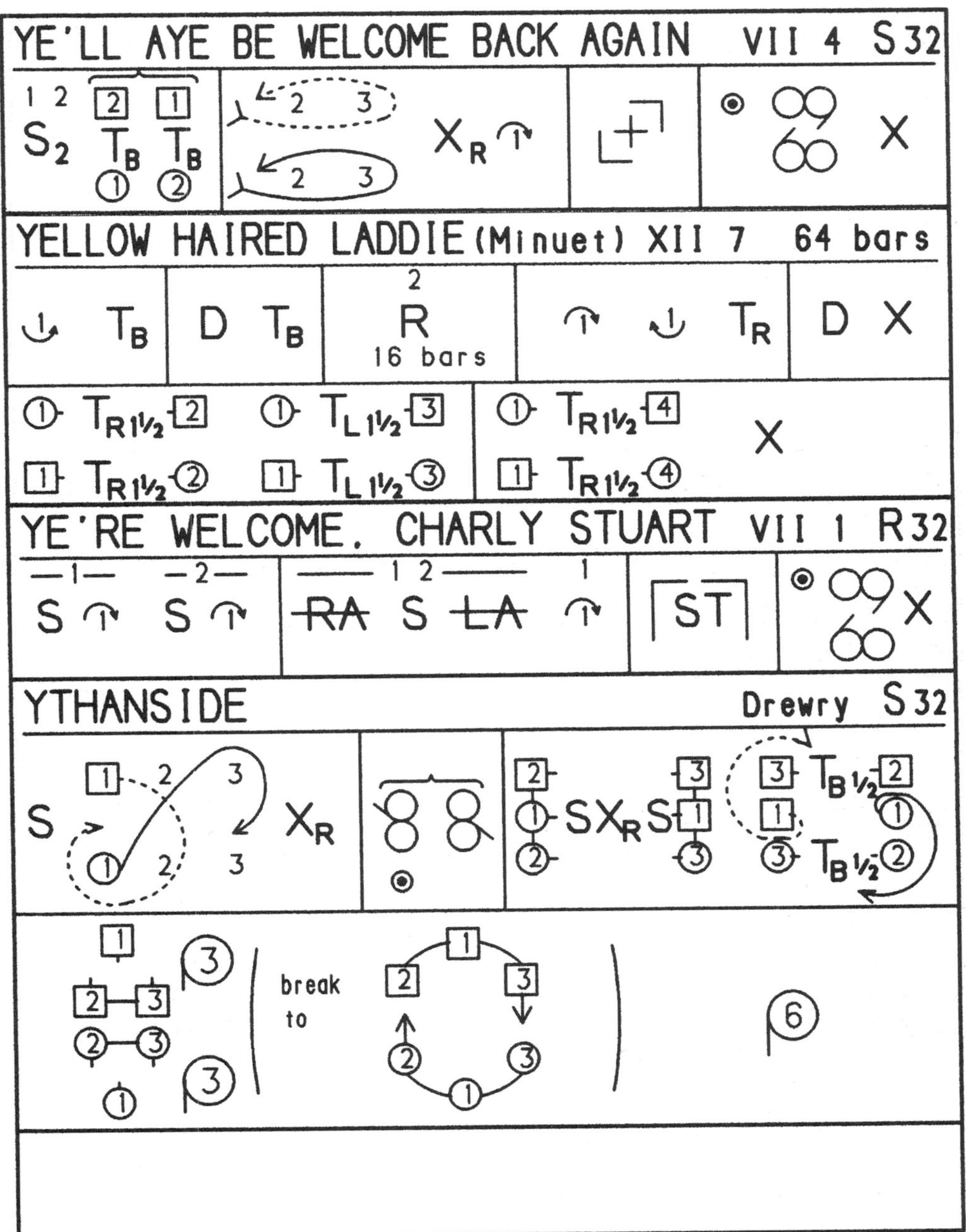
YE'LL AYE BE WELCOME BACK AGAIN VII 4 S32
YELLOW HAIRED LADDIE (Minuet) XII 7 64 bars
16 bars
YE'RE WELCOME, CHARLY STUART VII 1 R32
YTHANSIDE
Drewry S32
break to